Dante Now

The William and Katherine Devers Series in Dante Studies

Volume 1

THEODORE J. CACHEY, JR., AND
CHRISTIAN MOEVS, EDITORS

EDITED BY *Theodore J. Cachey, Jr.*

Dante Now

CURRENT TRENDS IN DANTE STUDIES

University of Notre Dame Press
Notre Dame and London

Manufactured in the United States of America

Library of Congress Cataloging-in-Publication Data

Dante now : current trends in Dante studies / edited by T. J. Cachey, Jr.
    p.   cm.
    Papers presented at a conference held at the University
of Notre Dame, Notre Dame, Ind., Oct. 29–30, 1993.
    Includes index.
    ISBN 0-268-00875-2 (pb)   0-268-00879-5 (cloth)
    1. Dante Alighier 1, 1265–1321—Criticism and interpretation—Congresses.
I. Cachey, T. J. (Theodore J.)   II. University of Notre Dame.
PQ4383.D36 1995   94-39220
851′.1—dc20   CIP

Contents

Part 2. "Minor Works"

Part 3. Reception

Preface

The William and Katherine Devers Program in Dante Studies at the University of Notre Dame supports rare book acquisitions in the university's John A. Zahm Dante collection, funds an annual visiting professorship in Dante studies, and supports electronic and print publication of scholarly research in the field. In collaboration with the Medieval Institute at the university, the Devers program has initiated a series dedicated to the publication of the most significant current scholarship in the field of Dante studies.

In keeping with the spirit that inspired the creation of the Devers program, the series takes Dante as a focal point that draws together the many disciplines and forms of inquiry that constitute a cultural tradition without fixed boundaries. Accordingly, the series hopes to illuminate Dante's position at the center of contemporary critical debates in the humanities by reflecting both the highest quality of scholarly achievement and the greatest diversity of critical perspectives.

The series publishes works on Dante from a wide variety of disciplinary viewpoints and in diverse scholarly genres, including critical studies, commentaries, editions, translations, and conference proceedings of exceptional importance. The series is supervised by an international advisory board composed of distinguished Dante scholars and is published regularly by the University of Notre Dame Press.

The Dolphin and Anchor device that appears on publications of the Devers series was used by the great humanist, grammarian, editor, and typographer, Aldus Manutius (1449–1515), in whose 1502 edition of Dante (second issue) and all subsequent editions it appeared. The device illustrates the ancient proverb *Festina lente*, "Hurry up slowly."

Theodore J. Cachey, Jr., and
Christian Moevs
Editors

ADVISORY BOARD

Albert Russell Ascoli, Northwestern
Zygmunt G. Barański, Reading
Patrick Boyde, Cambridge
Alison Cornish, Yale
Robert Hollander, Princeton
Giuseppe Mazzotta, Yale
Lino Pertile, Edinburgh
Michelangelo Picone, Zurich
John A. Scott, Western Australia
Tibor Wlassics, Virginia

Theodore J. Cachey, Jr.

Introduction

Writing nearly twenty years ago on the occasion of the publication of Charles S. Singleton's translation and commentary of the *Commedia*, George Steiner noted "in the largesse of Professor Singleton's presentation more than a hint of melancholy, of doubt as to those whom his labours might serve."[1] The Bollingen Dante clearly represented a watershed in the modern American academic canonization of Dante's poem, yet Steiner sensed an unmistakable air of scholastic purism about the enterprise. He observed pointedly that there were no references in the commentary to Eliot, Pound, Mandelstam, or other "poets, re-readers, exploiters who have helped the *Commedia* live at large (174)"; nor even, one might add, to Singleton's nineteenth-century American predecessors of this kind such as Emerson and Longfellow, who provided the historical foundation and framework for Singleton's own engagement with the poet.[2] The publication of Singleton's "heuristic" prose translation and three volumes of commentary suggested to Steiner a decline in Dante's contemporary literary currency and led him to speculate whether the poem itself was any longer accessible within a cultural environment characterized by an aesthetic of the fragmentary, where reading habits appropriate to the challenge of the classic text were rapidly being lost, where the noise level of contemporary life, its "bursts of static, stimuli," had rendered "impossible the necessary immersion in and self-gathering towards the jealous exigencies of Dante's text" (180).

Steiner's fears were not new. The 1970s were not the first time that the literary viability of Dante's poem, overwhelmed by scholarly exegesis, appeared threatened. As Brian Richardson illustrates in his contribution to this volume, the *Commedia* was at times marginal to major literary trends during the Renaissance, before it disappeared nearly completely from the cultural marketplace during the seventeenth century. But Steiner's prediction of an imminent decline in Dante's fortune appears now to have been mistaken. For the poem has survived remarkably well the passing of that literary modernism whose Dante Steiner particularly admires, and even shows signs of successfully making the transition into the new age of computerized textual environments "after the book."[3] And while this is not the place to rehearse the impact of Singleton's teachings on American Dante studies (a task admirably treated by several recent commentators),[4] a great revival and intensification of interest in Dante's poetry "as poetry" has characterized the post-Singletonian period, stimulated no doubt in part by the continuing utility of Singleton's landmark edition. Indeed, Dante's *Commedia* has prodigiously displayed throughout its history what Italo Calvino observed to be typical of the literary classic generally speaking: a capacity to generate incessantly dust-clouds of critical discourse about itself and no less continually to shake them off.[5]

By any measure, the current moment in Dante's critical fortune is one of exceptional intensity. Dante in America is central to ongoing debates in the humanities about the relationship between literature and philosophy, between literature and history, about allegory and / or representation, about the formation and function of the Western literary canon, about issues of gender, intertextuality, and translation. Work is appearing internationally at a rate and a volume never before witnessed. Some indication of this broader ferment, and of the increasing dialogue between previously more or less autonomous national traditions of Dante criticism is provided by the contributions of two distinguished British colleagues to the present volume.[6] Meanwhile, the heralded publication of a new poetic translation of the *Inferno* attests to Dante's continuing translatability and relevance to the contemporary American literary scene, to the fact that "the poem is written in a language that we speak *now*, no matter which language we speak."[7]

The question George Steiner raised concerning Dante's contemporary status has grown only more urgent given current high levels of engagement with the text from a wide variety of perspectives. Among readers of the *Commedia*, there is a growing recognition of the extent to which, as Giuseppe Mazzotta observes in these pages, "we owe our existence to it as much as it owes its existence to us" (63). The statement had special resonance given the particular context of its enunciation during a conference held at the University of Notre Dame, a Catholic university with intellectual and cultural origins deeply rooted in Dante's text. The extended inquiry into the status of "Dante Now" undertaken at Notre Dame during the 1993–1994 academic year sought in the first place to assess Dante's current position at a university with long traditions of faculty and student engagement with Dante, where every year approximately five hundred students engage in the study of some aspect of Dante's works "across the curriculum"—in the Medieval Institute, in the Departments of Philosophy, Theology, English, Romance Languages, Government, and the Program of Liberal Studies.

The university's John A. Zahm, C.S.C., Dante collection represents the material expression of Dante's original and historic centrality to Notre Dame's academic and cultural identity. Notre Dame's assessment of its engagement with Dante accordingly took as its point of departure an investigation into the history and contents of the Zahm collection. Roughly one hundred years after its establishment, the collection provided an appropriate focal point, since it genealogically links Notre Dame to an earlier *fin de siècle*, a similarly vital phase in the history of Dante studies in North America. The unique process of Dante's canonization as an American classic, begun by the poet-scholars Emerson and Longfellow, found at the time academic expression in the formation of three major North American Dante collections, at Harvard University, Cornell University, and the University of Notre Dame. The Zahm collection, however, which included over three thousand rare titles at the time of Zahm's death in 1921, represents an as yet unwritten chapter in the history of what Angelina La Piana called "Dante's American pilgrimage." Research into the Zahm collection naturally required a more general exploration of both the history and the current state of Dante studies which went beyond the walls of a single institution.

During the fall of 1993, "Renaissance Dante in Print (1492–1629)," a traveling exhibition of forty editions at the heart of the Zahm collection, and "Dante Now: Current Trends in Dante Studies," a conference held at Notre Dame 29–30 October, initiated a year-long discussion of Dante.[8] A second exhibition held at the Newberry Library in Chicago and a second conference dedicated to "Printing and Vernacular Literature in the Italian Renaissance" continued that conversation.[9] The exhibitions and the conferences were originally designed both to focus attention on Dante's position at Notre Dame and to establish a dialogue between that particular university community and the principal currents of Dante studies within the larger academic and literary world. Now that exchange promises to continue in the future, thanks to the generosity of William and Katherine Devers in establishing the Program in Dante Studies at the University of Notre Dame.

Dante Now: Current Trends in Dante Studies is the first volume in the William and Katherine Devers Series in Dante Studies. Like the conference from which the book derives, it is organized in sections reflecting three broad areas of interest in current research that distinguish the post-Singletonian period: Dante's poetics, "minor works," and reception. The priority which Singleton's school gave to theological and allegorical modes of interpretation in the analysis of the *Commedia* has given way to a renewed preoccupation with the problem of Dante's poetics, broadly conceived.[10] And this renewed attention to Dante's poetry has in turn stimulated increased attention to his "minor works," which, with the exception of the *Vita nuova*, had been neglected during the Singletonian ascendancy. Thus, works that had been considered merely ancillary to the theological and allegorical interpretation of the poem have become central to the study of the poet's language, style, and ideology.[11] Finally, the question of Dante's reception represents an important avenue of current research within the context of a broader concern with "cultural studies" and in a time of continuing debate about the history, role, and function of the Western literary classics. To be sure, some significant trends in Dante studies, and many significant voices currently at work in the field, could not be represented here, but these essays nevertheless offer a compelling portrait of the current ferment surrounding Dante now, both within and outside academic boundaries of Dante studies.

The essays in part 1, by Zygmunt Barański, Christopher Kleinhenz, and Giuseppe Mazzotta, show how readers and critics are still struggling, after nearly seven hundred years, to come to adequate terms with the absolute *novitas* of Dante's poem in the history of literary expression before or since, with the incredible density, resonance, and extension of Dante's literary and cultural memory, and with Dante's novel claims for the preeminent role of poetry as a form of knowledge. Barański's "Poetics of Meter" provides a vivid archaeological study of Dante's poetics by tracing the poet's self-exegesis as it is inscribed in the very poetic structures and rhetorical terminologies employed in the poem. The difference between the values of conventional poetic structures and rhetorical practices and those Dante fashions for the poem reveals the poet's artistic primacy vis-à-vis Romance, classical, and even biblical predecessors. Barański shows how the "canto," "canzone," and "terza rima" synthesize and surpass secular Romance and classical precedents. Dante's "cantica," on the other hand, establishes the poem's connection to the Canticum Canticorum and the Book of Psalms, and here Dante as *scriba Dei* appears to vie even with the biblical authors David and Solomon. In "Dante's Poetics of Citation," Kleinhenz, presents, with his visual clarity, a representative typology illustrating how and why Dante incorporates citations of earlier works in his poem. Kleinhenz focuses upon several *loci classici* that promise to continue to provide focal points of discussion for some time to come, beginning with the extraordinary moment in *Purgatorio* 29 when the poet, distinguishing between his vision and that of the biblical prophet Ezechiel, observes that with regard to the number of wings sported by the four animals representing the Gospels, John in the Apocalypse "agrees with me" ("Giovanni è meco").

Providing a kind of synthetic, albeit provisional, closure to the discussions of part 1, Giuseppe Mazzotta goes to the heart of the issue of Dante's poetics by asking why we still read the *Commedia*. He begins by asking us as readers to assume the perspective of the poet's consciousness, to put aside the "scholar's conceits," and to attempt to "come to terms with a consciousness that transcends our own." Dante's readers and critics must recognize as Dante did "the illusion that knowledge is power" and turn to poetry as "the language of our contingent historicity forever irreducible to the conventional canons of preestablished philosophical discourses" (66). For Mazzotta, readers must turn to the classics and to Dante's poem especially to discover its truth: "not a truth which is a whim or a *doxa*, but the truth about what a text is" (67). Mazzotta calls for a "philology of the imagination" that would bring together genealogy (Boccaccian, rather than Nietzchean or Foucaultian) with hermeneutics (Vichian rather than Derridean) and that would resolve the critical impasse of current neohistoricisms incapable of accounting for the aesthetic function of the text beyond questions of ideology. Mazzotta argues for Dante's centrality to ongoing and future theoretical speculation about the possibility of any kind of encounter with "other" worlds and "other" times.

Part 2 shows how the so-called opere minori are anything but minor to the study of Dante now. Edward Vasta and Dino Cervigni confront the problem of the oral versus the written in Dante's culture. Ronald Martinez considers Dante's poetic form in relation to the truths of natural science and metaphysics, while Albert Ascoli situates Dante within ongoing theoretical debate about the relationship between history and literature. Cervigni and Vasta reveal how the accepted canonical structure of the *Vita nuova* into forty-two numbered chapters represents an imposition of the conventions of print culture upon a work produced by a manuscript culture. Finding the chapter divisions established by Michele Barbi in his 1907 critical edition to be inconsistent and sometimes arbitrary, they propose new criteria for the division of the work which would, in their view, make possible "a full-scale orality/literacy study of the *Vita nuova*."

In "Nasce il Nilo," Martinez extends to the great canzone of exile "Tre donne intorno al cor mi son venute" a line of research that he and Robert Durling have brilliantly developed in their book *Time and the Crystal* with regard to Dante's *Rime petrose*. The crisis of exile rages in the poet's life and consciousness and, as before in the *petrose*, "the poet's best solution again proves to be a test of craft" (117). The political and ethical situation of the poet seems at an impasse that he attempts to resolve through the fashioning of a stanzaic and metrical form imitative of specific aspects of the cosmos. The result is a poem that parallels structures of the cosmos and the human body, indeed that points to the poet as a microcosm of the entire cosmos, "focusing the natural and metaphysical realms within the little world of [Dante's] body and mind" (117). Martinez's reading combines the highest level of formal precision with impressive erudition regarding the historical, literary, philosophical, and theological sources and contexts for Dante's poetry, nowhere better exemplified than in his learned gloss on Dante's verses at the canzone's midpoint, on the source of the Nile, which represent for Martinez the focus of the "poem's strategic mediation of inner and outer worlds, psychology and cosmology, moral virtue and natural order" (117).

The palinode represents Dante's most effective means of overcoming the estrangement of the self from history. According to this trope, Dante continually evokes his own previous texts and those of others only to mark the limitations of their doctrinal contents and rhetorical practices, thereby setting his *Commedia* apart from all previous human authorities. In the last twenty years the palinode has accordingly become the paradigmatic model for literary critical accounts of Dantean intra- and intertextuality. Albert Ascoli, however, proposes to shift the critical perspective from "inside" to "outside" the framework of the palinode. In "Palinode and History" he explores how history transcends the Dantean oeuvre by illustrating the breakdown of the palinodic structure under extreme forms of historical pressure. The *Monarchia*'s undecided chronological position, its engagement with, and suppression of, the political-historical order, reveal to us both the contingency and the rhetoricity of the palinode, its status as a rhetorical trope. Divergences between *Monarchia* and *Convivio*, between *Monarchia* and the *Commedia* (in particular the account of the proper relation between pope and emperor in *Purgatorio* 16), suggest the fragility and instability of the palinode, that is, of attempts by Dante and his critics alike to impose an idealized historical narrative on his life and works. Ascoli reveals instead Dante as "historical subject"—a poet who is produced by the same history he seeks to dominate through representation.

The contributions to part 3, on reception, range from R. A. Shoaf's reflections on Dante's problematic presence in late medieval England to Kevin Brownlee's treatment of the poem's transmission across both national and gender boundaries in late medieval France, from Brian Richardson's account of Dante's editorial fortune during the Renaissance to Nancy Vickers's discussion of a controversial contemporary video translation of Dante's *Inferno*. All raise important methodological issues while addressing the history and modalities of Dante's enlivening influence as a literary classic. Shoaf's essay "Noon Englissh

Digne" examines the notoriously difficult and much debated question
of Dante's literary influence in late medieval England, investigated
in relation to passages from Dante and Chaucer as well from the
Gawain poet. The essay raises the important question of the nature of
literary texts themselves as evidence, in the absence of forceful contextual arguments, for intertextual communication between authors
across space and time. For Kevin Brownlee the intertextual history
of Dante and Christine de Pizan provides an excellent laboratory for
an examination of the processes whereby national traditions, literary
works, and individual authors are "engendered." Brownlee uncovers
Christine de Pizan's "rewriting" of Dante's *Commedia* in her *Livre de
longe estude*, in which an appropriation of Dante as a literary "father
figure" accompanies a no less complex representation in the poem of
Christine's father, Thomas de Pizan, who was born in Italy, and was
himself a figure of authority at the French court of King Charles V.
Brownlee shows how both biological and literary genealogies are con-
structed by Christine in order to establish her own difference and
autonomous literary authority.

Brian Richardson's "Editing Dante's *Commedia*" illustrates Dante's
relevance to current research in book history and to analysis of the
processes of canonization by which literary works have historically
achieved their status as classics.[12] He identifies the editors of Dante's
text during the Renaissance and assesses the quality and character
of their work both as textual critics and as providers of interpretive
guidance for readers. Richardson's essay shows how printers, editors,
and their reading publics create new versions of the classic work:
it is through these that the classic continually renews its life. The
final essay, "Dante in the Video Decade," by Nancy Vickers, radically
shifts the chronological context from the Renaissance to the contemporary, but she illustrates the same phenomenon. Her presentation
of Peter Greenaway and Tom Phillips's 1990 video "translation" of
the beginning of the *Inferno* in "A TV Dante" attests yet again
to Dante's unequaled "translatability," this time across technological
and representational canons characteristic of the mass media. Vickers
adopts a formalist and philological mode to trace the polysemous
intertext in the Greenaway-Phillips *Inferno* of still-photographic de-
pictions of human and animal mobility by the cinematic pioneer
Eadweard Muybridge, whose work the video's creators regarded as
"the timeless abstracts of being and moving."

At the 1993 conference, Vickers's paper was complemented by a screening of "A TV Dante" and an accompanying lecture by John Welle on Dante's cinematic history, stretching back to a 1911 silent film version of Dante's *Inferno*.[13] Welle's presentation is one example of contributions to the conference that could not be presented here but are nevertheless worthy of recall, including formal responses to the three panels by Madison Sowell of Brigham Young University, Paolo Cherchi of the University of Chicago, and Dolores Frese of Notre Dame.

A special Notre Dame panel on the Monday following the conference addressed the topic "Dante: The Contemporary Status of the Classic" and featured Notre Dame faculty, including Lawrence Cunningham, a theologian; Kent Emery Jr., a medievalist; Henry Weinfield, a poet and critic; and Joseph Buttigieg, a translator and commentator of Antonio Gramsci's works. This panel effectively brought the inquiry full circle, returning it to the original institutional context from which it had departed. Cunningham illustrated the theological penetration of Dante's poetry, both in the figure of the stupid immensity and immobility of Dante's Satan, representing evil as the death of the intellect, and in the image of lady poverty climbing up to join Christ on the cross in *Paradiso* 11 ("ella con Cristo pianse in su la croce"). Emery offered reflections on the problem of the relation between poetry and theology during the medieval period and emphasized the primacy that Dante attributes to the poetic imagination vis-à-vis theological and philosophical materials, particularly in relation to those mysteries which are ineffable and beyond the final comprehension of the human mind. Weinfield presented a series of acute observations on Dante's influence in the creation of a visionary, but nontheological, tradition of poetry that broadly speaking coincides with romanticism, and discussed passages from Gray and Shelley. Buttigieg addressed the question of what it means to confront the whole issue of the classic literary text honestly, recalling the responses of a range of distinguished readers, from Antonio Gramsci who once wondered if anyone read Dante with love any longer besides "philologists who perform these strange philological rites, which are only understood, of course, within the circle of other scholars," to Samuel Beckett, who quit his teaching job at the University of Dublin, and when asked by a relative what he intended to do for the future, replied "Well, what I want to do with my life is sit, fart, and think of Dante."

The Notre Dame panel demonstrated how the presence of the John A. Zahm Dante Collection still finds today its living intellectual complement in the minds of Dante's many readers among faculty and students at Notre Dame. Like the collection, Dante's poem provides a link not only between members of a particular intellectual community and its past, but also to larger literary and cultural trends which take Dante as their focal point beyond the walls of any single academic institution. The intention behind the creation of the William and Katherine Devers Program in Dante Studies at the University of Notre Dame is thus to provide a point of reference for continuing conversations at Notre Dame as well as for future developments within the field of Dante studies and within the humanities generally.

At the end of his essay "Dante Now" George Steiner may have put his finger on precisely that quality of Dante's poetry which has guaranteed its continuing vitality for nearly seven hundred years, when he observed that "The *Divina commedia* performs that mystery of rooted motion without which there is no public sense or private weight to our lives" (185). In the narrative rhythms of the poem's *terza rima*, whose driving forward movement is constantly counterbalanced and controlled by echoes and reevocations of a poetic and narrative past, lies perhaps the mystery of "rooted motion" that the history of the poem's reception performs, in its constant movement forward into uncharted territories, in its continual evocations of a shared past. Today when our cultural life appears most vulnerable and ephemeral, this particular truth of Dante's poetry is particularly compelling and may explain why the noise level of contemporary society has not rendered inaccessible the "jealous exigencies of Dante's text" but, rather, made them the more imperative.[14]

The Dolphin and Anchor device that has been adopted by the Devers Program as its emblem and which appears on publications of the Devers series expresses this quality of rooted motion in Dante's poetry, and the force of his poem in history. Originally the mark of the great humanist, grammarian, editor, and typographer, Aldus Manutius (1449–1515), the device illustrated for Aldus the ancient proverb *Festina lente*, "Hurry up slowly." Within the new context of the Devers program it is meant to evoke in the leaping dolphin the endless mobility and innovation of the literary and critical traditions surrounding Dante's works, while the anchor suggests the role of the

Commedia itself, the focal point for the ceaseless interactions of poetics and hermeneutics, of literature and history, which the classic text continually renews.

ACKNOWLEDGMENTS

The conference for which these essays were invited was made possible through the generosity of the Paul M. and Barbara Henkels Visiting Scholars Program at the University of Notre Dame, as well as through the support of the university's Institute for Scholarship in the Liberal Arts, Medieval Institute, Departments of Romance Languages, English and the Program of Liberal Studies. Special thanks for their support of this endeavor go to Jennifer Warlick and Robert P. Burke, Director and Assistant Director respectively of the Institute for Scholarship in the Liberal Arts, to John Van Engen, Director of the Medieval Institute and Stephen Gersh, Acting Director of the Medieval Institute during the 1993–94 academic year, to JoAnn DellaNeva, Chair of the Department of Romance Languages and Literatures, to Stephen Fallon, Chair of the Program in Liberal Studies, and to Christopher Fox, Chair of the Department of English. Finally, I would like to express my gratitude to Jeannette Morgenroth, of the University of Notre Dame Press, for her always efficient and ever graceful editorial management of the volume and its editor.

NOTES

1. George Steiner, "Dante Now: The Gossip of Eternity," in *On Difficulty and Other Essays* (Oxford University Press, 1978), 164–185.

2. Giuseppe Mazzotta, "The American Criticism of Charles Singleton," *Dante Studies* 104 (1986): 27–44.

3. For example, the Dartmouth Dante Project currently provides on-line access to the poem and some forty-six commentaries across a chronological period ranging from 1322 to 1983. It is available at the following electronic address: dante@baker.dartmouth.edu.

4. Franco Fido, "Un grande dantista americano: Charles S. Singleton," *Autografo* 5 (1988): 57–72; Dante Della Terza, "Charles S.

Singleton: An Appraisal," *Dante Studies* 104 (1986): 9–25; Zygmunt G. Barański, "Reflecting on Dante in America: 1949–1990," *Annali d'italianistica: Dante and Modern American Criticism* 8 (1990): 58–86.

5. Italo Calvino, "Perchè leggere i classici," in *Perchè leggere i classici* (Milano: Mondadori, 1991): "Un classico è un'opera che provoca incessantemente un pulviscolo di discorsi critici su di se, ma continuamente se li scrolla di dosso" (14).

6. The international dimension of increased activity surrounding Dante was recently given formal recognition and greater focus at the first meeting of the International Dante Seminar, held at Princeton, 22–23 October 1994, with participating scholars from Australia, Canada, England, Ireland, Italy, Switzerland, and the United States.

7. The translation is Robert Pinsky's *The Inferno of Dante* (New York: Farrar Straus Giroux, 1994), and the citation is from the foreword to that volume by John Freccero (xix). See also *Dante's Inferno: Translations by Twenty Contemporary Poets*, ed. Daniel Halpern with an afterword by Giuseppe Mazzotta (Hopewell, N.J.: Ecco Press, 1993).

8. For a brief description of the exhibition, see Theodore J. Cachey, Jr., "Renaissance Dante in Print (1472–1629)," in *A Newberry Newsletter* 55 (Spring 1994): 2–4. An expanded Internet version of the exhibit, featuring over four hundred full-color images and accompanying commentary is available at the following URL address: http://tuna. uchicago.edu/Dante/Dante_Ex1.html. For a preliminary historical sketch of Zahm's collecting activity, see Louis Jordan, Christian Dupont, and Theodore J. Cachey, Jr., "The John A. Zahm Dante Collection," in *What is Written Remains: Historical Essays on the Libraries of Notre Dame*, ed. Maureen Gleason and Katharina J. Blackstead (Notre Dame and London: University of Notre Dame Press, 1994), 85–104.

9. Both events were organized together with the Newberry Library's Center for Renaissance Studies, with the collaboration of the center's director, Mary Beth Rose, and Paul F. Gehl, custodian of the John M. Wing Collection, Newberry Library. "Vernacular Literature and Printing in Renaissance Italy," supported in part by the National Endowment for the Humanities, featured lectures by JoAnn DellaNeva, Domenico De Robertis, Paul Gehl, Daniel Javitch, Louis Jordan, William Kennedy, Deborah Parker, Brian Richardson, and Elissa Weaver.

10. Steven Botterill, "Dante in North America: 1991–93," *Lectura dantis* 14–15 (1994): 116–129, and particularly, 123–124.

11. Steven Botterill, "*Dante Studies* and the Study of Dante," *Annali d'italianistica* 8 (1990): 88–103, and in particular 97–98.

12. The Richardson paper, originally presented in conjunction with the exhibit at the Newberry Library of the Zahm collection's Renaissance holdings was graciously made available by its author to be included in this collection.

13. John P. Welle, "Dante in the Cinematic Mode: An Historical Survey of Dante Movies," in *Dante's Inferno: The Indiana Critical Edition*, ed. and trans. Mark Musa (Bloomington, Ind.: Indiana University Press, forthcoming, 1995).

14. Calvino's definitions of the classic come to mind again in this context: "13. A classic is that which tends to relegate actuality to the status of background noise, but at the same time cannot do without this background noise. 14. A classic is that which persists as background noise even there where the most incompatible actuality dominates" ("È classico ciò che tende a relegare l'attualità al rango di rumore di fondo, ma nello stesso tempo di questo rumore non può fare a meno. 14. È classico ciò che persiste come rumore di fondo anche là dove l'attualità più incompatibile fa da padrona" ["Perchè leggere i classici," 19]).

Part 1

Poetics

The Poetics of Meter

TERZA RIMA, "CANTO," "CANZON," "CANTICA"

The Problem of the *Canto*

An arresting detail catches the eye in the trecento commentaries to Dante's *Commedia*. With the exception of Guido da Pisa, Giovanni Boccaccio, and Francesco da Buti, the rest of the commentators are uncomfortable with the poet's choice of *canto* to refer to the poem's one hundred constituent parts: "e dar matera al ventesimo canto" (*Inf.* 20.2), "e li altri due che 'l canto suso appella" (*Inf.* 33.90), "Sí cominciò Beatrice questo canto" (*Par.* 5.16), and "nel modo che 'l seguente canto canta" (*Par.* 5.139). In place of the poet's designation, they substitute *capitulum* or *capitolo*. For instance, Pietro Alighieri explains that "Forma tractatus est divisio ipsi libri, qui dividitur et partitur per tres libros; qui libri postea dividuntur per centum capitula; quae capitula postea dividuntur per suas partes et rhythmos";[1] while the Ottimo paraphrases *Paradiso* 5.139 as follows: "come contiene nel seguente capitolo."[2] That the commentators should have rejected Dante's terminology is far from unjustified. Ever since classical times, *cantus*, when applied to literature, had simply meant a poetic composition;[3] it had never been utilized as a precise technical term with which to tag the discrete parts of a long narrative poem (whether written in Latin or in the vernacular). The proper term for such major divisions—as the commentators and Dante himself[4] well knew—was of course *capitulum*[5] or, possibly, *liber*.[6] In their annotations, as the two examples I have just cited reveal, the poet's fourteenth-century readers normally responded to his use of *canto* by providing a clarificatory synonym for it—a procedure typical of the commentary tradition.[7] They rarely posed themselves the question, however, why Dante should have decided to apply such an idiosyncratic label to the one hundred units making up his "comedía."[8] The commentators obviously appreciated the peculiarity of Dante's usage, hence their literal gloss, but they then did not take the matter beyond this first basic interpretive level.

In their turn, modern Dantists do not even go so far. The term *canto* has now become so closely involved with the *Commedia* that it no longer seems to require an explanation, never mind be the cause of surprise. Indeed, it would be correct to say that neither the origins of the *canto*, nor its status as a metrical, epistemological, and structural form, nor the reasons for Dante's strange choice of the term have aroused much scholarly interest. The entry for *canto* in the *Enciclopedia dantesca* emblematically records this indifference; it simply notes that "Il termine indica ciascuna delle parti in cui si divide ogni cantica della *Commedia*."[9] Such critical neglect is odd in the light of the key position which the *canto* enjoys in the organization of the poem, and thereby the importance it would appear to have for our appreciation of the *Commedia*.[10] I should like to suggest that, given Dante's customary careful use of technical literary terminology, and given his obvious familiarity with the normal language of textual division, he purposely employed "canto" in a new and seemingly 'inappropriate' manner so as to draw attention to his use of the word. In my work on Dante's poetics,[11] I have noted that it is a commonplace of his self-exegesis always to talk about the *Commedia* in a vocabulary which a contemporary audience would have known. Yet, at the same time, a semantic discrepancy is invariably apparent between the conventional values of a term and the way in which Dante applied the concept to his poem. As a result, his readers are encouraged to reflect on his peculiar usages and thus begin to appreciate the *novitas* of his work, as well as its idiosyncratic, but continuing, relationship to the tradition. And this last factor is crucial. Dante must have believed that, despite first appearances to the contrary, something did link his experimental *canto* to current notions of the term. If this had not been the case, his use of "canto" to describe and define his poetry would have been pointless, not to say meaningless, and therefore uninterpretable. It is thus in contemporary usage and in the *Commedia* itself (especially in those sections of the poem where the word actually appears) that we need to seek the beginning of an answer to the problem of Dante's *canto*.

The poet first mentions the division of his poem into *canti* in the *exordium* to *Inferno* 20, where he defines the *Commedia*'s major metrical and narrative units:

> Di nova pena mi conven far versi
> e dar matera al ventesimo canto
> de la prima canzon, ch'è d'i sommersi.

> (*Inf.* 20.1–3)

Since the early 1960s, most critics have underlined the technical precision of these lines and their importance for Dante's metaliterary self-reflection.[12] The poet, in fact, made this feature of the *terzina* explicit by modeling it on the *accessus ad auctores*, the general prologues to literary and philosophical commentaries; thus, lines 1–3 are typical of discussions of the *forma tractatus* and of the *materia* of a text.[13] Earlier this century, scholars, disturbed by the tercet's 'prosaic' tone, tended, on the contary, to downgrade its importance[14] (though, fortunately, only Herbert Douglas Austin was so discomforted by it as to suggest that it should be expunged from the *Commedia* as an interpolation).[15]

While recognizing the lines' breadth of reference, recent discussions have preferred to fragment the *terzina* rather than to analyze it as a single unit. In particular, attention is separately paid to the possible meanings of "nova," of "mi conven far versi," of "canzon," and of "sommersi." Yet it would appear that Dante intended these lines to be read in quite a different way. In order to elucidate the organization and the poetics of the *Commedia*, he established a sophisticated system of interconnections among the tercet's various elements. At the most basic level, the syntax of the sentence confirms that at least the opening two-and-a-half lines need to be read as one—a detail which modern editors acknowledge by introducing a single pause into the sentence, a comma after "canzon." As a result of this, special emphasis is placed on the term; and it is further highlighted by its position at the end of the hemistych. That Dante should underline his choice of "canzon" is not surprising. His use of the word here seems even more aberrant, and therefore potentially more significant, than his use of "canto"; and it is worth noting that this term, too, is placed in a metrically marked position at the end of the line. Indeed, by continuing to exploit the formal characteristics of the hendecasyllable, the poet also draws attention to the tercet's two remaining literary terms—"versi" appears at the end of the line, while "matera" is found at the end of the hemistych. The skill with which Dante constructs the opening of *Inferno* 20 and the parallels which he creates between its four technical words are clear evidence both of the terms' interconnections and of their importance. Such attention to its composition befits a *terzina* which, it should be recalled, stands as Dante's first explicit internal definition of the *Commedia*'s meter and structure.[16] To put it simply, he declares that his poem has a most unusual form of organization; in Pietro Alighieri's commonplace language, it is divided into both *libri* and *capitula*—a unique arrangement for an epic poem (I shall return shortly to this crucial issue). And Dante immediately refines his description. The precision with which he affirms that we are about to read "*il ventesimo canto / de la prima canzon*" also reveals for the first time that this first *canzone* will have its numerical counterpart or counterparts elsewhere in the text. Up to this point, the poem provides no clue that it is to have such an unexpected and original design.[17] Further and more generally, Dante's eccentric use of "canto" and "canzon" affords immediate proof of the uniqueness of his "comedía" in relation to established literary canons, just as his conventional recourse to "versi" and "matera" serves as an equally timely reminder of its debts to the tradition. *Inferno* 20's *incipit* revitalizes the hoary *topos* of the novelty of the "matera" which the writer is about to present. The newness of Dante's "nova pena" spreads to every part of this crucial *terzina*, and, by extension, to the *Commedia* as a whole.

All that I have said so far is not difficult to discern; it involves what might be called the surface meaning of the lines. However, what is more intriguing and important, if the complexity and originality of the *Commedia* are to be appreciated, are the reasons (1) why Dante should have felt it necessary to organize his poem in the peculiar manner that he did; (2) why he decided to raise these matters at this particular juncture of his poem; and (3) why he chose to describe his work with the strange terms found in *Inferno* 20. The remainder of this study attempts to provide some answers to these three questions. However, given the considerable degree of overlap among my proposed solutions, my answers will not be as neatly compartmentalized as the three questions which they hope to elucidate. The history of Dante's "canto" and "canzon," as befits the all-embracing ambitions of his "comedía," is one of synthesis and variety, as well as of order.

"Canzon" and "Canto"—De vulgari eloquentia and the Commedia

Not unexpectedly, unlike his use of "canto," Dante's choice of "canzon" has attracted considerable critical attention. The infernal *canzone* not only sits uneasily with the synonymous "cantica" utilized at the end of *Purgatorio* (33.140), but its relationship to the illustrious lyric genre of the same name also seems especially problematic. It is now widely, and not unreasonably, accepted that, by means of "canzon," Dante was suggesting some kind of, probably contrastive, analogy between his 'lyric' and 'comic' poetry. However, less agreement exists as to what such an analogy might actually involve. Some critics claim that, given the *canzone*'s traditional association with the *stilus altus*, Dante's infernal "canzon" is simply a pointer to *Inferno* 20's 'tragic' register, especially in the light of the *canto*'s debts to classical literature.[18] This is an unsatisfactory explanation since it ignores, first, that "canzon" refers primarily to structural and thematic features rather than to stylistic ones, and, second, that it embraces the *Inferno* as a whole and, as Dante makes clear by his use of the epithet "prima," it can be applied to each of the *Commedia*'s major constituent parts and thus has a bearing on the poem as a whole. Furthermore, this suggestion fails to account for the *canto*'s stylistic variety which cannot easily be subsumed under the category of the 'tragic'. Other scholars argue more persuasively that, by means of "canzon," Dante was deliberately recalling the *De vulgari eloquentia*,[19] his major critical and theoretical contribution on this lyric form. Telling support for this position comes from *Inferno* 20's closing line—"Sí mi parlava, e andavamo introcque" (130)—which ends with a word that Dante had condemned in the treatise as unfit for the *volgare illustre* of the *canzone tragica* (1.13.2).[20] Thus, thanks to the verbal *rapprochements* between the *Commedia* and the *De vulgari eloquentia*—scholars go on to conclude—the poet underlined the ideological and artistic differences which distinguish the two principal moments of his poetic career. From this perspective, "canzon" touches on the *Commedia* in its entirety: "Il teorizzatore cioè della canzone come propria della poesia tragica si serve del termine— canzone—per indicare poesia comica per eccellenza."[21]

Though I largely agree with this line of argument, I also believe that *Inferno* 20 has more to reveal about the metaliterary interplay between the *De vulgari eloquentia* and the *Commedia* than has been recognized so far. To date, critics have restricted themselves to drawing broad comparisons between the two works—comparisons which, paradoxically, they have based on single words considered in isolation from the rest of the *canto* and of the chapters of the treatise from which they have been taken. Yet, as with its opening tercet, the whole thrust of Dante's presentation in *Inferno* 20 is towards a totalizing reading. It is surely not by chance that, in the *canto*, Dante should have strategically brought together technical vocabulary, allusions to the *De vulgari eloquentia*, an evaluation of classical *tragedie*, and a startling synthesis of 'high' and 'low' stylistic forms.[22] As we shall see, these elements illuminate each other in turn, thereby providing both an explanation for Dante's original use of literary terminology in the *canto*'s *incipit*, and general insights into the workings of the "comedía."

Dante placed the formal description of his poem at the head of a group of *canti* which, stretching from *Inferno* 20 to *Inferno* 23.57, represents an unusual section in the makeup of the *cantica*. It constitutes the most explicitly 'anti-tragic' part of the poem, and thus it crucially serves to illustrate Dante's new ideas on the 'comic' register.[23] More specifically, and in keeping with the concerns of their *exordium*, these *canti* yield considerable information on the structure of the *Commedia*; indeed, they could be said to offer an extended practical commentary on aspects of *Inferno* 20.1–3.

The three *canti* of barratry (*Inf.* 21–23) are the most conspicuous, if not quite the first,[24] instance in the *Inferno* of a lack of correspondence between the structure of the *canto* and of another narrative unit, such as a division of the afterlife, an infernal inhabitant, a group of sinners, etc. As the poem moves from *Inferno* 21 to *Inferno* 23, the 'space' created between the close of a *canto* and the opening of the following one ceases to be employed as a kind of break—a brief pause, like that enjoyed by Virgil and the pilgrim by the sepulcher of Pope Anastasius (11.1–15), in the onward flow of the story. Instead, a more fluid relationship, akin to enjambment, is established between the beginnings and the endings of these three *canti*. This is a striking new development in the organization of the *Commedia*, and it is a ploy which becomes typical in the *Purgatorio* and the *Paradiso*.[25] Nevertheless, that such a shift should occur precisely at this point cannot but cause a degree of perplexity. Dante, it should not be forgotten, has just highlighted the specificity of the *canto* ("il ventesimo canto / de la prima canzon"), a fact which, somewhat bewilderingly, he almost immediately calls into question. If, on the one hand, the image of the *canto* presented by *Inferno* 20 as a fairly well-defined unit conforms, in general terms, to the image which can be extrapolated from Dante's practice up to this point, then the next three *canti*, on the other hand, underscore its structural fragility and go some way to deconstruct its aura of self-sufficiency. Indeed, by doing this, and despite their particular narrative continuity, *Inferno* 21–23 help to bring to the fore the fact that, unlike the *laisses* of, say, the *Chanson de Roland* (see below, "Epic Structures"), none of Dante's *canti* so far can claim to have a single narrative or stylistic focus. Despite the clearcut individuality of each *canto*, a feature confirmed by the organization of their rhyme scheme (a point to which I shall return in greater detail in this section and below, in "The Flexible *Canto*") the *canti* are not self-standing compositions but subordinate parts of larger textual, narrative, and stylistic entities.

Approximately two-thirds of the way through the first *cantica*, Dante felt it was time to exploit that knowledge and those expectations of his poem's organization which, by this point, he could reasonably expect his readers to have acquired, in order to stimulate reflection on the nature of the *canto* (and of the *Commedia* in general). He prefaced this operation by defining it in relation to the *Commedia*'s other metrical components, and by finally giving a name to this new form (and the *canto*'s *novitas* could not have escaped anyone's notice, since nothing quite like it had previously graced the epic tradition).[26] In particular, Dante appeared to be raising a number of fundamental questions: if the canto is, narratively and stylistically, a diffuse, flexible, and possibly even arbitrary form, why does he bother to use it instead of an open-ended and continuous structure like that of the *romans*? In fact, why does he further complicate his poem by introducing an additional system of subdivision and another original organizational tier—the *canzone*? Yet again, Dante is prodding his readers to interpret, to act as commentators of his poem—a duty which he openly exhorts them to undertake a few lines later on: "Se Dio ti lasci, lettor, prender frutto / di tua lezione, or pensa per te stesso" (*Inf.* 20.19–20). And to succeed in this task, he provides them with an authoritative guide.

As might be imagined, this guide is the *De vulgari eloquentia*. If this were not the case, it is difficult to see why Dante should have made such an effort to raise the treatise's shadow in this already crowded metaliterary context. The metrical term which most powerfully, because most unexpectedly, unites the treatise with the *Commedia* is—as we have seen—*cantio/canzone*. Thus, in keeping with Dante's standard self-exegetical procedures, it seems feasible that the 'comic' "canzon" not only establishes a contrastive relationship with its 'tragic' counterpart (whose *caposcuola*, Virgil's *Aeneid*, is *Inferno* 20's principal intertext) but also, *mutatis mutandis*, has certain facets in common with the traditional 'high' *canzone*. And the poet's discussion of the *cantio* in the *De vulgari eloquentia* does indeed have uncanny links with *Inferno* 20.1–3. It is obvious that, like the lyric *canzone*, Dante's epic "canzon" is the shell which contains other structures: "cantio . . . est equalium stantiarum sine responsorio ad unam sententiam tragica coniugatio" (*DVE* 2.8.8). In fact, if we ignore for the moment the two epithets—"equalium" and "tragica"—which principally drive a wedge between them, the structural similarities between the two kinds of *canzone* are quite striking. Both do not include refrains (*responsoria*) between their main constituent units (*stantia/canto*), and each is dedicated to a single concern (*una sententia*); as regards the "prima canzon," this is naturally the "sommersi."[27] Furthermore, the specific structural relationship which exists between "cantio" and "stantia" also holds good for "canzon" and "canto": "Nam quemadmodum cantio [/"canzon"] est gremium totius sententie, sic stantia [/"canto"] totam artem ingremiat" (*DVE* 2.9.2). *Inferno* 20's *ars* is how it gives poetic form ("dar versi") to the "matera" of the "nova pena." And the 'comic' *canto* has other affinities with the *canzone* stanza. Metrically and structurally they are both independent organic units: "stantiam esse sub certo cantu et habitudine limitata carminum et sillabarum compagem" (*DVE* 2.9.6), while the confines of the *canto* are fixed, first, by its opening and closing with a double rhyme (the so-called *rime rilevate*) rather than with a triple one, and, second, by ending with the single line of a new tercet[28]—effects which are achieved thanks to the 'artistic' manipulation of its "versi."[29] Finally, as well as both being 'closed' structures, they are also 'open' ones, since they respectively unite with other *stantiae* and *canti* to create *canzoni*. By exploring the possible analogies (and we should not forget the centrality which deduction *per analogiam* enjoyed in the Middle Ages) between chapters 8 and 9 of book 2 of the *De vulgari eloquentia* and lines 1–3 of *Inferno* 20, we can gain illuminating insights into the character of the *Commedia*'s principal constituent parts.[30]

At this point, however, if the 'comic' and the 'lyric' are not to be perceived as somehow synonymous, it is imperative to restore the two 'missing' adjectives, "equalium" and "tragica," to the treatise's definition of *cantio* in chapter 8. In the following chapter, Dante goes on to explain what he means by "equalium stantiarum": "nec licet aliquid artis sequentibus arrogare, sed solam artem antecedentis induere" (*DVE* 2.9.2); and his definition of the *stilus tragicus* is equally restrictive: "illa que summe canenda distinximus isto solo sunt stilo [tragico] canenda: videlicet salus, amor et virtus et que propter ea concipimus, dum nullo accidente vilescant" (*DVE* 2.4.8; and cp. 2.2.1–9). It is the *De vulgari eloquentia*'s championing of a formally balanced and restricted treatment of a narrow subject matter which immediately discloses the abyss which divides the 'tragic' *cantio* and its *stantiae* from the equivalent components of the "comedía." Thus, if one undertakes a general assessment of the *canto* based on any small consecutive number of these, what emerges is a stylistic, structural, and thematic variety quite alien to the conventions of the lyric *canzone*. It is enough to think, since we are in its vicinity, of the richness of that group of eight *canti* which begins with *Inferno* 16 (where Dante first introduces the title of his poem)[31] and ends with *Inferno* 23. The *canti* supply the hard, practical evidence of the novelty of Dante's epic poetry, especially in contrast to the monotony of the *stantiae*. In fact, the formal and ideological polyvalence of the *canti* is what distinguishes the "comedía" from all other human books.

The Flexible *Canto*

The epistemological effectiveness of medieval analogy lay in its ability to highlight variance as well as similarity between things; and how Dante took advantage of the *De vulgari eloquentia* in *Inferno* 20 is a classic example of how he worked both with and against the tradition to explain his experimentation. In a similar manner, while pinpointing the common features of his hundred *canti*, Dante also indicated the uniqueness of each of these, as his lapidary "ventesimo canto / de la prima canzon" enshrines. Like the stanza, they are self-contained; however, Dante's new 'comic' outlook, as their changes in length testify,[32] no longer permits 'harmony' between them. The *Commedia* depends for its very artistic and ideological existence and resolution on their differences: the "nova . . . matera" in the ever new "versi" of each new *canto*. The single *canti*, however, are not left isolated; they are organically and logically integrated, first, into the scheme of their particular "canzon," and, then, into the totalizing and unifying embrace of the "comedía." It is obvious that traditional literary practices, like those examined in the *De vulgari eloquentia*, could only tangentially provide the forms for the *Commedia* and account for its *novitas*. Dante had to seek new models and new points of reference. He thus turned—as is well known—to God's two all-embracing books, the universe and the Bible.[33] In imitation of what he had learned from the synthesizing conventions of scriptural *sermo humilis* and from the "volume" which "binds" the plurality of "ciò che per l'universo si squaderna" (*Par.* 33.86–87), Dante similarly tried to incorporate 'everything' into a single text and to present this, in each instance, according to the style which he deemed most appropriate. This radical literary intent found formal fulfillment in the invention of the *canto*, a structure which, unlike conventional poetic frameworks subservient to the *genera dicendi*, was both all-receptive and able to establish links with God's 'writing'. Thus, the *dispositio* of the *canti* into structures based on the numbers three and ten has its artistic and symbolic point of origin in the *ordo* and character of divine creation;[34] and the same claim can be made for their wide-ranging style and content. It is thus indicative that, just before and after he defined the structure of his poem in *Inferno* 20, Dante should have laid special emphasis on God's artistry:

> O somma sapïenza, quanta è l'arte
> che mostri in cielo, in terra e nel mal mondo,
> e quanto giusto tua virtù comparte!
>
> (*Inf.* 19.10–12)

and "non per foco ma per divin' arte" (21.16).

The *canto* is a form of enormous flexibility. This seems to be the main lesson of *Inferno* 20.1–3. Its strength lies, first, in its structural ability both to stand alone and to become part of a larger whole, and, second, in its compositional possibility not to be tied to any one style or subject. Indeed, the *canto* is able to perform stylistic and thematic switches and syntheses at will, unconstrained by traditional notions of *convenientia* or of metrical 'harmonization', but driven only by the divinely willed demand that the poet "tutta sua visïon fa manifesta" (*Par.* 17.128). A less ambitious poet than Dante would have restricted himself to instituting stylistic shifts between *canti* rather than within them. It goes without saying, however, that such a solution would have singularly failed to provide a proper sense both of the complexity of the created universe and of the import of the poem's God-given message.

The other three references to the *canto* in the *Commedia* all similarly emphasize its flexibility. In *Inferno* 33.90—"e li altri due [Ugolino's children] che 'l canto suso appella"—the poet highlights the continuity, despite the changes in tone, time, and speaker, between Ugolino's story and Dante-*poeta*'s invective against Pisa. The two allusions in *Paradiso* 5—"Sí cominciò Beatrice questo canto" (16) and "nel modo che 'l seguente canto canta" (139)—underscore the limits of the individual *canto* while recognizing its contacts with the rest of the poem and its role in the narrative unfolding of the *Commedia*.[35] The *canto* is the fundamental artistic and ideological unit of the poem. Just as every part of creation is a 'trace' of the creator,[36] each *canto*, on account of its versatility, stands as a microcosm of the all-embracing "comedía." By hinting once again at his work's debts to the *Deus artifex*, Dante neatly and consistently clarifies and legitimates his literary experimentation and its forms.

Although the analogy I have suggested between the *exordium* of *Inferno* 20 and the *De vulgari eloquentia* helps to cast light on the *Commedia*'s arrangement, and partly also on the reason for Dante's choice of "canzon" as the tag with which to describe and explain his poetry (but see below), it fails to illuminate his thinking behind the selection of the term "canto." If anything, Dante's statement in the treatise that "Tota . . . ars cantionis circa tria videtur consistere: primo circa cantus divisionem" (*DVE* 2.9.4), where "cantus" is equivalent to *melodia*,[37] merely serves to underline the very different *divisio cantuum* of the *Commedia*. It is noteworthy, however, that Boccaccio, followed by Buti, did justify Dante's *canto* in terms of the similarities between musical and poetic scansion.[38] This interpretation is, of course, unsatisfactory since it ignores the structural, ideological, and stylistic functions of the 'comic' *canto*. In any case, Dante leaves no doubt in the *Commedia* that he is sensitively aware of the different possible meanings of *canto*.[39] When he appeals to the "sante Muse" for help in *Purgatorio* 1.8, he draws a precise demarcation between poetry ("canto") and music ("suono")—"seguitando il mio canto con quel suono / di cui le Piche misere sentiro / lo colpo tal" (10–12)—which recalls his technically more explicit discussion of the same distinction in the *De vulgari eloquentia*:

> Preterea disserendum est utrum cantio dicatur fabricatio verborum armonizatorum, vel ipsa modulatio. Ad quod dicimus quod nunquam modulatio dicitur cantio, sed sonus, vel thonus, vel nota, vel melos. Nullus enim tibicen, vel organista, vel cytharedus melodiam suam cantionem vocant, nisi in quantum nupta est alicui cantioni; sed armonizantes verba opera sua cantiones vocant, et etiam talia verba in cartulis absque prolatore iacentia cantiones vocamus. (*DVE* 2.8.5)

If Boccaccio's reading of *canto* is correct, then it would necessarily mean that, on the one hand, Dante employed the term to associate the *Commedia* with "modulatio" (for instance, in *Inferno* 20), while, on the other, he used *canto* to present his work as a "fabricatio verborum armonizatorum" in opposition to music (as he did in the 'prologue' to the *Purgatorio*). This seems extremely unlikely, as it would require Dante to have defined his poem in two mutually exclusive ways while utilizing the same word. Indeed, when Dante directly applied *canto* to his poem, it was always with expressly literary connotations.[40] Thus, I believe that he chose the term to refer to each of the one hundred parts of the *Commedia* precisely because of its traditional meaning as poetry or poetic composition in general. The all-embracing character of the *canto*—as we have seen—can potentially contain within its boundaries any type of poetry. Dante's new plurilingual *canto*, *vestigium* of the "comedía," makes concrete in a similar microcosmic and symbolic manner the abstract notion of 'poetry', which, hitherto, on account of the precepts of rhetorical *convenientiae*, had found practical expression in a fragmented manner through a system of discrete, as well as stylistically and thematically constrained, literary genres.

My suggestion that Dante selected "canto" because of its broad connections with poetry finds immediate support in his choice of "canzon," which, tellingly, can be justified for exactly the same reason. With his customary acumen and eye for detail, Gianfranco Contini was the first, as far as I know, to point out that, in *Inferno* 20, and once again thanks to the *De vulgari eloquentia*, "canzon" should be associated with poetry in general, since "ballates et sonitus et omnia cuiuscunque modi verba sunt armonizata vulgariter et regulariter, cantiones esse dicemus" (*DVE* 2.8.6; and cp. 2.3.4).[41] Nor is Dante's definition unorthodox; similar usages of *cantio/canzone* can be found in a range of Italian writers from Brunetto to Bembo.[42] Dante's "canto" and "canzon" come together in an effective alliance to sustain the idea of the literary all-inclusiveness of the *Commedia*. Furthermore, as I have shown elsewhere, Dante's decision to describe his poem as a "comedía" stems from the fact that, among all the medieval genres, only 'comedy' was associated with such a wealth of literary situations that, akin to the meaning of "canto" and "canzone" as poetry in general, it could stand for literature *tout court*.[43] The precision, coherence, and skill with which Dante clarifies his poem is impressive.

Before I leave the matter of the poet's possible reasons for applying *canto* and *canzone* to the *Commedia*, I should like to rectify any possible misconceptions which may have arisen from the sharp distinctions which I earlier drew between poetry and music. While I am far from persuaded that Dante intended any narrow or too specific associations between his versifying and the practices of musicians, I have little doubt that, by making recourse to *canto*, *canzone* (and *cantica*), given their traditional associations with song, he did aim to imply certain broad similarities between the *Commedia* and music. In particular, since musical harmony with its mathematical basis had long been equated with the order of divine creation, the poem's 'musical' qualities were yet another means of bringing to the fore both the *Commedia*'s dependence on the *Deus artifex* and its own numerically balanced organization.[44] As I hope is becoming clear, Dante reiterated in different ways certain basic facts about his great poem in order to ensure their implications would not be lost. Repetition is a fundamental characteristic of the *Commedia* (it is enough to think of the *canto*'s structural functions or the constant narrative recapitulations which punctuate the pilgrim's journey); at the same time, variety, the poem's other key pole, can only be fully appreciated and offset in opposition to paradigms of sameness. *Variatio*, the interplay between coincidence and diversity, was a technique which Dante was more than happy to learn from traditional rhetorical practice.

Epic Structures

Thus, *per variationem*, Dante's unique decision to arrange the *Commedia* into *canti* and *canzoni* also helps highlight another aspect of its poetics. These two peculiar structures, precisely because of their peculiarity, cannot but draw attention to the problematic relationship which pertains between them and the traditional divisions of other literary texts circulating at the beginning of the trecento. To note this fact is not something new. For instance, it has been stated that "L'idea . . . di costruire un'unità metricamente autonoma, dell'estensione . . . del canto, è indubbiamente nuova, anche se può trovare un suggerimento nei 'canti' in cui è divisa la grande poesia epica o narrativa latina (classica e medievale). Rispetto infatti anche a quei 'canti' latini, Dante innova in senso romanzo, attraverso l'invenzione di una struttura variabile, ma conclusa."[45] However, like most analyses of the *Commedia*'s metrical forms, this assessment is too reductive. It offers no evidence for the claim that Dante was adapting Latin models, nor does it explain what it means by "Romance renewal";[46] furthermore, it remains silent about the implications of Dante's inventiveness (the aspect on which my discussion has tended to concentrate). Like the glosses of the trecento commentators, it barely goes beyond the 'literal' level of Dante's *canto* and *canzone*.

Once again the *exordium* to *Inferno* 20 helps to disentangle the knotty issue of the nature of the contacts between the organization of the *Commedia* and that of other works. Achille Tartaro observes that, in lines 1–3, Dante "si procura d'identificare la propria opera, segnalandone le coordinate culturali accanto alle unità compositive."[47] In line with this comment, therefore, it is suggestive that other scholars have associated this troublesome *terzina* with a range of different poetic genres. D'Ovidio and Parodi felt that it had a 'popularizing' bias; the former declared that "il capitolo comincia alla buona, con una prefazioncella un po' da cantastorie,"[48] while the latter asserted that "il canto comincia con un'intonazione un po' da poemetto popolare."[49] And this line of analysis has been accompanied by the idea that "canzon" is supposed to recall the *chansons de geste*.[50] Conversely, as I mentioned earlier, other critics have interpreted *Inferno* 20's *incipit*, and especially the value of "canzon," in terms of the loftiest, 'tragic' creations of the classical tradition. The diversity of literary echoes which may be heard in the opening tercet—echoes which find support in the stylistic and thematic *variatio* of the rest of the *canto*—encourages the view that, in *Inferno* 20.1–3, Dante was underlining the need to measure his poem's structures against those of other texts, both Latin and vernacular; an approach which, naturally, also finds support in the association with poetry in general of "canto" and "canzon."

As is now widely recognized, the *canto* of the soothsayers stands as one of Dante's major statements on classical literature. During the course of his evaluation, the poet reveals what he considers to be the ideological and rhetorical limitations of pagan Latin writing, especially in relation to his Christian poetry. However, Dante did not restrict his criticism of classical poetry to these two aspects; I believe that, in the light of *Inferno* 20.1–3, he also highlighted its structural deficiencies. The lengthy (often stretching for nearly a thousand lines), cumbersome, and narratively amorphous 'books' of Virgil, Ovid, Lucan, and Statius, adopted also by their later Latin imitators, are supplanted by the short, nimble, and narratively better focused *canti* of his *Commedia* which rarely run to more than fifty *terzine*. The form of the *canto* is the first mark of the radical differences between the two types of epic: the 'monolingualism' of the *tragedie* has no need for that sophisticated sense of structural discrimination which is the *sine qua non* of the 'plurilingual' "comedía." Dante's *canti* may well owe something to the *libri* of his Latin predecessors, since he probably took from them the idea that epics ought to be subdivided. However, both the number and the stylistic and thematic span of his *canti*, as well as their assimilation into three *canzoni*, disclose that Dante had a more developed awareness of *dispositio* than other writers. Nor is it fortuitous that, given the relatively marginal concern with *dispositio* in much classical and medieval literary theory and practice,[51] Dante should have emphasized structural matters as part of his strategy to fix his own artistic primacy.

If few links can usefully be forged between the *canto* and the Latin epic *liber*, its ties with the *laisse* of the *chanson de geste* appear, at first sight, to be made of stronger stuff. Both the "comedía" and the *chanson* are fashioned from a large number of metrically independent units incorporating differing numbers of lines of the same length;[52] and, in both cases, these units are significantly shorter than their Latin counterparts. However, they are also crucially distinguished by two major formal discrepancies: first, unlike the *canto*, all the lines of the *laisse* have the same assonantic ending or are based on the same rhyme, and, second, the length of the *laisse* is both much shorter—seldom reaching one hundred lines—and much less stable than that of the *canto*. Though the span of the *laisse* did increase with the passage of time, it is most unlikely that Dante knew poems, such as the *Couronnement de Louis* and the *Moniage Guillaume*, where this happens.[53] In fact, the *Roland* is the only *chanson de geste* which it is generally accepted that Dante had read.[54] If this is indeed the case, then, the critical distinctions which Dante wished to draw between the *chansons* and the *Commedia* are all the more striking given the brevity of the *Roland*'s *laisses* and the almost perfect correspondence between these and narrative divisions—a correspondence whose rigidity recalls the narrow inflexibility of the equally censored lyric *stantia*.[55] Thus, even before the fluid presentation of the episode of barratry, simply the *canto*'s greater length guarantees a narrative diversity which the *Roland* cannot match. As Erich Auerbach succinctly put it when discussing *Inferno* 10's shifts of focus:

> The scenes [of the *canto*] are not set stiffly side by side and in the same key—we are thinking of . . . the *Chanson de Roland*—they rise from the depths as particular forms of the momentarily prevailing tonality and stand in contrapuntal relation to one another. . . . The events are not—as we put it in connection with the *Chanson de Roland* . . . —divided into little parcels; they live together, despite their contrast and actually because of it.[56]

Yet again, thanks to his structural inventiveness, Dante has little difficulty in asserting the fuller and more complex view of things which the *canto* and the "comedía" can offer in comparison to the *laisse* and the *chanson*.

As befits the brainchild of an arch-syncretist, the *canto* succeeds in integrating the diffuseness of the Latin *liber* with the highly restricted purview of the French *laisse*. By being able to absorb and supersede two such diametrically different forms, the *canto* makes a clear declaration of its literary uniqueness and its superiority in relation to both traditions. In addition, neither the structure of the classical epic nor that of the *chanson* can even begin to compete with that numerically significant and subtle synthesis between the parts and the whole which characterizes the *Commedia*'s organization as it strives to 'imitate' the unity of God's art—a synthesis, as we have seen, which is made possible largely thanks to the flexibilty and range of the *canto*. From this perspective it also becomes clear why Dante rejected a *roman*-type structure for his poem. The uninterrupted, monotonous, and repetitive flow of the octosyllabic rhyming couplets of the *romans* presents an undifferentiated view of things which is contrary to the *Commedia*'s highly nuanced yet totalizing sense of structure and of the complexity of reality.[57] As Dante's sustained critique of conventional literary forms reveals, none of them could even begin to accommodate this "vision." Only his *canto* could do this, not least because it was based on and incorporated the different dominant architectonic features of the principal narrative verse forms of his day. Thus, as the poet had succeeded in bringing together the *liber* and the *laisse*, so he also managed to fuse the *chanson* and the *roman*. One effect of Dante's decision to divide the *Commedia* into *canti* is that it allowed him to fuse the pauses of the *chanson de geste* with the flow of the *roman*, thereby giving his poem a cogent, orderly, and harmonized narrative development. Tradition and innovation, as is typical of Dante's art and self-commentary, achieve a perfect balance in the *canto*, whose invention is not presented merely as a piece of poetic bravura but is cogently legitimated as a desideratum in the light of the deficiencies of other forms. Finally, the ways in which Dante redimensions French narrative poetry through his creation of the *canto* is consistent with his overall limitative assessment of Gallic culture in the *Commedia*. The *canto*, like the poem as a whole, is the practical confirmation of that victory of Italian literature over French writing which Dante had promised, albeit obliquely, in the *De vulgari eloquentia*.[58]

Lyric Structures

There is little doubt that, in *Inferno* 20, "canzon" effectively and efficiently recalls both the Latin and the vernacular epic; however, it also has the further function, which I have already begun to discuss, of drawing attention to the Italian lyric tradition. It is thus suggestive when examining the *canto*'s structural properties vis-à-vis the tradition that the works which most closely approximate to its average length are three of Dante's own erotic allegorical *canzoni*—"Io sento sì d'Amor la gran possanza" of 106 lines, "Le dolci rime" of 146 lines, and "Poscia ch'amor" of 133 lines—and two of his great ethical poems written after his exile—"Tre donne" of 107 lines and "Doglia mi reca" of 158 lines. In the duecento lyric, *canzoni* of more than one hundred lines are extremely rare. The only other Italian poet to compose them with any kind of regularity is Guittone d'Arezzo.[59] It is thus not at all improbable that, as far as the basic shape of the *canti* of the new extended "canzon" is concerned, this finds its likeliest points of reference, first, in Dante's own lyric poetry and, second, in opposition to Guittone's versifying. At one level, the *canto* acknowledges the key role which the poet's lyric experience had in his artistic and intellectual journey to the *Commedia*. Especially in "Tre donne" and "Doglia mi reca," Dante showed himself a master at manipulating narrative and didactic forms of over one hundred lines—a skill which is at the basis of the composition of the "comedía." At another level, however, by transferring the structures of the *canzone tragica* (including the hendecasyllable)[60] to the new *canzone comica*, Dante was revealing his dissatisfaction with the older form; a dissatisfaction which, once again, was almost certainly conditioned by the established *canzone*'s stylistic and thematic restrictiveness (*DVE* 2.4.6–8). At the same time, Dante was also rejecting the claim he had earlier made in the *De vulgari eloquentia* concerning the literary primacy of 'tragic' poetry (*DVE* 2.3.2–3). He emblematically enshrined this 'transfer of power' both by bequeathing the name of the erstwhile favorite to his new creation and by dramatically changing the appearance of the form which traditionally had gone under this designation. And such a bequest was, to say the least, inappropriate. It made over a term, *canzone*, which the poet himself had closely united with the 'high' style, to another genre, the 'comic', which, as far as the tradition was concerned, most certainly had no right to it. In these circumstances, it is indeed difficult to think how Dante could have made more categorical his rejection of the oppressive precepts of the *genera dicendi* and of the literature which these sustained.

The possible allusion to Guittone discernible in Dante's use of "canzon" and in the length of the *canto* helps better to focus his critique of the vernacular lyric. Specifically, it provides a delimitative assessment of the most inventive and wide-ranging Italian poet writing in the *volgare* before Dante. This is not the place to go into the thorny question of Dante's relationship to Guittone.[61] Suffice it to say that, in the *Commedia*, Dante not only criticized Guittone explicitly during the course of the pilgrim's encounter with Bonagiunta da Lucca, but also did this implicitly by means of the poem's form. He revealed the proper genre—the *canzone comica* and not the lyric *canzone*—in which the older poet and his followers should have carried out their artistic experimentation.[62]

The Problem of the *Cantica*

By concentrating on the metaliterary reverberations of *Inferno* 20.1–3 and on the interplay in the tercet both between "canto" and "canzon," and between these and the secular literary tradition, I have neglected the third term with which Dante, just as unexpectedly and originally, defined the structure of the *Commedia*:

> ma perché piene son tutte le carte
> ordite a questa cantica seconda,
> non mi lascia più ir lo fren de l'arte.
>
> (*Purg.* 33.139–141)

There are two reasons for my omission. First, *Inferno* 20.1–3 provides a much fuller description of the character and logic of the *Commedia's* structure, style, and content than does *Purgatorio* 33.139–141. Second, Lino Pertile has recently published two excellent articles on a number of the principal reasons behind Dante's choice of this term.[63] Essentially, what Pertile has shown, is that the poet's use of "cantica" is closely tied to the rich commentary tradition to the *Canticum Canticorum*, not least because of the traditional association between the biblical book and comedy. My present study as a whole and particularly what follows are meant to complement his work. Just as "canzon" highlights the role played by the secular literary tradition in the *Commedia*, so "cantica" divulges its connections with the religious one. More importantly, by introducing the two terms as synonyms for one of the primary structures of the *Commedia*, Dante declares that his poem constitutes a balanced synthesis of both literary currents.

Although "cantica" underscores the special links which the "comedía" enjoys with scriptural *sermo humilis*, something in fact which the medieval concept of 'comedy' also does in other ways,[64] like "canto" and "canzon," *canticum* also refers to poetry in general.[65] The carefully programmed manner in which Dante selected the terms with which to define the *Commedia*, whereby these both complement and confirm each other's clarificatory functions in relation to the poem, can find no better illustration than this. Finally, "cantica" introduces a further set of important metaliterary religious connotations into the *Commedia*. By means of its links with the biblical *canticum novum*, it suggests that the poem is a celebration of God and his creation—to use Dante's terminology, that it is a "teodía" (*Par.* 25.73).[66] Furthermore, the association with *canticum novum* also pinpoints the role which God wants the poem to play in his scheme of earthly spiritual renewal.[67] As Cacciaguida explains to the pilgrim, it is the latter's duty to report his otherworldly experiences as precisely as possible because, by doing this, he would be fulfilling his divinely ordained responsibilities (*Par.* 17.124–142). In fact, Dante's ancestor gives him a practical lesson in the kind of language he is to use by veering between Latin (15.28–30) and the vulgarities of the *parlato* (17.129); and it is a plurilingualism—it should be remembered—which is sanctioned by God, since, as Cacciaguida speaks, he is in communion with his Maker (15.61–69). Dante's experimentalism is no mere artistic whim; it is the direct result of his miraculous journey and mission: "Et [Dominus] immisit in os meum canticum novum" (Ps. 39:4).

Biblical Structures

As I have already discussed, the *Commedia*'s style and structure are the tangible guarantors of its closeness to the divine; and this is especially so as regards its numerically significant two-tiered organization into *canti* and *cantiche*. However, this structure also has specifically textual implications. To put it starkly, the *Commedia*'s division into *canti* and *canzoni* is, arguably, its most original formal feature, since, as far as I have been able to ascertain, no other narrative poem before Dante's had been organized in this manner. Given the poet's claim, for instance in *Inferno* 28,[68] that his poem is superior to prose, and in particular to historical prose, and given its dialectical relationship with the philosophical *summa*, the encyclopedia, and the 'dictionary',[69] it is not unlikely that Dante was trying to show that part of the success of his poetry was that, like prose, it could be flexibly and rationally compartmentalized. In this context, it is important to remember that, during the course of the thirteenth century, the *ordinatio* and *compilatio* of texts, with their attendant emphasis on subdivision, had become increasingly central in the production of books.[70] As a result, the *Commedia*'s structure was also a sign of its 'modernity' and literary sophistication.

Even if no secular poem can serve as a model for the *Commedia*'s structure, there is a type of poetry with which it does have a noticeable affinity. The Bible, too, gathers up a considerable number of independent poetic texts into larger structures, which then unite with other *libri* to constitute the divine book as a whole. This characteristic of Scripture, which the new contemporary concern with textual division could not but highlight,[71] is especially apparent as regards the Book of Psalms and the Song of Songs. I have already noted the metaliterary interplay which Dante established between the *Canticum Canticorum*, the "cantica," and the "comedía." It is thus satisfying to recognize that, as the poet assiduously cultivated his poem's links with the Bible, he created, as he did for the Canticles, a similarly fascinating set of connections between his work and the Psalms. Indeed, I would argue that the very idea of giving the *Commedia* a tripartite structure which is narratively and morally based on the three realms of the afterlife came to Dante from the hermeneutic tradition to the Psalms. In the prologue to Thomas Aquinas's commentary, after categorizing the "modus seu forma" of the book as "deprecativus vel laudativus," the great Doctor divides the work he is about to discuss into three groups of fifty psalms each. "Per instinctum inspirationis divinae," these respectively deal with the "status poenitentiae," the "status iustitiae" and the "laus gloriae . . . aeternae."[72] The correlations between, on the one hand, this evaluation of the Book of Psalms and, on the other, the *Commedia*, its moral and artistic structure, and its relationship to the divine will are imposing. The importance of the Psalms for an understanding of the *Commedia*'s textuality and structure is further confirmed when we learn that *canticum*, not least in the guise of *canticum novum*, was often used as a variant for *psalmus*.[73]

That of all the books of the Bible, Dante should have decided to establish particular metaliterary links, thanks also to *cantica*'s connotative range, between his poem and the Book of Psalms and the Song of Songs has a precise cultural significance. From the twelfth century onwards, exegetes had paid increasing attention to the literal sense of Bible. Indeed, it was widely acknowledged that, while God was the source of Scripture's moral, figural, and analogical meanings, its earthly authors were responsible for its surface values, including its stylistic elaboration. God had chosen certain human beings as his *scribae* not only because of their moral worth but also because of their literary abilities. And David and Solomon were precisely two of the *scribae* who specially fascinated medieval exegetes.[74] Dante was well aware of these trends in biblical scholarship. He presented himself as an artistically responsible *scriba Dei*, and also recognized a similar role for David, who, in Paradise, is both rewarded for, and able to appreciate, the worth of his poetic endeavours, the "effetti" of his own "consiglio":

> Colui che luce in mezzo per pupilla,
> fu il cantor de lo Spirito Santo,
> che l'arca traslatò di villa in villa:
>   ora conosce il merto del suo canto,
> in quanto effetto fu del suo consiglio,
> per lo remunerar ch'è altrettanto.
>
>   (*Par.* 20.37–42)

However, rather than just simply place himself on a par with David, Dante, as he did with secular authors, measures himself against him and suggests his own artistic superiority. David's poetic powers were limited to the writing of a "teodía," while Dante was the *auctor* of a "comedía," one of whose many literary purposes, and not its exclusive intent, was that of celebrating God.[75] Dante similarly challenged Solomon, whose canticle was often presented as the supreme form of poetry: "Salomon inspiratus divino spirito, composuit hunc libellum de nuptiis Christi et Ecclesiae. . . . Unde et Cantica Canticorum vocavit hunc libellum: quia omnia alia Cantica superexcellit . . . dicuntur Cantica Canticorum ob excellentiam et dignitatem. Est autem in hoc obscurissimus iste liber, quae nullae ibi commemorantur personae, cum tamen stylo quasi comico sit compositus."[76] Once again, in comparison to Solomon's 'comedy', the greater stylistic complexity and narrative range of Dante's "comedía" is apparent, not least because, unlike the scriptural "libellum," his work is not just a "cantica" but also a "canzon." Where all this leaves the *Commedia* in the poetic pantheon is more than self-evident.

The Problem of the *terza rima*

By examining the metrical structures of the *Commedia* and the designations which the poet assigned to these, considerable information about the work and its composition can be unearthed. And the bulk of this knowledge derives from the *novitas* of the forms, whose metrical innovativeness is not restricted—as is widely believed—simply to Dante's invention of the *terza rima*.[77] As we have seen, every tier of the *Commedia* is notable for its originality, an originality whose implications can only be appreciated by assessing each structure's relationship both to the other parts of the poem and to the literary tradition in general. Thus, as a final example of this process, what is formally most significant about the *terza rima* is how it synthesizes different rhyme schemes: for instance, those of the *serventese caudato* and of the *sestina* together with the tercets of the sonnet (especially those with alternate rhyme as in the *Fiore*) and the triple rhyme patterns which characterize so many of Dante's own *canzoni*. The *Commedia*'s rhyme, too, indicates its ability to absorb and transcend any kind of poetry, thereby revealing its differences from conventional writing and its ideological continuity with the poem's other structures. In addition, the *terza rima* is formally integrated with these. For instance, the solitary last line of each *canto* serves as a means of hooking on to the next one, while the *rime rilevate* are the necessary demarcatory boundaries without which the *canto* cannot exist as an independent unit. Indeed, the *terza rima*, the *canto*, and the *cantica*, on account of the 'unbreakable' determinacy of their forms, come together to guarantee the *Commedia*'s textual integrity,[78] as they do to provide answers to Dante's experimentation.

NOTES

I should like to thank Maggie Barański, Giulio Lepschy and Lino Pertile for their valuable comments on an earlier version of this study. I am especially grateful to Theodore J. Cachey, Jr., for his suggestions and for his friendship. All quotations from and references to Dante's works are taken from the following editions: *Vita nuova*, ed. Domenico De Robertis, vol. 1, part 1 of Dante Alighieri, *Opere minori* (Milan and Naples: Ricciardi, 1984); *Rime*, 2 vols., ed. Gianfranco Contini, vol. 1, part 1, 251–552, of *Opere minori* (Milan and Naples: Ricciardi, 1979–1988); *Convivio*, ed. Cesare Vasoli and Domenico De Robertis, vol. 1, part 2 of *Opere minori* (Milan and Naples: Ricciardi, 1988); *De vulgari eloquentia* (*DVE*), ed. Pier Vincenzo Mengaldo, vol. 2, 1–237, of *Opere minori* (Milan and Naples: Ricciardi, 1979); *Epistole*, ed. Arsenio Frugoni and Giorgio Brugnoli, vol. 2, 507–643 of *Opere minori* (Milan and Naples: Ricciardi, 1979); *La Commedia secondo l'antica vulgata*, 4 vols., ed. Giorgio Petrocchi, Società dantesca italiana, Edizione nazionale (Milan: Mondadori, 1966–1967).

1. *Il "Commentarium" di Pietro Alighieri*, ed. Roberto Della Vedova and Maria Teresa Silvotti (Florence: Olschki, 1978), 3.

2. *L'ottimo commento della "Divina Commedia": Testo inedito di un contemporaneo di Dante*, ed. A Torri, 3 vols. (Pisa: Niccolò Capurro, 1827–1829), vol. 3.

3. "Cantus," in *Thesaurus Linguae Latinae* (Leipzig: Teubner, 1900–), 3:295.

4. Dante used "capitolo" with a certain regularity to refer to the various parts of each of the four books of the *Convivio*, while he employed "capitulum" in both the *De vulgari eloquentia* and the *Monarchia*. In the *Convivio*, he also labels the constituent elements of the Book of Proverbs by means of this term ("nel vigesimo secondo capitolo de li Proverbi" [4.7.9]).

5. "Capitulum," in *Thesaurus*, 3:351.

6. "Liber," in *Thesaurus*, 7.2:1274–1275.

7. On the medieval commentary tradition, see at least Gérard Paré, Adrien Brunet, and Pierre Tremblay, *La Renaissance du XII siècle: Les écoles et l'enseignement* (Paris and Ottawa: Vrin-Institut d'Etudes Médiévales d'Ottawa, 1933); Ceslaus Spicq, *Esquisse d'une histoire de l'exégèse latine* (Paris: Vrin, 1944); R. W. Hunt, "The Introductions to the *artes* in the Twelfth Century," in *Studia Medievalia in Honorem R. M. Martin* (Bruges: 'de Tempel', 1948), 85–112; Jean Daniélou, *Les figures de Christ dans l'Ancien Testament* (Paris: Beauchesne, 1950); Henri de Lubac, *Exégèse médiévale*, 2 vols. (Paris: Aubier, 1959–1964); Franz Quadlbauer, *Die antike Theorie der "genera dicendi" im lateinischen Mittelalter* (Vienna: Hermann Böhlaus, 1962); Winthrop Wetherbee, *Platonism and Poetry in the Twelfth Century* (Princeton: Princeton University Press, 1972); Paolo Bagni, "*Res ficta sed non facta*: Il campo concettuale del commento," in *Studi di estetica* 1 (1973): 113–163; Edouard Jeauneau, "*Lectio philosophorum*": *Recherches sur l'école de Chartres* (Amsterdam: Hakkert, 1973); *Medieval Literary Critcism*, ed. O. B. Hardison, Jr., et al. (New York: Frederick Ungar, 1974); Armand Strubel, "*Allegoria in factis* et

allegoria in verbis," *Poétique* 23 (1975): 342–357; Judson B. Allen, *The Ethical Poetic of the Later Middle Ages* (Toronto: University of Toronto Press, 1982); Glending Olson, *Literature and Recreation in the Later Middle Ages* (Ithaca, N.Y.: Cornell University Press, 1982); Beryl Smalley, *The Study of the Bible in the Middle Ages,* 3d ed. (Oxford: Blackwell, 1983); Claudia Villa, *La "Lectura Terentii"* (Padua: Antenore, 1984); *Le moyen âge et la Bible,* ed. Pierre Riché and Guy Lobrichon (Paris: Beauchesne, 1984); Jean Pépin, *La tradition de l'allégorie de Philon d'Alexandre à Dante* (Paris: Études Augustiniennes, 1987); Jon Whitman, *Allegory: The Dynamics of an Ancient and Medieval Technique* (Oxford: Clarendon Press, 1987); Christopher C. Baswell, "Medieval Readers and Ancient Texts: The Inference of the Past," *Envoi* 1 (1988): 1–22; Ralph J. Hexter, *Ovid and Medieval Schooling: Studies in Medieval School Commentaries on Ovid's "Ars amatoria"* (Munich: Arbeo-Gesellschaft, 1988); A. J. Minnis, *Medieval Theory of Authorship,* 2d ed. (London: Scolar Press, 1988); *Medieval Literary Theory and Criticism c. 1100–c. 1375: The Commentary Tradition,* ed. A. J. Minnis and A. B. Scott (Oxford: Clarendon Press, 1988); Rita Copeland, *Rhetoric, Hermeneutics, and Translation in the Middle Ages: Academic Traditions and Vernacular Texts* (Cambridge: Cambridge University Press, 1991); *"Ad Litteram": Authoritative Texts and Medieval Readers,* ed. Mark D. Jordan and Kent Emery, Jr. (Notre Dame, Ind.: University of Notre Dame Press, 1992); *The Cambridge History of Literary Criticism,* vol. 2: *The Middle Ages,* ed. A. J. Minnis (Cambridge: Cambridge University Press, 1995). See also Bruno Sandkühler, *Die frühen Dantekommentare und ihr Verhältnis zur mittelalterlichen Kommentartradition* (Munich: Hueber Verlag, 1967); and below, note 11.

8. Unlike the other commentators, Boccaccio, Francesco da Buti, and Benvenuto, and subsequently Giovanni da Serravalle, do try to account for Dante's selection of the term "canto": (1) "sì come i musici ogni loro artificio formano sopra certe dimensioni di tempi lunghi e brievi, e acute e gravi, e delle varietà di queste con debita e misurata proporzione congiunta, e quello poi appellano 'canto', così i poeti: non solamente quegli che in latino scrivono, ma eziandio coloro che, come il nostro autore fa, volgarmente dettano, componendo i loro versi, secondo la diversa qualità d'essi, di certo e determinato numero di piedi intra se medesimi . . . per che pare che a questi cotali versi, o opere composte per versi, quello nome si convegna che i musici alle loro invenzioni danno, come davanti dicemmo, cioè 'canti', e per conseguente quella opera, che di molti canti è composta, doversi 'cantica' appellare, cioè cosa in sé contenente più canti" (Giovanni Boccaccio, *Esposizioni sopra la "Comedia" di Dante,* ed. Giorgio Padoan [Milan: Mondadori, 1965], Accessus 15–16); and "Chiamano . . . i comedi le parti intra sé distinte delle loro comedìe 'scene' . . . dove il nostro autore chiama 'canti' le parti della sua *Comedìa*" (Boccaccio, *Esposizioni,* Accessus 23); (2)

"perchè si chiamano cantiche le sue principali parti, a che si può dire: Perchè sono composte di diversi canti . . . e ciascun canto di versi misurati con certo numero di sillabe, distinti per ternari sì, che cantar si possono, e così tornando dall'ultimo al primo. Perchè sono li versi distinti in ternario sì, che cantar si possono, si chiamano i capitoli canti" (*Commento di Francesco da Buti sopra la "Divina commedia" di Dante Allighieri*, ed. Crescentino Giannini, 3 vols. [Pisa: Fratelli Nistri, 1858–1862], 1:7); (3) "Quorum librorm quilibet dividitur per capitula, quae appellantur cantus propter consonantiam rhythmorum; et quilibet cantus per rhythmos" (Benvenuti de Rambaldis de Imola, *Comentum super Dantis Aldigherij "Comoediam,"* curante Jacobo Philippo Lacaita, 5 vols. [Florence: G. Barbèra, 1887], 1:21); and (4) "Quare dicitur cantus, dictum fuit in uno preambulorum, scilicet propter dulcedinem modi dicendi in carminibus, vel in rithymis" (Fratris Iohannis de Serravalle, *Translatio et Comentum totius libri Dantis Aldigherii* [Prato: Giachetti, 1891], 252). Although the explanations provided by the four commentators, as will become clear from my discussion, barely touch upon the implications of Dante's choice of "canto," the effort and ingenuity they put into clarifying the term is evidence of the sense they had of its importance.

The novelty of the poet's usage of "canto" can also be gauged from the fact that, as far as I have been able to ascertain from the standard works of reference, his is the earliest attested use of the term in the neo-Latin tradition with the meaning of "each of the parts into which a poem is divided." It is, of course, through Dante's vernacular application of "canto" that Latin *cantus* came to acquire the same meaning (as is confirmed by a perusal of classical and medieval Latin dictionaries in which, surprisingly, no mention is made of this important technical usage).

9. Lucia Onder, "Canto," in *Enciclopedia dantesca*, 5 vols. and appendix (Rome: Istituto della Enciclopedia Italiana, 1970–1978), 2:795. Ignazio Baldelli's excellent entries on Dante's metrics in the *Enciclopedia dantesca*, as well as his synoptic overview of the poet's stylistic development ("Lingua e stile delle opere in volgare di Dante," in *Enciclopedia dantesca*, appendix, 55–112), also pay no attention to Dante's *canto*.

10. Notable exceptions to the general lack of critical interest in Dante's *canto* are: Ernest H. Wilkins, "Cantos, Regions, and Transitions in the *Divine Comedy*," in *The Invention of the Sonnet and Other Studies in Italian Literature* (Rome: Edizioni di Storia e Letteratura, 1959), 103–110; Ettore Paratore, "Analisi 'retorica' del canto di Pier della Vigna," *Studi danteschi* 42 (1965): 281–285; Guglielmo Gorni, "La teoria del 'cominciamento'," in *Il nodo della lingua e il Verbo d'Amore* (Florence: Olschki, 1981), 164–186; Guido Di Pino, *Pause e intercanti nella "Divina Commedia"* (Bari: Adriatica, 1982), 11–38; Pietro G. Beltrami, *La metrica italiana* (Bologna: il Mulino, 1991), 91–92; Teodolinda Barolini, *The Undivine Comedy: Detheologizing Dante* (Princeton:

Princeton University Press, 1992), 21–47, 257–265; Joan Ferrante, "A Poetics of Chaos and Harmony," in *The Cambridge Companion to Dante*, ed. Rachel Jacoff (Cambridge: Cambridge University Press, 1993), 153–158. See also Giovanni Getto, "Lettura del canto XXIX del *Paradiso*," *Aevum* 22 (1948): 257; Edoardo Sanguineti, *Interpretazioni di Malebolge* (Florence: Olschki, 1961), 71, n. 4; Gianfranco Contini, "Filologia ed esegesi dantesca" [1965], in *Un'idea di Dante* (Turin: Einaudi, 1976), 123–125; Marino Barchiesi, "Arte del prologo e della transizione," *Studi danteschi* 44 (1967): 115–207. See also John Ahern's studies cited below in note 78.

11. See Zygmunt G. Barański, "'Significar *per verba*': Notes on Dante and Plurilingualism," *The Italianist* 6 (1986): 5–18; "Dante's (Anti-)Rhetoric: Notes on the Poetics of the *Commedia*," in *Moving in Measure: Essays in Honour of Brian Moloney*, ed. Judith Bryce and Doug Thompson ([Hull:] Hull University Press, 1989), 1–14; "*Comedía*: Notes on Dante, the Epistle to Cangrande, and Medieval Comedy," *Lectura Dantis* 8 (1991): 26–55; "'Primo tra cotanto senno': Dante and the Latin Comic Tradition," *Italian Studies* 46 (1991): 1–31: "*La Commedia*," in *Manuale di letteratura italiana*, vol. 1: *Dalle origini alla fine del quattrocento*, ed. Franco Brioschi and Costanzo Di Girolamo (Turin: Bollati Boringhieri, 1993), 541–560; "Dante Alighieri: Experimentation and (Self-)Exegesis," in *The Cambridge History of Literary Criticism*.

12. For a detailed discussion of *Inf.* 20.1–3 (though with few effective points of contact with my analysis), see Marino Barchiesi, "Catarsi classica e 'medicina' dantesca," in *Letture Classensi IV* (Ravenna: Longo, 1973), 14–33. See also Ettore Caccia, "Canto XX," in *Lectura Dantis Scaligera*, 3 vols. (Florence: Le Monnier, 1967–1968), 1:675–677; Sanguineti, *Interpretazioni*, 69–72; Giorgio Barberi Squarotti, "*Inferno* XX," [1965] in *L'artificio dell'eternità* (Verona: Fiorini, 1972), 235–239; Raffaello Ramat, "Lezione sul XX dell'*Inferno*," *L'Alighieri* 2 (1965): 27–28; Silvio Pasquazi, "Il canto XX dell'*Inferno*," in *Nuove letture dantesche*, 8 vols. (Florence: Le Monnier, 1966–1976), 2:183–184, 187–189; Robert Hollander, "The Tragedy of Divination in *Inferno* XX" [1976], in *Studies in Dante* (Ravenna: Longo, 1980), 133–140; Ignazio Baldelli, "Il canto XX dell'*Inferno*," in *Inferno: Letture degli anni 1973–'76*, ed. Silvio Zennaro (Rome: Bonacci, 1977), 478–480; Ettore Paratore, "Il canto XX dell'*Inferno*," *Studi danteschi* 52 (1979–1980): 169; Achille Tartaro, *Canto XX dell' "Inferno"* (Naples: Loffredo, 1982), 6–7; Teodolinda Barolini, "XX," in *Dante's "Divine Comedy": Introductory Readings*, vol. 1: "*Inferno*," ed. Tibor Wlassics (Charlottesville: University of Virginia Printing Office, 1990), 263. The various post-1960 commentaries to the *Commedia* which I have consulted on this tercet do not include anything which may not be found in the above *lecturae*. See also Leo Spitzer, "The Addresses to the Reader in the *Commedia*," *Italica* 32 (1955): 162–

163, n. 3; Chandler B. Beall, "Dante and His Reader," *Forum Italicum* 13 (1979): 308.

13. On the standard formulas of the *accessus ad auctores*, see Hunt, "Introductions"; Minnis, *Medieval Theory*, 9–72.

14. See Guido Marco Donati, *Il canto XX dell'Inferno* [1906] (Florence: Sansoni, n.d.), 10–11; Luigi Pietrobono, *Il canto XX dell' "Inferno"* [1916] (Rome: SEI, 1965); Francesco D'Ovidio, "Esposizione del canto XX dell'Inferno," in *Nuovo volume di studii danteschi* (Caserta and Rome: APE, 1926), 316–317. The idea of the tercet's 'prosaicness' has persisted to this day; see, for instance, Dante, *The Divine Comedy*, trans., with introduction, notes, and commentary, Mark Musa, 3 vols. (Harmondsworth: Penguin Books, 1984), 1:255. Another way in which Dantists have dismissed these fundamental lines is by describing them as the product of a 'tired' poet; see, for instance, Pietrobono, *Il canto XX*, 5; Dante Alighieri, *La Divina Commedia*, ed. Attilio Momigliano, 3 vols. (Florence: Sansoni, 1970 [1945]), 1:147; Dante Alighieri, *Commedia*, ed. Anna Maria Chiavacci Leonardi, 3 vols. (Milan: Mondadori, 1991–), 1:599.

The fourteenth-century commentators, too, as they did with so much of the *Commedia*'s metaliterary infrastructure, only paid, at best, scant attention to *Inf.* 20.1–3. Among those who gloss, or rather paraphrase, these lines are Jacopo Alighieri, *Chiose all'"Inferno,"* ed. Saverio Bellomo (Padua: Antenore, 1990), 165–166; Guido da Pisa, *Expositiones et Glose super Comediam Dantis*, ed. Vincenzo Cioffari (Albany, N.Y.: State University of New York Press, 1974), 375, 382; *Comedia di Dante degli Allaghieri col commento di Jacopo della Lana bolognese*, ed. Luciano Scarabelli, 3 vols. (Bologna: Regia Tipografia, 1866), 1:342; *L'ottimo commento*, 1; Benvenuti de Rambaldis de Imola, *Comentum*, 2.63–64; and *Commento di Francesco da Buti*, 1.7. Graziolo de' Bambaglioli, Pietro Alighieri, and the anonymous author of the *Chiose selmiane* pass them over in silence.

15. Herbert Douglas Austin, "'The Submerged' (*Inf.*, XX, 3)," *Romanic Review* 23 (1932):39–40.

16. At this juncture, the problem arises of what, if any, technical information concerning the structure of his poem Dante may have included in the *incipit* to the *Commedia*. A similar problem is whether he prefaced each *cantica* and *canto* with a rubric of the type printed between square brackets in Petrocchi's critical edition (such a decision, it should be noted, would have necessitated the poet revealing in advance not only the terminology so dramatically unveiled in *Inf.* 20 but also the peculiar structure of his work). The manuscript evidence regarding the *Commedia*'s rubrication is inconclusive: see Giuseppe Vandelli, *Per il testo della "Divina Commedia,"* ed. Rudi Abardo (Florence: Le Lettere, 1989), 277–292, 297–301; Giorgio Petrocchi, "Introduzione," in *La Commedia secondo l'antica vulgata*, 1:472–

473; Antonio E. Quaglio, "Titolo," in "Commedia," in *Enciclopedia dantesca*, 2:79. However, in the light of the carefully programmed manner—as I shall discuss—in which Dante introduced *Inf.* 20.1-3 into the structure of the *Commedia*, I believe that it is highly unlikely that he would have spoilt the tercet's effect by anticipating its substance. Lino Pertile adduces other telling evidence as to why it would have been difficult for Dante to have written the kind of rubrics published by Petrocchi (see "*Canto-cantica-Comedía* e l'Epistola a Cangrande," *Lectura Dantis* 9 [1991]: 115-118).

17. *Inf.* 20.1-3 must have had an especially startling and dramatic impact on the *Inferno*'s first readers given the *cantica*'s original independent dissemination. On the *Inferno*'s earliest diffusion, see Gianfranco Folena, "La tradizione delle opere di Dante Alighieri," in *Atti del Congresso internazionale di studi danteschi*, 2 vols. (Florence: Sansoni, 1965-1966), 1:41-43.

18. See Sanguineti, *Interpretazioni*, 72; Barberi Squarotti, "*Inferno* XX," 237. For a telling critique of these positions, see Pasquazi, "Il canto XX," 187-189. Robert Hollander also argues that "at this point [*Inf.* 20], as at perhaps no other point in the *Inferno*, Dante's poetry *is* tragic" ("Tragedy," 139), while, at the same time, acknowledging the *canto*'s stylistic hybridism. However, his list of *Inf.* 20's 'tragic' characteristics ("First, it [the *canto*] is about to narrate the bitterly painful experience of its protagonist; second, the subject of the entire *cantica* is seen as being 'i sommersi,' those whose lives on earth have ended in the ultimate unhappiness of damnation; third, it occurs in the canto which more than any other in the *Commedia* addresses the question of Virgil's status as tragic poet" ["Tragedy," 139]) relates somewhat tangentially to medieval notions of tragedy, especially as defined by the poet in the *De vulgari eloquentia* (which Hollander recognizes, correctly, as having a determining effect on any interpretation of "canzon" ["Tragedy," 138-139]): "Per tragediam superiorem stilum inducimus. . . . Si tragice canenda videntur, tunc assumendum est vulgare illustre, et per consequens cantionem ligare. . . . Stilo equidem tragico tunc uti videmur quando cum gravitate sententie tam superbia carminum quam constructionis elatio et excellentia vocabulorum concordat . . . illa que summe canenda distinximus isto solo sunt stilo canenda: videlicet salus, amor et virtus et que propter ea concipimus, dum nullo accidente vilescant" (2.4.5-8). Furthermore, by explaining Dante's use of "canzon" with reference solely to *DVE* 2.8.3-4, Hollander delimits much too narrowly, as we shall see, the connotative and exegetical potential of the equation between the *De vulgari eloquentia* and the *Commedia* (see also below, note 20). On the concept of tragedy, see Henry A. Kelly, *Ideas and Forms of Tragedy from Aristotle to the Middle Ages* (Cambridge: Cambridge University Press, 1993). By dissenting from the proposals put forward by the proponents of *Inf.* 20's *stilus tragicus*, I do not wish to create the impression that the *canto* does not include 'lofty' elements. I object to the totalizing and

dominant slant which they give to the 'tragic'. My view is that the 'high' is only one register among many, and that, as is usual in the *Commedia*, Dante's main focus in the *canto* is on the 'comic'. I am less inclined to disagree, however, with Hollander and Lino Pertile ("*Cantica* nella tradizione medievale e in Dante," *Rivista di storia e di letteratura religiosa* 18 [1992]: 412) when they suggest that, in line with the widely current structural definition of tragedy as a narrative which begins well and ends badly, "canzon" highlights the common 'tragic' ending of Hell's inhabitants. On the other hand, it is problematic to label *Inferno* a tragedy in structural terms, since more than any of the three parts of the *Commedia*, it has a quintessentially 'comic' organization, since it begins badly in the dark wood and ends positively with the travelers exiting to "riveder le stelle" (34.139). *Inferno* is thus a comedy which embraces a whole series of mini-tragedies (as well as a whole host of other genres); in this way, too, Dante underlined the dominant 'comic' character of his poem.

Other scholars are more cautious when talking about *Inf.* 20's 'tragic' register. They note that the *canto* synthesizes "un tono popolare ma non privo di una sua larghezza epica," and that "*canzone* . . . è la spia stilistica più significativa ad indicare lo sliricarsi del tono e insieme il suo epicizzarsi" (Caccia, "Canto XX," 676).

19. See Ignazio Baldelli, "Canzon," in *Enciclopedia dantesca*, 1:801, and "Il canto XX," 478–480; Barchiesi, "Catarsi," 28–29, 119; Hollander, "Tragedy," 138–139; Paratore, "Il canto XX," 168. For a wide-ranging analysis of the poetics of the *Commedia* in terms of the *De vulgari eloquentia*, see Antonino Pagliaro, *Ulisse: Ricerche semantiche sulla "Divina Commedia,"* 2 vols. (Messina and Florence: D'Anna, 1967), 2:529–583.

20. Several critics, usually to defend their 'tragic' reading of the *canto*, have tried—unconvincingly in my opinion—to loosen the links between "introcque" and the rest of *Inferno* 20. They argue that the Latinism, rather than an integral part of *canto* 20, in fact connects with the three *canti* of barratry which follow, since it acts as a stylistic signpost for their 'low' register (see Caccia, "Canto XX," 719, n. 2; Sanguineti, *Interpretazioni*, 97). Their arguments fail to persuade because "introcque" is such a fundamental component of *Inf.* 20. Although Dante is certainly establishing a bridge between *Inferno* 20 and 21, what is most striking about his strategic usage of "introcque" is the way in which he encloses the "ventesimo canto" between two words which unambiguously recall the *De vulgari eloquentia*. For better balanced discussions of "introcque," see Barchiesi, "Catarsi," 119; Hollander, "Tragedy," 214–215.

21. Baldelli, "Il canto XX," 479 (and compare his "Canzon," 801; and "Terzina," in *Enciclopedia dantesca*, 5:584). See also Barchiesi, "Catarsi," 28–29, 32; Paratore, "Il canto XX," 168–169.

22. See the *lecturae* listed in note 12. In addition, see Ernesto G. Parodi, "La critica della poesia classica nel ventesimo canto dell'*Inferno*," *Atene e Roma* 11 (1908): 183–195, 237–250; Robert Hollander, *Il Virgilio dantesco: Tragedia nella "Commedia"* (Florence: Olschki, 1983), 81–115.

23. In fact, Dante's questioning of conventional 'tragic' and 'comic' forms, as well as the concomitant definition of his new "comedía," is a constant feature of his poem; see Zygmunt G. Barański, "The 'Marvellous' and the 'Comic': Toward a Reading of *Inferno* XVI," *Lectura Dantis* 7 (1990): 72–95; "*Comedía*"; "'Primo'"; "Dante Alighieri."

24. See, in particular, the transitions between *Inf.* 6 and 7, and 7 and 8. See also Barolini, *Undivine Comedy*, 258–261.

25. See Wilkins, "Cantos, Regions, and Transitions"; Gorni, "La teoria," 164–186; Barolini, *Undivine Comedy*, 257–265; Ferrante, "A Poetics," 158.

26. On the novelty of the *canto* as an epic form, see the section, "Epic Structures."

27. In this context, it is noteworthy that Barchiesi should suggest that the phrase "ch'è d'[i sommersi]" is equivalent to the Latin formula used in titles: *quae est de* ("Catarsi," 24–25).

28. See Baldelli, "Terzina," 585; Gorni, *Il nodo*, 164–165, 181–182, 207; Zygmunt G. Barański, "Re-viewing Dante," *Romance Philology* 42 (1988): 65–66; Beltrami, *La metrica*, 90–92. For an excellent 'allegorical' reading of the *terza rima* and its assimilation into the *canto*, see John Freccero, "The Significance of *terza rima*," in *Dante, Petrarch, Boccaccio: Studies in the Italian Trecento in Honour of Charles S. Singleton*, ed. Aldo S. Bernardo and Anthony L. Pellegrini (Binghampton, N.Y.: State University of New York Press, 1983), 3–17.

29. The precise value of "versi" in this context is far from clear. It seems to cover three main areas of meaning: (1) "far versi" is equivalent to the generic 'to compose poetry' which "tria videtur consistere: primo circa cantus divisionem, secundo circa partium habitudinem, tertio circa numerum carminum et sillabarum" (*DVE* 2.9.4); (2) more specifically, "versi," as is clear from the quotation just given, equals *carmina* and probably also, by extension, *sillabae*, given the close association of these last two terms in Dante (see *DVE* 2.9.6; 12.4); (3) in the particular context of the *Commedia*, "versi" may stand for what we now call *terza rima* or *terzina*, and what the early commentators at times labelled *ternario*. "Versi," thus, appears to focus on the 'line', the hendecasyllables of the *Commedia*, one of the three elements, together with the "canto" and the "canzon," which constitutes the poem's *forma tractatus*. In addition, some of the poem's fourteenth-century readers gloss "versi" as *rithimi* (see, for instance, the passage from Benvenuto quoted in note 8)— I do not find this interpretation especially persuasive, given the care with which Dante always keeps *rithimus* distinct from *carmen* and *sillaba* in the

DVE (see, in particular, 2.9.4–5). It may equally be the case, however, that Benvenuto, who did not know the *DVE*, could have been using the term not with the meaning of 'rhymes' but with that of 'verses', since both meanings were current in the Middle Ages: "*Rithimus* sonus cantilene, et *rithimus* grece numerus, quia in numero quodam sillabarum vel vocum; unde *rithimus-a-um*, dulciter sonans, vel quia fit ex rithimis, et *rithimor -aris* id est consonare, vel rithimos facere" (Uguccione's definition of *rithimus* quoted in Brugnoli's notes to Epistle 13, in *Opere minori*, 2:612–613). The fact that, in the Epistle to Cangrande, under the *accessus* heading which deals, in a manner which recalls *Inf.* 20.1–3, with the *forma tractatus* of the *Commedia*, the letter's author should state that "quilibet cantus dividitur in rithimos" would be further evidence, for me, of the Epistle's inauthenticity. It seems unlikely, not to say pointless, that Dante, who certainly did know the *DVE*, would have described the basic organization of his poem by intentionally going against his own previously carefully established usage of *carmen-verso* in opposition to *rithimus*. First, it would have meant repudiating the terminology which had been fixed, in part—as we have seen—by means of a *rapprochement* with the *DVE*, within the *Commedia* itself. Second, if Dante were the author of the letter, it is not at all clear why he would have wanted to alter the terms in which he had already defined his poem, thereby creating terminological confusion, and this at a crucial point: the presentation of his poem's *forma tractatus*. In the *Commedia*, it is important to remember the basic nature of the line remains constant. The *verso* is not a key issue; its definition is not linked to the formal and ideological changes which the poem undergoes, such as the changes signaled by the terminological switch from "canzon" to "cantica," a process which, in any case, occurs not outside, but inside, the *Commedia*. To have used *rithimus* instead of *carmen* would have suggested that the line, like the *cantica*, alters its character during the course of the poem. Furthermore, in the light of the three meanings of *rithimus* current in the fourteenth century, Dante would have only compounded the confusion caused by his switch, since it is not at all clear what "rithimos" stands for in the letter. For Dante, to have substituted the precise *carmen* for the imprecise *rithimus* seems to make little sense and goes against the consistently sophisticated coherence of his metaliterary practices. Such exegetical sloppiness is, on the other hand, far from untypical of the anonymous author of the Epistle (see Barański, "*Comedía*"). Let me offer another example of the gap in critical and writerly perception which separates Dante from the author of the letter. If one compares *Inf* 20.1–3 with paragraph 9—"Forma tractatus est triplex, secundum triplicem divisionem. Prima divisio est, que totum opus dividitur in tres canticas. Secunda, qua quelibet cantica dividitur in cantus. Tertia, que quilibet cantus dividitur in rithimos"—what is immediately striking is the fact that they present the poem's *forma tractatus* in diametrically contrasting modes. Dante, with his poet's sensibility and experience, works his way up from the line, while the poetically inexperienced author of the Epistle works his way down, grandiosely but unrealistically, from the *cantica*. For an excellent discussion of Dante's use of *rithimus* and *rima*, see Brugnoli, notes to Epistle 13, in *Opere minori*, 2:612–613. See also Mario Pazzaglia, *Il verso e l'arte della canzone nel "De vulgari eloquentia"* (Florence: La Nuove Italia Editrice, 1967), 141–176; Antonio da Tempo, *Summa Artis Rithimici Vulgaris Dictaminis*, ed. Richard Andrews (Bologna: Commissione per i testi di lingua, 1977), 118, 120, 128–129. See also Alessandro Niccoli, "Verso," in *Enciclopedia dantesca*, 5:981–982.

30. As regards my discussion in this section, it is noteworthy that Beltrami should assert that, in the light of *Inf.* 20.1–3, "l'uso terminologico di Dante . . . spinge a credere che Dante pensi il canto come una stanza di canzone *sui generis*; una canzone 'comica' nello stile, che consente una relativa elasticità nella misura delle stanze-canti" (*La metrica*, 91). A final similarity between the stanza and the *canto* may be noted in the fact that just as, in a *canzone*, the first stanza establishes the basic metrical patterns for the *stanze* which follow it (*DVE* 2.9.2), so *Inferno* 1 fixes such patterns for the remaining ninety-nine *canti*.

On Dante's theoretical reflection on the *canzone*, see Pazzaglia, *Il verso*; Baldelli, "Canzone," 796–802; Gérard Gonfroy, "Le reflet de la *canso* dans le *De vulgari eloquentia* et dans les *Leys d'amors*," *Cahiers de civilisation médiévale* 25, no. 3–4 (1982): 187–196.

31. As well as *Inf.* 16.128, Dante alludes to the title and genre of his poem in *Inf.* 21.2. After providing the structural and metrical description of his poem in the *incipit* to *Inf.* 20, he repeats the term, *comedía*, which defines its register and subject matter. It is clear that Dante wanted these two *exordia* to be read together as a major metaliterary statement on the *Commedia*.

32. A breakdown, in table form, of the length of each *canto* may conveniently be found in Charles S. Singleton, "The Poet's Number at the Center," *Modern Language Notes* 80, no. 1 (1965): 5; and in Ferrante, "A Poetics," 154.

33. See Charles S. Singleton, *Dante's "Commedia": Elements of Structure* [1954] (Baltimore and London: Johns Hopkins University Press, 1977).

34. See Ernst Robert Curtius, *European Literature and the Latin Middle Ages* [1948] (London and Henley: Routledge and Kegan Paul, 1979), 501–509; Singleton, "Poet's Number," 10. Curtius remarks that "the wonderful harmony of Dante's numerical composition is the end and the acme of a long development. From the enneads of the *Vita nuova* Dante proceeded to the elaborate numerical structure of the *Commedia*: 1 + 33 + 33 + 33 = 100 cantos conduct the reader through three realms, the last of which contains ten heavens. Triads and decads intertwine into unity. Here number

is no longer an outer framework, but a symbol of the cosmic *ordo*" (*European Literature*, 509). See also the discussion below on the relationship between music and the *Commedia*.

35. See also Fausto Montanari, "Canto V," in *Letture dantesche*, 3:79–81; Manlio Pastore Stocchi, "Il canto V del *Paradiso*," in *Nuove letture dantesche*, 5:373.

36. See, for instance, M. D. Chenu, "Grammaires et théologie aux XIIe et XIIIe siècles," *Archives d'histoire doctrinale et littéraire du moyen âge* 10 (1935–1936), 5–28; Curtius, *European Literature*, 544–546; Marie-Thérèse d'Alverny, "Le cosmos symbolique du XIIe siècle," *Archives d'histoire doctrinale et littéraire du moyen âge* 20 (1953): 31–81; Hampus Lyttkens, *The Analogy between God and the World: An Investigation of Its Background and Interpretation of Its Use by Thomas of Aquino* (Uppsala: Almqvist and Wiksells, 1953); Thomas Camelot, "La théologie de l'image de Dieu," *Revue des sciences philosophiques et théologiques* 40 (1956): 443–471; Robert Javelet, *Image et ressemblance au douzième siècle*, 2 vols. (Paris: Letouzey et Ané, 1967); Werner Beierwaltes, *Identität und Differenz* (Frankfurt am Main and Bern: Peter Lang, 1980); Gerhart B. Ladner, *Images and Ideas in the Middle Ages*, 2 vols. (Rome: Edizioni di Storia e Letteratura, 1983); Kent Emery, Jr., "Reading the World Rightly and Squarely: Bonaventure's Doctrine of the Cardinal Virtues," *Traditio* 39 (1983): 183–218; Friedrich Ohly, "*Deus geometria*: Appunti per la storia di una rappresentazione di Dio," in his *Geometria e memoria*, ed. Lea Ritter Santini (Bologna: il Mulino, 1985), 189–247.

37. Mengaldo, notes to *DVE*, in *Opere minori*, 2:207.

38. See the passages quoted in note 8.

39. As well as using "canto" to refer to the subdivisions of the *Commedia*, Dante employs it to mean "poetry" and "poetic composition," and the human voice singing or articulating melodiously. See Onder, "Canto."

40. Further evidence against Boccaccio's explanation of "canto" in terms of the *Commedia*'s dependence on music comes from Dante's definition of *poesis* in the *DVE* as "fictio rethorica musicaque poita" (2.4.2). At no stage in his career did Dante modify the view that it is not music which subsumes poetry, as was widely deemed among his contemporaries, but that it is poetry which embraces music (see Pazzaglia, *Il verso*, 177–204; Gonfroy, "Le reflet," 196). If anything, this position became even more entrenched in the *Commedia* (see Zygmunt G. Barański, "Teoria musicale e legittimazione poetica nella *Commedia* di Dante," in *Letteratura italiana e la musica*, ed. Jorn Moestrup [Florence: Olschki, 1994]).

41. Contini, *Un'idea*, 124. In this context, Dante's words of praise for the lyric *canzone* in *DVE* 2.3.3–9, and especially for its range, can take on revealingly suggestive new meanings when applied to his comic, all-embracing "canzon." This is particularly so as regards evaluations such as

"Quod autem tota comprehendatur in cantionibus ars cantandi poetice, in hoc palatur, quod quicquid artis reperitur in omnibus aliis et in cantionibus reperitur, sed non convertitur hoc" (8), and "quicquid de cacuminibus illustrium capitum poetantium profluxit ad labia, in solis cantionibus invenitur" (9). In addition, such statements furnish further proof of the DVE's crucial role in clarifying the Commedia. As regards the relationship between Dante's comic canzone and the lyric form of the same name, if one recalls that "con l'esperienza dantesca [as a lyric poet] si attua una decisiva grammaticalizzazione della canzone volgare, di cui verrà mortificato l'impressionante potenziale di polimorfismo vivo nel Duecento, promuovendo canoni e modelli in base illustre" (Guglielmo Gorni, "Le forme primarie del testo poetico," in Letteratura italiana, ed. Alberto Asor Rosa [Turin: Einaudi, 1984], 3.1:456), then, the infernal "canzon" represents a return, on Dante's part, to the less rigid and more 'open' view of the canzone.

42. Mengaldo's notes to DVE, in Opere minori, 2:204.

43. Barański, "'Primo'," 16–22.

44. Barański, "Teoria musicale."

45. Baldelli, "Terzina," 585.

46. Baldelli, in "Lingua e stile," 81, does qualify the phrase "in senso romanzo, attraverso l'invenzione di una struttura variabile, ma conclusa" by adding "quindi avvicinabile alla canzone con congedo," an interesting suggestion in the light of my 'lyric' discussion of the canto.

47. Tartaro, Canto XX, 6.

48. D'Ovidio, "Esposizione," 316.

49. Ernesto G. Parodi, "Il canto XX dell'Inferno" [1900], in Letture dantesche, ed. Giovanni Getto, 3 vols. (Florence: Sansoni, 1955–1961), 1:401.

50. See, for instance, Caccia, "Canto XX," 676; Pasquazi, "Il canto XX," 183.

51. See Les arts poétiques du XIIe et du XIIIe siècle [1923], ed. Edmond Faral (Paris: Librairie Honoré Champion, 1971), 55–60; Douglas Kelly, "The Scope of Treatment of Composition in the Twelfth- and Thirteenth-century Arts of Poetry," Speculum 41 (1966): 261–278, and "Theory of Composition in Medieval Narrative Poetry and Geoffrey of Vinsauf's Poetria Nova," Mediaeval Studies 31 (1969): 117–148.

52. On the laisse, see Jean Rychner, La chanson de geste: Essai sur l'art épique des jongleurs (Geneva and Lille: Droz-Librairie Giard, 1955), 68–125; Angelo Monteverdi, "La laisse épique," in La Téchnique littéraire des chansons de geste (Paris: "Les Belles Lettres," 1959), 127–139; Wilhelm T. Elwert, Traité de versification française des origines a nos jours (Paris: Klincksieck, 1965), 153–156; Paul Zumthor, Semiologia e poetica medievale [1972] (Milan: Feltrinelli, 1973), 325–333. On the limited use of lasse in medieval Italy, see Beltrami, La metrica, 88, 258–259.

53. See Rychner, *La chanson*, 68–69, 107–125; Monteverdi, "La laisse," 129.

54. On Dante and the *Chanson de Roland*, see the commentaries to *Inf.* 31.16–18.

55. See Rychner, *La chanson*, 124.

56. Erich Auerbach, *Mimesis* [1946] (Princeton, N.J.: Princeton University Press, 1968), 178–180.

57. On Dante and the *romans* tradition, and in particular his contacts with the *Roman de la Rose*, see Contini, *Un'idea*, 245–283; Luigi Vanossi, *Dante e il "Roman de la Rose": Saggio sul "Fiore"* (Florence: Olschki, 1979); Earl J. Richards, *Dante and the "Roman de la Rose": An Investigation into the Vernacular Narrative Context of the "Commedia"* (Tübingen: Max Niemeyer Verlag, 1981), a study to be read with considerable caution; John Took, "Dante and the *Roman de la Rose*," *Italian Studies* 37 (1982): 1–25; *Lettura del "Fiore,"* ed. Zygmunt G. Barański, Patrick Boyde, and Lino Pertile (Ravenna: Longo, 1993) [= *Letture Classensi XXII*]. Dante's rejection of the structures of the *romans* also involves a criticism of the form, rhyming couplets of *settenari*, chosen by Brunetto Latini, in the wake of French examples, for his allegorical-didactic 'voyage', the *Tesoretto*.

58. See Contini, *Un'idea*, 106; Barański, "'Significar,'" 6–8, 11, 14–15.

59. See Teodolinda Barolini, *Dante's Poets: Textuality and Truth in the "Comedy"* (Princeton, N.J.: Princeton University Press, 1984), 107, n. 21. Barolini makes the important observation for my present argument that the *Commedia* is "the equivalent of many canzoni stitched together" (108).

60. I do not have the space here to go into the implications of the *Commedia* being written in hendecasyllables. Suffice it to say that, as the supreme Italian verse form (*DVE* 2.5.3), the hendecasyllable subsumes all the other types of poetic line. It thus has the same totalizing character as the "canto," the "canzon," the "comedía," and, as we shall see, the *terza rima*.

61. However, see, at least, Barolini, *Dante's Poets*, 85–123, 173–187.

62. Contini makes some suggestive observations about the ways in which "canzon" in *Inf.* 20 serves as a "bridge" connecting the *Commedia* with the structures of lyric poetry in general (*Un'idea*, 58–59). I believe that two particularly important areas for future researchers to explore as regards this field are (1) the links in organization between the *Commedia* and the *corone* of sonnets, and (2) the formal and ideological ties between the "sacrato poema" and a narrative sequence in sonnet form such as the *Fiore*. It would be astonishing if Dante had not established significant and revealing interconnections between the *Commedia* and the sonnet, given the latter's traditional standing as the lyric 'comic' meter (*DVE* 2.3.2, 4.1). Unfortunately, as with the hendecasyllable, I am unable to explore these fascinating matters in this study. See, however, Contini, *Un'idea*, 107; Lino Leonardi, "Sonetto e terza

rima (da Guittone a Dante)," in *Omaggio a Gianfranco Folena*, 3 vols. (Padua: Editoriale Programma, 1993), 1:337–351.

63. See Pertile, "*Canto*"; and "*Cantica.*"

64. Barański, "'Primo'," 21.

65. "Canticum," in *Thesaurus*, 3:284–285. Indeed, and obviously significant as far as Dante's choice of the term is concerned, *canticum* was used to refer both to the secular comedians, Plautus and Terence, and to the biblical one, Solomon (284). If I have a criticism to make of Pertile's excellent work on "cantica," it is that he ties Dante's usage of the term a bit too closely to the Song of Songs (but see "*Cantica*," 404–405), when, in fact, like the concept of comedy, *canticum* in medieval literary criticism was associated with a variety of different genres, thereby, making it an especially apt tag with which to describe the *Commedia*. I hope to return in the near future to this and other issues connected with Dante's definition of each of the three *cantiche*.

66. See, for instance, Ps. 95:1, 97:1; Sancti Bernardi, *Sermones super Cantica Canticorum* 1.9, in *Opera*, ed. Jean Leclercq et al. (Rome: Editiones Cistercienses, 1957), 1:6–7. I shall return to the question of celebrating God in the next section, "Biblical Structures."

67. See Pertile, "*Cantica*," 409–411. See also Domenico De Robertis, *Il libro della "Vita Nuova"* [1961], 2d edition (Florence: Sansoni, 1970), 117–120; Henri Rondet, "Le thème du Cantique Nouveau chez Saint Augustin," in *L'Homme devant Dieu. Mélanges offerts au père Henri de Lubac*, 3 vols. (Paris: Aubier, 1963–1964), 1:341–353.

68. Barański, "'Primo'," 6–9.

69. See Zygmunt G. Barański, "Dante fra 'sperimentalismo' e 'enciclopedismo'," in *L'enciclopedismo medievale*, ed. Michelangelo Picone (Ravenna: Longo, 1994).

70. See M. B. Parkes, "The Influence of the Concepts of 'Ordinatio' and 'Compilatio' on the Development of the Book," in *Medieval Learning and Literature: Essays Presented to R. W. Hunt*, ed. J. J. G. Alexander and M. T. Gibson (Oxford: Clarendon Press, 1976), 115–141; A. J. Minnis, "Late-Medieval Discussions of 'Compilatio' and the Role of the 'Compilator'," *Beiträge zur Geschichte der deutschen Sprache und Literatur* 101 (1979): 385–421; Neil Hathaway, "*Compilatio*: From Plagiarism to Compiling," *Viator* 20 (1989): 19–44; R. H. Rouse and M. A. Rouse, "*Ordinatio* and *Compilatio* Revisited," in *Ad Litteram*, 113–134.

71. On biblical *divisio*, see Beryl Smalley, *Study of the Bible*, 221–224, 366. On the Psalter and the Song of Songs, see James Kugel, *The Idea of Biblical Poetry: Parallelism and Its History* (New Haven, Conn.: Yale University Press, 1981); Minnis, *Medieval Theory*, 42–58; Ann W. Astell, *The Song of Songs in the Middle Ages* (Ithaca, N.Y.: Cornell University Press, 1990).

72. Thomas Aquinas, *In Psalmos Davidis expositio*, in *Opera Omnia*, 25 vols. (Parma: Ficcadori, 1852–1873), 14:149–150, and cp. 344, 351. See also Pertile, "*Cantica*," 408.

73. See "Canticum," in *Thesaurus*, 3:284–285. Dante underscored the proximity between *canticum* and *psalmus* by opening *Purgatorio* 33, the *canto* which closes with the reference to "questa cantica seconda" (140), with an allusion to Psalm 78 as "dolce salmodia" (2).

74. See Minnis, *Medieval Theory*. The Lamentations of Jeremiah was a further scriptural book which the Middle Ages deemed to be poetic and thus labeled a *canticum* (see, for instance, Hugonis de Sancto Victore, *Didascalicon*, ed. Charles Henry Buttimer [Washington, D.C.: Catholic University Press, 1939], 4.8). Although I am unable here to examine the links between the *Lamentationes* and the *Commedia*, it is obvious that, through this particular association, Dante's "cantica" also indicates the poem's prophetic and apocalyptic dimension.

75. On Dante and David, see Vincent Truijen, "David," in *Enciclopedia dantesca*, 2:322; Robert Hollander, "Dante's Use of the Fiftieth Psalm [1973]," in *Studies in Dante*, 107–113; A. Stäuble, "*Paradiso* XXV. 38 e i salmi dei pellegrinaggi," *Versants* 5 (1983): 3–21; Barolini, *Dante's Poets*, 275–279. Of limited use is Michel David, "Dante et sa théodie," in *Omaggio a Gianfranco Folena*, 1:429–446. On Dante and Solomon, see Paul Priest, "Dante and *The Song of Songs*," *Studi danteschi* 49 (1972): 79–113; Angelo Penna, "Cantico dei Cantici," in *Enciclopedia dantesca*, 1:793; Gian Roberto Sarolli, "Salomone," in *Enciclopedia dantesca*, 4:1079–1083; Lino Pertile, " 'Così si fa la pelle bianca nera': L'enigma di *Par.* XXVII, 136–138," *Lettere italiane* 43 (1991): 3–26, "Canto," and "Cantica."

76. *In Canticum Canticorum expositio* attributed to Thomas Aquinas but probably written by Haimo of Auxerre, in Thomas Aquinas, *Opera*, 14:354.

77. On the *terza rima*, see Giovanni Mari, "La sestina d'Arnaldo, la terzina di Dante," *Rendiconti dell'Istituto Lombardo di Scienze e Lettere*, ser. 2, 32 (1899): 953–985; Tommaso Casini, "Per la genesi della terzina e della commedia dantesca," in *Miscellanea di studi storici in onore di Giovanni Sforza* (Lucca: Tip. Ed. Baroni, 1920), 689–697; J. S. P. Tatlock, "Dante's *terza rima*," *PMLA* 51 (1936): 895–903; Singleton, *Dante's "Commedia*," 58–59; Mario Fubini, *Metrica e poesia* (Milan: Feltrinelli, 1962), 168–200; Gianfranco Contini, "La questione del *Fiore*," *Cultura e scuola* 13–14 (1965): 773; Tibor Wlassics, "Le caratteristiche strutturali della terzina," in *Interpretazioni di prosodia dantesca* (Rome: Signorelli, 1972), 9–23; Baldelli, "Terzina," 583–594; Vanossi, *Dante e il "Roman de la rose*," 219–221; Guglielmo Gorni, "Sull'origine della terzina e altre misure: Appunti di metrica dantesca," *Metrica* 2 (1981): 43–60; Freccero, "Significance of *terza rima*"; Franco Gavazzeni, "Approssimazioni metriche sulla terza rima," *Studi danteschi* 56 (1984): 1–82;

Beltrami, *La metrica*, 90–92; Guglielmo Gorni, "Postilla sull'ottava e sulla terza rima," in *Metrica e analisi letteraria* (Bologna: il Mulino, 1993), 295–310; Leonardi, "Sonetto."

78. See John Ahern, "Binding the Book: Hermeneutics and Manuscript Production in *Paradiso* 33," *PMLA* 97 (1982): 804; and "Dante's Last Word: The *Comedy* as a *liber coelestis*," *Dante Studies* 102 (1984): 2–3. See also Amelia E. Van Vleck, *Memory and Re-Creation in Troubadour Lyric* (Berkeley and Los Angeles: University of California Press, 1991).

Christopher Kleinhenz

Dante and the Art of Citation

The subject of this essay—biblical citation in Dante's *Divine Comedy* and, more generally, the nature and function of citation in the Middle Ages—was addressed in a recent "Peanuts" cartoon. In the first panel of the comic strip, Charlie Brown asks his sister Sally: "Have you seen my baseball glove around anywhere?" She replies in the middle panel by quoting Scripture: " 'I know not . . . am I the keeper of my brother's glove?' Genesis 4:9." In the final panel a dejected and resigned Charlie Brown concludes by saying, "I know the verse." What can we make of this? And how does it relate to the topic of this essay? In the first place, we all immediately recognize that Sally has adapted the biblical phrase to her own purposes, transforming Cain's curt but dramatic response to God's inquiry about Abel—"Am I my brother's keeper?"—into the ludicrous and mundane inanity of her not being the "keeper of her brother's baseball glove." The epic dimensions and character of the biblical drama are reduced, trivialized here to the unsuccessful quest for the baseball mitt. Charlie Brown does not denounce his sister, as we might expect he would, following the biblical intertext; rather, he simply says that he "knows the verse." As a learned reader of the Bible, Charlie recognizes its original meaning and implications for the present situation and understands, sadly, that the fate of the baseball glove, like that of Abel, is not promising; indeed, it is probably hopeless. Another reason for his gloom is that his innocent question has provoked a very hostile response, and from a family member to boot! Thus, it seems clear that Charlie and his sister need to get some counseling, or at the very least they should work on their interpersonal relations and communication skills. Given the biblical context, is this perhaps a dark allusion to the archetypal example of sibling rivalry—Cain and Abel? What Charlie Brown does not fully realize, of course, is that he and Sally are unconsciously following, now in the late twentieth century, the medieval pattern of textual citation—the incorporation and adaptation of authoritative source texts to respond to the needs of a new historical, literary, and cultural context.

The validation of discourse by reference to a source, to a commonly accepted authority, to a specific text or body of texts is a practice well known and well documented through the ages. While authors can never free themselves completely from their literary and cultural past, they deal with this heritage in different ways, and an understanding of these responses is crucial to the work of the critic and interpreter of texts. With Dante this sort of archeological excavation into and investigation of the textual *strata* of the *Divine Comedy* is a complex business, for his genius was so great that he constantly challenges us, his readers, to make sense of and to appreciate his intricate poetic and intellectual edifice.

Almost one hundred years ago Edward Moore noted in the introduction to his monumental work, *Scripture and Classical Authors in Dante*, that "Dante's reading was so extensive, and his mind was . . . so brimful of the varied learning thus acquired, that there is scarcely a page of his writings which does not exhibit its influence, and which consequently is not more fully and adequately appreciated when read in its light."[1] In his systematic examination of Dante's works, Moore identified more than fifteen hundred passages that fell within his three categories of "(a) direct citations, (b) obvious references or imitations, [and] (c) allusions and reminiscences."[2] Of these numerous passages, the Vulgate Bible garners the most references, over five hundred.

Following the general directions established by Moore, many scholars over the intervening decades have sharpened their critical focus on the manner in which and the purposes for which Dante incorporates and adapts these citations in his works.[3] Indeed, this has become one of the major areas of interest in recent Dante criticism: finding and discovering—some skeptics might be tempted to say, imagining and inventing—the subtext, source text, parallel text, intertext for Dante's text and then evaluating and determining the value of this textual relationship to our increased understanding of his works and of the nature of textual transmission, influence, and reception in the Middle Ages (and in subsequent centuries). We must then carefully consider the relationship that exists between Dante's texts and those of countless other writers—texts not only literary and historical, philosophical and theological, scientific and technical, but also cultural and popular, musical and visual—in short, the complete interaction between Dante's poem and the late Medieval world which it reflects, in which it was written, and which, so to speak, "produced" it.

Dante's art of citation is a vast and fertile field of investigation, and in the hundred years since Moore's pioneering work we have come to an increased understanding of how Dante incorporates the textual citation for his own purposes and how he is able to enhance the meaning of his text by evoking/invoking other texts and their context. In this essay, I would like to offer some thoughts on the nature of authority and then provide an overview of the broad outlines of Dante's practice of citation, which I have termed in other work his "poetics of citation."[4] Finally, I will illustrate this technique with a series of examples that, while not necessarily new and unusual, may present the framework for our continuing discussion of Dante's use of earlier texts.

There is a great and certain comfort we all experience when we are able to lend credence and give authority to our words, written or spoken, by appealing either to an outside source—the *auctores*, an encyclopedia or dictionary, history or the law, the common cultural legacy, and the like—or to an inside one—personal lived experience, valued advice from family members, results of previous research, and so on. Generally such authorities are named, and their contributions are conditioned by phrases such as "According to the President . . . ," "My grandmother always said that . . . ," "The following forecast is provided by the National Weather Service . . . ," "In an earlier study I argued that. . . ." In the *Divine Comedy* Dante sometimes signals his source in a precise way:[5] "come Livïo scrive, che non erra" (*Inf.* 28.12); "sì come ne scrive Luca" (*Purg.* 21.7); "Dice Isaia" (*Par.* 25.91). One extraordinary moment in the citing of authority occurs in *Purgatorio* 29, at the point in the procession of the Bible, the triumph

of the Church, when the four animals representing the Gospels appear
on the scene:

> coronati ciascun di verde fronda.
>
>   Ognuno era pennuto di sei ali;
> le penne piene d'occhi; e li occhi d'Argo,
> se fosser vivi, sarebber cotali.
>
>   A descriver lor forme piú non spargo
> rime, lettor; ch'altra spesa mi strigne,
> tanto ch'a questa non posso esser largo;
>
>   ma leggi Ezechïel, che li dipigne
> come li vide da la fredda parte
> venir con vento e con nube e con igne;
>
>   e quali i troverai ne le sue carte,
> tali eran quivi, salvo ch'a le penne
> Giovanni è meco e da lui si diparte.
>
> (*Purg.* 29.93–105)

Dante's written authorities are Ezechiel (1:4–14; 10:1–22) and the
Apocalypse of John (4:6–8), plus his own eye witness testimony here
in the Earthly Paradise atop the Mountain of Purgatory. While the
four animals are said to have four wings in Ezechiel, they in truth
possess six, just as John presents them and, more importantly, just
as Dante sees them, for, as the poet says, "John agrees with me"
("Giovanni è meco"). Note that he does not say "I agree with John"
but that "John agrees with me"! Dante draws his authority not merely
from the written text of the Bible but also and most importantly
from his own personal, eyewitness observation within the "historical"
constructs of the poem.

Some citations in the *Divine Comedy* refer to Dante's own works,
and these then belong to the category of inside sources. These autoci-
tations consist in the opening verse of one of his *canzoni*, thus opening
up the particular episode to reflect upon, to elaborate, to correct the
earlier text that has been evoked in this manner. Although these
moments are rare in the poem, the verses thus cited have a distinct
and important role to play in their new context: How does Dante, at
this particular moment in the Pilgrim's journey through the realms
of the afterlife, utilize his own literary past? Does the earlier moment
remain frozen in its original context? Or is its meaning adapted to
the new circumstances? In the second canto of *Purgatory* Casella

sings Dante's *canzone* "Amor che ne la mente mi ragiona" from the
Convivio, and this musical interlude has an immediate effect on those
who hear it:

> 'Amor che ne la mente mi ragiona'
> cominciò elli allor sì dolcemente,
> che la dolcezza ancor dentro mi suona.
>   Lo mio maestro e io e quella gente
> ch'eran con lui parevan sì contenti,
> come a nessun toccasse altro la mente.
>
> (*Purg.* 2.112–117)

And it is precisely the souls' absorption in the pleasing melody of the
song and the consoling nature of its words, in those earthly delights
that occasions Cato's abrupt arrival on the scene and his curt dispersal
of the crowd:

> Noi eravam tutti fissi e attenti
> a le sue note; ed ecco il veglio onesto
> gridando: "Che è ciò, spiriti lenti?
>   qual negligenza, quale stare è questo?
> Correte al monte a spogliarvi lo scoglio
> ch'esser non lascia a voi Dio manifesto."
>
> (*Purg.* 2.118–123)

The evocation of the *Convivio*, and thus of the love for the *donna
gentile* / Philosophy, is intended to demonstrate the progress in Dante
the poet's intellectual and spiritual growth and to highlight the se-
ductive attractions that still impede the movement of the Pilgrim.
In all of his works Dante is consistently moving toward a greater
and more all–encompassing vision of the universe, and he adroitly
incorporates previous works in later ones if generally only to revise
them, to point out their shortcomings and their relative position in
his personal, poetic, intellectual, and spiritual *iter*.[6]

In the Middle Ages authorities are cited as often as not, and
citations are sometimes marked in a distinctive way; but frequently
they are not, presumably because their nature and source were obvious
to the contemporary audience. While Dante on occasion identifies his
authority by name, as we have noted earlier, on other occasions he
uses antonomasia—for example, "il Filosofo" is always Aristotle (as
in *Convivio* 1.1.1: "Sì come dice lo Filosofo nel principio de la Prima

Filosofia").[7] In the second verse of his sonnet "Amore e 'l cor gentil sono una cosa" (*Vita Nuova*, 20.3),[8] Dante refers to Guido Guinizzelli as the "wise man"—"sì come il saggio in suo dittare pone"—alluding, of course, to the latter's famous doctrinal *canzone*, "Al cor gentil rempaira sempre Amore." In *Purgatory* 6 we find an instance in which Dante employs both strategies: naming and antonomasia. Virgil is responding to the Pilgrim's questions concerning the efficacy of prayer and specifically the validity of the passage in the *Aeneid* where it is said that the will of heaven is not moved by human prayers ("Desine fata deum flecti sperare precando" [*Aeneid* 6.373]). The Roman poet defends the validity both of his text and of the proper hopes of those in Purgatory:

> La mia scrittura è piana;
> e la speranza di costor non falla,
> se ben si guarda con la mente sana;
>   ché cima di giudicio non s'avvalla
> perché foco d'amor compia in un punto
> ciò che de' sodisfar chi qui s'astalla;
>   e là dov' io fermai cotesto punto,
> non s'ammendava, per pregar, difetto,
> perché 'l priego da Dio era disgiunto.
>
> (*Purg.* 6.34–42)

Virgil then defers to the higher authority of Beatrice:

> Veramente a così alto sospetto
> non ti fermar, se quella nol ti dice
> che lume fia tra 'l vero e lo 'ntelletto.
>   Non so se 'ntendi: io dico di Beatrice;
> tu la vedrai di sopra, in su la vetta
> di questo monte, ridere e felice.
>
> (*Purg.* 6.43–48)

In addition to the "double" reference to Beatrice, first identified by her role in the allegory of the poem ("lume . . . tra 'l vero e lo 'ntelletto") and then by her given name (Beatrice) which, of course, also carries allegorical significance with it, this passage invokes the Virgilian text and questions its authority. The sound and logical defense of the *Aeneid* is enhanced by Virgil's reference to it as "la mia scrittura." In Dante's poetic strategy the *Aeneid* becomes a sort of secular "scripture," where authority is clearly declared by the Florentine poet's use of the terms "scrittura" and "volume" to refer only to the Bible and the *Aeneid*.[9]

By and large, however, citations are generally not identified in Dante's text; rather, they are simply present as unintroduced and unadorned words, phrases, or sentences. Sometimes our attention is specifically directed to them because they are in another language, almost always Latin, but generally it is the reader's responsibility to notice the borrowing, to pursue its source, and to understand its function in Dante's text. In the past few years my research has focused on the general relationship between the *Divine Comedy* and the Bible and, particularly, on the use Dante makes of the Bible in his poem through the "art of citation." This investigation focuses primarily on Dante's technique of evoking a particular word, verse, or passage in the Bible through the use of an exact, modified, or incomplete representation either of the Vulgate or of an Italian translation or paraphrase of the Latin text. Moreover, through use of scriptural reference Dante not only invokes the text of the Bible but also evokes the rich commentary traditions—both verbal and visual—that are attached to that specific text. Thus, while the Florentine poet uses some scriptural citations simply for their immediate evocative value, he employs many others whose function in the text may be fully understood only through a careful consideration of these various sources, analogues, and materials, and their associations and interconnections. We might call this technique the "art" or "poetics of citation," the "poetics of allusion," the "poetics of reference," or even the "poetics of authority." And perhaps this last phrase most succinctly describes the goal toward which Dante was striving and the means of its accomplishment. The poetic text would thus proclaim Dante's personal, yet universal, vision; it would announce the means by which the "evil ways of the world," the "mondo che mal vive" (*Purg.* 32.103) would be corrected; it would contain the message that derives its moral and spiritual force precisely because it is rooted in and appeals to the authority of Holy Scripture, such that the *Comedy* itself becomes a sort of "new scripture."

Biblical citations in the *Comedy* take several forms. They may be exact, modified, or incomplete versions of the Latin text of the Vulgate or Italian translations or paraphrases thereof. These citations may be long or short, several lines, an entire verse or even a single word, just enough to trigger a response in the mind of the reader, to evoke that other text and its context and meaning. One example of exact citation from the Vulgate is the first verse from the Old Testament Book of Wisdom ("Diligite iustitiam qui iudicatis terram") that is presented in *Paradiso* 18:[10]

> 'DILIGITE IUSTITIAM', primai
> fur verbo e nome di tutto 'l dipinto;
> 'QUI IUDICATIS TERRAM', fur sezzai.
>
> (*Par.* 18.91–93)

These resplendent words, formed letter by letter by the luminous souls in the Heaven of Jupiter, are perhaps the most striking example of Dante's innovative artistry in the *Paradiso*. The problem of representation of material which largely defies description poses a very real challenge to the poet who must craft his paradisiacal imagery in terms of light and its brilliance, gradations, and refractions. Here the marvelous transformation of the M, the final letter of TERRAM, into the lily and, finally, into the eagle attests to the transformative power of the divine in the temporal sphere—from ideas in the mind of God that are made manifest in individual, visible letters that form whole words and sentences, and from these words and letters emerge forms (the lily, the eagle) that have symbolic value. Each stage in this transformative process is represented here in Paradise by these souls who by following the principle of justice fulfilled the divine Word on earth. The concept of justice is one of the most difficult for Dante—and for every human being—to grasp; indeed, the operation of divine justice is mysterious and ultimately unfathomable not only to human intellects in this life but even to those who are already among the blessed in Paradise.[11] In its urging of earthly rulers to "love justice," the biblical citation establishes the proper context for Dante's extended discussion of justice over the next three cantos.

Citations from the Vulgate are sometimes modified by the alteration of a word or the reordering of the phrase, the latter presumably to fit the requirements of Italian meter. An example of the latter variety is provided by the citation from Psalm 50 in *Purgatorio* 23:

> Ed ecco piangere e cantar s'udíe
> "*Labïa mèa, Domine*" per modo
> tal, che diletto e doglia parturíe.
>
> (*Purg.* 23.10–12)

The emaciated souls of the gluttons sing this psalm which provides an appropriate commentary on their own shortcomings and the reason they are on this purgatorial terrace, for it indicates what the proper use of the mouth should be—"Domine, labia mea aperies; et os meum annuntiabit laudem tuam" (Ps. 50:17). In the economy of the poem the singing of praise becomes analogous to the writing of poetry or, more precisely, the composition of the right and proper kind of poetry. Given this connection, in his bittersweet meeting with Forese Donati on this terrace the Pilgrim recalls their time together in Florence, and this invites us to recall and to reconsider their less than decorous poetic exchange in this new context. Those scurrilous sonnets represent as it were the improper use of the mouth and lips in poetic activity, not the joyful and devout singing of praise but rather the self-indulgent mouthing of insults and the voicing of coarse humor and base desires.

A more significant modification of a biblical citation occurs in *Purgatory* 30.19, where with the words "Benedictus qui venis" (Blessed are *you who come* [emphasis mine]) all of the participants in the triumphal procession announce the advent of Beatrice. The verse in the Gospel on which this one is modeled—"Benedictus qui venit" (Matt. 21:9: Blessed is *he who comes* [emphasis mine])—signals the arrival of Jesus in Jerusalem on Palm Sunday. Through Dante's slight but significant modification—*venis* for *venit*—he makes the phrase more direct and personal, and, even more importantly, by retaining the masculine inflection of *benedictus*, he stresses the important analogy between Christ and Beatrice, which is present throughout the entire episode and which lies at the heart of Dante's conception of Beatrice.

Some citations are purposefully "incomplete," for Dante gives only part—generally the first line—of the Latin text and expects the reader to fill in the missing portion. One well-known example occurs near the beginning of the *Purgatory*. As the ship guided by the angel approaches the shore of the Mountain, the souls "'*In exitu Isräel de Aegypto*' / cantavano tutti insieme ad una voce," and, as Dante specifies, "con quanto di quel salmo è poscia scripto" (*Purg.* 2.46–48). Although presenting only the first verse of Psalm 113, Dante the poet makes it clear that the *entire* psalm was sung, and consequently readers must fill in the omitted text for themselves and consider, therefore, the meaning and implications of the *entire* psalm in both the immediate and the more general context of the poem. The time in Purgatory is

Easter morning, and this psalm of exodus signals both Passover and Easter.[12] It is probably not without significance that in the much-debated Letter to Can Grande, which serves as an introduction to the poem as a whole, Psalm 113 is employed to illustrate the polysemous nature of the Bible, for this psalm presents best the notion of liberation and thus provides the most succinct statement of the movement of the poem as a whole:[13]

> Qui modus tractandi, ut melius pateat, potest considerari in hiis versibus: "In exitu Israel de Egipto, domus Iacob de populo barbaro, facta est Iudaea sanctificatio eius, Israel potestas eius." Nam si ad litteram solam inspiciamus, significatur nobis exitus filiorum Israel de Egipto, tempore Moysis; si ad allegoriam, nobis significatur nostra redemptio facta per Christum; si ad moralem sensum, significatur nobis conversio anime de luctu et miseria peccati ad statum gratie; si ad anagogicum, significatur exitus anime sancte ab huius corruptionis servitute ad eterne glorie libertatem. (13.7.21)

In some instances a Latin phrase is so charged with biblical echoes that its mere use is sufficient to evoke this larger context. In his narration of the life of St. Francis in *Paradiso* 11, Thomas Aquinas at one point uses the Latin phrase *et coram patre* (v. 62) to refer to Francis's meeting with his father in the episcopal court of Assisi. In this dramatic scene Francis, stripping himself naked, renounces his earthly father and all worldly possessions to wed, as it were, Lady Poverty with the blessing of the bishop and before the assembled people:

> ché per tal donna, giovinetto, in guerra
> del padre corse, a cui, come a la morte,
> la porta del piacer nessun diserra;
>   e dinanzi a la sua spirital corte
> *et coram patre* le si fece unito.
>
>   (*Par.* 11.58–62)

By using the phrase *et coram patre*, Dante evokes the passage in Matthew 10:32–33, where *patre* refers to God: "Omnis ergo qui confitebitur me coram hominibus, confitebor et ego eum coram Patre meo, qui in caelis est. Qui autem negaverit me coram hominibus, negabo et ego eum coram Patre meo, qui in caelis est." Francis's life was in many respects an *imitatio Christi*, and these well-known similarities form the basis for Dante's presentation of the saint. Thus, the use in *Paradiso* 11 of the phrase *coram patre* would appear to serve a dual—indeed, a pivotal function—first describing Francis's appearance before his carnal father, and second, and more importantly, referring to his mystical marriage with Lady Poverty before the bishop and God, his spiritual father. This transfer of allegiance from his earthly to his heavenly father is the beginning of Francis's own special mission on earth, one that accords in important ways with that of Christ.

Citations from the Vulgate have their vernacular counterparts, and the text of the Comedy is studded with examples of Italian translations and paraphrases of biblical words, phrases, or entire verses. In Inferno 10, for example, Farinata degli Uberti, the great Ghibelline warlord, addresses Dante as a fellow citizen of Florence, stating that he has recognized him through his Tuscan speech: "La tua loquela ti fa manifesto" (v. 25). As most commentators on the poem indicate, this phrase translates the words spoken to Peter after he has denied Christ for the third time—"Loquela tua manifestum te facit" (Matt. 26:73). However, these same commentators do not generally provide any further gloss. In an earlier essay I have attempted to demonstrate how meaning in this canto is generated by a remarkable conjunction of individual words, complete phrases, and images, through which Dante is able to draw our attention to the specific biblical text and its larger referential context of the passion, crucifixion, and resurrection.[14] We are first led to these considerations by the poet's insistence on the biblical citation—"la tua loquela ti fa manifesto"—which sets in motion the entire series of intertextual connections.

Another example of Dante's Italian adaptation of biblical phraseology occurs in Paradiso 29. In the midst of her diatribe against philosophers and false preachers Beatrice evokes the passage at the end of the Gospel of Mark—"Go ye into the whole world, and preach the gospel to every creature" (Euntes in mundum universum praedicate Evangelium omni creaturae" [Mark 16:15])—and adapts it to her immediate purpose by substituting the word ciance ("idle stories" or even "garbage") for Evangelium: "Non disse Cristo al suo primo convento: / 'Andate, e predicate al mondo ciance'" (Par. 29.109–110). The irony and bitter sarcasm of this distorted Gospel verse sums up the several points Beatrice is making about the lack of spiritual guidance on the part of the clergy. For example, the faithful, who are described typically as the flock of innocent lambs, are continually fed with the idle talk, the insubstantial hot air of the preachers: "le pecorelle, che non sanno, / tornan dal pasco pasciute di vento" (Par.

29.106–107). The movement in the verse cited almost verbatim after Mark's model—"Andate, e predicate al mondo ciance"—is similar to that found in the first verse of *Inferno* 34, where the ringing incipit of the hymn by Venantius Fortunatus, "Vexilla Regis prodeunt" is distorted, transformed to good infernal effect by the addition of the genitive *inferni* (of Hell). Thus, the first three words in the verse lead us to think of the triumph of Christ on the cross, of death being overcome by life. However, when we read the fourth word—*inferni*—we realize, suddenly and with surprise, that these *vexilla* are not those of Christ but rather the "banners" that belong to the king of Hell, Lucifer, who is immobile in the icy grip of Cocytus. Lucifer's banners, the grotesque batlike wings, just as Lucifer himself, cannot advance; they can only move to generate an icy wind that maintains the frigid conditions in this lowest region of Hell. In *Paradise* 29 the initial movement of the phrase suggests that it will be a direct and faithful citation of the Gospel—"Andate, e predicate al mondo"—but the use of *ciance* which belongs to a decidedly lower lexical register exerts a great effect on the reader/listener, one that shocks and clarifies at the same moment. To the power of the biblical citation is added the vigorous and dynamic force of a common, indeed crude, word that does not sidestep the issue.

In much the same way, Cacciaguida in *Paradise* 17 instructed Dante to divulge what he has seen ("tutta tua visïon fa manifesta" [*Par.* 17.128]) and to let those afflicted "scratch wherever it may itch" ("e lascia pur grattar dov' è la rogna" [*Par.* 17.129]). Cacciaguida continues by expanding on the metaphor of nourishment:

> Ché se la voce tua sarà molesta
> nel primo gusto, vital nodrimento
> lascerà poi, quando sarà digesta.
>
> (*Par.* 17.130–132)

Dante's voice is like that of the Old Testament prophets who inveigh against corruption and cry out for justice. His words—his poem—will be the "vital nodrimento" serving Christendom and the cause of justice in the early fourteenth century, as the word of Christ did—and should still do—in the Gospels and through the agency of the disciples who "to fight for kindling the faith made shield and lance of the Gospel" ("a pugnar per accender la fede / de l'Evangelio fero scudo e lance" [*Par.* 29.113–114]).

One final category of citation that I wish to explore briefly concerns the interplay of written text and visual image. We recall the poet's consummate artistry when in *Purgatorio* 10 he describes the relief sculptures on the wall of the first terrace depicting examples of humility:

> Là sù non eran mossi i piè nostri anco,
> quand' io conobbi quella ripa intorno
> che dritto di salita aveva manco,
>   esser di marmo candido e addorno
> d'intagli sì, che non pur Policleto,
> ma la natura lí avrebbe scorno.
>
> (*Purg.* 10.29–33)

and refers to One who made them:

> Colui che mai non vide cosa nova
> produsse esto visibile parlare,
> novello a noi perché qui non si trova.
>
> (*Purg.* 10.94–96)

God's artistry shines forth in the representation of the Annunciation:

> L'angel che venne in terra col decreto
> de la molt' anni lagrimata pace,
> ch'aperse il ciel del suo lungo divieto,
>   dinanzi a noi pareva sì verace
> quivi intagliato in un atto soave,
> che non sembiava imagine che tace.
>   Giurato si saria ch'el dicesse "Ave!";
> perché iv' era imaginata quella
> ch'ad aprir l'alto amor volse la chiave;
>   e avea in atto impressa esta favella
> "Ecce ancilla Deï", propriamente
> come figura in cera si suggella.
>
> (*Purg.* 10.34–45)

In terms of biblical citation Gabriel's initial address—"Ave"—and Mary's eventual response—"Ecce ancilla Dei"—define the boundaries of the biblical citation. The rapid succession of the two phrases as heard by Dante the Pilgrim in his mind is in part a function of the artistic medium that enables the observer to see the scene in its entirety and to "hear" the words in a virtually simultaneous fashion. Readers of Dante's text are invited to consider not only the two specified fragments of the biblical text but also to fill in the missing portion—some ten verses—in which the angel explains to Mary the cause of this miraculous event in order to allay her fears and doubts. Just as the artistic representation evokes the immediate scene and its multifold ramifications, so the spare words cited evoke the entire passage in the Gospel (Luke 1:28–38):

> Et ingressus angelus ad eam dixit: Ave gratia pleta: Dominus tecum: benedicta tu in mulieribus. . . .
> Dixit autem Maria: Ecce ancilla Domini, fiat mihi secundum verbum tuum. Et discessit ab illa angelus. (Luke 1:28 and 38)

In addition to the textual boundaries of the citation established by the words *Ave* and *Ecce ancilla Dei*, we are invited to consider the numerous artistic representations of this episode from the life of Mary and to bring them to bear on our understanding and appreciation of the *Comedy*. I think in particular of the marvelous annunciations done by Nicola Pisano and his son Giovanni for the pulpits in the Pisan Baptistery and Duomo, the Sienese Cathedral, and the church of Sant'Andrea in Pistoia, representations which Dante may have seen and retained in his visual memory for use at the appropriate moment in his poem.

Some evocations of sacred art are not necessarily accompanied by specific verbal citations but rather by the rich, visually oriented language of the poet whose vivid poetic descriptions conjure the object itself. Along these lines, it has been noted that the manner of some punishments in the *Inferno* reflects and incorporates certain elements of Christian iconography.[15] The punishment of the simonists is to be thrust head-first into an opening in the rock of Hell and to have their exposed feet burned with fire. When Dante and his guide Virgil are conversing with the upward turned and wildly kicking legs of Pope Nicholas III, the scene so created is virtually identical to that of Peter and Paul standing next to the fallen Simon Magus.[16] In addition to the episode in the Book of Acts (8:9–24) where Simon Magus attempts to purchase divine power from Peter and is soundly rebuked, we have the more fully developed account in the apocryphal Acts of Peter, in which Simon Magus issues a series of challenges to Peter. In the last of these Simon's flight aided by demons comes to a quick end because of Peter's prayers: Simon falls to the ground and breaks his shank in three places. Simon Magus's name has come to indicate all those who would traffic in sacred offices, and through this presentation Dante calls upon his readers to recall the standard iconography of this episode in the life of Peter and, thus, to enhance their appreciation of the present scene.

Moreover, in recent years critics have demonstrated how in the *Inferno* Dante incorporates standard images from Christian iconography to underscore the perversion of the holy and divine which these sinners represent and to highlight the appropriateness of the operation of divine justice in their punishment. The figure of the arch-heretic Farinata evokes and becomes the infernal perversion of the related images of Noah, of the resurrected Christ, and of Christ as the Man of Sorrows.[17] Similarly, Lucifer who stands waist deep in the frozen lake of Cocytus would represent the infernal perversion of the figure of the baptized Christ.[18] In an earlier study I argued, for a variety of reasons, that the devil who carries the soul of a sinner on his back represents the infernal, perverted form of Christ the Good Shepherd.[19]

A final example of this allusive practice, of Dante's appropriation of Christian imagery for his "word painting" in the poem, is found in *Paradiso* 30. In that episode Beatrice is showing the Pilgrim the beauties of the Empyrean and the Celestial Rose and indicates in particular the throne prepared for Henry VII:

> E 'n quel gran seggio a che tu li occhi tieni
> per la corona che già v'è sú posta,
> prima che tu a queste nozze ceni,
>   sederà l'alma, che fia giú agosta,
> de l'alto Arrigo, ch'a drizzare Italia
> verrà in prima ch'ella sia disposta.
>
> (*Par.* 30.133–138)

This image appears to evoke the motif found in Byzantine art of the "empty throne" (the *hetoimasia*), which derives in part from the description in the fourth book of the Apocalypse of the throne in heaven.[20] Although not common in Italy, this motif is found in certain key locations: in the sanctuary arch mosaic in Santa Maria Maggiore in Rome, in the Last Judgment mosaic in the cathedral at Torcello in the Venetian lagoon, and in cupola mosaics of the

Orthodox and the Arian Baptisteries in Ravenna. In this last example
the empty throne surmounted by the bejewelled cross represents the
throne that has been prepared for the Second Coming of Christ;
the twelve processional figures—Peter, Paul, and ten apostles—carry
crowns. In addition to being a part of the iconographic scheme in
mosaics, the empty throne is a regular feature in the arrangements
of Byzantine churches, where an elaborate, empty chair is sometimes
placed at the "back" (east) wall of the sanctuary. While not suggesting that Dante was using this motif in exactly the same sense, I do
believe that he was consciously drawing upon its physical features
to suggest that Henry VII possessed certain Christ-like qualities that
would have made him an excellent Christo-mimetic emperor. The
epistles Dante wrote on the occasion of Henry's descent into Italy
are replete with allusions to Christ, such that Henry becomes a mes-
sianic figure, the savior who would heal the wounds of Italy, one for
whom the heavenly throne is prepared.[21] The combination of biblical
citation and iconographic allusions contributes to and enhances the
drama and meaning of this passage in *Paradiso* 30.

Investigations of Dante's art of citation in its many verbal and
visual variations certainly have the potential to make us ever more
keenly aware of the poet's artistry in the *Divine Comedy* and to allow
us to understand and appreciate it more fully. Indeed, the *Comedy*
is truly the sacred poem fashioned jointly by heaven and earth, the
"poema sacro / al quale ha posto mano e cielo e terra" (*Par.* 25.1–2).

NOTES

1. Edward Moore, *Scripture and Classical Authors in Dante*, Studies in Dante,
first series (Oxford: Clarendon Press, 1896; reprint, 1969), 1.

2. Moore, *Scripture and Classical Authors*, 4.

3. Earlier studies have provided scholars with a catalogue (albeit incomplete) of those passages in the *Comedy* which betray definite origin
in or parallels with the Bible: e.g., Celestino Cavedoni, *Raffronti tra gli
autori biblici e sacri e la Divina commedia* (Città di Castello: Lapi, 1896);
and Felicina Groppi, *Dante traduttore*, 2d ed. (Roma: Herder, 1962). Other
studies have examined the presence of biblical language in Dante: e.g., Giulio
Marzot, *Il linguaggio biblico nella "Divina commedia"* (Pisa: Nistri-Lischi, 1956).
Other critics have treated the general question of Dante and the Bible in

excellent and insightful studies directed toward the elucidation of other no less pertinent matters, as, for example, the following:

Allegory: Charles S. Singleton, *Dante Studies*, vol. 1: *Commedia: Elements of Structure* (Cambridge, Mass.: Harvard University Press, 1954); and *Dante Studies*, vol. 2: *Journey to Beatrice* (Cambridge, Mass.: Harvard University Press, 1958). Robert Hollander, *Allegory in Dante's "Commedia"* (Princeton, N.J.: Princeton University Press, 1969). Giuseppe Mazzotta, *Dante, Poet of the Desert: History and Allegory in the "Divine Comedy"* (Princeton, N.J.: Princeton University Press, 1979). Pompeo Giannantonio, *Dante e l'allegorismo* (Firenze: Olschki, 1969). Jean Pépin, *Dante et la tradition de l'allégorie* (Montréal: Institut d'études médiévales, 1970). And Gian Robert Sarolli, *Prolegomena alla "Divina commedia"* (Firenze: Olschki, 1971).

Figural realism: Erich Auerbach, "'Figura,'" in *Scenes from the Drama of European Literature: Six Essays* (New York: Meridian Books, 1959), 11–76.

Typology: A. C. Charity, *Events and Their Afterlife: The Dialectics of Christian Typology in the Bible and Dante* (Cambridge: Cambridge University Press, 1966). And Johan Chydenius, *The Typological Problem in Dante* (Helsingfors: Societas Scientiarum Fennica, 1958).

Prophecy: Nicolò Mineo, *Profetismo e apocalittica in Dante* (Catania: Università di Catania, 1968).

Theological poetics: John Freccero, *Dante: The Poetics of Conversion*, ed. Rachel Jacoff (Cambridge, Mass.: Harvard University Press, 1986).

Church liturgy: Antonio C. Mastrobuono, *Dante's Journey of Sanctification* (Washington, D.C.: Regnery Gateway, 1990); and *Essays on Dante's Philosophy of History* (Firenze: Olschki, 1979).

Iconography: Giovanni Fallani, *Dante e la cultura figurativa medievale* (Bergamo: Minerva Italica, 1971). And Anthony K. Cassell, *Dante's Fearful Art of Justice* (Toronto: University of Toronto Press, 1984).

Other works have treated the general question of the influence of the Bible on Dante: e.g., *Dante e la bibbia*, Atti del Convegno Internazionale promosso da "Bibbia" (Firenze 26–27–28 settembre 1986), ed. Giovanni Barblan (Firenze: Olschki, 1988; Peter S. Hawkins, "Dante and the Bible," in *The Cambridge Companion to Dante*, ed. Rachel Jacoff (Cambridge: Cambridge University Press, 1993), 120–135; and David Higgins, *Dante and the Bible: An Introduction* (Bristol: University of Bristol Press, 1992). Numerous scholars have dealt with biblical influences on, and/or presences in, specific episodes in the *Comedy*: e.g., Margherita Frankel, "Biblical Figuration in Dante's Reading of the *Aeneid*," *Dante Studies* 100 (1982): 13–23; Peter S. Hawkins, "Transfiguring the Text: Ovid, Scripture, and the Dynamics of Allusion," *Stanford Italian Review* 5 (1985): 115–139, and "Scripts for the Pageant: Dante and the Bible," *Stanford Literature Review* 5 (1988): 75–92; Amilcare A. Iannucci, *Forma ed evento nella "Divina commedia"* (Roma: Bulzoni, 1984);

Robert E. Kaske, "Dante's 'DXV' and 'Veltro,'" *Traditio* 17 (1961): 185–254; and William A. Stephany, "Biblical Allusions to Conversion in *Purgatorio* XXI," *Stanford Italian Review* 3 (1983): 141–162.

4. Among my recent work on this topic are the following studies: "Biblical Citation in Dante's *Divine Comedy*," *Annali d'Italianistica* 8 (1990): 346–359; "Dante and the Bible: Intertextual Approaches to the *Divine Comedy*," *Italica* 63 (1986): 225–236; and "The Poetics of Citation: Dante's *Divina Commedia* and the Bible," in *Italiana 1988: Selected Papers from the Proceedings of the Fifth Annual Conference of the American Association of Teachers of Italian, November 18–20, 1988, Monterey, CA*, ed. Albert N. Mancini, Paolo A. Giordano, and Anthony J. Tamburri (River Forest, Ill.: Rosary College, 1990), 1–21.

5. All passages from the *Divine Comedy* are taken from Dante Alighieri, *La commedia secondo l'antica vulgata*, 4 vols., ed. Giorgio Petrocchi, Società dantesca italiana, Edizione nazionale (Milano: Mondadori, 1966–1967).

6. For studies on this particular moment, see, among others, John Freccero, "Casella's Song: *Purgatorio* II, 112," in *Poetics of Conversion*, 186–194 (originally published in *Dante Studies* 91 [1973]: 73–80); and R. A. Shoaf, "Dante's *colombi* and the Figuralism of Hope in the *Divine Comedy*," *Dante Studies* 93 (1975): 27–59.

7. The text of the *Convivio* follows the edition of Cesare Vasoli, vol. 1, part 2 of Dante Alighieri, *Opere minori* (Milano and Napoli: Ricciardi, 1988).

8. The text of the *Vita nuova* follows the edition of Domenico De Robertis, vol. 1, part 1 of *Opere minori* (Milano and Napoli: Ricciardi, 1980).

9. The word *volume* also refers to the Heavens (*Par.* 33.86) which is, of course, God's other Book. For the use of *scrittura* and *volume*, see Hollander, *Allegory*, 32–33, 78–79, 239.

10. All passages from the Bible follow the Vulgate: *Biblia vulgata iuxta Vulgatam Clementinam*, 6th ed., ed. Alberto Colunga and Laurentio Turrado (Madrid: Biblioteca de Autores Cristianos, 1982).

11. See, for example, *Par.* 19.40–90 and 20.130–138.

12. On this point, see Charles S. Singleton's commentary: Dante Alighieri, *The Divine Comedy: Purgatorio*, vol. 2: *Commentary* (Princeton, N.J.: Princeton University Press, 1973), 31.

13. The text of the *Epistole* follows that of Arsenio Frugoni and Giorgio Brugnoli, vol. 2 of *Opere minori* (Milano and Napoli: Ricciardi, 1979).

14. Kleinhenz, "Poetics of Citation."

15. See, among others, the excellent study by Cassell, *Dante's Fearful Art*, as well as my essay that provides an overview of the question, "Dante and the Tradition of Visual Arts in the Middle Ages," *Thought*, 65, no. 256 (1990): 17–26.

16. For a full treatment of this episode, see, among others, Charles S. Singleton, "*Inferno* XIX: O Simon Mago!" *Modern Language Notes* 80 (1965):

92–99; and Ronald B. Herzman and William A. Stephany, *"O miseri seguaci"*: Sacramental Inversion in *Inferno* XIX," *Dante Studies* 96 (1978): 39–65.

17. For a fuller treatment of this point, see the two studies by Anthony K. Cassell, *Dante's Fearful Art*, 15–31; and "Dante's Farinata and the Image of the *Arca*," *Yale Italian Studies* 1 (1977): 335–370.

18. See Cassell, *Dante's Fearful Art*, 96–104.

19. See my essay, "Iconographic Parody in *Inferno* 21," *Res Publica Litterarum* 5, no. 2 (1982): 125–137.

20. For a general discussion of this theme, see H. Leclercq, "Étimasie," in *Dictionnaire d'archéologie chrétienne et du liturgie*, ed. Fernand Cabrol and Henri Leclercq (Paris, 1922), 5.1:671–673. For its presence in Italian art, see James Hall, *A History of Ideas and Images in Italian Art* (New York: Harper and Row, 1983), 94–95.

21. In his fifth letter ("Universis et singulis Ytalie Regibus et Senatoribus alme Urbis . . ."), Dante alludes to Henry as the "sun that will rise in peace" ("Titan exorietur pacificus" [5.3]) and continues: "Letare iam nunc miseranda Ytalie etiam Saracenis, que statim invidiosa per orbem videberis, quia sponsus tuus, mundi solatium et gloria plebis tue, clementissimus Henricus, divus et Augustus et Cesar, ad nuptias properat. Exsicca lacrimas et memoris vestigia dele, pulcerrima, nam prope est qui liberabit te de carcere impiorum; qui percutiens malignantes in ore gladii perdet eos, et vineam suam aliis locabit agricolis qui fructum iustitie reddant in tempore messis" (5.5–6).

In his seventh epistle addressed to Henry ("Sanctissimo gloriosissimo atque felicissimo triumphatori et domino singulari domino Henrico . . ."), Dante compares the emperor's arrival in Italy as like the rising of the much-desired sun ("Titan, preoptatus exoriens") for which "nova spes Latio seculi melioris effulsit" (7.5) and speaks of the Italians as those who sang with Virgil about the reign of Saturn and the return of the Virgin ("Tunc plerique vota sua prevenientes in iubilo tam Saturnia regna quam Virginem redeuntem cum Marone cantabant" [7.6]), an obvious reference to the Fourth Eclogue and its presumed prophecy of the coming of Christ. A few lines later in this letter, Dante states his firm belief in and support for Henry: "in te credimus et speramus, asseverantes te Dei ministrum et Ecclesie filium et Romane glorie promotorem. Nam et ego qui scribo tam pro me quam pro aliis, velut decet imperatoriam maiestatem benignissimum vidi et clementissimum te audivi, cum pedes tuos manus mee tractarunt et labia mea debitum persolverunt. Tunc exultavit in te spiritus meus, cum tacitus dixi mecum: 'Ecce Agnus Dei, ecce qui tollit peccata mundi'" (7.8–10). Henry VII becomes in Dante's rich imagination a Christ figure.

Why Did Dante Write the *Comedy*?
Why and How Do We Read It?

THE POET AND THE CRITICS

I find the two questions that traditionally hover over the critical discussions of the *Divine Comedy* both exciting and perplexing. On the face of it, the first question, Why did Dante write the *Comedy*? entails and seems coextensive with the second one, Why and how do we read it? Yet the two questions are not at all quite identical with each other, and it is important that, at least provisionally, they be kept separate. True, we must, in the not-so-hazy and remote regions of our consciousness, remain aware that the *Divine Comedy* was written for us to read. And however unfathomable or secondary to the free play of language the *intentio auctoris* may be, there is the so-called intentionality of the text, the idea that a poem was conceived for us to read, was meant for reading, and that its existence is fulfilled by and through the act of reading. Yet, logically and chronologically, our reading of it reminds us that, as readers, though we may well be part of the poet's invention, we come after the poem and we owe our existence to it at least as much as it owes its existence to us.

The question, Why did Dante write the *Comedy*? is, thus, fundamental. It is fundamental, first of all, because it puts the focus not on us, not on the readers' interpretive experience, and it does not really ask why we read. On the contrary, the question probes the claim of hermeneutics' centrality, of the reader's priority or centrality vis-à-vis the poem. It asks of us, more precisely, to take the point of view of the poet's consciousness, and this request is tantamount to transcending the confines of our own narrow vision and alienating ourselves into the subjectivity of another, to entering an imaginary, disorienting space—the space of shades, mirrors, metaphoric language, and vain images, which all together make up the vast heterology—or *heteroglossia*—of the *Divine Comedy*. And one thing becomes immediately clear: in the space of the imaginary poetic world, which is literally the otherworld (and an alternate world to this world) and which is not of our own making, we are not ever (or just not yet) ourselves. The question, if anything, compels us to a quest, which may be a quest for discovering who we are by following winding, tortuous paths through the foreign lands of our inexorable exile. It demands of us that we strip ourselves of whatever scholar's conceits we harbor and come to terms with a consciousness that transcends our own. Only thus, only by entering the shadowy, enigmatic other and alternate world of infinite resonances, dark riddles, and polysemous allegories that we do not entirely know or grasp shall we resist the hermeneutical temptation of reducing the text to an approximation of ourselves.

It has often been said (by Santayana, I believe) that the only value of possessing great works of literature, such as the *Divine Comedy*, lies in what they can help us become, and this is undeniably true. Santayana's statement is also particularly suggestive in that it acknowledges the reader's state as a state of temporal flux, a becoming and a coming to a further form, the sort of spiritual movement of self similar to that which the opening paragraphs of the *Convivio* identify as the perfection which is our end:

> Sì come dice lo Filosofo nel principio de la Prima Filosofia, tutti li uomini naturalmente desiderano di sapere. La ragione di che puote essere ed é che ciascuna cosa, da providenza di prima natura impinta, è inclinabile a la sua propria perfezione; onde, acciò che la scienza è ultima perfezione de la nostra anima, ne la quale sta la nostra ultima felicitade, tutti naturalmente al suo desiderio semo subietti. Veramente da questa nobilissima perfezione molti sono privati per diverse cagioni, che dentro a l'uomo e di fuori da esso lui rimovono da l'abito di scienza. (*Convivio* 1.1–3)

The text goes on to allude to a tension between university and encyclopedia, which for Dante are two parallel forms of the organization of knowledge (*Convivio* 1.4). More centrally, there is a desire to know, Dante says, quoting Aristotle's *Metaphysics*, and this erotics of the mind inclines us to questing our perfection through "scienza" or knowledge.[1] *Convivio* maps the way to what purports to be an encyclopedic knowledge that would replace or substitute what the *studio*—the university education—cannot provide.

Essential to that process of knowledge as of ethics is hermeneutics, a mode which connects and involves both reading and writing, allegories and interpretations of philosophical poetry. The hermeneutics of *Convivio* is primarily a self-hermeneutics, a way of locating oneself—Dante's own displaced self—in the landscape of the desperate, political illusion that knowledge is power. Writing the *Convivio* is for Dante chiefly a self-reading. It is also a way for him to stake claims about the politics of his knowledge, that he can give counsel to the emperor. The inconclusiveness of the text depends on the discovery that the philosophical destination the would-be philosopher was seeking—the inevitably successful homecoming that Neoplatonic allegoresis promises and extracts from the *Odyssey* or the *Aeneid*—is really out of reach for the particular, irreducible history of the exiled Dante. Preestablished routes marked on the philosophical maps of knowledge, the would-be philosopher discovers, waylay this exile, who is nothing if not acquainted with grief, and they clash with the grim realities of his life.

Dante's intellectual discovery about the generalized, selfsame meanings made available by philosophical allegories forces us to add to Santayana's remark that poetic texts themselves have no a priori self-identical fixity of meaning but are part and parcel of the temporal mobility we claim for ourselves or Dante claims for himself in the *Divine Comedy*. Dante's *Inferno* evokes at the start an allegorical landscape—a metaphoric land of longing—where nothing is, as John Freccero eloquently puts it, what it seems.[2] What Freccero describes as the pilgrim's moral quandary, by virtue of the radical ambiguity that wraps it, is primarily poetry. This quintessentially poetic space comes through as a world where the traditional allegorical voice of nature (the *natura* of Bernard Sylvester, Alan of Lille, and Brunetto Latini) is stilled; where the Platonic correspondence between light and truth is fractured; where the philosophical readings of Virgil are bracketed. The crisis of hermeneutical signification is paramount for this radically displaced pilgrim. Dante's poetry arises out of this vast ambiguity of signs, and the pilgrim will turn to the shade of Virgil, to Virgil's mastery and to the poetry of the *Aeneid*, in the belief that poetry is the shadowy language of his contingent historicity forever irreducible to the conventional canons of preestablished philosophical discourses.[3]

Readers such as Santayana, who stands for most readers of Dante, turn to the *Divine Comedy* as Dante turned to the *Aeneid*, though not quite. If, in fact, we go to the *Divine Comedy* (and for that matter to the *Odyssey* or the *Aeneid*) in a spirit of edification, in the spirit of trying to determine how a great work can work for us or what it can do for us, we miss the point. We turn what is an unfamiliar, alien terrain into a domesticated commonplace of our own selves. It is not just that the self-reflection we recognize and embrace is arbitrary or premature. What is unsettling, rather, is that in seeking to utilize the text or in finding its relevance for our interpretive needs, we impose our own meaning on it; we circumscribe its significance within the boundaries of our own temporality, and, in the process, we may not be listening to its alien voices or to the resonant signs it ceaselessly emits. When readers read because they consider the poem a means to their own personal ends they are confirming, once again, their own superiority and lordship over the text, for indeed they make it the reified object of their illusions of mastery.

In some measure, this reclamation for oneself of what is a radically foreign figuration of the world and of ourselves in it is unavoidable: the hermeneutical fusion of horizons, the collapse of the distance between text and interpreter, the recognition of the play of identities and differences between text and reader are simultaneously the conditions and the objectives of reading. As one reads one unavoidably makes knowledge an act of recognition, the open-ended interpretive adventure, the performances of memory, discoveries, the simulations and trickeries of the imagination. Yet, if we simply view the *Divine Comedy* or the *Odyssey* as a means to our preestablished ends, we will not become anything that we were not always already: we will be stuck in place, like Belacqua or Penelope or Sisyphus or Brunetto Latini, who all variously experience what it means to be frozen in time and who all variously submit to the heroic or comical illusion of one's power over time by seeking to annihilate it or to mime its repetitive turns.

The question, Why did Dante write the *Comedy*? reminds us, cogently enough, that we ought to go to great works, such as the *Comedy*, the way Dante went to Virgil and the way Vico went to Dante or to Homer, to discover the truth of Virgil, of Dante, of Homer, not a truth which is a whim or a *doxa*, but the truth about what the text is. In the first book I wrote, *Dante, Poet of the Desert: History and Allegory in the "Divine Comedy,"* I clarified, at least for myself, the ambiguities of poetic language and the ambiguities of reading as mutually implicated configurations of the exilic imagination. A text, be it what Francesca reads in *Inferno* 5, or Statius reads in *Purgatorio* 22, or the *Comedy* itself, is a decisive locus of encounters and self-encounters. Only by submitting to the challenge of the text's otherness in relation to ourselves (and of our otherness in relation to ourselves) shall we emerge with the elusive / illusive perfection which is our end.

How can this truth about the *Divine Comedy* be discovered? One discovers the truth of Dante or Homer, as Vico argues, by following, first of all, a philological path. Philology has traditionally been the privileged path to a text's knowledge as knowledge of its alterity in relation to our self-interests or conceits. More cogently, philology is the *love of the word*, the love of the contingent, unique corporeality of every word; it is the recognition of history and time as the horizon of language. It may well be a sign of the times that in this our time faith in philology has weakened and that there are very few authentic philologists working on Dante today. One reason for the partial eclipse of this discipline (which is still known as Romance Philology and which of late has counted Dante scholars, such as Ulrich Leo, Leo Spitzer, and Eric Auerbach in its ranks) is that the great age of positivism with its unearthing of documentary sources is long gone, and scholars today have begun to reflect on the tendentious manipulations and ideological biases of those nineteenth-century masters, who were intent on concocting and peddling specific paradigms of textual origins for the vindication of one sort or another of political primacy.

We have rightly grown suspicious of the mechanical laws of cause and effect governing and lurking under the philologists' systematic obliteration of the power and originality of a text. The conventions regulating the positivists' laboratory are clear: under the guise of accounting scientifically for the text's existence in terms of its genealogical sources or of its constituent parts, they contest the claims of the uniqueness of the poet's imagination. The reconstruction of the reliable dynastic history of the manuscript tradition and its variants has spilled over into the determination of the less apparent intellectual or poetic influences in the constitution of a text. Yet, when it is applied to the identification of the intellectual strands of a text, this mode of philological analysis engenders some general fallacies. The first general fallacy of the dynastic-genealogical analysis of traditions and influences on the poem lies in the assumption that texts are natural entities—such is indeed the implication of the metaphor of origination—and their components can be scientifically gauged; second, a genealogical mode of textual analysis casts a text as the teleological endpoint of a purely linear temporal succession (without any apparent realization that the temporality of an imaginative construct is neither purely diachronic nor linear). The teleological trajectory of genealogy ends in the myth of what can be called *presentism* (in that there is an overt valorization of the present and of the self). Finally, the analysis of a text's components (as if a text were sugar or vitriol) reifies the text as an object whose existence lies so outside of one's own subjective concerns that one can treat it with a radical clinical distance.

The massive efforts of a scholar such as, say, Giuseppe Busnelli to reduce the *Divine Comedy* to the parameters of the theology of St. Thomas Aquinas have long appeared wrongheaded both on a question of principle and on a question of fact. In principle, Busnelli's research has ratified the subordination of poetry to the rigor, the standards, and the hegemony of a rational theology, which is what Aquinas held whereas Dante redefines theology's scope and structure. (I have documented this claim about theology's imaginative or fabulous essence extensively in my *Dante's Vision and the Circle of Knowledge* and I will not repeat here my arguments.)

In question of fact, on the other hand, Busnelli's claim that Thomism is the privileged and circumscribed context for Dante's poetry has been shown to be inadequate and even too naive. Largely in reaction to Busnelli, Bruno Nardi (and Gilson concurs with him in this) has rightly drawn attention to the limits of Dante's Thomism and has brought to light Dante's (and Cavalcanti's) awareness of the medieval philosophical dissidence which goes under the name of *radical Aristotelianism*. In recent years, Maria Corti has reopened the controversy of Dante's Averroism.[4] Corti has reproposed, without much success if one is to judge by the countless attacks to which her hypothesis has been subjected, Nardi's central idea that Dante subscribes to and endorses the language and thought of an abstract grammarian such as

Boethius of Dacia. The objection carries particular weight especially because, much as the cultists of St. Thomas Aquinas's influence on the *Comedy*, Corti's suggestion draws Dante's poetry under the sovereignty of one overarching philosophical doctrine.

For all the ceaseless reconfigurations of the poem's mobile contexts and registers, which philology in part pursues, and for all the blind belief that it establishes firm factual truths (which a subsequent scholar, ironically, ends up contradicting) and not merely unreliable, ephemeral aesthetic impressions, philology delivers, as hinted earlier, a crucial insight into the nature of any poetic text. The philologists' practice is shaped by the fundamental principle of the historical instability of language. Accordingly, a temporal wedge is posited in the semantics of every word: the temporal difference between past and present—so philologists think—cannot be abolished either by the assumption of unalterable semantic identities or by a mere act of interpretive power, which can be known by a seemingly innocuous phrase such as exegetical appropriation of the past. Confronted with the sense of the rupture between past and present, the philologists proceed as if the past were an unrecognizable other. But this past can be recuperated by the construction of an adequate historical context.

Unavoidably, other questions must now be raised. What is exactly "an adequate historical context"? Why should we not simply read the text? When is a context adequate to explain the infinite resonances of a poem such as the *Divine Comedy*? One first answer is that the text in itself, as if it were a formal self-enclosed universe or a self-sufficient monad, is a pure illusion. The *Divine Comedy* evokes many imaginative worlds and belongs to them, and these worlds together are the poem's vibrant core. A second answer is that the notion itself of adequate context is naive. It is naive because it depends on the philologists' belief that contexts, unlike texts, can be clearly defined and circumscribed and that they can, in turn, shed light on the obscurities of the poem. In fact, a context is by necessity as enigmatic and infinite as the text itself. Every word in a text potentially evokes a whole world of discourse, and the idea of philological *precision* is tantamount, literally, to a cutting and a closure of discourse.

To avoid such a misconception that texts can become wholly intelligible in terms of supposedly transparent contexts, philology may have to become what I would like to call a *philology of the imagination*, a phrase that implies that Philology, as in Martianus's myth, be yoked and submitted to the dark sovereignty of Hermes. Charles Singleton posited the story of Exodus as the sufficient paradigm that gives unity and intelligibility to the complex experiences dramatized by Dante's narrative. What is radically missing in Singleton's critical conception, however, is both the sense of plurality of hybrid traditions that would temper the conviction of the hegemony of Thomism and a view of poetry that would rescue the *Divine Comedy* from being a mere appendix of the Bible. On the other hand, the recent collaborative work of Robert Durling and Ronald Martinez on the *Rime Petrose* legitimately belongs, I believe, to a mode which I would call *archeological.*

I take the term *archeology* from Michel Foucault's *Archéologie du savoir.* Properly speaking, for Foucault the term is not at all coextensive with the age-old tradition of the history of ideas. A historian of ideas, such as A. O. Lovejoy, as the philologist Leo Spitzer lucidly pointed out years ago, largely aims at abolishing differences or specificities in the plurality of historical discourses and at delineating the perfect, homogeneous continuities of traditions and ideas. On the contrary, Foucault's archeology designates a level of meaning that eludes the consciousness of the writer; it recognizes the presence of symmetrical multiple discourses; it focuses on the ruptures, gaps, and transformations in the field of knowledge; and it reveals the breaks and complicities between, say, philology, biology, and economics.

With extraordinary intellectual consistency Durling and Martinez, on the other hand, cast astrology, numerology, lapidaries, Neoplatonism, patristics, and mythography as parts of Dante's poetic "composition" (as they refer to Dante's rhetorical/musical strategies but without an apparent theoretical/critical awareness of the implications of the procedure). Because Foucault's archeology—just as Dante's poetry (and all poetry)—reduces history to an archive of simultaneous phantasmic events, his thought has been criticized for not making allowances for temporal differences in his analysis of the diversities of discourses and of the rules that regulate them. We are never told by Foucault how fragments and scraps make up totalities; how exactly different discourses, say, grammar and economics converse with one another. But what Foucault leaves out is exactly what a poet such as Dante explicitly confronts.

Within the varied field of Dante studies there are philologists-critics (Curtius, Auerbach, Spitzer, Contini, Foster, Kaske, Sarolli, Simonelli, Corti, Pasquini, Barański) who have acknowledged what

Dante makes explicit. Unlike Foucault, whose thought lacks an aesthetics and tends to elide differences by drawing together literature
and extraliterary documents as if they were part of the same universe
of discourse, these scholars bring to the light the rhetoricity of the
poetic text. Within this perspective, *composition*—which means the
arrangement of the parts into a whole and which is to be taken as an
imaginative-aesthetic-rhetorical strategy—is the specific modality of
poetry. Such a notion of composition and encyclopedic poetry counters the critical tendencies of the neo-historicists who, in the wake of
Foucault's speculations on history and the interconnected structures
of thought, establish homologies between literature and history.

In recent years, neo-historicism has been shaping the critical reflections of some medievalists. The intellectual lucidity of their enterprise
is admirable, but there are, I think, some pitfalls in the neo-historicist
procedures. The fundamental and brilliant impulse behind the work of
the neo-historicists, at their best, is to strip literature of any romantic
aura of privilege by unveiling its complicities with history's structures
of power and politics. The homologies between, say, the poet and the
king that they establish, however, effectively reduce literature's steady
ambiguities to the univocity of literal statements and in the process
they cancel literature's anti-historical thrust, its radical untimeliness
which is simultaneous with its time-bound referentialities, its playful
evasiveness of and concomitant utopian resistance to the political
manipulations of knowledge for ends of power.

I have suggested earlier that Dante's *Convivio* tells the parable of
the failure to equate or even coordinate knowledge and power as if the
equation, which is in practice possible, could be morally desirable. The
Vita nuova, on the other hand, had already explored the singularity
of a poetic vocation and had pointed to Dante's sense of the neces-
sities of poetry. Let me briefly recapitulate Dante's argument for his
claims of poetry's singularity. The question, Why did Dante write the
Comedy? logically presupposes—to be sure—another question: Why
did Dante write poetry and not, say, a theological *summa*? What kind
of knowledge does poetry deliver that other discourses cannot deliver?
What is his sense of the necessity to be a poet? These questions are
the core of the autobiographical *Vita nuova*, which tells the story of
the love for Beatrice and of the lover's poetic apprenticeship as if
the two themes were two sides of the same reality. The quest for the
words of love is fleshed out as the love of the word.

The main intent of this text is to tell of Dante's youthful love for Beatrice and of how this love sets the lover on the path of a self-discovery. This love, Dante quickly finds out, cannot be explained through the objective, empirical reasons physicians would provide, for love is not purely a problem of humoral pathology. This love cannot even be explained as if it were a love for the good, the worthy passions for abstract ideas that philosophers from Plato to Boethius pursue. Either account of love as physics or as philosophy is inadequate. More than that, either account is false, for it gives general prefabricated answers; it says nothing about the enigma of Beatrice and the terror of the lover's encounter with her and reduces the uniqueness of her apparition to the measure of ordinary speech. Dante writes the poetry of the *Vita nuova* because he grasps that the language of poetry is alone equipped to convey the sense of her enigma and to fathom the surrender of his mind to the infinite prodigy of her apparition.

The other strand of the text dramatizes the poet-lover as still learning what poetry is, and it shows him as he asks the wrong questions about poetry as about much else. As a reader of his own poems, the lover believes that poetry is a question of craft, of technical constructions and divisions of stanzas from one another. The manuals of rhetoric, the art of persuasion and of writing well, had taught him that this is the material stuff of rhetorical composition. Yet, I take Dante's insistence on the formal structures of poetry to be nothing less than an indictment of what has come to be known as merely *formalist* criticism. I take this formalism to be for Dante the equivalent of the divisive, partial visions both of the physicians (who, in their diagnoses of love divide body from soul) and of the philosophers of sundry schools (who wallow in empty abstractions and forget love's body).

Dante writes the *Vita nuova* as an archive of memories and visionary expectations of the future, and the youthful text can be thus called a literal philology of the imagination. The poet's self is located in the landscape of this imagination: the imagination of love and the imagination of poetry are here intertwined. Now the poet-lover of the *Vita nuova* finds out that his poetic discourse is inadequate because he came to understand the law of his love for Beatrice as exclusive of all objective reality (politics, the social realities of the city, ethics, etc.). By the same token, up to now he had understood poetry as the secret code of a secret passion: caught in the ghostly world of his own mind, besieged by memories and fears, overwhelmed by the death of Beatrice, Dante had turned poetry into a solitary language of the hieroglyphs of love's compulsions.

But in the *De vulgari eloquentia* this view of poetry radically changes. The treatise theorizes a national idiom made of scraps drawn from the various dialects both dividing and making up the Italian language. It argues, more precisely, that a harmonious unity can be achieved only by joining together the various and discordant discourses of the tribe. Accordingly, Dante sees poetry here as part and parcel of the large reality of language (legal, political, moral, etc.) he seeks to forge, and its essence is invested with a new status. In an essay on Dante's theories of language, one of the founders of the Dante Society (which, by the way, is the oldest scholarly association in the United States) and a disciple of Emerson, Longfellow, had grasped one central principle of Dante's linguistic theories. Longfellow showed that the unified diversity of the language Dante envisions in the *De vulgari eloquentia* existed already everywhere in part, but nowhere else as a whole save in the pages of the *Divine Comedy*. Obliquely, Longfellow sees Dante as the poet-encyclopedist who in the *Divine Comedy* gives a representation of the many voices, cadences, styles, and, in one word, dialects of Italy.[5]

The history of Dante criticism across the centuries—from Benvenuto da Imola to Benedetto Varchi, from Vico to Gravina and to the present—has shown a steady awareness that the *Divine Comedy* ought to be read as the encyclopedic, all-inclusive, poetic reservoir of shared memories and languages, or to put it in Vichian terms, as the mental dictionary of the tradition (which I take to be Vico's way of talking about the philology of the imagination). It can be said that the most sustained and mutually exclusive interpretations of the *Divine Comedy* given in our times make the encyclopedic mode the distinctive rhetorical feature of the poem as well as the fruitful method of fathoming the multiple stratified intersections of discourses.

The sundry volumes of the *Enciclopedia dantesca* with its neat circumscription of entries, the volume edited by Aldo Scaglione and Giuseppe Di Scipio (*The "Divine Comedy" and the Encyclopedia of Arts and Sciences*), and Patrick Boyde's *Dante Philomythes and Philosopher: Man in the Cosmos* are works that explicitly recall the necessity of coming to terms with the vast compass of knowledge as a totality of correlations. I would inscribe within this tradition the work of archeologists-philologists such as Zygmunt Barański, Lino Pertile,

Durling, and Martinez, or such as Sarolli, whose *Prolegomena alla "Divina commedia"* seeks to retrieve even the most rarefied of symbolic resonances. Even John Freccero's *Dante: The Poetics of Conversion*, with its steady focus on the pilgrim's education of the soul, arguably places the encyclopedic project within the interiority of the self. But do these various perspectives really cohere with one another? What do they really reveal about the *Divine Comedy* that readers did not already know?

To answer these questions I must take a detour through the assumptions governing the possibility of an archeological or documentary-objective sort of analysis. I must go back to the premises of Foucault's archeology and point out another limit of the Foucaultian project. Sensing the inadequacy of providing only "archeological" descriptions of sundry textual representations as if they were objective documents, and prodded by the critique leveled by Derrida against his descriptive and objective procedures, Foucault retrieved the category of *genealogy* in his "Nietzsche, Genealogy, History."[6] Genealogy now comes to mean for him the "history of the present," in the sense that by its means he can explore the complicity between the historian/reader and the archeological discourses he examines or, to say it differently, the links between power and knowledge. From this Nietzchean perspective, which posits the arbitrariness of the reader's claims of "sovereignty over the events of the past" (Foucault, 153). Foucault's "genealogy" runs the risk, as hinted earlier, of turning into a cult of presentism wherein the historians's subjectivity is inevitably inscribed in the reading of the past. Plainly enough, genealogy is a version of hermeneutics, and the links between genealogy and hermeneutics were posited by Boccaccio.

As is apparent from his *Genealogy of the Gentile Gods*, Boccaccio, whom both Foucault and Nietzsche ignore, casts genealogy as the category for the temporal process of history, which is embodied by the ceaseless transformation of myths. History is a history of myth, a decentered succession of mythical memories. There is, thus, no possible recuperation of, or access to—so does Boccaccio start his encyclopedic account of poetic myths—history's origins either in their archaic literalism or from the standpoint of the present. Because there is no room for illusions of philological objectivity, genealogy turns into a hermeneutics, and, consistently, Boccaccio ends his *Genealogy of the Gentile Gods* with a theory of allegory and a defense of the allegorical substance of literary structures whereby the otherness of all imaginative experiences is ratified.

The distance between Boccaccio and Foucault is of some moment in this argument. Whereas Foucault never sees the links joining archeology to a hermeneutics, Boccaccio makes hermeneutics and allegory the inner core of poetic language. The links between theology and poetry (or to say it in a number of ways, between philology and hermeneutics, semiotics and hermeneutics, archeology and genealogy) are forcefully stated in Boccaccio's *Vita di Dante*: "I say that theology is no other thing than a poetry of God." The distance between the two terms is a version of the distance that exists between Dante and his critics. Whereas for Dante (and Boccaccio and Vico) the pluralities of fragmentary discourses are held together by the poetic imagination, Foucault, the hermeneuts, the archeologists, the neo-historicists, and the philologists posit the principle of Aristotelian, scientific rationality as the medium of knowledge. Foucault's assumption about the intelligibility and ultimate transparency of the world finds its counterpart in the critics' belief in the rational order of the poem. Whereas Foucault's mode of analysis ends up in the circumscription of discrete strands of knowledge (labor, wealth, grammar, etc.), almost all the critical works on Dante's encyclopedic vision end up providing and restating partitioned arguments, fragmentary entries, paragraphs of discourse (on, say, angels, light, love, motion, etc.)

Such an analytical procedure is certainly useful, and it may be correlated to a critical mode of analysis in Dante scholarship that apparently is the most remote from it. I mean the tradition of the *lectura dantis*. This exegetical convention can be described as an interpretive and somewhat personal reading of individual cantos of the *Divine Comedy*, and it depends on a long-standing critical (and fictional) assumption that each canto constitutes a self-enclosed, autonomous narrative unit. The practice of the *lectura dantis*, which has turned into a veritable scholarly ritual, has acquired the status of a pedagogical tool of *haute vulgarisation* and has become the focus of sociocultural events. The popularity and undisputed usefulness of this rhetorical genre notwithstanding, there is little doubt that there is nothing more artificial than the mechanical division of the poem's dramatic unity and sequence into discrete, fragmentary units that, more often than not, end up obscuring and effacing the sense of the poem as a unified whole. One could hardly stress too much the extent to which the economy and structure of the poem demand that each unit be read within the architectural design of the whole poem: textual symmetries, verbal echoes, figurative and conceptual parallelisms, thematic and metaphoric patterns across extended segments of the narrative, chiastic reversals and juxtapositions, semantic-phonetic resonances, etc.—these are some of the elements that force us to be wary of the pitfalls lurking beneath the folds of an otherwise useful critical convention.

What the archeological method of investigation, which I have brought into the realm of Foucaultian discourse, and the impressionistic *lectura dantis* share is the indifference to the workings of the imagination. The poetic imagination, as Dante fully grasped, is both the foundation and the privileged pathway for any possible conversation across disparate worlds and disparate times. The possibility (and the conditions of possibility) for such a conversation is the central issue confronting contemporary theoretical speculation at the highest levels (Serres, Lyotard, Foucault, Deleuze), and a poet such as Dante or a poetic thinker such as Vico, who acts out the principle of the synthetic faculty of the imagination, could turn out to be necessary points of reference in the debates that lie ahead.

I have discussed two questions. One question concerns the field of Dante scholarship in its wide productive practices (erudite glosses, philology, archeology, readings of various cantos) and have shown their conceptual premises, which, somewhat arbitrarily, I call *Foucaultian*. The second question concerns the contours of Dante's poem and his insight into poetry. A chasm exists, as I have argued, between, on the one hand, Dante's sense of poetry as the infinitely open language of ambiguities and of the endless imaginative quest of infinity, and, on the other hand, the critics' and scholars' search for definable quantities, precise categories, transparent referentialities. The opposition is crude, and I have repeatedly indicated how often Dante scholars go beyond Foucaultian paradigms of commentaries.

My own work on Dante so far has sought to propose arguments whereby both Dante criticism and contemporary speculations on literary theory can obtain a degree of clarity and renewed purpose. *Dante, Poet of the Desert: History and Allegory in the "Divine Comedy"* argued for the radical ambiguity of poetic language and of history, and the figuration of this ambiguity was exile. The power and danger of poetic language, this is the burden of that book, invests the poet's own enterprise in the belief that the poet's fundamental iconoclasm cannot, logically enough for his prophetic imagination, stop complacently and idolatrously at the threshold of his own self. The more recent *Dante's Vision and the Circle of Knowledge* presents the poem as a tightly knit encyclopedic web of disciplines and arts wherein there are occult layers of discourse to be deciphered, sediments of sense to be probed, and mobile patterns of relations to be analysed. The poem is the imaginative locus or crossroads of multiple and heterogeneous historical parameters wherein divergent and parallel disciplines are mapped.

There is in these two books a departure, as I see it, from traditional ways of understanding Dante's poetry, his discourse on knowledge and on the specific knowledge poetry engenders. An erudite critical essay by, say, Patrick Boyde, can be legitimately criticized on two major counts. First, he never establishes a difference between Dante's poetic text and the scientific traditions that the text absorbs. The specificity of poetry, of the visionary knowledge poetry provides, is, thus, blurred or altogether elided. Second, Boyde, unfolds his series of discrete glosses as if no interpretation were needed. His unstated assumption is that Aristotle and the uniformly Aristotelian intellectual discourse provides the unifying, overarching necessary context and exegesis of the text. *Dante's Vision and the Circle of Knowledge*, on the other hand, deliberately seeks not to muzzle or exclude the multiple and contradictory voices making up the *Divine Comedy*. Dante's imagination, very simply, cannot be reduced within the parameters of a single influence (be it Aquinas, Augustine, Averroes, the classics etc.). Accordingly, *Dante's Vision* articulates the disjunctions within a complex multiplicity of convergent and divergent discourses; it brings to the foreground the role of the imagination; and it never treats any of the categories of knowledge (language, the subject, grammar, logic, ethics, theology, etc.) as stable or fixed modalities or themes. Even so, I am painfully aware of how incomplete such a study is: questions of Dante's metaphysics, alchemy, the mechanical arts—to mention only a few gaps—need to be rethought. Nonetheless, the exegetical principle of *inclusiveness* strikes (what I hope is also welcome) a note of dissonance in the midst of ideological criticisms prevalent in the academic discourses of our times.

The departure is, in fact, methodological. It is, more specifically, a reaction to some current critical trends. One of these trends is deconstruction, which acknowledges (and this is its extraordinary power) the overlapping of discourses and yet is trapped within its assumption of the impasse of the mind (a principle which violates the notion of the endless mobility of the mind). Another is Foucault's archeology, which does not take into account hermeneutics. A third is neo-historicism, which is based on the Foucaultian elision of the specificity of literature and turns into a theory of power.

These trends have been subjected to a steady critique from a variety of perspectives. I have been helped in these elaborations by the radical new way of thinking set forth by Vico's *New Science* which, among other things, is a watershed in the traditional understanding of Dante.[7] But I have also been helped by those Dante scholars I have mentioned above, and especially by my teachers, Charles Singleton, John Freccero, Gian Roberto Sarolli, James Hutton, and Robert E. Kaske. In their sundry ways of producing a conjunction of philology and hermeneutics one can rediscover the possibility of infinite ripples of new commentaries, which are memories turned to the future; one can rediscover a new way of thinking—beyond the banality of calcified opinion—whereby forms and doctrines are and are not the same thing, whereby God and God's use-lessness can be fathomed; one can rediscover what a poet such as Dante knew all along—which is the reason why be wrote the *Divine Comedy* and why we cannot but continue reading it.

NOTES

1. See Giuseppe Mazzotta, *Dante's Vision and the Circle of Knowledge* (Princeton, N.J.: Princeton University Press), for an extensive discussion of the question of knowledge in Dante and his medieval sources.

2. John Freccero, *Dante, the Poetics of Conversion*, ed. Rachel Jacoff (Cambridge, Mass.: Harvard University Press), 1.

3. Giuseppe Mazzotta, *Dante, Poet of the Desert: History and Allegory in the "Divine Comedy"* (Princeton, N.J.: Princeton University Press, 1979), 150–159.

4. Maria Corti, *Dante a un nuovo crocevia* (Milan: Libreria Commissionaria Sansoni, 1981). See also Maria Corti, *La felicità mentale: Nuove prospettive per Cavalcanti e Dante* (Turin: Einaudi, 1983).

5. I have described this central trait of this text in the Afterword to Dante's *Inferno: Translations by Twenty Contemporary Poets*, ed. Daniel Halpern (Hopewell, N.J,: Ecco Press, 1993), 159–168.

6. This essay is to be found in Michel Foucault, *Language, Counter-memory, Practice: Selected Essays and Interviews*, ed. Donald F. Bouchard (Ithaca, N.Y.: Cornell University Press, 1977), 139–164.

7. See Giuseppe Mazzotta, *Critical Essays on Dante* (Boston: G.K. Hall, 1991), xviii-xix and 58–60.

Part 2

"Minor Works"

Dino S. Cervigni and Edward Vasta

From Manuscript to Print

THE CASE OF DANTE'S *VITA NUOVA*

In his 1907 edition of Dante's *Vita nuova*, Michele Barbi, following the initiatives of his predecessors—Torri in 1843, Witte in 1876, and Casini in 1885—divided Dante's autobiographical *libello* into forty-two numbered chapters.[1] Barbi also numbered the sentences within chapters, both poetry and prose, by grouping them arbitrarily into *commi*, containing one to four sentences each (see below, Appendix 2). This division and numbering, as Barbi explained in 1932 ("Introduzione," cccix), were meant to establish a uniform reference system for future editions, concordances, and dictionaries, and for Dante scholarship and criticism in general (see below, Appendix 2). Barbi's 1932 edition, which repeats the divisions of the 1907 edition, became the international standard text of the *Vita nuova*, and his divisions and numbering have been preserved, utilized, and repeated ever since.[2]

Barbi could not have known that his divisions brought to culmination the progressive imposition and enforcement, upon a work produced in a manuscript culture, of the modes of reading and interpretation internalized by his own print culture. It was in 1928 that Milman Parry initiated studies on orality vs. literacy that distinguish modes and techniques of oral poetic composition from those developed through the art of writing,[3] and only in recent decades have such distinctions revealed the diverse technological effects of language enacted not only through speech and writing but also through print and electronics. Only now, some four score years after Barbi's first edition (1907), do we know that print-culture features such as format, divisions, spacing, numbering, punctuation, even the visual presentation on the printed page, affects how readers read, experience, and understand a text. Only since Barbi's time have linguistics, literary criticism, semiotics, anthropology, psychology, and social and cultural studies in general taught us that our print culture techniques have produced literary, psychological, social, and political effects not produced in a manuscript culture. Such effects have been further complicated and extended in our century by the addition of the electronic culture, so that today's consciousness is affected by speech, writing, print, radio, film, television, and computers, all operating simultaneously, each with its area of utility and dominance, and each interacting with the others. Barbi could not have foreseen the reconsideration that today's scholars consequently bring to modern editions of medieval works.[4] Such reconsideration is absolutely essential for the *Vita nuova.*

Dante's *libello* offers itself as a key work for orality/literacy analysis in being a product of Europe's "High Middle Ages," a manuscript culture in which, as Brian Stock has shown, the technology of the written word was calling up abstract and intellectualized models that were changing the individual's internal experiences, interpretations, and judgments, and in which, as Walter Ong has demonstrated, the spoken word, despite the growing dominance of literacy over orality, still largely governed human relations and communicative expression.[5] Inevitably, the *Vita nuova* drew upon both medieval cultures, the oral and the literate, for it was at once generated from three main sources in which both cultures were interactive: Dante's literary knowledge and poetic intentions; his desire to address a real, as well as conceived, audience;[6] and his memories of actual experience.

On the one hand, therefore, the work is replete with evidence of oral consciousness. We find in it the personal authorial voice that addresses directly a particular and personal audience, including other poets.[7] Its narrator frequently uses the expression "Io dico che,"[8] along with verbs of speaking or saying when referring to poetic writing,[9] usages which suggest that the work is meant to be read *viva voce.*[10] The autobiographical work draws personal experiences and utterances from memory (*Vita nuova* 1), resulting in a text presented as rooted in the constantly shifting dynamics of remembrances and poetic literary concerns. Its narrative line is additive and aggregative, based on memory as much as, or more than, on a preordained narrative scheme. The account becomes caught up in explanations, and while chronologically controlled, it is governed only to a certain extent by a preeminently self-conscious and teleological design. Indeed, at a crucial point in his writing, which has by necessity become the "conclusion" of the *Vita nuova*, the writer-protagonist interrupts himself because he feels inadequate to perform the task undertaken at the *libello*'s beginning: namely, to transcribe what is written in the book of his memory. The narrative presents characters, particularly Beatrice and the protagonist, as strictly defined and ruled by a few powerful features. It offers prose explanations of the poetry, and it self-consciously insists upon the proper internal divisions of the poems into their thought units. It is replete with the additive use of temporal terms such as "after," "then," "later" (see below, Appendixes 3 and 4, for temporal phrases at the beginning of the present chapters). All such features exhibit communicative practices that scholarship since Parry has identified as operative in an oral culture.[11]

On the other hand, the *Vita nuova* is simultaneously and self-consciously directed to the thirteenth-century's expansive writing culture. Literacy and literature, founded on the written word, govern the work's ultimate authorial project, which is to raise a dialect of vernacular Italian, already widely written, to standards of art and expression comparable to those of written Latin poetry (*Vita nuova* 25). The work offers not unaltered memories but self-consciously transcribed memories; it addresses the entire subject of writing, from narrative to gloss to several poetic forms; and it introduces innovations (in both form and content) into previous traditions and current trends of literary production. The work addresses a literary world; it is replete with literary references, allusions, and borrowings; and it records the production and circulation of particular written poems. Unlike the externality of materials in oral productions, the materials of the *Vita nuova* are those of a writing culture: interior, interpretive, centered in individual self-consciousness. The materials come from a consciousness raising that was personally achieved by the narrator in the past and that is now brought forward in order to promote a wider consciousness raising to be achieved culturally in the future. In these efforts, the elevated, refined language of the work is not communal, as in oral productions, but private, as in literary productions: a written language appropriated to the particular style and personal voice of the individual author.

A full-scale orality/literacy study of the *Vita nuova* has not to our knowledge been undertaken, and we must leave that to others. Here we wish to focus on the effects of the print-culture element of chapter division and sentence numbering imposed during the nineteenth century and then canonized by Barbi, who added the numbering of sentences in order to facilitate print-culture scholarship. Divisions as such are certainly called for by the text itself; Dante's preoccupation with division is explicit in his *divisioni* of almost every poem. Although Boccaccio failed to see the value of these *divisioni*, hence his decision literally to marginalize them, they are instructive to us. They specify, first of all, not the prosodic divisions of the poems but their thought divisions; they signify not the structural divisions of versification and rhyme that a print culture makes visual through indentations and spacing but the divisions of thought units that frame meaning and interpretation. The *divisioni* further reveal an authorial self-consciousness about the poems as written texts, for they indicate that the meaning of the poems may neither be taken for granted nor be dependent upon oral give-and-take. At the same time, they reveal a manuscript culture's view of meaning as inherent in the text, as opposed to a print culture's view of meaning as the product of an interpretive mind and therefore distinct from the text.[12]

Dante also explicitly refers to his prose as involving paragraphs, and he speaks of some paragraphs as "greater" than others (*Vita nuova* 2.10; see below, note 1). In medieval manuscripts, according to Walter Ong, paragraphs are signified not by a break, space, and new line, but by the paragraph mark within the line. These paragraph marks, Ong insists, do not signify a unit of discourse; they merely provide an aid to visual location; in fact, Ong remarks, writing during this period still functions largely to reconstitute "the originally oral, spoken word in visual space."[13] On the other hand, Dante nowhere in his *libello* speaks of chapters. Barbi examined meticulously the forty-one manuscripts containing Dante's *Vita nuova*, most of which are fifteenth and sixteenth century, and reported in his 1907 and 1932 editions that while paragraph signs and lead sentences are not lacking here and there among the manuscripts, none of which is a holograph, no clear pattern of chapter divisions exists ("Introduzione," xviii). This finding left Barbi reluctant to introduce an extraneous element like chapter divisions, but he succumbed to such nineteenth-century scholarly concerns "pel comodo delle citazioni": for the ease of citations (see below, Appendix 2).

The effects of imposed chapter divisions are subtle but not insignificant. Such divisions are executed by a print-culture code and a graphic arrangement that add to the *Vita nuova* technological concerns absent from the original, and they thereby diminish the orality that Dante's writing preserves and uses. The degree of that orality's loss increases sight dominance and diminishes reading dominance, so that we see divisions of ideas more as visual units and less as units of thought and internal consciousness. We look at the work more and listen to it less, in other words, and consequently the distance between us and Dante—his life, experiences, objectives, intentions—is increased. Simultaneously, chapter divisions complete the print culture's textualizing of Dante's work; they draw the work out from Dante's own manuscript culture and into our print culture, thereby assimilating it, further than otherwise, into modern thought and consciousness.

The result diminishes auctorial control and increases reader control. Chapter divisions add not merely internal junctures, as do paragraphs, but internal closures. These closures subdivide the work into units of discourse and thereby render the text not only easier for the modern reader to cite but also easier to read; they render the text, in other words, more "consumer oriented." In subjecting the work more to the reader's consciousness and less to the author's, chapter divisions have the further effect of imposing on the reader's consciousness a significant degree of control. They organize the thought content of the text, structure it, rigidify its sequence, lock up thought into predetermined divisions, control it through an imposed format. They thereby limit, if not proscribe, the freedom and inducement to reconsider and discuss the microstructures of Dante's discourse.

The grid, furthermore, which distributes the author's meaning by imposing spaces and numbers that divide the text into chapters, paragraphs, and *commi*, is not the author's grid but that of the editor, who thereby perpetuates editorial control through imposing a single conception of unity on a given segment of text. Although Torri, Witte, Casini, and Barbi may not have thought in these terms, they held competing conceptions of unity, until Barbi succeeded, through academic standing and personal pleading (see Appendix 2), in gaining acceptance of his conception as the standard. We thus read the text through Barbi's consciousness, and to an extent we have since been more loyal to Barbi in these respects than to Dante. Because spaces and numbers separate meaning into the editor's grid, and not the author's, such editorial interferences affecting the relations between the elements and parts of the text represent control by a kind of cultural ruling class, the class composed of editors, publishers, and scholars who insist on staying within the lines laid down by Barbi's national standard edition.

Barbi, it should be repeated, was reluctant to impose chapter divisions, with their required numbering, and once he yielded to such editorial interferences for the sake of ease of citation, he was reluctant to deviate from the divisions of his predecessors, particularly those of Torri and Casini. At the same time, he offered no justifications for his own decisions in dividing each chapter into numbered *commi*, or sentence clusters. Further, in twelve instances Barbi introduced paragraphs that separate Dante's *divisioni* of his poems from the previous or following prose text, but in at least three instances where the same textual features exist and editorial criteria obtain, he did not introduce paragraph breaks. In the absence of a clear manuscript tradition of divisions into chapters, paragraphs, and sentence clusters, Barbi's divisions are often inconsistent and sometimes plainly arbitrary.

Barbi's own practices, therefore, as well as the *Vita nuova*'s editorial tradition, invite review and revision, so that readings of Dante's work may gain in fidelity to its medieval character and auctorial intention. New criteria of textual division are called for, and these criteria must be textually justifiable. Let us review, therefore, in outline, Barbi's editorial decisions regarding paragraph divisions.

Barbi classified the manuscript tradition of the *Vita nuova* according to two families, which he called "alpha" and "beta" and each of which generated two principal groups of manuscripts (see his ch. 4, "Classificazione dei testi"). On the basis of this fourfold manuscript tradition, Barbi drew up his scheme for chapter divisions. We have excerpted from Barbi's description of these manuscripts all those passages that offer explanation of the *Vita nuova*'s chapter divisions (below, Appendix 1). Barbi's descriptive observations, we must note, are not numerous (see Appendix 2), but the following recapitulation can be made from Barbi's descriptions of the manuscripts and from his general comments:

1. In describing the manuscripts, Barbi normally employs the term "paragraph." Dante himself uses the same term in *Vita nuova* 2.10. It would seem, therefore, that the term "chapter"—*pace* Witte—should be avoided (see note 1).

2. Barbi recognizes that the text's divisions are present here and there ("qua e là" ["Introduzione," cccviii]), and thus most divisions introduced in his critical edition do find some justification in some manuscript or other.

3. Precisely on the basis of the manuscript tradition, Barbi, as noted, would have preferred no marked distinction into chapters and no numbering between them ("Io non avrei voluto quindi introdurre nel testo una distinzione marcata di capitoli con la relativa numerazione fra l'uno e l'altro" ["Introduzione," cccviii]).[14] However, for the sake of ease of reference ("pel comodo delle citazioni") Barbi divides the text into forty-two chapters. Each chapter is separated from the following one by leaving ample space and placing at its head the number of the chapter in roman numerals, followed by square brackets enclosing the Witte / Casini numbering in small capitals when these differ from his own.[15]

4. Barbi opted also for a more detailed division of each chapter into *commi* ("commas"),[16] for which, needless to say, the manuscript tradition offers no justification. One must note, however, that Barbi's edition sets the numbering of these *commi* not in the text itself (as the numbering of the paragraphs) but along the margins of the text and thus arguably outside the text. In Barbi's view, these *commi*, which cluster together several sentences, should be based primarily on meaning ("Si doveva in questa suddistinzione tener conto soprattutto del senso")—a fundamental principle we fully endorse.[17] Barbi adds, however, that one should also be concerned with facilitating the scholars' needs and preserving typographical taste ("gusto tipografico").[18] In so doing, Barbi further demonstrates his concern not so much for reproducing a text as closely as possible to the author's original intention but rather for contemporary scholarship and print technology.

Barbi's critical edition incorporates further typographical arrangements of the text, most of which concern the alleged special status of the *divisioni*, the divisions of poems that Barbi views as different from the narrative:

1. Barbi's edition separates the poems' *divisioni* from the previous or following prose text and indents the initial line of the *divisione* at

VN 3.13; 7.7; 8.7; 8.12; 9.13; 12.16; 15.7; 16.11; 19.15; 20.6; 21.5; 22.11; 22.17; 23.29; 24.10; 26.14; 31.3 (first indented *divisione* before the poem); 33.4 (second indented *divisione* before the poem); 34.4 (third indented *divisione* before the poem); 38.7 (fourth indented *divisione* before the poem); 41.2–8 (fifth and last indented *divisione* before the poem).

2. By contrast, the *divisioni* before the poems are not indented at *VN* 32.4; 37.4–5.

3. Although not a *divisione*, the line is indented at *VN* 3.14 (after the *divisione*); 12.17 (after the *divisione*); 22.12 (which announces a sonnet and follows a *divisione*); and 40.8 (which declares the author's intention not to divide the following sonnet).

4. Several instances with analogous characteristics are treated differently, where the initial line is indented in some while in others it is not: 14.13 (indented, right after the poem; the narrator offers justification for not dividing the poem); 19.22 (not indented, whereas 12.17, which has the same characteristics, has an indented line); 26.8 (indented right after the poem; the narrator justifies not dividing the poem and continues the narrative); 38.5–6 (indented, although not a *divisione* but an explanation and justification of certain practices in the following sonnet; it is in fact followed by the *divisione*, which is indented); 35.4 (not indented, before the poem; the narrator states that the poem is obvious and thus needs no *divisione*); 36. 3 (not indented, before the poem; the narrator states that the poem is obvious and thus needs no *divisione*); 40.5–7 (not indented: an explanation of certain terms employed in the following sonnet; although not indented, it shares similar purposes with 38.5–6, which is indented); 32.4 and 37.4 (not indented, although here the same principle obtains as in 39.7, which is indented: "Questo sonetto non divido, però che assai lo manifesta la sua ragione," and 40.8, which is also indented: "Questo sonetto non divido, però che assai lo manifesta la sua ragione").

One can thus conclude that not only has the manuscript tradition no consistent divisions into chapters but also that Barbi's divisions into chapters and into *commi* (in addition to beginning several passages as new paragraphs) are either inconsistent or outright arbitrary. Barbi's handling of *divisioni*, whether they come after or before the poems (according as they are written *in vita* or *in morte* of Beatrice), is also based on unstated or inconsistent criteria that have brought about clearly unnecessary separations: for example, of Barbi's (but also Torri's and Witte's) chapter 25 from the *divisione* (*VN* 24.10–11) of which it is part, and arguably also from *VN* 26.[19] Barbi's edition also separates some *divisioni* from the previous or following text but not all of them; at times it begins a new paragraph within the chapter whereas it does not do so in other instances where the same principle obtains. Not only is there no clearly apparent justification for indenting the *divisioni* as separate paragraphs following the poems, some *divisioni* are linked unitively with the following material by pronouns, adverbs, references, or a specific topic. These incongruities, in part inherited from Barbi's predecessors, suggest that the ghost of Boccaccio, who removed the poems' divisions entirely from the text and placed them in the margins, still hovers over today's international edition of the *Vita nuova*.[20]

We can begin a search for new and justified criteria by noting that at the beginning of his writing, the text's narrator-protagonist proposes only a single, fundamental principle of narrative unity: "le parole le quali è mio intendimento d'assemplare in questo libello." The syntagm "le parole" suggests multiplicity and difference—hence disunity—only apparently, since Dante normally uses this plural to signify words insofar as they carry a complete meaning and thus constitute a discourse.[21] The three nouns and one verb that follow further propose: (1) a unifying purpose and direction toward a goal ("intendimento"), (2) an operation of writing equally directed toward a model ("assemplare," from *exemplum*, to put aside and to serve as a model),[22] and (3) an end product that is viewed as a specific written unit ("questo libello")[23] and that carries a meaning ("la loro sentenzia").[24]

Thus from the perspective of the text's foreshadowed structure and composition, no division is justified except between the prose and the poems. By their self-contained prosodic structures, the poems create distinctions between their incipit and explicit and the prose text that respectively precedes and follows them.[25] Other than the prose/poetry distinctions, furthermore, the fundamental principle that the text of the *Vita nuova* forms a narrative continuum requires that after the explicit of the poems the narrative should not be indented to mark a new paragraph, as it may be customary to do in contemporary editions, *unless other criteria require such an indentation*, which in our print technology stands for a new paragraph.

If the text of the *Vita nuova* is to be divided any further than into poetry and prose, then any subdivisions of the prose should be based

on clearly identifiable criteria. Toward this end, analysis of the incipit
of each chapter in Barbi's edition discloses five categories of textual
usage (see below, Appendix 3 and Appendix 4):

1. The opening chapter refers figurally to location: that is, to
   the place in the book of the narrator's memory from which
   his material is transcribed.

2. Twenty-two chapters begin with either a preposition, a phrase,
   a conjunction, or an adverb of time.

3. Nine chapters begin with an indeterminate temporal indication.

4. Four chapters begin with an introductory formula, such as
   "Dico che" or "Ora . . . dico che."

5. Six chapters begin with one of a miscellany of expressions.

A closer analysis reveals that the six chapter incipits listed under
category 5 seem to have no justification (except arguably VN 28) and
that the text they initiate in Barbi should be added to the chapter
that precedes each of them. Accordingly, Barbi's chapter 18 should
join chapter 17, which in fact announces it ("E però che la cagione
de la nuova matera è dilettevole a udire, la dicerò, quanto potrò più
brievemente" [Barbi's ch. 17.2]).[26] Barbi's chapters 25 and 26 have
spurred the recent intervention of Mario Marti, who rightly argues for
the elimination of chapter 25 and implicitly also for the elimination
of chapter 26.[27] Concerning Barbi's chapter 28 ("Quomodo sedet
sola civitas plena populo! facta est quasi vidua domina gentium"),
one could eliminate it in order to intensify the interruption of the
preceding canzone and thus intensify the announcement of Beatrice's
death, which Jeremiah's quotation announces, or one could keep
it separate, as it is, and thereby control and to a degree subdue
the interruption of the canzone and the announcement of Beatrice's
death, which VN 28 contains. Finally, by eliminating Barbi's chapters
36 and 37, which contain either a weak temporal marker ("poi" in VN
36) or no temporal indication (VN 37), the episode of the "donna
gentile" would constitute one coherent and self-contained account
(Barbi's ch. 35–38).
    Of the remaining categories of chapter incipit, the largest are those
of the temporal opening, which, using prepositions, conjunctions , adverbs, or a phrase indicating an undetermined period of time, initiate

thirty-one of Barbi's forty-two chapters. Two of the incipits listed under category 5 and beginning with the introductory formula "Dico che" or "Ora . . . dico che," although they too contain some temporal indication ("Dico che in questo tempo che" [VN 6.1]; "Dico che quando ella apparia da parte alcuna" [VN 11.1]), do not justify forming a separate chapter.[28] The last chapter incipit under this category ("Io dico che, secondo l'usanza d'Arabia" [Barbi's ch. 29]) is strictly linked with the previous chapter, which in fact announces it.[29]

The issues are, then: (1) whether the temporal criterion warrants dividing the text into chapters; (2) whether the temporal criterion can be accepted as the fundamental criterion for dividing the text of the *Vita nuova* further than the division established by poetry and prose;[30] and finally, (3) whether such a temporal criterion is sufficiently represented by the temporal phrases that mark the beginning of most chapters in the present editions of the *Vita nuova*.[31] We believe that the temporal criterion meets all of these conditions, and that its application would result in a new edition of the *Vita nuova*. Except for the first, each paragraph would be based on temporality, a fundamental feature of oral communication and a criterion utterly inseparable from narrativity.

These temporal expressions, therefore, together with the distinction between prose and poetry, provide the clearest patterns that create internal junctures within the text and the only patterns sufficiently extensive and consistent to provide an adequate number of divisions necessary for understanding and interpretation. Inasmuch as the narrative structure of the *Vita nuova* is temporal, and because temporality governs and integrates the sequence of poetic composition with the protagonist's encounters and experiences with Beatrice before and after her death, the pattern of prose-poetry combined with the temporal category provides the most integral bases and the clearest sanction for textual divisions.

We have put these divisions to the test by applying them tentatively to a part of *Vita nuova*, and we have found the work's effect changed to a surprising degree. Because it is impossible here, in limited space, to print and analyze a sufficiently extensive portion of Dante's redivided *libello* to illustrate the change, we recommend that anyone interested read, as an example, Barbi's chapters 3–4 as a single paragraph separated only into prose and poetry. The resulting single paragraph recounts the first meeting of Beatrice that gives rise to the first of the work's poems, the sonnet beginning "A ciascun'alma presa." The most important effect of the unification of these chapters is the clear integration of the poetic production with the experience of Love, an integration that increases the impact of this event, enhances narrative sense, reduces the treatise-like effect of Barbi's division, produces greater narrative energy, sharpens the narrative intention, and deepens the narrator's sincerity. Unified, the autobiographical event is more psychological than when divided, the narrative voice more intimate, and the narrator himself more present. In short, the orality of the work, the reader's relation to someone speaking, and therefore the reader's propensity to listen are not only enhanced but emerge as a felt condition natural to the text.

But readers must consider the changed effect for themselves, and such consideration might well open a new vein of scholarly interest. For now, we recommend the reconsideration of chapters, and we intend to publish fairly soon, the *Vita nuova* (Italian and English) redivided according to temporal and prose/poetry criteria only. For the sake of scholarly references, we are experimenting with including the National Standard Edition's paragraphs and sentence numbers in margins in order to preserve and utilize Barbi's by now extensively employed system of references without allowing that system to impose print-culture effects directly onto Dante's text. Such a format may well refine our experience, understanding, and criticism of Dante's text, and it may render the *Vita nuova* amenable to a full orality/literacy study.

APPENDIX 1

The Manuscript Tradition:
Barbi's Divisions into Chapters

Michele Barbi (*La vita nuova di Dante Alighieri*, critical ed. [Firenze: Bemporad, 1932]) classifies the manuscript tradition of the *Vita nuova* according to two families, "alpha" and "beta," each of which gives rise to two principal groups of manuscripts (ch. 4, "Classificazione dei testi"). We have excerpted from Barbi's description of these manuscripts, and have listed below, all those passages that describe the *Vita nuova*'s division into chapters (ch. 2, "Manoscritti"). When Barbi, in describing a manuscript, makes no comments concerning the manuscript's presence or absence of divisions into chapters, we have nevertheless listed the manuscript.

1. Vaticano Chigiano L, VIII, 305 (K)
   Le rime sono scritte a mo' di prosa, distinguendo i versi con lineette trasversali, non sempre però regolarmente. La *Vita nuova* è senza titolo ed *explicit*: non ha distinzioni di paragrafi, ma soltanto dopo la fine delle narrazioni si viene a capo per trascrivere la poesia e s'ha l'iniziale colorata, e col segno del paragrafo e l'iniziale colorata si torna ugualmente a capo per la divisione: ove dopo la divisione riprende la narrazione, fra l'una e l'altra non è fatta nessuna distinzione. (Barbi, xxi)

2. Vaticano Chigiano L, V, 176 (K²)
   La *Vita nuova* ha le divisioni in margine, come nella copia fatta dal Boccaccio (cfr. p. xvi), e reca in fatti a c. 13ª la nota giustificativa del Boccaccio stesso per aver tolto le divisioni dalla loro sede naturale: *Marauiglieannosi molti per quello che io aduisi*, ecc. La distinzione dell'opera in paragrafi, col mezzo sia di lettere miniate e capoverso, sia di sole iniziali minate, corrisponde a quella da noi seguita, eccetto il § II e III, il cui principio non ha alcun segno di distinzione. Le rime sono scritte a mo' di prosa. (Barbi, xxiv)

3. Vaticano Capponiano 262 (C)
   La *Vita nuova* ha le divisioni nel testo e senza alterazioni, e i versi scritti di seguito a mo' di prosa. Da principio non si fa, ordinariamente, capoverso se non per le poesie, che ha per di più anche l'iniziale miniata, e la divisione stessa è distinta dalla fine dei versi con una sola lineetta obliqua (al contrario troviamo il capoverso nel § XII dopo ciascuna delle due citazioni latine!); ma in seguito si distingue con capoverso anche la narrazione e, quando non è indivisibile da questa, pur la divisione. (Barbi, xxvi)

4. Bibl. dei Lincei 44, E, 34, già Corsiniano 1085 (Co)
   Capoversi nel testo non mancano, ma non sono così frequenti come in altri manoscritti e nelle moderne edizioni: c'è al § III (non è ben chiaro se anche al VI, VII e IX), ai §§ XIII–XV, XVII, XVIII, XX, XXII–XXVII, XXVIII (tanto per la rubrica come pel seguito), alla divisione del XXXI, e, naturalmente, al § XXXII e ai seguenti sino alla fine. (Barbi, xxvii)

5. Codice Martelli (M)

La *Vita nuova* è intera, con le divisioni al loro posto. Ha il titolo: *Incipit uita noua*, e porta infine: *Explicit liber. Deo gratias. Amen.* Quanto alla distinzione in paragrafi, si torna a capo, oltre che per il principio delle poesie e per il riprendere poi della prosa, anche dopo il termine poi delle divisioni, e vi si appone altresì il segno del paragrafo. A capo si torna pure a principio del § XXVI (sebbene il segno del paragrafo sia stato omesso) e del § XXXI: nessuna distinzione al principio dei nostri §§ II, III, IV (c'è bensì a III 14), V, VI, VII, XI, XII (c'è invece il segno del paragrafo, senza tornare a capo, a XXVIII 3) e XXX. (Barbi, xxviii)

6. Laurenziano XL, 31

Mancano le divisioni. Si ha il capoverso, oltre che per le poesie e al riprender via via della prosa dopo ciascuna di esse, ai § XIII, XXVI e XXXI, e anche a metà del § XXIX ([L]o *numero* . . .) e a metà del XXX ([S]e *alcuno* . . .). (Barbi, xxvii)

7. Laurenziano XL, 42

É mancante delle divisioni. L'iniziale dell'opera è in oro. . . . e miniate sono pure le iniziali sia delle poesie che delle prose che seguono. . . . e segnata intanto in carattere miniato la lettera da miniare, in principio dei nostri § IV, VI, VII e XVII. (Barbi, xix)

8. Laurenziano XC sup. 136

La *Vita nuova* ha dunque le divisioni nei margini. . . . La distinzione dei capoversi corrisponde a quella di K^2. (Barbi, xxxi)

9. Laurenziano XC sip. 137

Le divisioni della *Vita nuova*, in inchiostro rosso, sono nel testo, ma sempre dopo le poesie, e colle modificazioni introdotte dal Boccaccio. (Barbi, xxxi)

10. Laurenziano Ashburnhamiano 679

Alla *Vita nuova* mancano le divisioni. (Barbi, xxxii)

11. Laurenziano Ashburnhamiano 843 (A)

Le divisioni della *Vita nuova* sono al loro posto. Si fa capoverso al principio dei §§ V, VIII–X, XIII, XIV, XVI, XVII, XX, XXXI, e naturalmente, di tutti i seguenti. (Barbi, xxxii)

12. Laurenziano Acquisti e doni 224 (O)

13. Bibl. Nazionale di Firenze, Magliabechiano VI, 30 (Mgl)

14. Bibl. Nazionale di Firenze, Magliabechiano VI, 143

Oltre la grande iniziale in rosso con rabeschi violacei a principio dell'opera, ha iniziali miniate, più piccole, ordinariamente ai capoversi delle poesie e al riprendere della prosa, sia divisione o narrazione. Tra la divisione e il riprendere della narrazione, nella prima parte dell'opera, non c'è distinzione se non al § XIII, che comincia, facendo capoverso con lettera miniata; al § XXIII, che, pure a capoverso, ha un'iniziale maiuscoletta . . . ;

al § XXV con un semplice ritorno a capo e una maiuscoletta in nero; al § XXVII con un ritorno a capo e l'iniziale miniata; e così pure, terminata l'allegazione del passo di Geremia *Quomodo sedet* nel § XXVIII, al ricominciare del volgare, e, senza ragione, anche in fine della narrazione del § XXXIII, alle parole *Questa canzone e questo soprascritto sonetto,* ecc. (Barbi, xxxvi)

15. Bibl. Nazionale di Firenze, Magliabechiano VI, 187
La *Vita nuova* è priva delle divisioni. Ha iniziale miniata grande oltre che al principio d'ogni poesia e al riprender della prosa, anche al § XII e al § XXVI; il principio del § XVIII è distinto col capoverso e coll'iniziale colorata piccola . . . ; al § XXVIII la citazione latina ha l'iniziale colorata piccola, le parole volgari che seguono (*Io era nel proponimento . . .*) la grande. (Barbi, xxxvii)

16. Bibl. Nazionale di Firenze, Magliabechiano VI, 1103
. . . le divisioni nei margini. . . . Ha iniziali colorate a principio dei capoversi, i quali sono però in questo codice assai più rari che in altri, e basti notare che manca ogni segno di distinzione in principio dei §§ II, III, V, VI, VII, XI, XII, XVIII e XIX. (Barbi, xxxviii–xxxix)

17. Bibl. Nazionale di Firenze, Palatino 204 (Pal)

18. Bibl. Nazionale di Firenze, Palatino 561
Nella *Vita nuova* mancano le divisioni. Iniziali miniate si hanno non solo ad ogni poesia e al riprendere della prosa, ma anche a quegli altri punti che dal Torri in poi si considerano come principii di paragrafi, fatta eccezione per il § II e III che non hanno nel nostro codice, come in K^2, alcun segno di distinzione. (Barbi, xxxix)

19. Bibl. Nazionale di Firenze, Panciatichiano 9
La distinzione dei paragrafi è segnata da uno spazio bianco lasciato per la lettera iniziale, che doveva essere miniata, e non fu: ma fuori del principio delle rime e del riprender della prosa quel segno è raro, e manca, ad es., al § II, III, IV, VI, VII, XII, XVIII, XIX, e c'è invece a metà del XVIII [A]*llora mi rispuose quella che mi parlava,* dove logicamente non può stare. (Barbi, xl)

20. Bibl. Nazionale di Firenze, Panciatichiano 10

21. Bibl. Nazionale di Firenze, Conv. B, 2, 1267

22. Riccardiano 1050
La *Vita nuova* è senza divisioni. Iniziale colorata al principio di ogni poesia, e al ricominciare della prosa; maiuscolette vergate di rosso spesso anche a mezzo dei paragrafi; e iniziali grandi colorate, per distinguere pure i paragrafi, al § XVIII, al § XIX e al § XXVI; ma anche queste sono talvolta dove paragrafo nuovo non può cominciare. (Barbi, xliii)

23. Riccardiano 1118

24. Riccardiano 1054

25. Frammento dell'Archivio di Stato fiorentino
26. Braidense AG, XI, 5
27. Trivulziano 1058 (T)
28. Trivulziano 1050
29. Ambrosiano R 95 sup. (Am)
   Quanto alla distinzione dei paragrafi, si trova apposito segno in principio dei nostri III, IV, VIII, IX, XIII–XVII, XXI–XXIV, XXVI e XXVII; e oltre a ciò cominciano a nuova linea i § II, XX e XXVIII (e anche le parole che seguono quivi stesso alla rubrica latina), e, naturalmente, tutti i paragrafi che vengon dopo a quelli che terminano con una poesia. (Barbi, liii)
30. Biblioteca capitolare di Verona 445 (V)
   Il codice non ha segni speciali, e neppure iniziali colorate, per una distinzione del testo in paragrafi. L'amanuense fa capoverso, oltre che al principio delle poesie, a III 15 e al principio dei §§ VIII, XIII, XXIV, XXV e XXVII. (Barbi, liv)
31. Marciano ital. X, 26 (Mc)
   La *Vita nuova* ha le divisioni colle modificazioni introdotte nella copia del Boccaccio; non però nei margini, ma rimesse nel testo, sempre dopo le poesie, anche nella parte delle rime dolorose, nonostante la dichiarazione di Dante al § XXXI 2: "Ed acciò che questa canzone. . . ." Quanto alla divisione in paragrafi, soltanto al principio del § II e III non si ha né il capoverso né altro segno di distinzione. (Barbi, lv)
32. Marciano ital. IX, 191
33. Marciano ital. IX, 491
34. Codice Pesarese, oggi Maiocchi (P)
35. Biblioteca Nazionale di Napoli XIII, C, 9 (N)
36. Biblioteca universitaria e territoriale di Strasburgo, L ital. 7 (W)
   Nella *Vita nuova* si ha il capoverso ai §§ II, XV, XVI, XVII (anzi a questo paragrafo è lasciato il posto per l'iniziale miniata e segnato il *p* nel margine), XX, XXII, XXIII, XXIV, XXV, XXVI, XXVIII, XXX e XXXI, e naturalmente a tutti i successivi: talvolta, pur cominciando il paragrafo a principio di riga, la cosa è incerta perché la linea precedente è piena, e a principio della nova non si ha spazio bianco né iniziale distinta. (Barbi, lxii)
37. Codice Altemps
38. Bibl. capitolare di Toledo: cajon 104, num. 6, Zelada (To)
   Le divisioni della *Vita nuova* sono nei margini e colle modificazioni introdotte dal Boccaccio; e il codice è infatti, come mostrai sin dall'edizione del 1907 . . . ed è ora generalmente ammesso, della mano di lui. (Barbi, lxv)
39. Bibl. Bodleiana d'Oxford, Canonici Ital. 114
   Quanto alle divisioni della *Vita nuova* e alla distinzione in paragrafi, tutto è come in Marc. ital. X, 26. (Barbi, lxvi)

40. Bibl. dell'Università Cornell di Ithaca, New York. Mss. D. 51

41. Estratto del § VIII

A questi manoscritti che contengono della Vita nuova così la parte prosastica come quella poetica, sono da aggiungere, come dicemmo, altri [Mss. 42–80; Barbi, lxii–lxxxviii] che contengono tutte o in parte le rime con evidenti indizi di essere estratte da testi completi dell'opera. (Barbi, lxxi)

APPENDIX 2

Barbi's General Comments on Chapter Divisions

On a few occasions Barbi makes general observations concerning the division of the Vita nuova into chapters:

Occasione a divergenze fra gli editori e i commentatori della Vita nuova ha dato anche la divisione dell'opera in paragrafi. Una vera distinzione di tal genere Dante non fece, tanto più che per ogni poesia pause spontanee s'avevano, ordinariamente, alla fine sia della narrazione, sia dei versi, sia delle divisioni; ma dove pure il racconto si svolge senza riferimento di poesie, pause e capoversi doverono all'autor venir fatti, anche se non ebbe una premeditata disposizione della materia. Un'edizione moderna non può far a meno di una più accurata distinzione in paragrafi e sottoparagrafi, e, sebbene sia cosa esteriore, deve adattarsi quanto più strettamente è possibile allo svolgimento del trattato: onde l'opportunità di attendere alle divisioni date dai vari testi e di verificare se ci sia una tradizione costante. (Barbi, xviii)

In concluding his analysis of the manuscripts, Barbi notes:

Abbiamo visto, nel descrivere i manoscritti, che una vera e propria distinzione in capitoli, che si mantenga uguale in tutti i testi non esiste, ma che capoversi e segni paragrafali qua e là tuttavia non mancano. Io non avrei voluto quindi introdurre nel testo una distinzione marcata di capitoli con la relativa numerazione fra l'uno e l'altro; ma non si può ormai, pel comodo delle citazioni, rinunziare a tale distinzione e numerazione. Pel numero di questi capoversi o paragrafi, poiché la disparità dei manoscritti mi lasciava libero di farne più o meno, ho cercato di discostarmi meno che fosse possibile dalle due divisioni più in uso, del Torri e del Casini. Bene sarebbe stato che quella del Torri si fosse mantenuta costante in tutte le edizioni successive, anche se difettosa (il vantaggio vero di queste numerazioni è che rimangono fisse: cfr. p. CXXII); ma ormai che l'accordo è rotto, ho cercato d'evitare gl'inconvenienti tanto della divisione Torri (distinzione del § XXVI in due paragrafi) quanto di quella del Casini (mancanza di numero per il proemio, distinzione del § III in due paragrafi). Così la mia numerazione concorda con quella del Torri sino al § XXVI e dopo rimane inferiore d'una unità, e concorda con quella del Casini dal § III in poi.

Se non che pei bisogni dello studioso la divisione del testo in paragrafi non basta: ne occorre una più minuta in commi che dia modo di trovare alla prima un dato passo o una data voce, e che possa mantenersi inalterata in tutte le edizioni. Si doveva in questa suddistinzione tener conto soprattutto del senso, ma aver altresì riguardo da una parte al vantaggio dello studioso, che non vuol commi troppo lunghi, e dall'altra al gusto tipografico, che non vuol numerazioni troppo fitte e troppo irregolari. . . . io raccomando ai futuri editori queste mie suddivisioni, come anche quelle in paragrafi, perché siano accettate e tramandate quali sono: mutino pure nel mio testo quello che a loro parrà meno sicuro; ma non impediscano che una citazione fatta su questa o quella edizione possa valere per qualsiasi altra. (Barbi, cccviii–cccix)

APPENDIX 3

Incipit and Explicit of Barbi's Chapters

1. In quella parte del libro de la mia memoria. . . . Sotto la quale rubrica io trovo scritte le parole le quali è mio intendimento d'assemplare in questo libello; e se non tutte, almeno la loro sentenza.
2 [1]. Nove fiate già appresso lo mio nascimento era tornato lo cielo de la luce quasi a uno medesimo punto. . . . e trapassando molte cose le quali si potrebbero trarre de l'essemplo onde nascono queste, verrò a quelle parole le quali sono scritte ne la mia memoria sotto maggiori paragrafi.
3 [2]. Poi che furono passati tanti die, che appunto erano compiuti li nove anni appresso l'apparimento soprascritto di questa gentilissima. . . . Lo verace giudicio del detto sogno non fue veduto allora per alcuno ma ora è manifestissimo a li più semplici.
4. Da questa visione innanzi cominciò lo mio spirito naturale ad essere impedito ne la sua operazione. . . . E quando mi domandavano: "Per cui t'ha così distrutto questo Amore?", ed io sorridendo li guardava, e nulla dicea loro.
5. Un giorno avvenne che questa gentilissima sedea ove s'udiano parole de la regina de la gloria. . . . Con questa donna mi celai alquanti anni e mesi; e per più fare credere altrui, feci per lei certe cosette per rima, le quali non

è mio intendimento di scrivere qui, se non in quanto facesse a trattare di quella gentilissima Beatrice; e però le lascerò tutte, salvo che alcuna cosa ne scriverò che pare che sia loda di lei.

6. Dico che in questo tempo che questa donna era schermo di tanto amore. . . . E presi li nomi di sessanta le più belle donne de la cittade ove la mia donna fue posta da l'altissimo sire, e compuosi una pistola sotto forma di serventese, la quale io non scriverò se non n'avrei fatto menzione, se non per dire quello che componendola, maravigliosamente addivenne, cioè che in alcuno altro numero non sofferse lo nome de la mia donna stare, se non in su lo nove, tra li nomi di queste donne.

7. La donna co la quale io avea tanto tempo celata la mia volontade, convenne che si partisse de la sopradetta cittade. . . . Questo sonetto ha due parti principali; che ne la prima intendo chiamare li fedeli d'Amore per quelle parole di Geremia profeta che dicono: "O vos omnes qui transitis per viam, attendite et videte si est dolor sicut dolor meus", e pregare che mi sofferino d'audire; ne la seconda narro là ove Amore m'avea posto, con altro intendimento che l'estreme parti del sonetto non mostrano, e dico che io hoe ciò perduto. La seconda parte comincia quivi: *Amor, non già*.

8. Appresso lo partire di questa gentile donna fue piacere del segnore de li angeli. . . . La seconda comincia quivi: *poi che hai data*; la terza quivi: *E s'io di grazia*; la quarta quivi: *Chi non merta salute*.

9. Appresso la morte di questa donna alquanti die avvenne cosa per la quale me convenne partire de la sopradetta cittade. . . . La seconda comincia quivi: *Quando mi vide*; la terza: *Allora presi*.

10. Appresso la mia ritornata mi misi a cercare di questa donna. . . . E uscendo alquanto del proposito presente, voglio dare a intendere quello che lo suo salutare in me vertuosamente operava.

11. Dico che quando ella apparia da parte alcuna. . . . Sì che appare manifestamente che ne le sue salute abitava la mia beatitudine, la quale molte volte passava e redundava la mia capacitade.

12. Ora, tornando al proposito, dico che poi che la mia beatitudine mi fue negata, mi giunse tanto dolore, che, partito me da le genti, in solinga parte andai a bagnare la terra d'amarissime lagrime. . . . Potrebbe già l'uomo opporre contra me e dicere che non sapesse a cui fosse lo mio parlare in seconda persona, però che la ballata non è altro che queste parole ched io parlo: e però dico che questo dubbio io lo intendo solvere e dichiarare in questo libello ancora in parte più dubbiosa, e allora intenda qui chi qui dubita, o chi qui volesse opporre in questo modo.

13. Appresso di questa soprascritta visione. . . . La seconda parte commincia quivi: *e hanno in lor*, la terza quivi: *e sol s'accordano*, la quarta quivi: *Ond'io non so*.

14. Appresso la battaglia de li diversi pensieri avvenne che questa gentilissima. . . . Vero è che tra le parole dove si manifesta la cagione di questo
sonetto, si scrivono dubbiose parole, cioè quando dico che Amore uccide
tutti li miei spiriti, e li visivi rimangono in vita, salvo che fuori de li
strumenti loro. E questo dubbio è impossibile a solvere a chi non fosse in
simile grado fedele d'Amore; e a coloro che vi sono è manifesto ciò che
solverebbe le dubitose parole: e però non è bene a me di dichiarare cotale
dubitazione, acciò che lo mio parlare dichiarando sarebbe indarno, o vero
di soperchio.

15. Appresso la nuova trasfigurazione mi giunse uno pensamento forte. . . .
La seconda parte comincia quivi: *Lo viso mostra*; la terza quivi: *e per la
ebrietà*; la quarta: *Peccato face*; la quinta: *per la pietà*.

16. Appresso ciò che io dissi questo sonetto, mi mosse una volontade. . . .
Questo sonetto si divide in quattro parti, secondo che quattro cose sono
in esso narrate; e però che sono di sopra ragionate, non m'intrametto se
non di distinguere le parti per li loro cominciamenti: onde dico che la
seconda parte comincia quivi: *ch'Amor*; la terza quivi: *Poscia mi sforzo*; la
quarta quivi: *e se io levo*.

17. Poi che dissi questi tre sonetti. . . . E però che la cagione de la nuova
matera è dilettevole a udire, la dicerò, quanto potrò più brievemente.

18. Con ciò sia cosa che per la vista mia molte persone avessero compreso
lo secreto del mio cuore. . . . E però propuosi di prendere per matera de
lo mio parlare sempre mai quello che fosse loda di questa gentilissima; e
pensando molto a ciò, pareami avere impresa troppo alta materia quanto
a me, sì che non ardia di cominciare; e cosi dimorai alquanti dì con
desiderio di dire e con paura di cominciare.

19. Avvenne poi che passando per uno cammino lungo lo quale sen gia
uno rivo chiaro molto, a me giunse. . . . Dico bene che, a più aprire
lo intendimento di questa canzone, si converrebbe usare di più minute
divisioni; ma tuttavia chi non è di tanto ingegno che per queste che
sono fatte la possa intendere, a me non dispiace se la mi lascia stare,
ché certo io temo d'avere a troppi comunicato lo suo intendimento pur
per queste divisioni che fatte sono, s'elli avvenisse che molti le potessero
audire.

20. Appresso che questa canzone fue alquanto divolgata tra le genti. . . .
Poscia quando dico: *Bieltate appare*, dico come questa potenzia si riduce in
atto; e prima come si riduce in uomo, poi come si riduce in donna, quivi:
E simil face in donna.

21. Poscia che trattai d'Amore ne la soprascritta rima, vennemi volontade. . . . Poscia quando dico: *Ogne dolcezza*, dico quello medesimo che
detto è ne la prima parte, secondo due atti de la sua bocca; l'uno de li
quali è lo suo dolcissimo parlare, e l'altro lo suo mirabile riso; salvo che

non dico di questo ultimo come adopera ne li cuori altrui, però che la memoria non puote ritenere lui né la sua operazione.

22. Appresso ciò non molti dì passati, sì come piacque al glorioso sire lo quale non negoe la morte a sé. . . . Questo sonetto ha quattro parti, secondo che quattro modi di parlare ebbero in loro le donne per cui rispondo; e però che sono di sopra assai manifesti, non m'intrametto di narrare la sentenzia de le parti, e però le distinguo solamente. La seconda comincia quivi: *E perché piangi*; la terza: *Lascia piangere noi*; la quarta: *Ell'ha nel viso*.

23. Appresso ciò per pochi dì avvenne che in alcuna parte de la mia persona mi giunse una dolorosa infermitade. . . . Poscia quando dico: *Mentr'io pensava*, dico come io dissi loro questa mia imaginazione. Ed intorno a ciò foe due parti: ne la prima dico per ordine questa imaginazione; ne la seconda, dicendo a che ora mi chiamaro, le ringrazio chiusamente; e comincia quivi questa parte: *Voi mi chiamaste*.

24. Appresso questa vana imaginazione, avvenne uno die. . . . La terza parte si divide in due: ne la prima dico quello che io vidi; ne la seconda dico quello che io udio. La seconda comincia quivi: *Amor mi disse*.

25. Potrebbe qui dubitare persona degna da dichiararle onne dubitazione. . . . E questo mio primo amico e io ne sapemo bene di quelli che così rimano stoltamente.

26. Questa gentilissima donna, di cui ragionato è ne le precedenti parole, venne in tanta grazia de le genti. . . . La seconda comincia quivi: *La vista sua*; la terza quivi: *Ed è ne li atti*.

27. [28]. Appresso ciò, cominciai a pensare uno giorno sopra quello che detto avea de la mia donna. . . . / Questo m'avvene / ovunque ella mi vede, / e sì è cosa umil, che nol si crede. /

28. [29]. *Quomodo sedet sola civitas plena populo! facta est quasi vidua domina gentium.* . . . Onde prima dicerò come ebbe luogo ne la sua partita, e poi n'assegnerò alcuna ragione, per che questo numero fue a lei cotanto amico.

29. [30]. Io dico che, secondo l'usanza d'Arabia, l'anima sua nobilissima si partio ne la prima ora del nono giorno del mese. . . . Forse ancora per più sottile persona si vederebbe in ciò più sottile ragione; ma questa è quella ch'io ne veggio, e che più mi piace.

30. [31]. Poi che fue partita da questo secolo, rimase tutta la sopradetta cittade quasi vedova. . . . E simile intenzione so ch'ebbe questo mio primo amico a cui io ciò scrivo, cioè ch'io li scrivessi solamente volgare.

31. [32]. Poi che li miei occhi ebbero per alquanto tempo lagrimato. . . . / e tu, che se' figliuola di tristizia, / vatten disconsolata a star con elle. /

32. [33]. Poi che detta fue questa canzone, sì venne a me uno. . . . / in persona de l'anima dolente / abbandonata de la sua salute. /

33. [34]. Poi che detto èi questo sonetto, pensandomi chi questi era a cui lo intendea dare quasi come per lui fatto, vidi che. . . . / e lo intelletto loro alto, sottile / face maravigliar, sì v'è gentile. /

34. [35]. In quello giorno nel quale si compiea l'anno che questa donna era fatta de li cittadini di vita eterna. . . . / venian dicendo: "Oi nobile intelletto, / oggi fa l'anno che nel ciel salisti". /

35. [36]. Poi per alquanto tempo, con ciò fosse cosa che io fosse in parte ne la quale mi ricordava del passato tempo. . . . / Io dicea poscia ne l'anima trista: / "Ben è con quella donna quello Amore / lo qual mi face andar così piangendo".

36. [37]. Avvenne poi che là ovunque questa donna mi vedea, sì si facea d'una vista pietosa e d'un colore palido quasi come d'amore; . . . . / e voi crescete sì lor volontate, / che de la voglia si consuman tutti; / ma lagrimar dinanzi a voi non sanno. /

37. [38]. Io venni a tanto per la vista di questa donna, che li miei occhi si cominciaro a dilettare troppo di vederla. . . . / Voi non dovreste mai, se non per morte, / la vostra donna, ch'è morta, obliare". / Così dice 'l meo core, e poi sospira. /

38. [39]. Ricovrai la vista di quella donna in sì nuova condizione, che molte volte ne pensava. . . . / e la sua vita, e tutto 'l suo valore, / mosse de li occhi di quella pietosa / che si turbava de' nostri martiri". /

39. [40]. Contra questo avversario de la ragione si levoe un die, quasi ne l'ora de la nona, una forte imaginazione in me. . . . / però ch'elli hanno in lor li dolorosi / quel dolce nome di madonna scritto, / e de la morte sua molte parole. /

40. [41]. Dopo questa tribulazione avvenne, in quello tempo che molta gente va per vedere quella imagine benedetta. . . . / Ell'ha perduta la sua beatrice; / e le parole ch'om di lei pò dire / hanno vertù di far piangere altrui.

41. [42]. Poi mandaro due donne gentili a me pregando che io mandasse loro di queste mie parole rimate. . . . / So io che parla di quella gentile, / però che spesso ricorda Beatrice, / sì ch'io lo 'ntendo ben, donne mie care. /

42. [43]. Appresso questo sonetto apparve a me una mirabile visione. . . . quella benedetta Beatrice, la quale gloriosamente mira ne la faccia di colui *qui est per omnia saecula benedictus*.

APPENDIX 4

Categories of Usage in Chapter Incipits in Barbi's Chapters

1. *Figurative locus:*
   1. In quella parte del libro de la mia memoria
2. *Temporal beginning with conjunctions or prepositions of time:*
   2 [1]. Nove fiate già appresso lo mio nascimento
   3 [2]. Poi che furono passati tanti die
   8. Appresso lo partire di questa gentile donna
   9. Appresso la morte di questa donna alquanti die
   10. Appresso la mia ritornata mi misi
   13. Appresso di questa soprascritta visione
   14. Appresso la battaglia de li diversi pensieri avvenne che
   15. Appresso la nuova trasfigurazione mi giunse
   16. Appresso ciò che io dissi questo sonetto
   17. Poi che dissi questi tre sonetti
   20. Appresso che questa canzone fue alquanto divolgata[32]
   21. Poscia che trattai d'Amore ne la soprascritta rima[33]
   22. Appresso ciò non molti dì passati
   23. Appresso ciò per pochi dì avvenne che
   24. Appresso questa vana imaginazione, avvenne uno die
   27 [28]. Appresso ciò, cominciai a pensare uno giorno
   30 [31]. Poi che fue partita da questo secolo
   31 [32]. Poi che li miei occhi ebbero per alquanto tempo lagrimato
   32 [33]. Poi che detta fue questa canzone
   33 [34]. Poi che detto èi questo sonetto
   40 [41]. Dopo questa tribulazione avvenne, in quello tempo che
   42 [43]. Appresso questo sonetto apparve a me
3. *Indeterminate temporal indication:*
   4. Da questa visione innanzi cominciò lo mio spirito naturale
   5. Un giorno avvenne che
   7. La donna co la quale io avea tanto tempo celata la mia volontade, convenne
   19. Avvenne poi che passando per uno cammino
   34 [35]. In quello giorno nel quale si compiea l'anno che
   35 [36]. Poi per alquanto tempo, con ciò fosse cosa che io fosse in parte
   36 [37]. Avvenne poi che là ovunque questa donna mi vedea,
   39 [40]. Contra questo avversario de la ragione si levoe un die
   41 [42]. Poi mandaro due donne gentili a me

4. *An introductory formula followed by a temporal indication:*

    6. Dico che in questo tempo che

    11. Dico che quando ella apparia da parte alcuna

    12. Ora, tornando al proposito, dico che poi che la mia beatitudine mi fue negata,

    29 [30]. Io dico che, secondo l'usanza d'Arabia

5. *Other beginnings:*

    18. Con ciò sia cosa che per la vista mia molte persone avessero compreso

    25. Potrebbe qui dubitare persona degna

    26. Questa gentilissima donna, di cui ragionato è ne le precedenti parole, venne in tanta grazia

    28 [29]. *Quomodo sedet sola civitas plena populo! facta est quasi vidua domina gentium.*

    37 [38]. Io venni a tanto per la vista di questa donna, che

    38 [39]. Ricovrai la vista di quella donna in sì nuova condizione, che molte volte ne pensava

NOTES

1. *Vita nuova di Dante Alighieri*, 16th ed., ed. Alessandro Torri (Livorno: Coi Tipi di Paolo Vannini, 1843); *La vita nuova*, ed. Carlo Witte (Leipzig: Brockhaus, 1876); *La vita nuova*, ed. T. Casini (Firenze: Sansoni, 1885); *La vita nuova di Dante Alighieri*, ed. Michele Barbi (Milano: Hoepli, 1907). Hereafter, Torri, Witte, Cassini, and Barbi, respectively.

Whether Barbi considers these forty-two divisions of the text of the *Vita nuova* paragraphs or chapters seems uncertain, for his phraseology shifts (see above, Appendix 2). Torri proposed the concept of "paragraph" on the basis (accurate, in our view) of the presence of such a term in *Vita nuova* 2.10. "Da questo passo scorgesi che l'Autore dettò in paragrafi distinti la presente opera; ed è per ciò che noi credemmo ben fatto apporre ai medesimi il numero progressivo; col quale metodo, e coll'aver anche numerate le poesie che vi sono comprese, rendonsi più facili i riscontri, stante la precisione delle citazioni" (Torri 3, n. 34). Witte objects to such a term (and concept): "Le altre sottodivisioni s'intenderanno facilmente dalla nostra tavola. L'infima di esse non è indicata nei testi a penna che per capoversi. Il primo a distinguerle per numeri apposti fu il Torri. Applicandovi l'ultimo detto della prima di queste sottodivisioni ('quelle parole, le quali sono scritte nella mia memoria sotto maggiori *paragrafi*') egli credè dover chimarle 'Paragrafi'. Non mi sembra però che questo nome corrisponda alle intenzioni dell'autore. Nelle altre sue opere, come nella Monarchia, nel Convivio ecc. Dante stesso chiamò

'*Capitoli*' le sottodivisioni dei libri ossia dei trattati. Capitoli ancora da non pochi antichi sono detti li Canti della Commedia, e non si vede perché l'autore dovesse aver scelto pel presente libretto, il più semplice di tutti i suoi componimenti, un altro termine, termine che ricorda un po' troppo la pedanteria degli Scolastici. Questi 'maggiori paragrafi', ossia rubriche, non vogliono dir altro, che: oggetti di maggiore importanza a paragone delle altre che infino a quel punto si trovavano registrate nel libro della memoria dell'autore. Si è dunque restituito il nome di 'Capitoli' a quello tutto arbitrario di paragrafi" (Witte, "Prolegomena," xvi–xvii). The present essay objects not only to the division of the *Vita nuova* into chapters but also to the application of the concept of chapter itself to the *Vita nuova*. It is noteworthy that whereas Witte refuses to use the term "paragrafi" even though Dante himself employs it in *Vita nuova* 2.10, he nevertheless takes literally another term used in the text, "proemio" (*Vita nuova* 28.2), in order to view the opening (*VN* 1, according to the Torri and Barbi editions) as a proem to the *libello* ("Prolegomena," xvii).

2. *La vita nuova di Dante Alighieri*, ed. Michele Barbi (Firenze: Bemporad, 1932). Concerning these chapter divisions, Cesare Segre writes: "I manoscritti sono discordi nelle divisioni, o talora ne sono privi. Quando s'erano ormai imposte le divisioni del Torri (Livorno, Vannini, 1843), venne il Witte a mutarle, e il Casini se ne sentì autorizzato a mutarle ancora. Oggi tutti adottano, col testo, le divisioni del Barbi, e per questo penso utile fornire una tavola di corrispondenza. Eccola: I Torri Barbi = *Proemio* Witte Casini; II Torri Barbi = I Witte Casini; III Torri Barbi = II+III Witte Casini; IV–XXV Torri Witte Casini Barbi; XXVI Casini Barbi = XXVI+XXVII Torri Witte; XXVII–XLII Casini Barbi = XXVIII–XLIII Torri Witte" ("Presentazione," xvii, n. 23, in *La vita nuova*, ed. T. Casini, rev. Cesare Segre [Firenze: Sansoni, 1962]).

3. Milman Parry, *L'epithète traditionelle dans Homère* (Paris: Société Éditrice Les Belles Lettres, 1928).

4. For a brief introduction to such issues and their implications for medieval studies, see the six essays, with pertinent bibliography, published in *Speculum* 65, no. 1 (1990).

5. Brian Stock, *The Implications of Literacy* (Princeton, N.J.: Princeton University Press, 1983). Walter Ong, *Orality and Literacy: The Technologizing of the Word* (London: Methuen, 1982). Although Ong does not mention Dante's *Vita nuova*, his analysis of orality / literacy is the basis for our observations about the evidence of these two cultures in Dante's work. Other major studies relevant to medieval manuscript culture include: M. T. Clanchy, *From Memory to Written Record: England, 1066–1307* (Cambridge: Harvard University Press, 1979); Elizabeth Eisenstein, *The Printing Press as an Agent of Change: Communications and Cultural Transformations in Early-Modern Europe*,

2 vols. (New York: Cambridge University Press, 1979); John Miles Foley, "Oral Literature: Premises and Problems," *Choice* 18 (1980b): 487–496; Werner Kelber, *The Oral and the Written Gospel: The Hermeneutics of Speaking and Writing in the Synoptic Tradition, Mark, Paul and Q* (Philadelphia: Fortress Press, 1983); Marshall McLuhan, *The Gutenberg Galaxy: The Making of Typographic Man* (Toronto: University of Toronto Press, 1962); Marshall McLuhan and Quentin Fiore, *The Medium Is the Message* (New York: Bantam Books, 1967); William Nelson, "From 'Listen, Lordings' to 'Dear Reader,'" *University of Toronto Quarterly* 46 (1976–1977): 111–124; George Steiner, *Language and Silence: Essays on Language, Literature, and the Inhuman* (New York: Athenaeum, 1967). In Italian, one may consult several of the essays in *Letteratura italiana*, vol. 2: *Produzione e consumo*, ed. Alberto Asor Rosa (Torino: Einaudi, 1983).

6. John Ahern, "The Reader on the Piazza: Verbal Duels in Dante's *Vita nuova*," *Texas Studies in Language and Literature* 32 (1970): 18–39, in which Ahern applies to two passages in the *Vita nuova* (14; 18) this distinction of real and conceived audiences, using respectively the designations "social" and "literate"; and "The New Life of the Book: The Implied Readers of the *Vita nuova*," *Dante Studies* 90 (1992): 1–16.

7. In VN 30.3 the narrator-protagonist says that he writes for his first friend ("questo mio primo amico a cui io ciò scrivo"), which is usually understood to indicate that the *Vita nuova* is dedicated to Guido Cavalcanti. Cavalcanti is also referred to as friend in 24.3, 24.6, 25.10, 30.3, and 32.1. At the same time, one should bear in mind that Guido's name never appears in the *Vita nuova*, that the first reference to him appears in 3.14, and that, most importantly, numerous are the text's addressees: the many poets to whom the poet-protagonist sends the first sonnet of the *Vita nuova*, asking them for an interpretation of the first dream (*Vita nuova* 3.9–12); the many who answer him (*Vita nuova* 3.14), including the three poets whose answers are extant (Terino of Castelfiorentino or Cino of Pistoia, Dante of Maiano, and Guido Cavalcanti); and implicitly any reader who understands the poetics of love at work in the *Vita nuova*. Furthermore, the narrator never addresses Cavalcanti directly; that is, in the way he addresses, for instance, the "Ladies who have understanding of love" in *Vita nuova* 19.4. Finally, those who do not understand the poet-narrator's poetics of love are excluded by the narrator: *Vita Nuova* 19.6, v. 14; 19.20–22; 25.10. In the *De vulgari eloquentia*, where Dante refers to Guido in four instances (1.13.4, 2.6.6, 2.12.3, 2.12.8), Dante resumes this narrative strategy of referring to someone as "friend." However, here Dante refers in the third person not to Guido but to himself as friend ("amicus eius") of Cino of Pistoia (*DVE* 1.10.2, 1.17.3, 2.2.8, 2.5.4, 2.6.6; see also 1.13.4). Dante's complete moving away from Guido takes place in *Inferno* 10, where the *Commedia*'s protagonist encounters Cavalcante de' Cavalcanti, Guido's father (but see also *Purg.* 11.94–99). For an in-depth

study of Dante's treatment of poets in his works, see Teodolinda Barolini, *Dante's Poets: Textuality and Truth in the* Comedy (Princeton, N.J.: Princeton University Press, 1984).

8. The formula "dico che" emphasizes the voice of the author-narrator within the text and is quite common: *Vita nuova* 2.7, 6.1, 7.7, 8.7, 10.1, etc.

9. The most common verb the poet-protagonist employs in introducing or referring to his poems (or parts of them) is "dissi" (*Vita nuova* 7.2, 8.3, 14.10, 15.4, 16.1, 16.6, 17.1, 20.2, 21.1, 23.16, 24.6, 26.4, 26.9, 32.3, 33.2, 34.3, 36.3, 37.3, 38.4, 39.6, 40.5, 40.6, 41.1), followed by "propuosi di dire" or "propuosi di dicere" (*Vita nuova* 8.2, 14.10, 15.3, 20.2, 22.7, 23.16, 26.4, 26.9, 27.2, 35.4, 40.5). The next most frequent verb to announce a poem's composition is "fare," either by itself or in conjunction with "propuosi di" (*Vita nuova* 12.9, 22.8, 31.1, 32.3, 33.4, 39.6, 40.5, 41.1). The least common expression, finally, includes a verbal form of "scrivere" (*Vita nuova* 3.9, 7.2, 13.7, 24.6, 34.3). Concerning the usage of the verb "dire" in introducing or referring to the poems, one must be aware of the strong links between this verb and the related verb "dittare" (*Purg.* 24.54), which in its Latin correspondent ("dictare"), as Ernest Curtius remarks, "from the time of Augustine . . . acquires the meaning 'to write, to compose', and particularly 'to write works of poetry' " (*European Literature and the Latin Middle Ages*, trans. Willard R. Trask [Princeton, N.J.: Princeton University Press, 1953], 76). More recent studies, however, have emphasized, as James J. Murphy writes, that the term ("dictare") "reveals a concern for the oral-written relationship" (*Rhetoric in the Middle Ages: A History of Rhetorical Theory from St. Augustine to the Renaissance* [Berkeley: University of California Press, 1974], 195, n. 5). That Dante at times uses within the same context of the *Vita nuova* not only "dire" and "scrivere" (24.6: "propuosi di scrivere per rima"; "dissi questo sonetto"; also 34.3) but also "dire" and "fare" (32.3, 33.2–4, 39.6, 40.5–6, 41.1) should not be construed to signify the identity of those three terms, "dire," "scrivere," and "fare."

10. Riccardo Ambrosini ("Dire," in *Enciclopedia dantesca* [Roma: Istituto della Enciclopedia Italiana fondata da Giovanni Treccani, 1970–1978], 2:467–470), remarks that "Più diffuso nella *Vita nuova* che nel *Convivio*, ma assente nella *Commedia*, è l'uso del verbo in relazione all' 'arte del dire parole per rima', con evidente riecheggiamento dell'*ars dictandi*." Ambrosini neither excludes nor privileges the oral character of the verb "dire" in the *Vita nuova*: "Quest'uso tecnico e traslato di dire . . . si riferisce non necessariamente a un 'parlare ad alta voce' " (469). These brief comments should be integrated with more recent studies on the *ars dictandi* and its relation to orality: see Murphy, *Rhetoric in the Middle Ages*, 195, n. 5.

11. For issues concerning memory vis-à-vis orality and literacy, see Mary J. Carruthers, *The Book of Memory: A Study of Memory in Medieval Culture* (Cambridge: Cambridge University Press, 1990), 10–12, 159–160, 297, etc.

12. On the origin, function, and importance of the *divisioni* in the *Vita nuova*, see Thomas C. Stillinger, *The Song of Troilus: Lyric Authority in the Medieval Book* (Philadelphia: University of Pennsylvania Press, 1992), 44–117.

13. Ong, *Orality and Literacy*, at 124 and 123. Isidore of Seville's description of a paragraph is worth quoting: "[The sign of] Paragraphus ponitur ad separandum res a rebus, quae in conexu concurrunt, quemadmodum in Catalogo loca a locis et [regiones a] regionibus, in Agone praemia a praemiis, certamina a diversis certaminibus separantur" (*Isidori Hispalensis Episcopi Etymologiarum sive originum libri* XX, 2 vols., ed. W. M. Lindsay [Oxford: Clarendon Press, 1911], Lib. 1.21.8).

14. Previous scholars had already expressed the same opinion; namely, that the manuscripts justify no division of the text into chapters. Casini writes in the introduction to his 1885 edition of the *Vita nuova*: "Nei codici e nelle prime edizioni la *V.N.* non ha alcuna partizione per capitoli o paragrafi; primo a introdurla fu il Torri, che vi distinse quarantatré paragrafi; e la sua divisione fu accettata da' seguenti editori fino al Witte" (xxii).

15. Barbi's concern for recording the differences in the divisions of the chapters established by Torri, Witte, and Casini goes as far as to literally interrupt the narrative in the middle of the chapter at *VN* 3.3 and *VN* 26.8 in order to insert the different number of chapter divisions.

16. Witte and Casini had already started the practice of numbering the lines of their editions of the *Vita nuova*—a practice that Barbi continued. The numbering of lines obviously varies from edition to edition and thus cannot provide any standard system of reference.

17. In emphasizing the principle of meaning for dividing the text, Barbi continues (while also modifying) a practice that Torri begins in his 1843 edition and that, in his view, enables him to divide the *Vita nuova* into two parts; namely, *in vita* and *in morte* of Beatrice, in close imitation of the scholars' division of Petrarch's *Canzoniere*. According to this division into two parts, therefore, Torri's edition of the *Vita nuova* carries within the text itself and on the running heads, "Part 1" (= ch. 1–28, in Torri's numbering: *in vita*) and "Part 2" (= ch. 29–43: *in morte*). Most obviously, some of the events of the *Vita nuova* unfold when Beatrice is alive while others occur when she is dead. However, to derive from such an obvious observation, and to impose a twofold partition on the text itself confuses a personal and thus subjective reading of a text with the structure of that text. In fact, in the preface to his 1884 edition of the *Vita nuova* (*La Vita nuova di Dante Alighieri*, 2 ed., ed. Alessandro D'Ancona [Pisa: Libreria Galileo già ff. Nistri, 1884]). D'Ancona proposes a fivefold partition of the text, which Casini accepts with some modifications, although the latter does not introduce it in his edition of the *Vita nuova*. Here follows D'Ancona's fivefold partition as modified by

Casini: first part, VN 1–17, "Amori giovanili e rime sulla bellezza fisica di Beatrice (1274–1287)"; second part, VN 18–27, "Lodi della bellezza spirituale di Beatrice (1287–1290)"; third part, VN 28–34, "La morte di Beatrice e le rime dolorose" (1290–1291); fourth part, VN 35–38, "L'amore e le rime per la donna gentile (1290–1293)"; fifth part, VN 39–42, "Ritorno all'amore e al culto di Beatrice estinta (1294)" (Casini, xxiii). A further indication of such a concern for dividing and subdividing the text is to be found in Witte's edition of the *Vita nuova*, although Witte's complex divisions never make it into the text: "Proemio. Parte prima. Periodo primo, Sezione prima, 1–4; Sezione seconda, 5–9; Sezione terza, 10–16; Periodo secondo. Sezione prima, 17–21; Sezione seconda, 22–23; Sezione terza, 24–28; Parte seconda. Sezione prima, 29–35; Sezione seconda, 36–39; Sezione terza, 40–43" (Witte, xli–xiv).

18. "Se non che pei bisogni dello studioso la divisione del testo in paragrafi non basta: ne occorre una più minuta in commi che dia modo di trovare alla prima un dato passo o una data voce, e che possa mantenersi inalterata in tutte le edizioni. Si doveva in questa suddistinzione tener conto soprattutto del senso, ma aver altresì riguardo da una parte al vantaggio dello studioso, che non vuol commi troppo lunghi, e dall'altra al gusto tipografico, che non vuol numerazioni troppo fitte e troppo irregolari " (Barbi, cccix).

19. VN 25 begins with: "Potrebbe qui dubitare persona degna. . . ." The adverb of place "qui" links the discussion on love's personification with the previous division, which also deals with Love's personified appearance to the protagonist. The close connection between the previous division and the following discussion supports the argument in favor of combining ch. 24 and 25, which Mario Marti proposes in his essay, " ' . . . l'una appresso de l'altra maraviglia' (Dante, *Vita nuova*, XXIV)" (*Giornale storico della letteratura italiana* 158, no. 544 [1991]: 481–583), on several grounds: (1) in ch. 25, the text repeatedly refers to ch. 24 ("Io dico d'Amore" [25.1]; "che io dica di lui" [25.2]; "Dico che lo vidi venire" [25.2]; "Dico anche di lui che ridea, e anche che parlava" [25.2]), thereby evincing textual and thematic unity; (2) the conclusion of ch. 25 ("E questo mio amico e io ne sapemo bene di quelli che così rimano stoltamente" [25.9]) links itself directly with the narrator's decision, in the previous paragraph, "propuosi di scrivere per rima a lo mio primo amico" (24.6); (3) a similar argument could be made from the beginning of ch. 26 ("Questa gentilissima donna, di cui ragionato è ne le precedenti parole"), since the narrator speaks of Beatrice not in ch. 25 but in ch. 24; and, finally, (4) a similar strategy is also at work in VN 12, where right after the division of the ballade (12.16), the glossator raises the possibility of someone's questioning his poetic practice and then defers to the actual ch. 25 for a clarification of his poetics (12.17). The same argument could also be made from the long division in 19.15–22 as well as

from that in 38.5–7 (where the narrator explains such terms as heart and soul), in 40.6–7, and in 41.2–9. Marti, therefore, argues that the present ch. 25 should not be considered a digression, however precious and useful, but rather a harmonious element in the *Vita nuova's* structure, which follows this pattern: prose account, poetry, and division, before Beatrice's death; and after Beatrice's death, prose account, division, and poetry.

20. One should document here Boccaccio's decision to remove the divisions from the text of the *Vita nuova* and to transcribe them along the margins: "Maraviglierannosi molti, per quello ch'io advisi, perché io le divisioni de' sonetti non ho nel testo poste, come l'autore del presente libretto le puose; ma a ciò respondo due essere state le cagioni. La prima, per ciò che le divisioni de' sonetti manifestamente sono dichiarazioni di quegli: per che piú tosto chiosa appaiono dovere essere che testo; e però chiose l'ho poste, non testo, non stando l'uno con l'altre bene mescolato. Se qui forse dicesse alcuno—e le teme de' sonetti e canzoni scritte da lui similmente si potrebbero dire chiosa, con ciò sia cosa che esse sieno non minore dichiarazione de quegli che le divisioni—, dico che, quantunque sieno dichiarazioni, non sono dichiarazioni per dichiarare, ma dimostrazioni delle cagioni che a fare lo 'ndussero i sonetti e le canzoni. E appare ancora queste dimostrazioni essere dello intento principale; per che meritamente testo sono, e non chiose. La seconda ragione è che, secondo che io ho già più volte udito ragionare a persone degne di fede, avendo Dante nella sua giovinezza composto questo libello, e poi essendo col tempo nella scienza e nelle operazioni cresciuto, si vergognava avere fatto questo, parendogli ancora troppo puerile; e tra l'altre cose di che si dolea d'averlo fatto, si ramaricava d'avere inchiuse le divisioni nel testo, forse per quella medesima ragione che muove me; là onde io non potendolo negli altri emendare, in questo che scritto ho, n'ho voluto sodisfare l'appetito de l'autore" (Barbi, xvi–xvii, note; Boccaccio's text appears in the manuscript Laurenziano XV, sup. 136, and in the Toledo manuscript of the Bibl. capitolare di Toledo, cajon 104, num. 6, Zelada).

21. Domenico Consoli, "Parola," in *Enciclopedia dantesca* , 4:318–320.

22. "Lat. *exemplu(m)* (da *eximere* 'mettere da parte perché serva di modello' " (Manlio Cortelazzo and Paolo Zolli, "Esempio," in *Dizionario etimologico della lingua italiana*, 5 vols. [Bologna: Zanichelli, 1979–1988]).

23. A little book, in that the written book derives from the book of memory. Dante always refers to the *Vita nuova* as a *libello* (*VN* 12.17, 25.9, 28.2; *Conv.* 2.2.2), preceded by the demonstrative *this* (except in *Conv.* 2.2.2), whereas the book of memory (*libro*) is marked by the definite article *the* ("In quella parte *del . . .*). Insofar as *this* written *libello* derives from *the* unwritten *libro* of memory, the *libello* is not merely a diminutive in form but not in meaning (De Robertis, 1988 Ricciardi volume listed below, this note); rather, it implies dependence and derivation, and as such the expression

falls under the category of the topos of modesty and humility (as does, for example, the *munuscula mea*, "my little gifts," of *Ep.* 13.10, for which see the note by Frugoni and Brugnoli in the 1979 Ricciardi volume). *Opere minori*, vol. 1, part 1, ed. Domenico De Robertis and Gianfranco Contini (Milano and Napoli: Ricciardi, 1984) (*Vita nuova*, ed. Domenico De Robertis; *Il fiore* and *Il detto d'amore*, ed. Gianfranco Contini); *Opere minori*, vol. 1, part 2, ed. Cesare Vasoli and Domenico De Robertis (Milano and Napoli: Ricciardi, 1988); *Opere minori*, vol. 2, ed. Pier Vincenzo Mengaldo (Milano and Napoli: Ricciardi, 1979) (*De vulgari Eloquentia*, ed. Pier Vincenzo Mengaldo; *Monarchia*, ed. Bruno Nardi; *Epistole*, ed. Arsenio Frugoni and Giorgio Brugnoli; *Egloge*, ed. Enzo Cecchini; *Questio de Aqua et Terra*, ed. Francesco Mazzoni).

24. Substance or meaning (*sentenzia*, from the Lat. *sententia*). For Augustine (*De dialectica* 2), for instance, *sententia* applies "to any set of combined words which express any sort of complete meaning." The same usage is found in Capella, IV.390–392 (*De dialectica*, ch. 2, n. 1).

25. This criterion should not be taken as self-evident, for in a few manuscripts the poems are not divided according to lines but are written as prose.

26. Barbi's ch. 17 appears even less justifiable as it is presently because it counts only seven lines in his and also De Robertis's editions.

27. Marti, " . . . L'una appresso de l'altra maraviglia." The account in *VN* 26 in fact links itself with those previous episodes in which the narrator has spoken of Beatrice, particularly with the protagonist's encounter with Beatrice and Vanna (*VN* 24), in which Beatrice is described as a "marvel" walking along the street. Focusing on the "mode of praising" Beatrice (*VN* 26:3), the narrator thus resumes "the new matter" (*VN* 17) already announced in *VN* 18.6 ("those words that praise my lady"). In contrast with most other chapters (except ch. 18 and 25), this present account neither is introduced by a temporal phrase nor contains chronological or circumstantial elements. Its position at this juncture of the narrative, therefore, is justified by the narrator's decision to resume the "mode of praising" Beatrice (*VN* 26:3) primarily through the description of her effects on those who saw her and knew of her, including himself (*VN* 27). This renewed focus on the praise of Beatrice occurs just before the announcement of her death (*VN* 28).

28. We recommend that Barbi's *VN* 6 ("Dico che in questo tempo che questa donna era schermo di tanto amore, quanto da la mia parte, sì mi venne una voluntade di volere ricordare lo nome di quella gentilissima ed accompagnarlo di molti nomi di donne, e spezialmente del nome di questa gentile donna") be combined with the previous chapter, because of chapter 6's brevity (only eleven lines in Barbi's and De Robertis's editions) and more importantly because chapter 5 (which is also rather short: twenty-two lines) is strictly linked with it: " . . . feci per lei certe cosette per rima . . . e però le lascerò tutte, salvo che alcuna cosa ne scriverò che pare sia loda di lei"

[VN 5.4]). We also recommend that VN 11 be combined with the previous chapter on two grounds: (1) VN 10 announces the topic of Barbi's VN 11. (2) the adverb "quando" marks neither a specific time nor a transition of time, but rather an iterative action; and, finally, (3) because of the brevity of the two chapters. The introductory formula "Dico che" or "Io dico che" cannot be used as a criterion for forming chapters, since it is weakened by its high frequency within the text itself (VN 2.7, 6.1, 7.7, 8.7, 10.1, 11.1, 12.1, 12.17, 13.10, 14.4, 14.7, 14.14, 15.8, 16.11, 19.2, 19.5, 19.17, 23.2, 24.2, 25.2, 25.10, 26.8, 31.3, 34.4, 34.5, 38.6, 39.3).

29. "Onde prima dicerò come ebbe luogo ne la sua partita, e poi n'assegnerò alcuna ragione per che questo numero fue a lei cotanto amico" (VN 28.3 in Barbi's ed.).

30. On this concept, see primarily Paul Ricoeur, "Narrative Time," *Critical Inquiry* (Fall 1980): 169–190; and *Time and Narrative*, 3 vols., trans. Kathleen Blamey and David Pelauer (Chicago: University of Chicago Press, 1984–1988) (=*Temps et récit* [Paris: Seuil, 1983]).

31. The temporal phrase "Poi che," followed by a complete, dependent clause, marks the beginning of seven of the present chapters. In all its other occurrences, this temporal phrase cannot mark a break as strong as to call for a new chapter: "Poi che" occurs only an additional time at the beginning of a sentence, but in a direct discourse (VN 18.8); it occurs ("poi che") four additional times in the middle of the sentence (VN 18.3, 23.30, 24.10, 26.2); four times it is preceded by the conjunction "E" at the beginning of a sentence (VN 12.2, 18.3, 18.6, 32.2); finally, in one instance it is preceded by the adversative conjunction "Ma" (VN 18.4).

32. "Appresso che" occurs only here.

33. "Poscia che" occurs only here.

Ronald L. Martinez

"Nasce il Nilo"

JUSTICE, WISDOM, AND DANTE'S CANZONE "TRE DONNE INTORNO AL COR MI SON VENUTE"

As Dante's principal lyric expression of the theme of exile, "Tre donne intorno al cor mi son venute" has received steady if not lavish attention since modern study of it began in the last century.[1] With a few demurrals (Contini, for example) the poem has been deemed an artistic and moral triumph, in which the speaker meets exile and isolation with fortitude, indeed grandeur. Although interpretations of the poem's difficulties are varied, even recent contributions (e.g., Poole, Mercuri) do not much modify this dominant critical stance toward the poem.

In addition to pondering the problems posed by Drittura's unnamed offspring,[2] writers on the poem are called on to pronounce on the speaker's own intimations of a fault, perhaps political, perhaps erotic, that he feels he has expiated but that still stands between him and what he desires (stanza 5).[3] The exact nature of the poet's relation to exile and his adversaries remains obscure, however, while the poet's political and ethical situation seems at an impasse, such as we find, for example, in the *rime petrose*.[4] Indeed, Pézard has remarked how muted are the poem's affirmations; the promised redemption of the *sangue* of Justice and Amor (vv. 70–72) remains distant; the poet's desire, cut off from its precise goal, its *segno*, seems to be leading, in the fourth stanza, to death; even his willingness for reconciliation with

115

his enemies is frustrated (second *tornata*). It does not seem that views of the poem as a triumph of moral heroism (Barbi) or as a decisive conversion leading to the synthesis of the *Commedia* (Paasonen) can be sustained on a close study.

In addition to the puzzles of the implied narrative, the poem bristles with linguistic and rhetorical difficulties: the poem's *ornatus difficilis*, characterized by the explicitly allegorical language of the first *tornata* and the vivid metaphorical language of the second, constellates the text with equivocal terms and amphibologies.[5] At the same time, the poem intensively exploits synechdoche, the trope of fragmentation: not only do parts suggest wholes (Drittura described by her "nudo braccio," the "treccia bionda" of her daughter), but the elements invoked (the *colonna* of Drittura's arm, the *rocca* promised by Amor) sketch a lost wholeness glimpsed by the poet. In the face of a Justice "discinta e scalza" (v. 26) such fragmentary details suggest a poetics of at once wreckage and hope; not by accident, this same technique governs the references in the poem to the Golden Age, when Justice had reigned supreme. The vivid use of synechdoche means that while terms (including the identities of Drittura's offspring) elude precise definition, their range of suggestion is greatly expanded.

My own attempt to meet the challenges posed by "Tre donne" will be guided by work done by Durling and me on the *petrose*. We argue that the *rime petrose* mark a decisive step in Dante's development as man and poet, one that led in many respects to the *Commedia*. The concentration on the natural world and on concepts from natural science, especially astronomical and cosmological ones; and the attempt to make the stanzaic and metrical forms of the poems imitative of specific aspects of the cosmos, developing parallels between poem, cosmos, and the human body—these are aspects of the *petrose* that illuminate the poetics of "Tre donne."

In fact Dante drew on much of the same source material for the *petrose* and "Tre donne," including Lucan's *Pharsalia*, Seneca's *Naturales quaestiones*, and Boethius's *Consolatio philosophiae*; moreover, as we argued for the *petrose* and for "Donne ch'avete," there is in "Tre donne" a specifically Neoplatonic understanding of the relation of macrocosm and microcosm and of the hierarchy of being.[6] In both the *petrose* and "Tre donne," the exact description of solar motion proves important to unlocking the poems both thematically and as formal structures: in "Tre donne" the relevant natural scientific information (strongly mediated by scriptural and exegetical materials) is the lore regarding the Nile river.[7]

Traces of the *petrose* have of course been detected in the language of "Tre donne."[8] The links go well beyond the lexical, however. A key structural principle of "Io son venuto," the repeated turn to the condition of the speaker, marked by a coordinate conjunction (at times with adversative force) in identical position in the *sirma* of every stanza,[9] returns in "Tre donne" in the dramatic shift to the first-person voice of the speaker beginning stanza 5. In "Io son venuto" the shift has precise implications for how the canzone imitates the natural cosmos and serves to draw the essential contrast and parallels of the natural setting and the speaker; in "Tre donne" the delayed turn to the first-person voice of the poet cues our understanding that Dante has, as Bárberi-Squarotti and Boyde have observed, parsed himself out among the personifications of the first four stanzas of the poem.[10] Indeed the shift to the "Io" in "Tre donne," bringing the content of the poem to impinge fully on him, fulfills a key category of the *petrose*: underscoring the speaker as a microcosm of the entire cosmos, focusing the natural and metaphysical realms within the little world of his body and mind. In "Tre donne" the speaker's heart provides the court where the exiled Drittura comes to Amor; but it is the excursus spoken by Drittura in stanza 3 that most sharply defines the poem as a textual microcosm. In having Justice generate her offspring in (most readers agree) the Earthly Paradise, at the source of the Nile, Dante follows the tradition that makes of Paradise a garden of virtues in the mind as well as a remote place on the earth.[11] The topographical choice of the headwaters of the Nile announces the poem's strategic mediation of inner and outer worlds, psychology and cosmology, moral virtue and natural order.

Both the *petrose* and "Tre donne" have a specific function as artifacts. We argued that in the *petrose* the making of microcosms itself advances the speaker's transcendence of his predicament; in "Tre donne" a historically different, if in some respects structurally similar, crisis rages, and the poet's best solution again proves to be a test of craft. This time, however, the conversion of form into content has the goal of "showing Virtue her own feature," of revealing the "visible image of goodness" (*exemplar honesti*), as Lucan puts it (*Pharsalia* 9.563).[12] That is, of showing how both poem and poet are in some sense embodiments of the virtue cast out by the world: Justice.[13]

As I have anticipated, the most dramatic gesture in the poem comes in the first line of stanza 4 (v. 73), with the shift to the speaker's first person utterance:

> E io, che ascolto nel parlar divino
> consolarsi e dolersi
> così alti dispersi[14]

In the terms of the *Convivio*, as Philosophy is found when her "lover" or "friend" is discovered (4.30.5: "l'anima in cui essa alberga") so Justice is found in the "casa d'amico" that is the poet's heart; conversely, the poet becomes the vessel of exiled Justice. The poet's situation parallels that of Drittura in a negative sense but in a positive one as well: if the poet's heart is the last refuge of justice, it is only by virtue of bearing Amor and Drittura ("così alti dispersi") in his heart that he can maintain his dignity (v. 76: "onor mi tegno").

But once out of his inner world, the speaker is frustrated, cut off from the "segno" of his desire (v. 81–82), unable to secure peace from the Blacks (v. 104). Boyde's distinction of transferred and proper might then also correspond to different aspects of the speaker's possession of justice, expressed in terms of the traditional distinction between habit and perfect operation: that is, between willing, and actually doing, justice.[15] The distinction is echoed in Dante's discussion of justice in *Monarchia* 1.11.6–7, where justice faces two kinds of obstacle: not being perfectly willed ("contrarietatem . . . in velle") and not being accomplished for lack of power ("contrarietatem . . . in posse").[16]

Seen in these terms, the arrival of Drittura in the poet's heart and her recognition there by Amor, who "converts" his desire toward her might suggest that the poet comes to love justice and wills to do it.[17] The text goes on to suggest that the poet does reach out to do justice to others: he repents of a fault, a *colpa* (v. 88–90), and is willing to seek reconciliation with his enemies. He is moved both by concord, one of the "parts" of justice, and by charity, a virtue that, like justice, reaches out to others.[18] But these same passages suggest the poet's lack of power to realize what he wills with respect to his beloved *segno* and his enemies.[19] Although the poet possesses justice in his heart, he lacks the power to do justice to others.[20]

That the poem's most significant transition also maps the double vector of justice (possessed within, extended to others) suggests that the poem itself, as well as the poet, embodies the virtue of justice. This might be expressed thematically (the poem laments the exile of Justice) and in the poem's form, its verbal disposition: according to Aristotle, justice, like the beautiful, is a "proportion" (*Ethics* 5.3.1131b16). Perhaps the best reason for invoking the "justice" of beauty in "Tre donne" is the oft-remarked parallel between Drittura and the "bella donna" who typifies the canzone in the first *tornata* (vv. 91–92).[21] Indeed the pairing of Justice and the canzone is firmly buttressed by the poem's symmetry: Dante echoes the opening rhymes of the canzone, used of Drittura and her offspring (vv. 2–7: *fore, Amore, core*) with the final rhymes of the first *tornata*, used of the canzone's beauty, or "flower" (vv. 99–100: *fori, amorosi cori*). Such symmetry makes the canzone a verbal "sorella" of Drittura and pairs the poem's subject of justice with the sign of its external beauty, the flower.

But the canzone as "bella donna" is also sharply distinct from the downcast Drittura; the poem, received by a "uom di virtù," is asked to show "color' novi" (v. 98). Such an outcome seems to echo the future prospects for Drittura and her *gente* announced in vv. 69–72, so that the poem in "new colors" might represent a vision of Drittura reinstated; but this conclusion, though valid, is premature.[22] Rather, the distinction of Drittura and the canzone in "color' novi" follows the dichotomy of sententious content and formal beauty expressed in stanzaic construction and rhetorical *ornatus*.[23] Drittura's personification of upright virtue is implicit in the fact that she is a *donna* in and of herself ("sol di sè par donna"), for it was formulaic that probity, *honestas*, should be valued for itself alone.[24] Set against Drittura's austere sorrow the canzone decked out in "color' novi" might seem superficial: but in fact the poem's final self-presentation (vv. 91–100) dismantles the dichotomy of probity and beauty. By adorning and "showing" itself only to worthy readers, the poem sifts its audience with a moral criterion: those who ask ("e' ti priega") rather than those who sieze ("man piega") will be served. And the canzone is bidden to show more than outward color: the "inward parts" previously denied ("a tutta gente niega"), the parts that represent the profound *sensus* of the poem ("dolce pome"), will also be opened to the worthy. Not only does Dante fashion the poem's visible beauty ("il fior, ch'è bel di fori") for the sake of kindling the heart's desire for justice: he specifies that the full beauty of the canzone *will not appear* if the poem's justice is not perceived: there is no allowance here for an appreciation of the poem divorced from its meaning. But if the poem's "justice" of proportion is seen, then the poem will be transformed and literally appear in a new light.

"Tre donne" thus modifies the usual dichotomy of poetic *bellezza* (= *ornatus*) and *bontà* (= *sententia*) in the direction of identifying beauty as an essential property of the subject treated, the virtue of justice.[25] That the "beauty" of an abstraction is precisely its moral worth is also the burden of *Convivio* 3.15.11, where morality is said to be the "beauty" of philosophy, of the love for wisdom.[26] Displaying this "order of the moral virtues" as "beauty" is one of the specific artistic achievements of "Tre donne," and the final reference to the canzone showing "color' novi" should be thought of in terms of high medieval aesthetics, where the beautiful is conceived as a combination of *suavitas coloris*, the congruence of parts, and the splendor or radiance emitted by the formal perfection of the thing perceived.[27]

The identification of content and form in "Tre donne" may itself be a consequence of the poem's focus on justice, described by Aristotle as the sum of all the virtues, and by patristic writers as their harmony.[28] For Albertus Magnus and Aquinas, justice is preexcellent among the moral virtues precisely because it seeks the good of others and participates, by virtue of its desire for the rational, in the ordering of all things to their final ends.[29] But justice was also thought preexcellent or "brightest" (*praeclarissima*) because of Aristotle's comparison of it (*Ethics* 5.1.1129b) to the morning and evening stars, a comparison Albertus notes as prompted by the beauty of justice ("propter suum decorem").

If Drittura is indeed natural justice, then the coordination of moral virtue and beauty in "Tre donne" gives additional reason for taking Drittura as another name for Astraea, the "starry" *virgo* of Justice, as some scholars have proposed;[30] it also warrants the poem's elliptical, fragmentary allusions to the Golden Age, when justice was strongest (*potissima*): a power now lost, but potentially existing in the future.

Dante's figure of a sorrowing Justice is a descendant of the Astraea-Virgo-Justice of Virgil's Fourth Eclogue and Roman literary and legal traditions. The poem's allusion to the Golden Age has usually been based on Amor's prophecy of a *gente* who will restore the bridle and whip of moral self-control; this "people" evokes the "gens aurea" of Virgil's Fourth Eclogue and anticipates the "prima gente" of *Purgatorio* 1.24, who will once again see the constellation of the four virtues.[31]

The destitution of Drittura "povera in veste e a cintura," though a sign of exile, is also proof of her residence in a virtuous community free of luxury (such as Florence where Cacciaguida lived, a city—as d'Arco Silvio Avalle showed—defined with the topics of an austere Golden Age).[32] But these references are elusive, mere gleams of future possibility.[33]

However, in opening chapter 11 of the *Monarchia* with the reference to the return of Astraea and the citation of Virgil's Fourth Eclogue ("redit et virgo"), Dante implies that when justice is at its most powerful ("cum iustitia in eo potissima est") it shines and gleams—hence the emphasis on the name *Astraea* and reference to the "golden" centuries ("que etiam Aurea nuncupabant.") The notion is confirmed by the procession of luminaries in the same chapter: Dante cites Aristotle's comparison of justice to the morning and evening stars (*Ethics* 5.1) and then tops it by introducing the equinoctial balance of sun and moon ("Phebe similis, fratrem dyametraliter intuenti . . .") as a figure for the coming plenitude of justice. Torraca long ago observed that the encounter of Drittura and Amor appears closely linked to this passage of the *Monarchia*, where Dante has charity sharpen, clarify and strengthen justice (*acuit et dilucidat, vigorabit*); especially striking is the similarity in the language for the state of Love's weapons in "Tre donne" (*turbate, lucente*) and the language of the *Monarchia* for the states of Justice both impeded (*obnubilata*) and at maximum, in "fulgore sue puritatis." We find the same contrast in Dante's terms for the varying appearance of Wisdom to her lover in "Amor tu vedi ben" (vv. 77–78): "Tu sai che il ciel sempr'è *lucente* e chiaro, / E quanto in sé non si *turba* già mai." That is, eternal virtues like wisdom or justice may appear "tarnished," but this is always an effect of how they are perceived (or poorly served) by fallible human subjects. That the arrow of Amor in "Tre donne" will one day shine and gleam ("un dì sarà lucente") thus fits the pattern announcing the return of the shining "gens aurea" and tends to confirm the view that the poem itself will one day shine like Justice.[34]

Treating moral virtues as stars is of course a commonplace Dante frequently invoked.[35] Still, the identification of Drittura with natural justice and Astraea is especially fitting in light of the tradition that takes Astraea as the *beauty* of natural justice, as in Bernard Silvestris's commentary on the *Aeneid*, where Astraea is identified as Venus, the natural harmony and justice of the cosmos ("equalem mundanorum proportionem"): that is, precisely its beauty.[36] The relation established here between Venus and Astraea may lie behind the claim of Drittura to be the "sister" of Love's mother (v. 35: "son suora a la tua madre")—and thus, according to most commentators, the sister of Venus.[37] Such a role for Justice-Astraea also informs the relation between Drittura and the canzone itself, which will be beautiful and "radiant" when it displays its "color' novi": since in medieval aesthetics *color* implies light, new "color" must be the new light, the new radiance, of a justice that is *praeclarissima*.[38]

The full implication of the display of new "colors" to the worthy is that the poem, rightly understood, will become radiant: not through its rhetorical ornament but through its very form, as Dante's canzone "Amor tu vedi ben" is said to give off light ("la novità che per tua forma luce") by virtue of its intricate stanzaic form.[39] It is indeed implicit that a fully restored Drittura would be Astraea, the starry one, shining brightly as in *Monarchia* 1.11.1–2 in the presence of the Monarch, or at the approach of the "sun of Justice" (Henry VII in Dante's *Epistle* 7.5–6). Short of that palingenesis, however, the poem also shines for the reader who can perceive how justice is embodied in the poem itself. This sudden radiance, transforming the poem, would equal in intensity the poem's sudden turn to the poet beginning the fifth stanza; but where that shift brings the burden of Drittura's plight to the speaker, the prospective brightening of the *canzone* is rather like the action of justice itself, perfected in seeking the good of others.[40] Only in this way can the poet, frustrated as a political actor, reach out and "do justice" for the common good.

To conceive of "Tre donne" in light of its function as an artifact reshuffles our priorities in approaching the poem. Examination of the poem as a microcosm of justice may begin with the midpoint, Drittura's account of the source of the Nile, which has not been much discussed.[41] The central *sirma*, the focus of the whole poem for *formal* reasons, proves also to represent the source of the poet's *mente*, the inner chamber of his soul and place where his "divinity" is most manifest; it is thus also the space—mental and poetic—from which springs the poem's power for both self-consolation and moral self-challenge.[42]

Given traditional accounts of the Nile as one of the four rivers of Paradise, it must be in some sense an extension of the "fountain" of the four rivers, Wisdom, which flows directly *ex ore altissimi* (Wis. 24:7).[43] Identification of the source river itself as the stream (or *like* the stream) of creative wisdom is consequential for the canzone, for justice has, in Dante's culture, a strong traditional relation to wisdom.[44] The association of the two virtues is scriptural, as Dante, who incorporated the opening verse of Wisdom (1:1: "Diligite iustitiam, qui iudicatis terram") into the *Commedia* (*Paradiso* 18.91, 93), well knew.[45] Aquinas linked the two virtues as supreme in their spheres; as wisdom is the chief of the intellectual virtues, justice is the greatest of the moral.[46] The association was well disseminated enough for Justice to appear as the "daughter" or "emanation" of wisdom in Lorenzetti's fresco in the Sala dei Nove (reflecting Wisdom's status as "mater omnium virtutum").[47]

But a number of features specific to "Tre donne" also point in the direction of closely associating wisdom and justice. First in importance is the clear derivation of Drittura from Boethius's Lady Philosophy, herself usually taken as a figure of Sapientia in the Middle Ages,[48] Boethius's Lady Philosophy and Dante's Drittura are more than casually related: the torn garments of Drittura echo Lady Philosophy's mantle, rent by the disputing philosophical sects (*Consolatio philosophiae* 1.1.3);[49] Drittura and her host, the poet, are in exile, as Lady Philosophy herself is condemned ("quoque mecum rea") along with her disciple Boethius (1.3); even the "scene" of the poem, in which the three ladies sit around the poet's heart (v. 2: "seggensi di fore") may reflect the scene of Boethius's narrative, usually represented as occurring in his chambers, but also in his own mind (1.5), where he is visited by Philosophy, who sits next to him (1.1: "In extrema lectuli mei parte consedit")—all these aspects link "Tre donne" to Boethius's text and make the link of wisdom and justice compelling.[50] The shift to the "Io" beginning stanza 5 of the canzone is itself an instance of first-person report justified by Dante's criteria in *Convivio* 1.2.13, where one of the examples is Boethius.[51]

The oft-remarked vividness and "concreteness" of Dante's personification of Drittura thus owes much to Lady Philosophy as the intimate teacher and confidante (a distinctly maternal figure) of Boethius.[52] But the treatment of Drittura in specifically erotic terms depends more on the biblical and exegetical tradition of Wisdom as an object of love, as *druda* and *dilecta soror*, rather than *omnium mater* (Wis. 7:12).[53] This is much the same complex of associations that Dante focuses on the Philosophy of the *Convivio*, of course: the relation of the poet's Amor to Drittura in "Tre donne" should generally be seen as a pendant to the relationship between Amor and Sapientia elaborated in the second and third books of that work.[54]

The tradition of Solomon's Wisdom as the beloved *columba* of the Song of Songs authorizes the strongly erotic representation of Drittura and, in the first *tornata*, of the canzone itself.[55] The strongly marked gender of the name *Drittura* is part of a trend toward even greater concreteness and realism: in a sense, the strong gendering of Drittura and her misfortune are but two aspects of the same thing, indices of the tragic history tarnishing the radiance ("fulgor puritatis") of justice with violence and impotence.[56] This tragic, historical aspect of Drittura brings her into relation with an iconography of downcast female figures, such as the widowed Jerusalem of Lamentations[57] and Justice found trussed at the feet of Tyranny in Lorenzetti's fresco in the Sala dei Nove.[58]

Like her exile, the poverty and vulnerability of Drittura must reflect—given the shift beginning stanza 5—on the poet; and indeed Dante's poverty during the early years of his exile was acute.[59] The same paradox that makes Drittura, as a virtue, "sol di sé donna" operates here to exalt poverty in a manner reminiscent of Franciscan values. Indeed Dante's Drittura has much in common with the later representation in the *Commedia* of Poverty as the bride of Francis: a figure whose very loathsomeness because poor and outcast triggers a paradoxical language of sexual desire.[60]

The disastrous historical aspect of Drittura in stanzas 1 and 2, like that of the speaker in stanza 5, are in sharp and deliberate contrast to the excursus in stanza 3, where Drittura describes generations that are "ideal," indeed markedly Neoplatonic, in their unfolding. Recognizably Neoplatonic in origin, for example, is the greater distance of each successive child from the source, Drittura (v. 50: *da lato*; v. 54: *lontana*).[61] The detail implies, of course, the stepwise descent of levels of being from the One, hinted at in this case by the vertical arrangement of sun, leaf, shadow, and water (cf. especially vv. 46–48, discussed below).[62] Neoplatonic, too, is the optically "reflective" manner of Drittura's reproduction, a metaphor for cognitive "operation" leading to the intellectual "generation" of concepts.[63] Such a process of "reflective" generation recalls how the philosophical mind contemplates itself in contemplating truth, described in the *Convivio* in a passage Foster and Boyde cite as a parallel to Drittura's generations in "Tre donne," and which also has Neoplatonic roots.[64] The *Convivio* passage and that of "Tre donne" as well have affinities with Boethius's account of the procession of cosmic mind (*mens*) and the world soul (*anima mundi*) from the One, as presented in the gnomic central verses of *Consolatio* 3, m. 9 (v. 15–17), as well as anticipating Dante's adaptation of Boethius's verses to describe the individual's act of self-consciousness in *Purgatorio* 25.73–75 ("sé in sé rigira . . ."); that Boethius's verses can illustrate both macrocosm and human microcosm is typical of the Neoplatonic tradition and of Dante's poetics here in "Tre donne."[65]

Stanza 3 thus represents "ideal" Justice and her "parts" brought forth from the creative fount of Wisdom as personified virtues or goddessess: terms Dante himself uses to explain Platonic ideas in the *Convivio*.[66] This "emanationist" scheme is not necessarily recondite in Dante's milieu. In Lorenzetti's frescoes in Siena, whose program has been traced to Aristotelian and Thomist sources, Justice nevertheless "proceeds" from Sapientia, and Concord (one of the "parts" of Justice in accounts of the virtues) from Justice.[67] Such schemes, both in the "informal" forms in which the parts or subdivisions of virtues are referred to as "daughters" (cf. *filiae acediae, filiae superbia*, etc.) as well as in more ambitious schemes, such as those found among discussions of *Iustitia* by the jurists, owe much to Neoplatonic conceptions of "ideal" mental generation.[68] Perhaps the most striking parallel to Dante's generation of virtues from the stream of Wisdom, one with a fully Neoplatonic structure and that is also an allegory of pagan myth (*integumentum*)—though probably not directly known to Dante—is the birth of Minerva, or Wisdom, from the head of Jove in Remigius of Auxerre's commentary on Martianus Capella, which Remigius describes using a *catena* of texts from the books of Wisdom: Remigius has Pallas descend from on high (cf. Ecclus. 24:7); she is born from the head of Jove because Wisdom is generated from the mind of God (Ecclus. 24:5); and she has no mother because "eternal wisdom" has its beginning in the divine substance.[69]

The generations of stanza 3 suggest not only a Neoplatonic form but also adopt three fundamental, virtually archetypal, Neoplatonic terms for origination:[70] parthenogenesis (or "immaculate conception")

itself, by which Drittura and her offspring procreate; the river, itself
here said to be "born"; and the sun, the "gran lume."[71] If we grant
the Neoplatonic logic of the fable, we can transfer to the sun its
Neoplatonic attributes as we find them, in Cicero's familiar *Somnium
Scipionis*: the sun is the "mind of the universe" and "heart of the sky";
the "chief and regulator of the other lights" and a "fount of celestial
light."[72] With specific relevance to "Tre donne," both in Neoplatonic
lore and Aristotelian thought (and in Christian cosmology as well),
the sun is the remote cause of earthly fecundation ("tutte le cose
col suo calor vivifica," Dante says of the sun in *Conv.* 3.12.7), while
the Nile typifies the nourishing and fecundating power of water and
earth.[73] When we register the fact that the "conceptions" of Drittura's
offspring require the action of both sun and water—the ladies *reflect*
their optical images in the river—then the cooperation of vivifying
sun, fecundating river, and "optical" generations of Drittura appears
as a version of the divine marriage or *hieros gamos* between sky and
earth: in this case dramatizing the procession of justice from wisdom
both in the divine mind and in the human microcosm.[74]

The esoteric account of the Nile source is underscored by its central
structural position in the poem, which includes all possible mid-
points—verses 45–46 (midpoint of the five stanzas); verses 50–51
(midpoint of the poem including first *tornata*); and verses 54–55
(midpoint including both *tornate*). Most significant for "Tre donne"
is the suggestion that the site of Drittura's generation is ulterior
and "higher" with respect to the space containing the action of
stanzas 1, 2, and 4. This site is in a sense the textual-microcosmic
equivalent of the traditional datum that the source of the Nile was
secret:[75] if the events in stanza 3 are "in" the poet, they are in
his deepest, highest "mind."[76] The shift in stanza 3, cued by Drittura's expression "Tu sai . . . ," works as do certain digressions in the
Commedia, where speakers break away from the dramatic foreground
to clarify points of dogma or lore.[77] Like Virgil's exposition to the
pilgrim, asking him to imagine the site of Jerusalem in his mind,
"dentro raccolto" (*Purg.* 4.67–68), Drittura's shift requires not only a
change from a dramatic to a discursive mode, but also a movement
above and within (*intra et supra*) to the sphere of contemplation in
the mind.[78]

One consequence of the shift at verses 44–45 is to mark Drittura's
account as a formal microcosm of the canzone itself. The ten-line

sirma, which encloses the excursis on the Nile, is also the measure of the first *tornata*: it represents the modular unit of the canzone. But this relation of the *tornata* to the *sirma*—conventional to the canzone form—is remarkable in the case of "Tre donne" because ten is also the square root of the number of lines in the whole canzone (excluding the second *tornata*). "Tre donne" alone among Dante's canzoni exhausts the traditional full measure of one hundred, the number of completeness otherwise reserved for the *Commedia*.

The modularity of the *sirma* emerges further in its syntactical subdivisions. Although the *sirma* has no formal subdivisions, no *versus*, Contini notes that if we except stanza 4, the *sirma* is consistently subdivided into groups of four and three lines (4, 3, 3): this means that four stanzas have, if we add in the *piedi*, five discrete "parts." The full potential of this subdivision of the *sirma* is realized only in stanza 3, where each grouping of lines corresponds to the "origin" of one of the three ladies. In stanza 3, the first line (the *concatenatio* of the *sirma* with the *piedi*) serves as the incipit to Drittura's discourse; each subsequent three-line section describes the origin of one of the ladies. The second "birth" is that of Drittura's daughter (*generai*); the third that of Drittura's grandchild (*generò*). The "birth" of Drittura locates itself in the first line of the first group, that is, with the birth of the Nile itself.

The arrangement of the three terms for birth, *nascere* for the Nile and two instances of *generare*, is clearly motivated: the first occurs in the first line of the first group, the second in the second, the third in the third. The order of terms in the three groups of three lines graphs the procession of each entity from the previous. The scheme is consistent with the distribution of modifiers indicating spatial relationships (which, as we saw, articulate the Neoplatonic "emanation" scheme) in which the third *donna* is marked as *lontana* in the third line of the third group; the second *donna*, as *allato* in the second line of the second group. In this way, the subject of the *sirma*—the procession of the three ladies—is tightly wedded to the syntactic subdivisions. The Neoplatonic logic of emanation, by which virtues are generated from the stream of Wisdom, is embodied in the poem's stanzaic form and rhetorical *ornatus*, so that the *bellezza* and *bontà* of the poem are fused, exemplifying the "justice" of rational order.[79]

But a difficulty in the central lines of the poem has not yet been explained. The verses that mention the sun (vv. 46–48)—

> di fonte nasce il Nilo picciol fiume
> quivi dove'l gran lume
> toglie a la terra del vinco la fronda

—have been construed in several ways. The simplest is that the equatorial sun withers the osiers and deprives the earth of their shade.[80] Another reading, taking *fronda* as grammatical subject, has the leaves take the sun from the earth: that is, casting shadows.[81] In the rhetorically bolder reading preferred by Contini and Foster-Boyde, the sun directly overhead deprives the ground of the shade cast by the osiers (*ombra* itself is elided, and must be understood); this reading emphasizes the hierarchy of a Neoplatonic reading of the *sirma:* sun, leaf, shade, ground.[82]

If the reading preferred by recent editors is adopted, then Dante's lines might identify a specific time or times when the sun is directly overhead. Granted that the source of the Nile was placed at the Equator, then the passage might indicate two occasions during the year when the sun is directly overhead at noon: the vernal and autumnal equinoxes. A sun near the zenith resonates with the figurative noonday sun of the celestial paradise;[83] Dante's choice would thus suggest an equinoctial configuration symbolizing the equity of justice.

But Dante distinguishes between the generations in perfect tense (*generai, generò*) and the birth of the Nile, in the present (*nasce*). And like the birth of the river, the action of the sun is given in the present tense (*toglie*). *Quivi* in verse 48 fixes no specific moment, and verses 47–48 are periphrastic, defining place and circumstances. A faithful translation of the sense of verses 47–48 might be: "there where the sun ["habitually," understood] removes shadows from the ground." That is, the expression takes for granted the regular and cyclical movements of the sun. The precise referent for Dante's phrase is thus *part of the cycle of the sun's annual motion:* its gradual *contraction of shadows* as it moves toward the zenith at the equinox. As we will see, beyond justifying the periphrasis for the location, this specification is important for identifying Dante's literary source, and for confirming the meaning of the passage.[84]

First, however: Why has Dante chosen to mention the Nile at all? Since most readers quickly move to the authorized equivalence of the Nile and the Gihon, Why did Dante not simply use *Giòn* or leave the river unnamed? On the contrary, in a canzone dominated by personified abstractions (Amor, Morte, Larghezza, Temperanza, Drittura), the Nile alone has a proper name.

Of the rivers known to antiquity, the Nile was acknowledged to have the most remarkable properties; its great length, supposedly meandering course, Northward flow, hidden origin, and surprising property of rising during the hot summer months, rather than during the winter, as expected of rivers, were much discussed as geophysical "problems."[85] The reasonable assumption is that Dante names the Nile in order to invoke the river's special properties. More important, how Dante names the Nile—in conjunction with the sun's movement to its highest point at the equinoxes—allows us to pinpoint Dante's chief source. As Casari and Torraca knew, that source is Lucan's discussion of the Libyan desert and course of the Nile, in the ninth and tenth books of his historical epic, the *Pharsalia*.[86] Although all of Lucan's information on the Nile was available in Seneca and Pliny, only in the *Pharsalia* do we find it gathered into brief compass in the context of political themes—civil war, exile—linked to Dante's canzone of exile.

Dante takes from Lucan the idea that, because the source of the Nile is at the equator, shadows will disappear twice a year at the equinoxes, when the sun is directly overhead. At these times, despite groves and oases, the sun removes all shade:[87]

> Hic quoque nil obstat Phoebo, cum cardine summo
> Stat librata dies; truncum vix protegit arbor:
> Tam brevis in medium radiis compellitur umbra.[88]
>
> (9.528–530)

Lucan also accounts for the approximately hundred-day cycle of the Nile, though in one of his most confused passages (*Pharsalia* 10. 210–218). It is enough for our purposes to say that Lucan reiterates, though garbles, the traditional view of how the Nile begins to rise shortly after the summer solstice, becoming stronger when the sun passes from Cancer to Leo simultaneous with the morning rising of Sirius, the Dog Star, announcing the hottest days of the summer. The river begins to return to its banks only at the autumnal equinox,[89] correlating the river's diminution with the equinoctial parity of day and night, after which shadows reemerge and fall to the south.[90] There is thus the closest assocation in Lucan's accounts between the cycle of the Nile's flooding and the movements of the sun in the sky; indeed Lucan describes the flooding of the Nile as a kind of solar tide.[91]

The river, Lucan finally explains, increases in the summer but decreases in the winter because its waters are coeval with the creation, thus governed by the creator: "quasi ille creator / Atque opifex rerum certo sub iure coercet" (10.262–267).[92]

Lucan's account of the Nile's origin at the equator (*Pharsalia* 10.287: "medio consurgis ab axe"); of its growth from solstice to equinox (as shadows disappear); and of the river's course, from south to north, but also to east and west, solves the riddles of the Nile. It also correlates the Nile with the sun: like the sun, the river moves through the four cardinal points, but where the sun heats, the river cools; the river moves from south to north, while the sun, in the period of its correlation with the Nile's flow, moves from north (summer solstice) to south (approaching the autumnal equinox). Putting Lucan's passages together suggests a chain of cause and effect linking the government of the waters by the creator, the movements of the sun in the sky between solstice and equinox, and the cycle of the Nile's flooding. The Nile increases to meet the sun's intensity during the "dog days," tempering the violent heat of the equatorial region; this balance of natural powers, which explains the odd rising of the river, is a recurring feature of literature on the Nile and suggests the "wisdom" of cosmic order.[93]

Returning to "Tre donne," we can now discern that the segment of the sun's course there implied—the period of diminution of shadows, which begins at the solstice and continues to the equinox—is precisely the part of the sun's course that coincides with the rise and fall of the Nile. Verses 46–48 may be construed as a miniature system, governed by the sun in the medial *settenario* (v. 47): the origin of the river precedes in v. 46, and the diminution of shadows to zero (which accompanies the growth of the river) follows in v. 48. In view of this information, we can remark as significant the antithesis between the "gran lume" and the "picciol fiume" that is the Nile: beyond coordinating the action of the sun and the action of the river, *picciol* has the force of a potential oxymoron when said of the Nile: it surely assumes our understanding of the Nile as (eventually) the largest and longest river known to antiquity.[94] The Nile's yearly flood is only implied, but it is *deeply implied* as an irresistible future condition, as the secret promise of great, even salvific power. From this perspective, the hopes for palingenesis scattered through "Tre Donne" rest on the implicit promise of restorative power suggested by the cycle of the Nile.

But even if we reject the implication of the Nile's annual flooding in verses 46–48, the *Pharsalia* still influences Dante's account of the Nile in "Tre donne": if we consider the status of the river as aboriginal and abyssal, governed by the *opifex rerum* himself; and if we consider the association of the river's flow with the orbits of the sun and other planets, Lucan's version of the Nile appears closely compatible with the action of the "river" of biblical Wisdom. This generic account is made specific for "Tre donne" by the words of Sapientia in Ecclesiasticus 24:32–47, where she compares herself to the four rivers of Paradise, including the Gihon (or Nile), and where her sagacity furnishes the precepts enshrined in Mosaic Law: a passage probably familiar to Dante because of Aquinas's use of it in his opening glosses to Peter Lombard's *Sentences*. The passage in Ecclesiasticus is modeled in turn on the speech of personified Sapientia in Proverbs 8:22–30, where Sapientia speaks as demiurge, co-present with God in setting the heavens in motion and restraining the upwelling of waters from the primeval abyss. She says, in Dante's translation of the passage that virtually concludes the third book of the *Convivio* (3.15.16):

> Quando iddio apparecchiava li cieli, io era presente; quando con certa legge e con certo giro vallava li abissi, quando suso fermava [l'etera] e suspendeva le fonti de l'acque, quando circuiva lo suo termine al mare e poneva legge a l'acque che non passassero li suoi confini. . . .

Wisdom's tasks are closely analogous to the relation between the sun, "mind of the universe," and the abyssal waters in Lucan's poem.[95] By implication, the law that governs the Nile, opening and closing the abyssal gates of the river according to the position of the sun and planets exemplifies Wisdom's rule over the cosmos: of Drittura/Astraea as *natural* law, ordered to the end of Justice.

The depth of Dante's working out of the Nile-Wisdom relation may reflect another traditional fountain playing a part in Dante's plan here: the fountain "quia ascendebat e terra, irrigans universam superficiem terrae" (Gen. 2:6). Augustine uses this mysterious fountain to signify the work of the six days as God's a priori creation of the *rationes seminales*, or "seminal reasons" that would unfold through time (*De genesi ad litteram* 5.7.20–22); this fountain may also, Augustine speculates, be the origin of the subsequent "common" source of the virtues, Wisdom (5.7.22). For present purposes, it is significant that only one terrestrial river bears comparison (three times) with this aboriginal fountain: the Nile, whose off-season flooding and recession Augustine uses to illustrate how such a spring might "water the whole earth": "this flooding might happen during recurring seasons, just as the Nile at a certain period overflows its banks and floods the plains of Egypt and at another returns to its banks" (5.10.25).[96] Augustine has absorbed Seneca's and Lucan's Stoic understanding of the Nile as a river that expresses the direct intervention of divine influence in nature.

To summarize: Drittura's excursus on the Nile brings together all the possible intensities of the canzone: it is the formal "fulfillment" of the canzone's "art" in being the full realization of the ten-line articulated *sirma*: thus the pattern, "heart," and microcosm of the hundred-line poem, it frames the virgin births of Drittura's offspring, at a site where humankind (or those who follow justice and wisdom; but also a place in the depths of the poet's mind) drinks directly from the stream of divine wisdom; it suggests a correlation of celestial influence and terrestrial waters that harks back to the shape of the cosmos at creation and hints at a faith in the providential rectification of history—only glimpsed here, however. Most significantly, it unifies the formal values of the poem with the virtue that it celebrates, showing how the "architectonic" virtues of justice and wisdom are ordered in harmony with the final *telos* of cosmic justice.[97]

The scene of Drittura at the Nile source, with its concentrated formal and allusive power, stands in marked contrast to the speaker's difficult historic circumstances: the exile of Drittura (stanzas one and two), and the frustration of the speaker (stanza five, *tornata*), flank the central excursus. Were Dante dividing "Tre donne" he might distinguish the first and last stanzas because the speaker is present in both in first-person pronominal forms ("mi son venute . . . quel ch'io dico"; "E io . . ."); these extreme stanzas are thus set off from the three central stanzas, given over to the conversation of Amor and the "tre donne."[98] The distinction proposed here is confirmed by finite verbs in initial positions in stanzas 2 and 4 (*Dolesi* and *Fenno*), while stanza 3, the central stanza, displays an identical term (*Poi*) for beginning both *piedi* and *sirma*, unifying the formal parts of the stanza. Further symmetry is visible in the triple use of *sono* in stanza 2 (noted by Vallone)—"*son* la più trista"; "*son* suora"; "*son* Drittura"—answered by Love's insistence on the eternal status of himself and his kin, using conjugated forms of *essere*: "non noi, che *semo* de l'etterna rocca"; "se noi *siamo* or punti"; "noi pur *saremo*."[99]

Links between stanzas 1 and 5—which fall outside the central panel of three stanzas—are weaker, and relational elements when found are contrastive. Stanza 1, depicting the ladies arranged around the speaker's heart, the "casa d'amico," is circular and dancelike in structure (note "mi son venute" in v. 1 and "venute son" in v. 17, and the symmetry of vv. 4 and 11); but stanza 5 finds *Morte* at the door of this same house, and instead of a graceful pattern of syntax and sorrowful ladies around the speaker's heart, there are closely marshaled adversatives, conditions, and conclusions ("E io . . . che," "se . . . E se . . . ," "Ma . . . Onde") that build up the impasse around the speaker.

Thus the fable of the three ladies stands above and beyond the conversation of Drittura and Amor: and even farther from the poet's painful exile. But the fable, by position and internal structure, acts as the "origin" or "fountain" of the canzone itself, much as the "fountain" of the Earthy Paradise is the source of the virtues or the Nile itself the source of the waters that keep all Egypt from dessication. In this sense, the central excursus functions as an ascent to the highest part of the mind, what Dante refers to as the "rocca della mente" in *Convivio* 2.2.3.[100] Given the status of the poet as a condemned exile, this ascent is also a withdrawal or escape: if Drittura, like Astraea, has been chased from the world of men, the poet withdraws, in the course of the poem, to the source of his being within his mind. The speaker's ascent, through Drittura's discourse, to the fountain of wisdom emulates the retreat of Boethius's Philosophy from those who would violate her and the forced return of Boethius himself to his mind, the dwelling-place of Philosophy.[101] Following this Boethian vein, the fountain over which Drittura gives birth—the fountain of Sapientia, God's wisdom—is arguably not distant from the fountain to which Philosophy, in her prayer to God in book 3, meter 9, wishes her protegé might rise: it draws on the Neoplatonic, and in this context markedly Boethian, topic of the return of the soul to its source and home (cf. *Consolatio* 4.1, 4 m.1, 4 m.6): "Da pater augustam menti conscendere sedem / da fontem lustrare boni" (grant, father, that the mind climb to your august throne, grant that it find the fount of good).[102] The lore of Wisdom implicit in the Nile myth justifies the speaker's sense, in stanza 5, of witnessing a "divine conversation" ("parlar divino") and of being, through witnessing it, himself divine.[103]

Such contact with the mind's divine source is one of the principal self-consolations offered by the poem: but it is not the only one in "Tre donne." If the divine source in "Tre donne" appears as the fountain of Wisdom, the influence of the sapiential books on the conception of "Tre donne" goes beyond ordering the creation: she traditionally also acts as moral bastion and comfort to those who love her. The teachings of Wisdom and of her "daughter" Justice are timeless, and those who contemplate her truths communicate with an eternal realm; she promises not to fail her votaries. Dante writes in Convivio 3.14.7, glossing the canzone "Amor che nella mente": "ché la sapienza, ne la quale questo amore fere, etterna è. Ond'è scritto di lei: 'Dal principio dinanzi da li secoli creata sono, e nel secol che dee venire non verrò meno'" (Ecclus. 24:14). Such passages, and others in the Wisdom tradition promising that the good and the just will endure,[104] arguably inform the confident assertions of Amor in "Tre donne": "noi pur saremo" (24.3–7). "Noi siam dell'etterna rocca," Amor proclaims. The stronghold promised is the palace of Wisdom, the earthly paradise of the virtues in the mind, the august seat of the good, the *fons boni*. As the Nile source, Wisdom permeates the entire fabric of the poem as she permeates the fabric of the cosmos: the poem builds Wisdom's temple, but only by hints, in fragments, like the gleams of the Golden Age that appear in the poem through the same kind of fragmentary technique.[105]

Although the ascent into the *mente* and the account of the generations of the Nile is merely implicit, suggested by the position of the central *sirma* as a further space-within-the-space of the speaker's heart, there is evidence that more closely links Dante's account of the Nile at its source and the poem's representational scheme in the first four stanzas (within his "secreto dentro," as he says in *Conv.* 2.7.6). In the *Commentarii in Somnium Scipionis* of Macrobius, a work Dante probably knew by 1304, Macrobius illustrates the status of the soul as the origin or source of motion (meaning mental acts like judgment, love of virtue, etc.). He seizes on the word "source" (*fons*) as an implicit fluvial metaphor and compares the soul's origin to the springing-up of a river:

Just as the sources are not easy to discover from which pour forth the Nile, the Po, the Danube, and the Don, and as you, in wonder at the vastness of such streams and curious about their beginnings, run back in your thoughts to their sources and realize that all this flood originates in little bubbling springs, so when you pause to think about the motion of bodies, whether they be divine or earthly, and wish to seek their beginning, let your mind run back to the soul as the source, the motion of which, even without bodily activity, is evidenced by our thoughts, joys, hopes, and fears. Its motion is the discernment of good and evil, love of the virtues, yearning for the vices, from which flow all the streams of action that arise in us. . . .[106]

In addition to naming the Nile as first analogue for the soul, Macrobius recalls here several *topoi* regarding the Nile—curiosity about its source, its small beginnings, even its status as fount, river, and lake, which Anselm seized on to compare it to the Trinity.[107] But most striking in the passage is its self-consciously mimetic structure: considering the origin of the Nile, at first glance merely an analogy for the consideration of the soul, itself initiates the mental return to the origin that constitutes the key spiritual tropism of Neoplatonism. There could be no better example of how the act of making the poem of consolation for exile is itself the first step in that consolation. If the relation of the Nile to the sun exposed in stanza 3 figures the cosmic plan of "artifex Sapientia," Macrobius's passage authorizes taking the generations of Drittura as an image of the soul's imitation of the divine mind, an imitation that marks the beginning of its return to that origin. The poem provides the formal space, the *stanza*, where the cosmic plan and the poet's individual return may coincide.

NOTES

1. Contributions to understanding the poem include Adolfo Gaspary, *Storia della letteratura italiana*, trans. Nicola Zingarelli (Turin: Loescher, 1887), 1:219, 453; Cornelia Casari, "Appunti per l'esegesi di una canzone di Dante," *Giornale Dantesco* 8 (1900): 264–284; Nicola Zingarelli, *Il canzoniere di Dante* (Florence: Sansoni, 1905); Giosuè Carducci, *Delle rime e della varia fortuna di Dante* (Bologna: Zanichelli, 1913), 73–198, 207–251; Francesco Torraca, "La canzone 'Tre donne,'" in *Nuovi studi danteschi nel VI centenario della morte di Dante* (Naples: Federico e Ardia, 1921), 229–270; Thérèse Labande-Jeanroy,

"La chanson de Dante 'Tre donne intorno al cor mi son venute,'" *Études italiennes* 8 (1926): 193–215; Kenelm Foster, "Dante's Canzone 'Tre donne,'" *Italian Studies* 9 (1954): 56–68 (reprinted in *God's Tree: Essays on Dante and Other Matters* [London: Blackfriars, 1957]); André Pézard, *La rotta gonna*, vol. 1 (Florence and Paris: Sansoni-Didier, 1967), 86–88; Nicolò Mineo, *Il duecento dalle origini a Dante* (Bari: Laterza, 1970), 511; Patrick Boyde, *Dante's Style in his Lyric Poetry* (Cambridge: Cambridge University Press, 1971), 147–151; Aldo Vallone, *Lettura interna delle Rime di Dante* (Rome: Signorelli, 1972), 64–121; Giorgio Bárberi Squarotti, *L'artificio dell'eternità* (Verona: Fiorini), 144; Anna-Maria Aino Paasonen, "Dante at the Turning Point: The Canzone 'Tre donne al cor mi son venute' as a New Key to the 'Commedia'" (dissertation, University of California at Los Angeles, 1977); Ignazio Baldelli, "Lingua e stile dalle petrose a 'Tre donne,'" *La rassegna* 82 (1978): 5–17; Gordon Poole, "Dante's *canzone*, 'Tre donne intorno al cor,'" *Dante Studies* 98 (1980): 123–144; Roberto Mercuri, "Dante, Petrarca, Boccaccio: Storia, geografia e intertestualità," in *Letteratura italiana: Storia e geografia*, vol. 1: *L'età medievale* (Turin: Einaudi, 1987), 235–237. Important annotation is found in Gianfranco Contini, *Dante Alighieri: Rime* (Turin: Einaudi, 1970 [1946]), 172–179; Daniele Mattalia, ed., *Dante Alighieri: Le rime* (Turin: Paravia, 1943); André Pézard, *Dante: Oeuvres complètes* (Paris: Gallimard, 1965); Michele Barbi and Vincenzo Pernicone, *Dante Alighieri: Rime della maturità e dell'esilio* (Florence: Le Monnier, 1969), 583–590; Kenelm Foster and Patrick Boyde, *Dante's Lyric Poetry* (Oxford: Oxford University Press, 1967), 2:281–293. I would like to thank Paolo Cherchi and Giuseppe Mazzotta for useful remarks on an earlier version of this essay.

2. In Gaspary's wake, most editors still follow Pietro di Dante's commentary on *Inferno*, canto 6, where he argues that the scene in stanza 3 represents the birth of *ius gentium* (the law of nations) from Drittura (natural and divine justice) and of positive law (*ius civile*) from the *ius gentium*. In partial confirmation of Pietro's gloss, F. Mazzoni, "Per la storia della critica dantesca," *Studi danteschi* 30 (1951): 157–202, cites Graziolo da Bambaglioli's commentary on the *veltro* (*Inf.* 1.101), which quotes "Tre donne" and describes the poem as Dante's lament "in persona iustitie et aliarum virtutum" for the contempt and oblivion into which justice has fallen. Pietro's view (an eclectic summary of Roman and Canon Law) was attacked, and modified, by Torraca (Drittura represents habitual justice, the acquired moral virtue; "natural justice" is the daughter) and recently by Poole, who reduces Pietro's category of "divine and natural" to the merely "natural" and makes other minor changes. For Labande-Jeanroy, the trio of ladies represents the Roman Empire deriving from the fountain of *pietas* (cf. *Monarchia* 2.5.5; *Epist.* 5.7–8); for Vallone the three ladies are the three branches of philosophy, natural, ethical, and logical; for Paasonen, they are the three theological virtues

(following the late-fourteenth-century Magliabechiano VII.152 commentary on "Tre donne"). My own view is that by multiplying the offspring of Justice while omitting to name them Dante gives himself latitude: Drittura and her daughters probably include both natural and legal justice (distinguished by Aristotle in *Ethics* 5.7: roughly, Pietro's *ius divinum et naturale* and *ius gentium*), not excluding the acquired virtue of habitual justice (Torraca).

3. The debate between Umberto Cosmo ("Se io ebbi colpa," *Cultura*, n.s. 12 [1933]: 652–657), arguing for the fault as a specific injustice offered Florence shortly after the poet went into exile (perhaps his alliance with the Whites against the Blacks), and Michele Barbi ("Per l'interpretazione della canzone 'Tre donne,'" *Studi danteschi* 17 [1933]: 97–103; 20 [1937]: 17–25), who suggested the general inherited fault of mankind, remains unresolved; see the resumé of positions in Foster and Boyde (*Dante's Lyric Poetry*) and the arguments in Foster and H. S. Vere-Hodge (*The Odes of Dante* [London: Oxford University Press, 1963]: 258–265).

4. See Robert M. Durling and Ronald L. Martinez, *Time and the Crystal: Studies in Dante's 'rime petrose'* (Berkeley and Los Angeles: University of California Press, 1990), 45–52 (on the problematic of the *petrose*).

5. Explicitly allegorical are the "panni," "dolce pome," "color novi," and "fior" of the personified poem in the first *tornata*; the "neri veltri" and "bianche penne" of the second *tornata*, though referring to Blacks and Whites, are also far from transparent (cf. Pézard, *Rotta gonna*, 87–88). Some equivocal terms are v. 8, "s'aita" (see Contini's discussion); v. 37, "conta" (derived from *cointe*, or *compta*?); v. 62, "turbate." Amphibologies are v. 26, "sol di sè par donna" ("mistress of herself only," or, "mistress by virtue of her very self?"); v. 48, "toglie a la terra del vinco la fronda"; v. 87, "posto la chiave" ("key put to the lock," or "key turned in the lock"?). For obscure lines where the problem is determing what is referred to and why, see vv. 44, 68, 79, 81, 88; for some of these, see Boyde, *Dante's Style*, 148–151.

6. Cf. Durling and Martinez, *Time and the Crystal*, 375, 418, 421 (Lucan); 350–351 (Seneca); 8–9, 53–54, 66–68 (Boethius); and especially 53–70, 339–349 (Neoplatonism in the canzone).

7. For solar motion and canzone structure, see Durling and Martinez, *Time and the Crystal*, 72–79 and 109–138; Dante's discussion of the solar orbit in *Convivio* 3.5–6 and 12 is, I believe, closely linked to the context of "Tre donne."

8. Baldelli calls attention to *rimas caras* in the texture of the poem (especially *donna : colonna, raggio : oraggio, nuda : chiuda*) that betray a *petrose* pedigree; while the inversion of the *sententia* in the *tornata* to "Così nel mio parlar" ("ché bell'onor s'acquista in far vendetta") in the final line of "Tre donne" ("ché'l perdonare è bel vincer di guerra") is strong evidence of a more than casual relation between the two texts. Note the echo of "Io son

venuto al punto della rota" in the first and penultimate lines of the first stanza of "Tre donne intorno al cor mi son venute" ("*venute son* come a casa d'amico").

9. See "Io son venuto," v. 10 ("e però . . ."); v. 23 ("e Amor . . ."); v. 36 ("e'l mio . . ."); vv. 49–50 ("e la crudele spina . . . però"); vv. 62–63 ("e io . . . non son però . . ."). For discussion of the stanza of "Io son venuto," see Durling and Martinez, *Time and the Crystal*, 72–79.

10. Boyde (*Dante's Style*, 148) points out the rhetorical effectiveness of the shift, literally a trope, in which the fiction of the poet containing the personifications of the first three stanzas is dropped and the poet-as-subject comes into the foreground: " . . . justice, personified as the three ladies, has been driven out and exiled from human society. What he [Dante] has done, therefore, is to take terms that can be used properly of his own case, and apply them in a transferred sense to the general situation. Or, to put it another way, the terminology of the two propositions is identical; but in the first case it is used 'properly,' in the second, 'tropologically.'"

11. This tradition regarding the Earthly Paradise goes back to Philo of Alexandria (*De opificio mundi* 1.6) and Origen, and influenced Ambrose and Augustine; see Charles S. Singleton's citations, *Dante Studies*, vol. 2: *Journey to Beatrice* (Cambridge, Mass.: Harvard University Press, 1958): 178–182. Augustine and Aquinas argued for the Earthly Paradise as both geographical place and allegory; cf. *Super libros Sententiarum* 2, dist. 17, q. 3, a. 2, sol. (cited in Singleton, *Journey*, 156), where Aquinas mentions the Nile. See also J. Daniélou, *From Shadows to Reality: Studies in the Biblical Typology of the Fathers* (Westminster, Md.: Newman Press, 1960), 57–65.

12. My own view is thus close to that of Mercuri, "Dante, Petrarca, Bocaccio," 237—"la canzone ricompone la scompostezza cui il mondo ha ridotto le tre donne"—but the problem is how the "ricomposizione" is achieved.

13. Dante gives no instances (other than the virtues themselves) of the *buoni* (v. 80) he might be honored to fall alongside. One tacit exemplum is Boethius; another is Cato of Utica; a third is Ripheus, implicitly paired with Cato by Boethius in the *Consolatio philosophiae* 4.6 (John A. Scott has announced a study of this pairing in an essay forthcoming in *Studi danteschi*). Cato, as exile, defender of a lost cause, and strict adherent of virtue is a logical parallel to the exiled poet (for Cato as exemplum in *Monarchia* 2.5.15, see T. Silverstein, "On the Genesis of *Monarchia* II.v," *Speculum* 13 [1938]: 326–349). Note that Cato, like the poet, is the last refuge of virtue (Lucan, *Pharsalia* 2.243–244: "omnibus expulsae terris olimque fugatae / virtutis iam sola fides") and ever the servant of justice (388–389: "iustitiae cultor, rigidi servator honesti, / in commune bonus" and "durae . . . virtutis amator" [9.561]). The medieval tradition of Lucan's Cato as exemplar of the four virtues is reviewed in Violetta de Angelis, "' . . . e l'ultimo Lucano,'"

in *Dante e la "bella scola" della poesia,* ed. Amilcare A. Ianucci (Ravenna: Longo, 1993), 145–206.

14. References to "Tre donne" are to Contini's edition of the *Rime*; to the *Commedia*, to *La commedia seconda l'antica vulgata,* 4 vols., ed. Petrocchi Società dantesca italiana, Edizione nazionale (Milano: Mondadori, 1966–1967). For Dante's other works, see *Monarchia,* ed. Bruno Nardi, vol. 2 of *Opere minori* (Milan and Naples: Ricciardi, 1979); and *Epistole,* ed. Arsenio Frugoni and Giorgio Brugnoli, vol. 2 of *Opere minori* (Milan and Naples: Ricciardi, 1979); *Vita nuova,* ed. Domenico de Robertis, vol. 1, part 1 of *Opere minori* (Milan and Naples: Ricciardi, 1984); *Convivio,* ed. Cesare Vasoli and Domenico de Robertis, vol. 1, part 2 of *Opere minori* (Milan and Naples: Ricciardi, 1988).

15. See *Convivio* 3.17.7–8: "L'undecima [vertù] si è giustizia, la quale ordina noi ad amare e operare drittura in tutte le cose": abstract Justice is the ideal "governing" virtue, Drittura the virtue in the soul (habit) and extended to others (operation). Cf. Aquinas, *Summa theologiae* 1.2, q. 66, art. 4 (ed. P. Caramello [Rome: Marietti, 1950]): "iustitia inter omnes virtutes morales praecellit, tanquam propinquior rationi. Quod patet et ex subiecto, et ex obiecto. Ex subiecto quidem, quia est in voluntate sicut in subiecto: voluntas autem est appetitus rationis, ut ex dictis patet (q. 8., art. 1; q. 26, art. 1). Secundum autem obiectum sive materiam, quia est circa operationes, quibus homo ordinatur non solum in seipso, sed etiam ad alterum. Unde iustitia est praeclarissima virtutum, ut dicitur in V. *Ethic.*"

16. The importance of this chapter for "Tre donne" was pointed out by Torraca (*"La canzone,"* 240).

17. Love or *dilectio* is an important aspect of possessing a virtue (cf. *Convivio* 3.11.5–6), and justice is supremely lovable among virtues (*Convivio* 1.12.9; see also Aquinas, *Sententia libri Ethicorum* 1, lec. 13.156–160). Amor acts in "Tre donne" both as the poet's innate *genius,* the "fonte del gentil parlare" as he is called in the sonnet "Due donne in cima de la mente mia" (his *dictator,* as in *Purg.* 24.51), and his eros or desire, closely identified with his will, his *voluntas* (see *Convivio* 1.12.9–10: "quella [virtù] è più amabile in esso che è più umana, e questa è la giustizia, la quale è solamente ne la parte razionale o vero intellettuale, cioè ne la volontade"). To my knowledge, only Paasonen (*Dante at the Turning Point,* 126–128) has suggested that the arrows of Love are the alternate whips and bridles of desire and restraint of desire (cf. "come affrena e come sprona," in the sonnet to Cino), rather than simple references to Ovid's shining and leaden arrows; these whips and bridles are "taken from love," as in *Purg.* 13.38–40 (*ferza, freno*) and are associated with imperial law as well ("guida o fren" [*Purg.* 16.93]). If these identifications hold, the Amor of "Tre donne," given Torraca's identification of Amor in "Tre donne" as *recta dilectio,* as in *Monarchia* 1.11.13 (see also *Epist.* 11.15:

"Non caritas, non Astrea"), and Dante's conception of Amore counseled by reason (as in Vita nuova 2.9) are very close to the "abito eligente" of the noble soul ("Le dolci rime," 81–88, and Convivio 4.17.7–8). See also Convivio 4.17.7 ("nascono [le virtù] tutte da un principio, cioè da l'abito di nostra buona elezione") and 4.21.13–14.

18. See Monarchia 1.11.13 (karitas linked to justice) and 1.13.7, where Dante cites the Aristotelian definition of justice as a virtue that acts for the common good ("iustitia sit virtus ad alterum"; cf. also Convivio 1.12.9–10 and Vasoli's note). Pietas, religio, misericordia, gratia, and concordia are all traditionally sub-parts of justice; cf. Odon Lottin, "Le traité d'Alain de Lille sur les vertus, les vices et les dons du Saint-Esprit," Medieval Studies 12 (1950): 20–56; especially 30. I am taking v. 108, "perdonar è bel vincer di guerra," to mean that both the poet and his enemies must open the "chamber of forgiveness" (see next note).

19. In Monarchia 1.12.10 Dante quotes Aristotle's observation in the Politics (3.4.1276b30) that no man can be a good citizen in a bad city; or, mutatis mutandis, in a world not governed by the Monarch.

20. Discussion of the second tornata is beyond the scope of this paper; but the final line, which Pézard (Oeuvres, 212) derived from a Senecan sententia in the Fiore de' Filosofi, can be traced to the entry on magnanimity (a species of fortitude) in the Tractatus de quattor virtutibus of Hildebert of Lavandin (vol. 171, 1055–1064, of Patrologiae Cursus Completus, Series Latina, 221 vols., ed. J. P. Migne [Paris, 1841–1864]), a versified version of the pseudo-Senecan Formula vitae honestae of Martin of Braga (ed. C. W. Barlow [New Haven: Yale University Press, 1950], 241). Hildebert gives "Nobile vindictae genus est ignoscere victo" (The noble kind of vengeance is to forgive the vanquished); while Martin of Braga writes: "Scito enim honestum et magnum vindictae esse genus ignoscere" (Know truly that the great and honorable form of vengeance is to forgive). Dante's passage also seems influenced by St. Paul in Romans 12:21: "Noli vinci a malo, sed vince in bono malum."

21. Vallone, Lettura, 115–116; Paasonen, Dante at the Turning Point, 192–221; Mercuri, "Dante, Petrarca, Bocaccio," 237. For a census of Dante's various personifications of canzoni in tornate, see Paasonen (197–201); note especially the canzoni of the Vita nuova described as figliuole and the reference to a poem (thought to be the ballata "Voi che savete") as a sorella of the canzone "Amor che nella mente" (Convivio 3.15.19–20; Dante's gloss given below). See also Convivio 3.9.2, said of poems: "puote l'uomo dire sorella de l'opera che da uno medesimo operante è operata; che la nostra operazione in alcuno modo è generazione."

22. See Paasonen, Dante at the Turning Point, 192–194, whose account imposes a nuptial metaphor on the first tornata that the text does not bear out; see also Mercuri, "Dante, Petrarca, Bocaccio," 237.

23. The relation of *vertù* and *bellezza* is also presented as a dichotomy in the sonnet "Due donne": the impasse is resolved with a distinction uttered by Love, the poet's "fonte di bel parlar," between *diletto* and *operazion*. In "Tre donne" itself, "bellezza" and "vertù" are twice predicated of the ladies who approach the poet's heart (vv. 5, 12); this is also the fundamental dichotomy in the canzone "Doglia mi reca," often thought of as closely contemporary with "Tre donne," (vv. 7–8, 12–13, 16–18, etc.).

24. Cf. Cicero, *De inventione* 159: "Quod aut totum aut aliqua ex parte propter se petitur, honestum nominabimus"; and *De finibus bonorum et malorum* 2.45 ("Honestum igitur intelligimus quod tale est, ut detracta omni utilitate, sine ullis praemiis fructibusve per se ipsum possit iure laudari"), which Paolo Cherchi, in his *lectura* of *Purgatorio* 7 (*Lectura dantis* 12, supplement [1993]: 98–114) notes is cited by Dante at *Convivio* 4.6.9–10. Cf. also "Honestum est quod sua vi nos trahit et sua dignitate nos allicit" (*Des Moralium Dogma Philosophorum des Guillaume de Conches*, ed. J. Holmberg [Uppsala: Almqvist and Wiksells, 1929], 7).

25. Cf. "Voi ch'intendendo," vv. 53–61, which sharply distinguishes *ragione* and *bellezza*, and Dante's gloss in *Convivio* 2.11.2–5; in *Convivio* 1.1.14–15, Dante notes that his poems were not understood, "sì che a molti loro bellezza più che loro bontade era in grado": the work being undertaken is intended to remedy this problem.

26. "E da sapere che la moralitade è bellezza de la filosofia; ché così come la bellezza del corpo resulta da le membra in quanto sono debitamente ordinate, così la bellezza della sapienza, che è corpo di Filosofia come detto è, risulta da l'ordine de le virtudi morali, che fanno quella piacere sensibilemente." This is a version of the Greek ideal of *kalós kagathós*; for this and for the Ciceronian tradition of beauty and decorum (*pulchrum, decens*) and virtue (*honestum*, see Umberto Eco, *The Esthetics of Thomas Aquinas*, trans. Hugh Bredin [Cambridge, Mass.: Harvard Univ. Press, 1988], 85–87).

27. Eco, *Esthetics*, 72, cites Augustine's Third Letter to Nebridius: "Omnis pulchritudo est partium congruentia cum quadam suavitate coloris," a view Dante partially echoes in *Convivio* 1.5.13. See also Albertus Magnus, *De pulchro et bono* (cited in Eco, *Esthetics*, 112): "Ratio pulchri in universale constitit in resplendentia formae supra partes materiae proportionatas vel super diversas vires vel actiones"; compare *Convivio* 4.8.1.

28. Aristotle, *Ethics* 5.3.1129b25: "In iustitia autem simul omnis virtus est . . . Hec enim igitur non pars virtutis, sed tota virtus est" (text in Albertus Magnus, *Super Ethica* (books 1–5, ed. W. Kübel [Aschendorff: Monasterium Westfalorum, 1968–1972], 322). In the parsing of the cardinal virtues among the four rivers of the Earthly Paradise by the Church fathers, Justice was compared to the Euphrates, which since unassociated with any specific geographical area was said to embrace all the other rivers (cf. Genesis 2:14);

Singleton, *Journey*, 181–182, cites Ambrose and Augustine (*De genesi contra Manicheos*, vol. 34, 203–204, of Patrologiae Cursus Completus, Series Latina, 221 vols., ed. J. P. Migne [Paris, 1841–1864]): "Quartus fluvius . . . iustitia enim ad omnes partes animae pertinet, quia ipsa ordo et aequitas animae est, qua sibi ista tria concorditer copulantur, prima prudentia, secunda fortitudo, tertia temperantia; et in ista tota copulatione atque ordinatione justitia."

29. Cf. Albertus Magnus, *Super Ethica* 5, lec. 3 (ed. Kübel, 377): "Quod sic probat Tullius in libro de officiis, quia ab exercitio aliarum virtutum aliquando aliquis retrahitur, ab exercitio vero iustitiae nunquam, Unde patet, quod haec est propinquius attingens communitatis bonum; ordinat enim ad alterum, secundum quod est perfectio hominis, inquantum est civilis, et per hunc modum dicitur perfectissima."

30. See S. Santangelo, *Dante e i trovatori provenzali* (Catania: Giannotta, 1921), 149–150; Foster and Boyde, *Dante's Lyric Poetry*, 2:285; and for Astraea in the *Purgatorio*, see Singleton, *Journey*, 184–203.

31. For the departure of Astraea, repelled by the violence of mankind, see Ovid, *Metamorphoses* 1.90–150; the story was retold by Lactantius, and there are adaptations in the *Roman de la rose* (5535–5554, 20115–20220) and the *Ovide moralisé* (1.1004–1033). E. H. Kantorowicz, *The King's Two Bodies: A Study on Medieval Political Theology* (Princeton, N.J.: Princeton University Press, 1957), 108–110 gives examples of Justice-Astraea portrayed by the jurists showing both *gravitas* and sadness (at the failure of men to follow her precepts); Kantorowicz traces some of these details (e.g., "reverendae cuisudam *tristitiae* dignitate") to Aulus Gellius, *Noctes Atticae* (14.4).

For the relationship between "gente" in "Tre donne," "Gens aurea" in the Fourth Eclogue, and "prima gente" in the *Purgatorio*, see Singleton, *Journey*, 184–203.

32. d'Arco Silvio Avalle, *Modelli semiologici nella Commedia di Dante* (Rome: Bompiani, 1975), 183. The Nile source in the Earthly Paradise (Foster and Boyde, *Dante's Lyric Poetry*, 2:285–286) is consistent with the theme of the Golden Age as well (Isidore's description of the Earthly Paradise [*Etymologiae* 14.3.2] as a place of perpetual spring echoes Ovid's account); for Pézard (*Oeuvres*, 209) it is the reference to a "vergin onda" (v. 49) that evokes Astraea, the *virgo*. Seneca, *Naturales quaestiones* 3.30.7 (ed P. Oltremare [Paris: Belles Lettres, 1929]), also echoes Ovid and Virgil in describing the regeneration of the world after the cataclysm (" . . . et antiquus ordo revocabitur. Omne ex integro animal generabitur dabiturque terris homo inscius scelerum et melioribus auspiciis natus").

33. Dante's sonnet "Se vedi li occhi miei," often associated with "Tre donne" (cf. Contini) describes Justice as lying naked and dead (v. 12: "questa vertù che nuda e fredda giace"), echoing Ovid, *Metamorphoses* 1.149 ("victa

iacet pietas"). Like "Tre donne," the sonnet draws on the topics of the Golden Age in its depiction of virtue outraged.

34. Although not mentioned in Ovid (*Metamorphosis* 1.468–470) Love's stimulating arrow was traditionally of gold; Ovid says its point was gleaming and sharp ("cuspide fulget acuta"). Dante's *acuit et dilucidat* (*Monarchia* 1.11.13) almost surely echoes Ovid's text.

35. Since stars project power (*virtù*), the association is logical; for virtues as stars in the *Purgatorio*, cf. Singleton, *Journey*, 200–203. See also *Convivio* 3.9.15, where the whole point of the comparison is that the meaning of the poem (the nature of wisdom) is like a star, first seen dimly because of the observer's defect, then seen clearly (and note the use of *trasmutarsi* in this passage, e.g., 3.9.12).

36. See Bernard Silvestris, *The Commentary on the First Six Books of the "Aeneid" of Vergil Commonly Attributed to Bernardus Silvestris*, ed. J. W. Jones and E. F. Jones (Lincoln, Neb., and London: University of Nebraska Press, 1977), 9: "Legitimam Venerem legimus esse mundanam musicam, id est equalem mundanorum proportionem, quam alii Astream, naturalem iustitiam vocant. Hec enim est in elementis, in sideribus, in temporibus in animantibus." For the Scholastic notion of "natural" justice as cosmic order, see Albertus Magnus, *Comentarii in secundum librum Sententiarum*, dist. 16, art. 5, sol.: "Iustitia autem naturalis dicitur ordo rectus virium inferiorum ad superiores, et superioris ad Deum, et corporis ad animam et mundi ad corpus. Et in hoc ordine creatus est homo." See Singleton, *Journey*, 222–253.

37. In *Convivio* 2.13.13–14, Dante makes Venus, shining as both Lucifer and Hesperus (the morning and evening stars), the planet symbolizing rhetoric; this is noteworthy in view of Aristotle's identification, in *Ethics* 5.3, of justice as "more lovely than the morning or evening star"—preparing a link between rhetorical *venustas* and the virtue of justice, now in cosmological terms.

38. Cf. *Convivio* 3.9.6 "propriamente è visibile lo colore e la luce." For radiance or *claritas*, see Aquinas, *Summa theologiae* 2.2, q. 145, art. 2, c.: "ad rationem pulchri sive decori concurrit et claritas et debita proportio"; and Eco, *Esthetics*, 252, citing Aquinas on Pseudo-Dionysius, *Commentarium De divinis nominibus* 4.6: "forma autem est quaedam irradiatio proveniens ex prima claritate; claritas autem est de ratione pulchritudinis." The first book of the *Convivio* begins (1.1.13: "la luce la quale ogni colore di loro sentenza farà parvente") and ends (1.13.12–13: "questo sarà luce nuova, sole nuovo . . .") with reference to the commentary illuminating the canzoni for readers.

39. For discussion, see Durling and Martinez, *Time and the Crystal*, 151–162, 387–396.

40. Aristotle, *Ethics* 5.1.1129b (text in Albertus Magnus, *Super Ethica* [ed. Kübel, 322]): "Propter hoc ipsum autem et *alienum bonum videtur esse* iustitia

sola virtutum, quoniam ad alterum est; alii enim conferentia operatur, vel principi vel communi."

41. Foster and Boyde (*Dante's Lyric Poetry*, 285–286) give the best recent account; but Karl Witte, *Dante Alighieris lyrische Gedichter: II, Anmerkungen* (Leipzig, 1842), especially 132–138, was aware of the scriptural background (explored below in the text); see Carducci, *Delle rime*, 185–186.

42. *Convivio* 3.2.14–16: "[l'anima umana] participa de la divina natura a guisa di sempiterna intelligenza . . . la divina luce raggia in quella, e pero è l'uomo divino animale da li filosofi chiamato. In questa nobilissima parte de l'anima sono più vertudi, sí come dice lo Filosofo nel sesto de l'*Etica*. . . . E tutte queste nobilissime vertudi, e l'altre che sono in quella eccellentissima potenza, si chiama insieme con questo vocabulo, del quale si volea sapere che fosse, cioè *mente*. Per che è manifesto che per *mente* s'intende questa ultima e nobilissima parte dell'anima." See also 3.2.24: "Onde si puote omai vedere che è mente che è quella fine è preziosissima parte de l'anima che è deitade. E *questo è il luogo* dove dico che Amore mi ragiona de la mia donna" (emphasis mine).

43. Foster and Boyde, *Dante's Lyric Poetry*, in the wake of Mattalia, identify the the Nile with the fountain of Wisdom. Singleton, *Journey*, 159–183, showed that Dante's account of the rivers of Paradise in *Purg.* 32–33 draws on the tradition, derived from Philo and represented in Ambrose and Augustine, of the four rivers emanating from the fountain of Wisdom (the common source) and consisting in the four cardinal virtues (variously assigned to the rivers; the Gihon, associated with the Nile, is temperance for Ambrose, fortitude for Augustine). The association of Wisdom with streams is traditional: see Prov. 8:22–31, Ecclus. 24:40 ("Ego sapientia effudi flumina; ego quasi trames aquae immensae de fluvio . . . et sicut aquaeductus exivi de paradiso") and 47:16 ("Et impletus es, quasi flumen, sapientia").

44. Witte and Torraca note Ecclus. 24:37: "et assistens quasi Gehon in die vindemiae," said of the biblical Sapientia, but do not develop the idea.

45. And see *Convivio* 4.6.18 and 4.16.1, which translate Wis. 6:23, the doublet to 1.1. The association of wisdom and justice is frequent in Wisdom tradition; see Wis. 1:15, 3:1, 6:23; Prov. 8.14–16, 8.20. The association of Wisdom and Mosaic Law in Ecclus. 24:33 is fundamental; (Wisdom speaks): "Legem mandavi Moyses in praeceptis iustitiarum."

46. Wisdom and justice as "architectonic" virtues are the focus of consecutive articles in Aquinas, *Summa theologiae* 1.2, q. 66, art. 4, 5.

47. See Nicola Rubinstein, "Political Ideas in Sienese Art: The Frescoes by Ambrogio Lorenzetti and Taddeo di Bartolo in the Palazzo Publico," *Journal of the Warburg and Courtauld Institute* 21 (1958): 179–207, especially 182–185.

48. See Marie-Thérèse d'Alverny, "La sagesse et ses sept filles," *Mélanges Felix Grat* (Paris, 1946), 245–277; and "Notes sur Dante et la Sagesse,"

Revue des études italiennes 11 (1965) [*Dante et les Mythes*]: 7–24; and Pierre Courcelle, *La "Consolation de philosophie" dans la tradition littéraire* (Paris: Études Augustiniennes, 1967), 29–66. Zingarelli (cited by Paasonen, *Dante at the Turning Point*, 164) suggested that the speaker's beloved *segno* was Sapientia; Pézard, *Oeuvres*, notes in "Tre donne" v. 31 ("O di pochi vivanda") an echo of Wis. 16:20 ("paratum panem de caelo") in reference to the "food of Wisdom."

49. Dante's injunction on putting hands to the canzone (v. 91: "non ponga uom mano") may echo "vestem violentorum quorundam sciderant manus" in *Consolatio philosophiae* 1.1 (trans., *The Consolation of Philosophy* [Cambridge, Mass.: Harvard University Press, 1973]). For this and other Boethian parallels, see Bruno Nardi, "Le rime filosofiche e il *Convivio* nello sviluppo dell'arte e del pensiero di Dante," in *Dal "Convivio" alla "Commedia"* (Rome: Istituto storico italiano per il medio evo, 1960), especially 17–20.

50. For the iconography of Boethius's chambers, see Courcelle, *La "Consolation,"* plates 21–60. Note also the parallel of Amor's unused weapons ("Tre donne" vv. 59–62) and Philosophy reminding Boethius of his neglected "philosophical" weapons (1.3); "talia contuleramus arma quae nisi prior abiecisses."

51. The *Convivio* is of course shot through with parallels between the exiled Dante and Boethius; see especially 2.12.3, noted by Carducci, where Boethius is "cattivo e discacciato" (cf. "Tre donne" v. 10: "discacciata e stanca"), and 2.15.1, where Dante attributes his acquaintance with Philosophy to Boethius. Strikingly, the majority of Dante's uses of *consolar, consolazion* in his work refer to Boethius or figures like him (cf. "Tre donne" v. 74: "consolarsi e dolersi").

52. Cf. *Consolatio philosophiae* 1.2: "nostro lacte nutritus."

53. Cf. *Convivio* 2.15.5 ("dico lei [Sapienza] essere di tutto madre." But see Prov. 7:4 ("dic sapientia, soror mea es, et prudentiam voca amicam tua") and 8.17 ("ego diligentes me diligo, Et qui mane vigilant ad me, invenient me"); Wis. 6:13 and 24:5; also Sg. 4:8: ("Tota pulchra es, amica mea, Et macula non est in te. Veni de Libano, sponsa mea").

54. Dante adopts Solomon's *columba* as the symbol of divine wisdom, the object of theology (and so correlated with the Empyrean) in *Convivio* 2.14.20, where it is immediately preceded by moral philosophy or "giustizia legale" (2.14.15); see also 3.12.13 (Philosophy is the *druda* desired by her lovers). For Dante's use of Sapientia in the *Commedia*, see Singleton, *Journey*, 122–138; Peter Armour, "Matelda in Eden: The Teacher and the Apple," *Italian Studies* 38 (1983): 1–27; and for the *Convivio*, Maria Corti, *La felicità mentale* (Torino: Einaudi, 1983), especially 74–78.

55. The periphrastic v. 28 ("... in parte che il tacere è bello") is the only direct, nonmetaphorical reference in Dante's works to the sex of the

female. The emphasis may imply that Drittura is a victim of rape; note the related implication that some readers of the poem would "lay hands" on the canzone and strip it of its clothing (vv. 90–92); for this suggestion, see Vallone, *Lettura*, 116.

56. The beloved *columba* is traditionally immaculate (Sg. 4.7), like Wisdom herself (cf. Wis. 7.26: "speculum sine macula") and like ideal Justice, whom Dante compares to an abstract, pure whiteness (*albedo*) in *Monarchia* 1.11.4.

57. Also a seated figure; cf. Lam. 1:1, "quomodo sedet solitaria civitas," and, for the plural, "sederunt in terra" of the *virgines* of Jerusalem, Lam. 2.10. To my knowledge only Paasonen (*Dante at the Turning Point*, 49) has raised this parallel; a more elaborate parallel links "Tre donne" v. 25 ("la faccia lagrimosa") and vv. 11, 15 ("cui tutta gente manca . . . or sono a tutti in ira ed in non cale") with Lam. 1:2: ("Et lacrymae eius in maxillis eius; Non est qui consoletur eam, Ex omnibus charis eius, Omnes amici eius spreverunt eam, Et facti sunt ei inimici").

58. Other instances of this iconography are the monochrome fresco of Injustice in Giotto's Scrovegni chapel, showing a woman despoiled of her clothes, likely to be raped. Lauro Martines, *Power and Imagination: City-States in Renaissance Italy* (New York: Alfred A. Knopf, 1979), 114–115 cites the Anonimo Genovese's portrayal of Genoa (1290s) as a mother torn and lacerated by her factions ("lay hands on her person. . . . tear her dress to pieces"); a similar portrayal, personifying Pisa (1285), is found in Guittone d'Arezzo's poem "Magni baroni certo e regi quasi." Paasonen refers (*Dante at the Turning Point*, 50) to passages in Guittone's letter to the Florentines.

59. The nexus of poverty, sorrow, exile, impotence, and consolation in "Tre donne" is echoed in Dante's letter (*Epist.* 2) to the sons of count Alessandro da Romena probably written in 1304 (a time possible for the composition of "Tre donne") where Dante expresses his sorrow ("doleat progenies . . . doleant omnes . . . me miserum dolore oportet, qui a patria pulsus et exul immeritus infortunia mea rependens continuo . . .") for the death of their uncle and laments his own poverty, due to his exile ("paupertas quam fecit exilium") that prevents attendance at funeral exequies. In addition to the thematic associations, the rhetorical insistence on forms of *dolere* and *dolor* (six instances) seems to parallel "Tre donne," with eight instances (vv. 9, 19, 22, 30, 38, 44, 66, 74).

60. Drittura is "discinta e scalza," like the followers of Francis's Lady Poverty (*Par.* 11.83: "scalzasi Egidio . . ."). Carducci noted the parallel between "Tre donne" v. 108 ("camera di perdon savio uom non serra") and "la porta del piacer nessun diserra," said of Lady Poverty (*Paradiso* 11.60).

61. See Albertus Magnus, *De causis et processu universitatis a prima causa* 1.4.4 (ed. W. Fauser [Aschendorff: Monasterii Westfalorum, 1993]): "Propter

quod Platonici dicebant, [*Timaeus* 27–29, 48, 50] quod fluens a primo bonitas forma quidem est in proximis, imago autem in distantibus, in ultimis autem obscura reflexio sive resonantia sive umbrosa primi represaentatio. Tamen omnis virtus istius fluxus a primo est. . . ."

62. In *Conv.* 3.6.11–12 Dante follows the *Liber de causis* in explaining how the celestial intelligences contemplate Lady Philosophy: "E qui è da sapere che ciascuno intelletto di sopra, secondo è scritto nel libro de le Cagioni, conosce quello che è sopra sé e quelle che è sotto sé. Conosce adunque Iddio sì come sua cagione, conosce quella che è sotto sé come suo effetto. . . ." For a full-scale exposition of these doctrines, see Albertus Magnus, *De causis* 1.4.6 and 2.3.5.

63. For this process said specifically of composing canzoni, see *Convivio* 3.9.4: "così puote l'uomo dire sorella de l'opera che da uno medesimo operante è operata; chè la nostra operazione in alcuno modo è generazione."

64. Philosophy, Dante writes, contemplates herself, "che altro non è a dire, se non che l'anima filosofante non solamente contempla essa veritade, ma ancora contempla lo suo contemplare medesimo e la bellezza di quello, rivolgendosi sovra sé stessa e di sé stessa innamorando per la bellezza del suo primo guardare" (*Conv.* 4.2.17–18; see also 3.6.11–12). For the Neoplatonic inspiration of the passage, Vasoli cites the *Liber de Causis* and Albertus Magnus's commentary on it: "in omni opere sive actione intelligibili ad essentiam propriam reducitur. Haec autem reditio completa est. . . ."

65. See Boethius, *Consolatio philosophiae* 3, m. 9, vv. 15–17: "Quae cum secta duos motum glomeravit in orbes / In semet reditura meat mentemque profundam / Circuit et simili convertit imagine caelum" (and Soul, cut in two, has globed its motion in two orbs, goes forth to return to itself, turns about the depth of Mind, and curves the heaven to a like pattern). Dante translates the adjacent verses (8–11), also relevant, at *Conv.* 3.2.17–18 ("Tutte le cose produci da lo superno essemplo, tu, bellissimo, bello mondo ne la mente portante"). Boethius's poem and Dante's text in *Purg.* 25 have often been linked; for the import of Boethius's meter in Dante's poetics more generally, see Durling and Martinez, *Time and the Crystal*, 8–18, 53–54, 66–68, 124–126, 227–236, 333–336.

66. *Convivio* 2.4.5–6: "e volsero che sì come le intelligenze de li cieli o sono generatrici di quelli, ciascuna del suo, così queste fossero generatrici de l'altre cose ed essempli, ciascuna de la sua spezie; e chiamale Plato *idee*, che tanto è a dire quanto forme e nature universali. Li gentili le chiamano Dei e Dee, avvegna che non così filosoficamente intendessero quelle come Plato, e adoravano le loro immagini. . . ." Dante mentions among these goddesses "Minerva, la quale dissero dea di sapienza" (Vasoli, in Dante, *Convivio*, 147–148, cites the *Liber de causis*). Kantorowicz, *The King's Two Bodies*, 110, traces the consideration by the jurists of Justice as a Platonic idea.

67. See Kantorowicz, *The King's Two Bodies*, 111–112; and Rubinstein, "Political Ideas," 182–186.

68. Brunetto Latini sees Virtue as an empress with a number of daughters: "Esser nate di lei / quattro regine figlie" (*Tesoretto*, 1246–1247: the four cardinal virtues), who are subsequently parsed out "Or mi parean divise / E'n quattro parti mise . . . E poi, di grado in grado, / Ciascuna va più rado" (1251–1252, 1261–1262: the "parts" of each virtue, as liberality and severity are parts of justice). Kantorowicz, *The King's Two Bodies*, 107–109, notes the elaborate *Quaestiones de iuris subtilitatibus* attributed to Placentinus (d. 1192) where a melancholy Justice presides over a court of daughters (Aequitas, balancing her mother's scales, along with the civic Virtues— traditional "parts" of Justice—*religio, pietas, gratia*).

69. See Remigius of Auxerre, *Commentum in Martianum Capellam* 1.24.14 (ed. Cora E. Lutz [Leiden: E. J. Brill, 1962]). Lucan, *Pharsalia* 9.350–354, also presents a "reflective" Minerva that may have influenced Dante: "Voltus vidit aqua posuitque in margine plantas / et se dilecta Tritonida dixit ab unda" (9.353–354).

70. Pézard (*Rotta gonna*, 87) hears an echo of "super flumina confusionis . . . exules in Babylonis deflevimus" of Psalm 136 (cf. *Epist.* 7.4, 6, 60) in v. 49 ("sovra la vergin onda"). Note also the idea of God brooding over the waters in the original creation, as in *Par.* 29.12 ("lo discorrer di Dio sovra quest'acque") which echoes Dante's rendition in *Convivio* 3.7.2 of the *Liber de causis* on the action of the first cause: "Onde scritto è nel libro de le Cagioni: 'La prima bontade manda le sue bontadi sopra le cose con uno discorrimento.'"

71. Metaphors of radiation, fluvial flow, and generation figure in Neoplatonic accounts of the emanation of the hypostases, such as Macrobius, *Commentarii in Somnium Scipionis* 1.14.5 (ed. J. Willis [Leipzig: Teubner, 1970]): (emphases indicate the "emanations" and figurative terms for light, generation, and water flow): "Secundum haec ergo cum ex summo deo mens, ex mente anima fit, anima vero et condat et vita compleat omnia, quae secuntur, cunctaque his unus fulgor *illuminet* et universis appareat, ut in multis speculis, per ordinem positis vultus unus cumque omnia continui successionibus se sequantur *degenerantia* per ordinem ad imum *meandi*." See also *Commentarii* 1.17.12, and *Saturnalia* 1.18.17.

72. See Macrobius, *Commentarii* 1.20.2–3: "dux et princeps ait et moderator luminum reliquorum, mens mundi et temperantio"; also 1.20.4 ("fons . . . lucis"), 1.20.7 ("cor caeli"). For Dante, in *Convivio* 3.12, the sun is the most adequate physical representation of God. Vasoli glosses the Neoplatonic (Pseudo-Dionysius and the *Liber de causis*) backgrounds for Dante's account of the sun in *Convivio* 3.7.3 and 3.14.3.

73. Seneca, *Naturales quaestiones* 3.25.11, reported the view that the waters of the Nile not only aided conception but also restored fertility (see also 4a.2.10).

74. There is thus a parallel between the generations of Drittura and the descent of divine *virtù* into Philosophy at the climax of "Amor che ne la mente" (cf. v. 37: "In lei discende la virtù divina").

75. See Ovid, *Metamorphoses* 2.254–255: "Nilus in extremum fugit perterritus orbem / occuluitque caput; quod adhuc latet"; and Lucan, *Pharsalia* 10.190–191: ". . . fluvii causas per saecula tanta latentes / ignotumque caput." There is a parallel here with the secret origins of wisdom in the depths of God: see Ecclus. 1:5–6: "fons sapientiae verbum Dei in excelsis . . . radix sapientiae cui revelata est?" See also Job 28:2, 20–28.

76. For the Neoplatonic notion of the "apex mentis" in lyric poetry, see our discussion in Durling and Martinez, *Time and the Crystal*, 410. The source of inspiration is of course frequently figured a well or spring; cf. the "interno fonte" on which Dante's pilgrim would draw for his profession of faith (*Par.* 24.51), a fountain derived from the "fonte ond'ogne ver deriva" (*Par.* 4.116; see also 20.118, 31.93, and *Purg.* 15.131). Fountain and the river suggest poetic stimulus as well, from the "rivo chiaro molto" that accompanies the inspiration of "Donne ch'avete" in *Vita nuova* 19 to the traditional characterization of Virgil as he who "spand[e] di parlar sì largo fiume" (*Inf.* 1.69).

77. The construction is also in "Amor che ne la mente," verses 77–78: "tu sai che'l ciel sempr'è lucente e chiaro, / e quanto in sé non si turba già mai." See also *Purg.* 17.93 ("e tu'l sai") beginning Virgil's discussion of universal Love. Drittura's formulaic "come saper dei" resembles Buonconte's "ben sai" (*Purg.* 5.109), identifying a turn to learned material, in fact Aristotle's account of the formation of rivers from rainfall (*Meteorologica* 1.9–11, 13; 2.2), which refutes the stoic-Platonic views of Seneca and Lucan, for whom great rivers draw on abyssal reservoirs.

78. Drittura's mention of her eyes just before unfolding her genealogy suggests that, as Dante says of the eyes of Lady Philosophy, she refers to proofs, *dimonstrazioni*; see *Convivio* 2.15.4, 3.15.21.

79. Dante cites at *Convivio* 4.8.1 Aquinas's preface to his commentary on the *Ethics* (*Sententia libri Ethicorum* 1.1.1, cited by Vasoli, in Dante, *Convivio*, 606): "Sicut Philosophus dicit in principio *Metaphysicae*, 'sapientis est ordinare, cuius ratio est, quia sapientia est potissima perfectio rationis, cuius proprium est cognoscere ordinem . . . ordo autem actionem voluntariarum pertinet ad considerationem moralis philosophiae. . . .'"

80. Pézard's reading, for whom the scene points to an apocalyptic scorching of the earth (*Oeuvres*, 208–209). For the Nile flooding of the earth (the

cataclysm), see Seneca, *Naturales quaestiones* 3.27–30; and R. M. Durling, "'Io son venuto': Seneca, Plato and the Microcosm," *Dante Studies* 93 (1975): 95–129, especially 97–100.

81. Foster and Boyde (*Dante's Lyric Poetry*, 2:288–289) quote passages showing that deep shade is conventional for the Earthly Paradise (cf. *Purg.* 28.31–33).

82. The Magliabechiano commentary (7.1152), followed by Edmund Gardner ("Notes on the Lyrical Poetry of Dante," *Modern Language Review* 19 [1924]: 306–314; and 20 [1925]: 331), understands that the sun generates osier plants from the ground without seed (thus "taking the leaves from the ground") merely with its great "virtù" (cf. Gen. 2:9: "produxitque Dominus Deus de humo omne lignum . . ."), a reading syntactically consistent with Contini's and Pézard's.

83. The sun is near the zenith when the pilgrim approaches Eunoè (*Purg.* 33.103–105) prior to beginning his ascent in *Paradiso*. The balance of the sun and moon near the equinox is the object of Dante's simile at *Par.* 29.1–6 (cf. Alison Cornish, "Planets and Angels in *Paradiso* XXIX: The First Moment," *Dante Studies* 108 [1990]: 1–28); and see *Monarchia*, 1.11.5: "Phebe similis, fratrem dyametraliter intuenti . . ." where the astronomical "balance" suggests justice (cf. Durling and Martinez, *Time and the Crystal*, 208–209, 420).

84. If this seems excessive attention to the sun's orbit, compare Dante's discussion of v. 19 of "Amor che nella mente" ("Non vede il sol che tutto il mondo gira") in *Convivio* 3.5–6. Use in *Convivio* 3.5.12 of the ninth book of the *Pharsalia* (mention of Cato, the Garamantes, etc.) suggests parallels with "Tre donne." See also Durling and Martinez, *Time and the Crystal*, 232–240.

85. The Nile course is treated at length in Pliny, *Natural History* 5.55–56; Seneca devotes a whole (now fragmentary) book of *Naturales quaestiones* to it, plus sections of book 3, on rivers (the Nile is of "propriae naturae ac singularis" [3.1.2]); for Lucan, see below.

86. See especially Lucan, *Pharsalia* 10.188–331, a speech to conquering Caesar by Acoreus, priest of the Egyptian religion. Lucan's errors of geography and astronomy are legion, as Housman pointed out (Lucan, *Bellum civile*, ed. A. E. Housman [Oxford, 1958], 330–332). But Sacrobosco adopts a number of passages from Lucan correctly perceiving that they are accounts of the equator (see Lynn Thorndike, *The Sphere of Sacrobosco and Its Commentators* [Chicago: University of Chicago Press, 1949), 103–107.

87. Pliny's *Natural History* (5.55–56) clearly correlates the river's flow with the disappearance of shadows: "id evenire a canis ortu per introitum solis in leonem, contra perpendiculum fontis sidere stante, cum eo tractu adsumantur umbrae. . . ."

88. Singleton, in his commentary, correlates this passage with *Purg.* 30.89: "la terra che perde ombra . . .", clearly also a parallel with vv. 46–48 of "Tre donne." See also Lucan, *Pharsalia* 10.304–306.

89. In Lucan's most succinct description of the phenomenon: "Nilus neque suscitat undas / ante Canis radios nec ripis alligat amnem / Ante parem nocti Libra sub iudice Phoebum (*Pharsalia* 10.225–227).

90. "Iussus adest, auctusque suos non ante coarta, / Quam nox aestivas a sole receperit horas" (Lucan, *Pharsalia*, 10.217–218); see also 10.226–228: "nec campus liberat undis, / donec in auctumnum declinet Phoebus et umbras / Extendat Meroe. . . ."

91. See Lucan, *Pharsalia* 10.215–216: tunc Nilus fonte soluto, / exit ut oceanus lunaribus incrementis." Lucan's uncle Seneca compares the final flooding of the earth to an equinoctial (thus particularly strong) tide in *Naturales quaestiones* 3.28.6.

92. Lucan follows Seneca (*Naturales quaestiones* 3.22), for whom the Nile (like the Danube) is an abyssal river, the source of its waters established from the origin of the present world. David Quint, in his *Origin and Originality in Renaissance Literature* (New Haven, Conn.: Yale University Press, 1983), discusses the rivers of Paradise and the Jordan as "sources" of authority for Renaissance writers; much of what Quint says goes for Dante as well (the Jordan is the last terrestrial river mentioned in the *Commedia*, and just possibly also the first).

93. For the Nile's flow as balancing the sun's heat, see Seneca, *Naturales quaestiones* 3.10.3 and 4a.2.1: "natura . . . ita disposuit ut eo tempore innundaret Aegyptum quo maxime usta fervoribus terra undas altius traheret . . ."; see also Lucan, *Pharsalia* 10.230–233. For the principle of a "tempered" cosmos, see Isidore, *De natura rerum* 13.1, describing how the "waters above" cool the cosmos heated by the sun.

94. Torraca noted Lucan's use of *parvus* for the Nile at its source, *Pharsalia* 10.295: "Arcanum natura caput non prodidit ulli, / nec licuit populis *parvum* te, Nile, videre. . . ."

95. Note the verbal echo of Lucan's phrase for the creator's governance of the waters "*certo* sub *iure* coercet" in Dante's "con *certo giro* vallava li abissi." Dante attributes the solar orbit laboriously described in *Convivio* 3.5.22 to Wisdom: "O ineffabile sapienza che così ordinasti. . . ."

96. Augustine, *De Genesi ad litteram* 1.160 (trans. J. H. Taylor as *The Literal Meaning of Genesis* [New York: Newman Press, 1982]).

97. Cf. *Monarchia* 2.2.5: "Et iterum ex hoc sequitur quod ius in rebus nichil est aliud quam similitudo divine voluntatis. . . ."

98. This structure informally echoes the division of "Donne ch'avete" and "Amor che ne la mente," both of which use the final stanza as a *tornata* and the first stanza as a *propositio*.

99. For the close parallels between the first and last rhymes in the poem, see above. For additional contrasts, consider the "feminine" stanza 2, in effect a blazon, sketching Drittura in face, hands, arm, foot, and secret parts, versus the "masculine" stanza 4, where Love shows off his blunted weapons.

100. In *Conv.* 2.6.2, a propos of "Voi ch'intendendo" (cf. v. 2: "il ragionar ch'è nel mio core"), Dante observes that the "heart" is not always taken as the organ but as the "secreto dentro" of the person (and cf. 2.6.7–8); this is how I take it here.

101. In a passage with direct bearing on the Drittura of "Tre donne," Philosophy explains that when attacked by the barbarous men who have torn her dress, "nostra quidem dux copias suas *in arcem contrahit*" (our captain [Wisdom] withdraws her forces into her citadel [Boethius, *Consolatio philosophiae* 1, pr. 4]).

102. Dante cites verses from bk. 3, m. 9 in his discussion of the "nobilissima parte dell'anima," the *mente*, in *Convivio* 3.2.17–19, by virtue of which humans can be referred to as divine ("e però è l'uomo divino animale da li filosofi chiamato . . ."); cf. above, note 64.

103. Aquinas, *Summa contra gentiles* 2.1 (trans. Anton C. Pegis [Notre Dame, Ind.: University of Notre Dame Press, 1975]): "the pursuit of wisdom is most perfect . . . because, insofar as man gives himself to the pursuit of wisdom, so far does he even now have some share in true beatitude." Seneca, addressing Lucilius in the prefaces to the *Naturales quaestiones*, presents natural-historical study as a way of turning away from politics and returning to the self: such activity is "divina conversatione." See also *Naturales quaestiones* 3, pref. 2: "sibi totus animus vacet et ad contemplationem sui saltem in ipso fine respiciat"; 3, pref. 11: "Quid est praecipuum? Erigere animum supra minas et promissa fortunae"; and 4a, pref. 20: "Fugiendum ergo et in se recedendum est; immo etiam a se recedendum"; see also 3, pref. 18, and 4a, 1.1.

104. Compare Ecclus. 24:46: " . . . non desinam in progenies illorum usque in aevum sanctum"; in the Middle Ages, these words were attributed to Sapientia, not Ben Sirach. See also Wis. 1:15: "Iustitia enim perpetua est, et immortalis . . ."; 5:16: "iusti autem in perpetuum vivent. . . ." See also Aquinas, *Summa contra gentiles* 1.2: " . . . through wisdom we arrive at the kingdom of immortality, for 'the desire of wisdom bringeth to the everlasting kingdom [Wis. 6:21].'"

105. Dante sprinkles through the poem—all stanzas *except* the third—terms related to dwellings: thus *casa* in stanza 1, *rocca* in stanza 4, and *camera* in the second *tornata*; and, in stanzas 2 and 5, the synechdoches *colonna* and *chiave*). The architectural synechdoche suggests the attribute of Sapientia, the column or pillar, may be behind Dante's use of *colonna* for Drittura: see Prov. 9:1: "Sapientia aedificavit sibi domum, Excidit *columnas* septem"; these seven columns were often identified with the virtues.

106. Macrobius, *Commentarii in Somnium Scipionis* (trans. W. H. Stahl as *Macrobius: Commentary on the "Dream of Scipio"* [New York: Columbia University Press, 1952], 243).

107. See Pézard's citation (*Rotta gonna*, 86) from Anselm (vol. 158, 280–281, of Patrologiae Cursus Completus, Series Latina, 221 vols., ed. J. P. Migne [Paris, 1841–1864]): " . . . Tres igitur sunt, fons, rivus, lacus, et unus Nilus."

Palinode and History in the Oeuvre of Dante

In terms of the focus of this book, *Current Trends in Dante Studies*, the overall aim of my essay is threefold: (1) to review a topic, the "palinode," which has been at the heart of American Dante studies for the last twenty years and which in fact can be understood broadly as a figure for most of the work in this period on Dantean inter- and intratextuality; (2) to bring Dante studies into productive relationship with two major trends in method on the American literary scene generally, namely, "rhetorical" and "historical" reading (in this case, rhetorical reading *as* historical reading);[1] and (3) to continue my own ongoing attempt (in which I am clearly not alone)[2] to redefine the ways in which the *opere minori* of Dante can and should be read—to the point of interrogating what it means to think of such uniquely ambitious intellectual projects as *Convivio, De vulgari eloquentia*, and *Monarchia* as minor works and as pendants from, and dependents of, the colossal achievement of the *Commedia*.

At least since the work of Gianfranco Contini and Charles S. Singleton, Dante criticism on both sides of the Atlantic has focused intensely on Dante's characteristic propensity for overt reflection on the nature of his own poetic practice,[3] and especially his self-placement within a complex vision of literary history that includes both classical and contemporary poets, and perhaps even the Bible itself. In North America this tendency has been stimulated and oriented by theories of "intertextuality"[4] and by important studies of how medieval and Renaissance authors write literary history allusively and "from the inside."[5] Within the vast economy of Dante's literary self-awareness and auto-referentiality, the term *palinode*, literally a "singing again" or "recantation," describes a particular form of revisionism[6]—namely, the explicit and / or allusive invocation and transformation of materials from prior Dantean texts within their successors, above all the *Commedia*'s critical evocation of its author's earlier efforts.

Twentieth-century Dante criticism has focused obsessively on its author's propensity for repeating, correcting, and even overtly contradicting himself from one work to the next at a number of different levels—concept, image, narrative, character, and so on. The exemplary sequence, of course, is the one that leads from the *Vita nuova*, with its explicit focus on Dante's love for a human, if virtually inaccessible, woman, Beatrice; through the apparent turn in *Convivio* to an allegorical "donna gentile," who represents Dante's first mournful, then joyful, recourse to the "consolation of philosophy"; and on to the return of Beatrice in *Purgatorio* 30, now explicitly revealed as a *figura Christi* and mediator of Dante's salvation. However one charts this sequence, and there have been an extraordinary number of variants,[7] there is no doubt that Dante wrote it at each stage to be seen as a sequence, or that there is some sort of maturation or ascent dramatized in each successive passage from one text to the next. This, in fact, is already the case in the relationship of the *Vita nuova* to the previously composed poems it surrounds with narrative and commentary, transforming them from lyric moments not dramatically different than those found in Cavalcanti and Guinizzelli, and in the Provençal and "Sicilian" poets before them, into something quite different.[8]

More generally speaking, in the Italian context, and even to some extent in our own, speculative theories of chronology (e.g., Bruno Nardi's placement of the *Monarchia* in 1308)[9] and of belated textual revision (e.g., Luigi Pietrobono's claim that Dante "retrofitted" the ending of the *Vita nuova* to support his later rejection of the *Convivio*'s philosophical stance)[10] have been deployed to create a coherent and evolutionary interpretation of Dante's literary career and intellectual biography, usually with the *Commedia* as ideal telos.[11] These discussions, which were characteristically guided by commitment to the primacy of Dante's "thought," then found powerful and appropriate correction in Contini's examination of the evolution of Dante's career primarily in terms of stylistic, rhetorical, and narratological considerations, and particularly in his seminal insistence on Dante's ceaseless linguistic "experimentalism" and the rhetorical deployment of the first-person voice (culminating in the pilgrim / poet tension that structures the *Commedia*).[12]

The dominant American variant of this critical strategy emerged in the early 1970s largely through John Freccero's elegant reading, with its debt both to Contini and to Bloomian theories of literary revisionism, of "Casella's Song" as a poetic recantation of the consolatory Boethian poetics of *Convivio*.[13] The structure of palinode was clearly congenial to Freccero, since in the domain of literary intertextuality it approximates the psychic and narrative structures of conversion which form the basis of his reading of the *Commedia*. In addition, to return to where we started, Freccero's essay has the special virtue of suggesting that the palinode is in fact potentially paradigmatic for many, if not all, forms of Dantean intertextuality and literary history. The same essay which shows how "Amor che nella mente mi ragiona" is reinterpreted and recanted as it is recontextualized also suggests a revision of an earlier portion of the *Commedia* (i.e., *Inferno* 5) as well as of important literary-philosophical precursors, notably Boethius.[14] In other words, the pattern of repetition and recantation is fundamental not only among the various Dantean texts but also within individual texts (as Singleton in "The Vistas in Retrospect" and Robert Hollander in *Allegory in Dante's "Commedia"* had earlier suggested)[15] and between Dante's texts and his various classical and medieval *auctores*—as the work of many different scholars on Dante and Virgil, Ovid, Statius, Cavalcanti, Daniel et al. has repeatedly shown over the last twenty years.[16]

The basic argument of most recent "intertextual" work on palinodic structure and on precursor poets is as follows: Dante evokes his own previous texts or those of others in a variety of ways (verbal or conceptual echo, generic modeling, narrative episode, dramatic representation), only to define a limit to their value as models, usually in the form of a critique of the doctrinal substance conveyed by their literary practice (*Convivio*'s philosophical stance, Virgil's and Ovid's paganism, and Cavalcanti's epicureanism being only the most obvious examples).[17] In this account, Dante again and again leads his readers to the same conclusion—namely, that the union of Christian theology and poetic representation sets his *Commedia* apart from practically everything else that has ever been written, with the unique (and even then at times not absolutely clear) exception of the Bible itself.

Furthermore, Dante's inscriptions of literary history can also be characterized as typological, that is, as conforming to the pattern of salvation history as defined in the Bible, where the Christ event imposes the complete reinterpretation of the significance of the Hebrew Bible as the Old Testament.[18] And for that matter, one could argue that Auerbach's notion of *figura*, that is, the interpreting recontextualization of historical events in the eschatological frame of the *Commedia*, is part of the same phenomenon.[19] An example of the convergence of literary palinode with historical *figura* is the case of Guido da Montefeltro—whose belated conversion is celebrated in *Convivio* 4.28.8 then subverted in *Inferno* 27, where his ultimate damnation is revealed. Guido's sorry tale at once corrects an "error" in the earlier text and sets the historical record straight from the "infallible" perspective of eternity. A similar phenomenon can be registered, as we shall see, in the treatment of Frederick II and his family. In other words, this structure is a means for re-presenting a series of histories: Dante's internal creative biography, the literary history of his relations with other poets, as well as the political-social history of his time. Just as the *Commedia* confronts, interprets, and ultimately aims to dominate the realm of human history by appearing to transcend it, so Dante confers upon himself a typological and eschatological perspective, *as if* at the end of literary history, fulfilling and transcending those who have written before, including his own earlier incarnations.[20]

It is now possible to suggest how a reexamination of the palinode involves a reconsideration both of the rhetorical organization structuring Dante's texts and of the ways in which those texts may be understood *historically*—both as products and as interpretations of history. The topic of Dante and history is not exactly new, of course. Auerbach went so far as to argue that Dante was essentially a "poet of the secular world" in the sense that the most fundamental achievement of his art was the "full" representation of historical reality.[21] Giuseppe Mazzotta, in *Dante, Poet of the Desert*, turned from a model of virtually transparent mimesis or figural imitation to a powerful account of the problematic "poetics of history" by which Dante confronted from the perspective of language "history as the economy of redemption and as the realm of exile."[22] What these accounts share, for all their differences, is a focus on how history appears, in its particular contingencies and as a conceptual domain, within the economy of Dante's representations.[23] While I do not want to underestimate the importance of these accounts for understanding "from the inside" Dante's representation and understanding of history, what I wish to focus on is what they perforce set aside, namely, the question of how an unfolding set of historical events and circumstances made Dante and his representations possible in the first place—how history implies, subsumes, and, as it were, transcends the Dantean oeuvre, just as much as the other way around.[24] My hope is not so much to deny the existence of the palinode, as some recent critics have done,[25] but to see it clearly as a powerful rhetorical device rather than as a true expression of Dante's experience.[26] It can then become a tool for historicizing Dante's literary career, always mindful that to identify the marks of history upon the Dantean texts, one must first come to terms with the textual strategies by which they seek to master history by representing it.

What makes such a question so difficult to answer, other than the intrinsic complexity of charting the lines of force from world to text and back again, is that the palinode is designed specifically to anticipate the question and to prevent the asking of it. Dante's palinodes are rhetorical-conceptual devices for containing and dominating the unruly differences of the self and of history. He establishes a narrative with continuity between beginning and ending (by the recurrence of common elements, for example, Beatrice and the Dantean "I"), but also with the focused and meaningful disruption of what Aristotle would have called *peripeteia* (reversal) and *anagnoresis* (recognition) and what Freccero, with reference to Augustine, calls *conversion*. Thus, contradictions of the self and of history are at once acknowledged and contained by their placement within a hierarchical narrative order, where what comes above and last subsumes and interprets what comes below and before.

Against the fictive power of palinodic structure stands the factual power of history. One might indeed expect that the palinode would find its limits under extreme forms of historical pressure. The most obvious example, of course, would be the intervention of death—a death so sudden or disruptive that no room for the writing of a *retractio* remained. In Italian literary history, useful examples appear in the later cases of Poliziano's *Stanze* and Boiardo's *Orlando innamorato*, the one left unfinished after the assassination of its Medicean protagonist / patron, the other after the author's own demise. One could argue that the motive engine for Dante's first and most powerful recourse to the palinode in the *Vita nuova* itself was precisely the death of Beatrice,[27] and that he later, apotropaically, converted his own death (made more pressing by the untimely, and poetically prefigured, death of his sometime "primo amico" Guido Cavalcanti) into the palinodic perspective par excellence, the world of divine justice beyond individual lives and beyond history itself.[28] Nonetheless one would have to acknowledge Dante's luck in surviving barely long enough to close the "sacro poema" whose visionary and revisionary power depends to no little extent on its seamless totality.[29]

Death is not the only way in which history makes itself felt or resists authorial attempts to bring it under control by giving it a definite shape. Nonetheless, it would have taken something or someone quite extraordinary to resist incorporation and appropriation within the providentially poetic order of the *Commedia*, something, or someone, that was crucial in the most basic way to Dante's historical experience and to his project for interpreting it and that therefore could not easily be reduced to the mere effluvia of contingency. Such elements, I submit, can be found, first, in the one major treatise Dante actually completed, *Monarchia*, which also constitutes, with a few of the epistles, his most direct literary attempt to influence the course of contemporary political history and, second, in a crucial historical personage, the Emperor Frederick II, whose powerful hold on Dante's poetic and political imagination is betrayed by his recurrent appearances in the postexilic works.

The case of *Monarchia* is especially intriguing because its relationship to the *Commedia* is much less easily fixed than that of the *Vita nuova*, *Convivio*, and *De vulgari eloquentia*.[30] The political discourse of the *Commedia* undoubtedly shares some of the *Monarchia*'s principal theses—the parallelism of imperial and salvation history (*Inferno* 34; *Paradiso* 6-7), the complementary functions of pope and emperor (*Purgatorio* 16), and so on. But it also clearly betrays the same kinds of differentiating shifts that characterize the *Commedia*'s relationship to the other treatises. For example, where *Monarchia* openly attacks the Decretalists' allegorization of the "duo magna luminaria" of Genesis and the subordination of the "lunar" empire to the "solar" papacy (3.4), *Purgatorio* 16 offers its own revised allegorization of two separate but equal "suns" figuring the two great institutional authorities.[31] For Nardi, who believed that *Monarchia* preceded the *Commedia*, a version of the palinode is clearly at work here too. *Monarchia* is the logical consequence of Dante's drive toward a fully articulated philosophical rationalism in *Convivio*, and it brings into the open a radical, for Nardi averroistic, split between the domain of nature and active human reason, on the one hand, and on the other, the realm of grace and acquiescing human faith. The institution of a hierarchy in the *Commedia* which subordinates nature to grace, reason to revelation, Virgil to Beatrice, is thus a corrective to both *Convivio* and *Monarchia*.[32]

The problem with this hypothesis is that in order to conserve the palinodic narrative as such, Nardi has to date *Monarchia* to 1308, although there is no hard evidence that allows one to do so, any more than it is possible to link the treatise securely to the slightly later period of Henry VII's foray into Italy (1310–1313), despite the temptation to see Henry as the "objective correlative" to Dante's utopian emperor. It is much easier to date the treatise to a point after Dante had completed the *Paradiso*, to which there is one explicit reference in the text. Critics, however, have frequently tried to dismiss this reference as a later interpolation, based partly on peculiarities in the manuscript tradition but more on their own sense of what the shape of Dante's career should look like.[33] If *Monarchia* comes later, it means that the transcendent synthesis of the *Commedia* was not absolute but contingent and, as it were, generic, linked to the perspective offered by the particular literary form and stance embodied in the *Commedia* and not to a permanent and essential "conversion" of Dante's self and his poetics.[34] My point, however, is not that Nardi's dating, or any of the others, is demonstrably incorrect, though I do strongly incline to the later date myself. Rather, right or wrong, in the absence of definitive evidence the case of *Monarchia* suggests the fragility and instability of the palinode, that is, of the attempts by Dante and his critics alike to impose an idealized historical narrative on his life and works.

Let me come at the same point from another angle. The pattern of allusion and repetition-in-difference in Dante's oeuvre is not limited to the *Commedia* vis-à-vis the other texts. Clear echoes also connect certain of the *opere minori* to others. And in most such cases it is much more difficult to establish the hierarchical narrative and conceptual order that so clearly characterizes the *Commedia*'s relationship to the treatises. The *Convivio*'s love story is overtly set in relation to the *Vita nuova*'s, particularly through the dramatization of a struggle between two thoughts of love. However, Dante is careful to avoid stating that love of Lady Philosophy replaced love of Beatrice who, he says, continues to dwell in his soul (*Convivio* 2.2.1; cf. 2.8.8). Rather, it is the *Commedia* that seemingly creates a radical opposition between the two. In other cases, apparent contradictions are even less easily resolved into a palinodic hierarchy, an important example being the *divario* between *Convivio* and *De vulgari eloquentia* over the relative nobility of "grammar" (i.e., Latin) and *volgare* (i.e., Italian). And in such cases the suspicion arises either that Dante adopts different and even opposed positions according to the specific and contingent needs of a given argument (that is, he is shamelessly rhetorical in his deployment of concepts), or that his notion of dialectic permits the determination of truth value according to specific context (i.e., that he allows for a double or multiple truth, accepts the "sic et non").[35]

An especially interesting instance of this phenomenon, at least from the point of view of this essay, is the pattern of connections that link *Convivio*, book 4, and *Monarchia*.[36] This pattern forms the basis for Nardi's claims that *Monarchia* derives directly and almost immediately from *Convivio*; but, as we shall see, with the evident resemblances there are also differences—in the form of omissions, additions, and contradictions—between the two works which invite a somewhat more sustained examination than is usually given them. In book 4 of *Convivio*, a discussion of the nature of imperial authority arises in the course of a digression whose governing purpose is to show that Dante's definition of *nobilitas* as an individual, divinely conferred quality which is the ground of all human virtue (4.18–19) does not contradict the authority either of Emperor Frederick II (to whom is attributed the notion that nobility derives from ancient lineage and its attendant wealth, i.e., that it is familial and transpersonal), or of Aristotle, who seems to give Frederick and his followers indirect support by his assertion that anything believed by a large number of people is necessarily rooted in truth (4.3). *Monarchia* obviously picks up and develops several of Dante's claims in *Convivio* (especially 4.4–5): the necessity of a single, universal monarchy; the supreme role of the emperor as "cavalcatore della volontà umana" (ch. 9.10) and as ultimate judge over human actions; the directly mandated assignment of empire and emperorship to the Roman people; the privileged place of the Roman Empire in the economy of salvation history. Moreover, the evidence adduced concerning the providential nature of Roman history in *Monarchia* book 2 reflects the same close reading of Virgil's *Aeneid* as the latter part of *Convivio* book 4 (and, obviously, as the *Commedia* itself).[37]

In fact, although the thorny question of the relationship of emperor to pope, which constitutes the polemical burden of *Monarchia*, is not discussed in *Convivio*, nonetheless, the earlier treatise does preview the rhetorical and conceptual strategies through which Dante will address the problem in book 3 of *Monarchia*. Though *Convivio* goes to some lengths to define the emperor's and empire's absolute dominion in the judicial and political domain of the "ragione scritta" (4.9.9) the point of the digression is to circumscribe their authority, to show where it does *not* hold sway, namely, in the realm of philosophical and especially ethical reasoning (4.6, 8–9). That domain, instead, belongs to the philosopher, embodied first of all by Aristotle but also, implicitly, by Dante himself. Dante specifies the absolute *auctoritas* of emperor and philosopher in distinct realms of human experience and then insists on the necessary complementarity and interdependence of the two (4.6.17–20). This conceptual structure, which Gilson designated as the "aporia dantesca,"[38] is then repeated in *Monarchia*—although the philosopher as textual protagonist has disappeared altogether, only to be replaced by the pope, who occupies an equivalent dialectical position vis-à-vis the emperor.

Elsewhere I have argued that this strategy of defining, but also delimiting, absolute authority allows Dante to create a conceptual and rhetorical space for his own *auctoritas* to emerge in both of these texts.[39] Here instead I want to emphasize how the evident transfer or displacement of both a complex of concepts (regarding imperial authority) and an argumentative strategy (the separation and interdependence of authorities) works to create not only a continuity but also a notable shift between the two treatises—one which cannot be adequately grasped in the terms of the palinode. One might argue that by substituting the pope for the philosopher as the intellectual / spiritual "other" of the emperor, Dante replaces reason with faith as the most important mode of human vision, thus following the typical pattern of palinodic revision as deployed in the *Commedia*. Yet this is precisely what *Monarchia* does not do. The function of the empire is to fulfill the terrestrial *bonum* of rationality and justice (1.11; 3.15).[40] The exercise of the emperor's judging will both exemplifies and enables the full realization of the "possible intellect" (1.3–5). Moreover, the treatise itself explicitly adopts the perspective of rationality (e.g., 1.2.4–8; 3.2) notwithstanding a number of recourses, under evident constraint, to arguments from both faith and experience (e.g., 2.1.7–8; 2.7). And the principal function of the argument concerning the separate but equal relationship of pope and emperor in book 3 is to limit rather than to affirm papal authority.

The disappearance (or, perhaps better, *sublimation*) of the figure of the philosopher between *Convivio* and *Monarchia* thus requires a different and nonpalinodic explanation, namely, that the philosopher would be an obvious *terzo incomodo* in this context. Since the emperor's judicial authority in the domain of natural reason is characterized by being unitary and undivided (this is the burden of book 1, especially ch. 7–10), the reassertion of the philosopher's intellectual authority as a necessary complement to it would compromise and vitiate it (by dividing what is by definition indivisible), just as it would introduce an unbalancing asymmetry in the neat duality of book 3. The suspicion, then, would be that the echoing of *Convivio* in *Monarchia* is not a deliberate revisionary evocation, a palinodic recantation, of an earlier text by a later one. Rather, it rehearses a conceptual and rhetorical strategy which had served Dante's turn in the past—one that unveils not the transcending emergence of new and stable meaning but instead an essential rhetoricity which subtends and potentially evacuates meaning. This is not to discount the seriousness of the politics articulated in *Monarchia*. I would argue in fact that it is the very importance Dante attaches to them that drives him to deploy an intrinsically flawed line of argument.

Even more specific evidence for this hypothesis comes at the one point where *Monarchia* flatly contradicts *Convivio*, on a topic that constitutes the very substance of book 4 of the earlier treatise. As mentioned before, *Convivio* systematically asserts that nobility is individual and divinely infused, not genealogical, racial, social, and / or economic in origin, attributing the opposing position to Frederick and his vulgar followers (4.canzone.21–40; 4.3.5–10). Furthermore, it has long been noted that the opinion attributed to Frederick in *Convivio* is not easily to be found in the emperor's surviving writings and that one sonnet attributed to him actually takes a line very close to Dante's own.[41] Rather, it can best be located in Aristotle's *Politics* [4.8.1294a.20–21]. In *Monarchia*, however, Dante specifically adduces *as his own* the Aristotelian definition of nobility, now attributing it to its proper source: "est enim nobilitas virtus et divitie antique, iuxta Philosophum" (Nobility is virtue and ancient wealth, according to the Philosopher [2.3.4]).[42]

If we discount the unpersuasive scholarly attempts to claim that Dante had not yet read the Aristotelian treatise when he wrote *Convivio*,[43] this reference at the very least exposes a disingenuous and strategically motivated line of argument in the earlier work. It does not, however, then place *Monarchia* in a position of palinodic superiority, since, as *Convivio* does make clear, the imperial / Aristotelian definition of nobility is at odds with the Christian notions of free will and the autonomous value of the individual soul. Instead, I conjecture, the open use of the Aristotelian definition in *Monarchia* is dictated by a shift of conceptual domains and is equally strategic in nature. In the domain of (Christian) ethics, which is the domain of *Convivio*, nobility must be individual. In the domain of politics, especially imperial politics, the need for institutional continuity—within the Roman people, and from one emperor to the next—requires a social and transpersonal concept of nobility.[44] And so Dante adopts one without hesitation, despite a full awareness of the problems it presents from other perspectives. In short, the contradictions between *Convivio* and *Monarchia* do not become the basis of a hierarchically articulated palinode or establish Dante's transcendent authority over his material, rather the parallel passages in the two texts are mutually "subversive," in the limited sense that the juxtaposition reveals that *both* treatises deliberately suppress relevant conceptual steps for strategic, that is, for contingent—rhetorical and historical—reasons. The relation between the treatises is thus based at least as much on convenient forgetfulness as it is on a confessional and recantatory remembering, and it points obliquely to the contingent constructedness of the author's intellectual history.

This idea finds further confirmation if we look at the single greatest change in the material that is passed on from *Convivio* to *Monarchia*— an alteration not by addition or revision but, rather, by suppression. As we have already seen, in *Convivio* the discourses about imperial authority and the role of the Roman *imperium*, as well as the discourse concerning nobility, are all inextricably linked to a specific historical figure, Frederick II of Swabia, designated by Dante precisely as the "last emperor of the Romans" (4.3), since none of his German-born successors had been properly installed in office or had made the obligatory effort to take up his place in the center of the empire, Italy (as Frederick, whose court was in Sicily, obviously had done, virtually alone among the Holy Roman emperors).[45] *Monarchia*, however, is the only one of Dante's four major postexilic writings in which there is no reference to Frederick, although the material linked to his name in *Convivio* is largely conserved, and although it is the one work in which one would most expect to find him, given its exclusive focus on imperial politics.

In a recent essay, Roger Dragonetti has argued that Dante's treatment of Frederick embodies the power of poetry to absorb and transform the raw materials of history through its representations.[46] The question, I will suggest, is more complex than Dragonetti allows it to be. In any case, it is clear that, at least after 1301, Frederick played a decisive role in Dante's historical imagination—in his politics, in his linguistics and attendant poetics, and, above all, at the point of intersection between them, the place where power, knowledge, and imagination meet and, one desperately hopes, collaborate, offering Dante a point of insertion back from his state of exile into the ethical and political life of his day.

In *Convivio*, Frederick's crucial place in any even minimally historicized understanding of the institution of empire and of the political circumstances in Italy during the thirteenth and early fourteenth centuries is clearly acknowledged. In addition, it is arguable, he becomes the figurative stand-in for the hypothetical audience of the treatise—the men of politics and commerce, illiterate in Latin, who need a divulgative tutelage in ethical philosophy to guide them in their activities (1.10.5). Thus, Dante implicitly stages himself, via his poetry and commentary, as the philosopher who stands as necessary complement to the emperor, identified through Frederick. *De vulgari eloquentia* makes the point even more plainly. Dante's account of the development of the illustrious Italian vernacular places its origins, at least as far as poetry is concerned, at the court of Frederick, as patron of Giacomo da Lentini (Il Notaio), Pier delle Vigne, and others, and as a poet himself (1.12.1–4), while Dante, in the company of Cino da Pistoia and Guido Cavalcanti, figures as the consummate and climactic voice of the *volgare illustre*, the lineal descendant of the *scuola siciliana*. And his later definition of the *volgare illustre* as properly *aulic* and *curial*, that is, as the language which could be spoken and written in the central royal court of Italy, clearly looks back to Frederick's court as an empirical model for what once was and perhaps again will be (1.18.2–5). And here again he posits a complementary relationship between the poet guided by the "gratioso lumine rationis" (1.18.5) and his powerful patron.

Nor is the value Dante attributes to Frederick in *Convivio* and *De vulgari eloquentia* exclusively, neutrally historical and political— rather he confers on him an ethical worth equivalent to his historical importance: Frederick and his son Manfred are praised to the skies in *De vulgari eloquentia* 1.12.4: "those illustrious heroes, Frederick Caesar and his well-born son, Manfred, displayed the nobility and rectitude of their souls and, while Fortune allowed, behaved with humanity, disdaining what is bestial" ("illustres heroes, Fredericus Caesar et benegenitus eius Manfredus, nobilitatem ac rectitudinem sue forme pandentes donec fortuna permisit humana secuti sunt, brutalia dedignantes").[47] It is particularly noteworthy that Dante here assigns Frederick the three attributes which are most fundamental and laudable in the language of *Convivio* and *De vulgari eloquentia*: illustriousness, nobility, rectitude. Nonetheless, there are egregious problems implicit in linking Dante's imperial and poetic hopes to the "last emperor." Even in the quoted passage, the qualifier "donec fortuna permisit," which allows for an eventual descent from humanity into bestiality, foreshadows the contingencies which clearly remove Frederick from any possible idealization.

As Dragonetti observes, these problems emerge full blown (and I would add, in a clearly figural-palinodic mode) in the *Commedia*, beginning with Frederick's damnation as a faithless epicurean in *Inferno* 10, a canto which calls sharp attention to the Guelf / Ghibelline, church / empire conflicts that had originated with Frederick, that still ravaged Italy during Dante's youth, and that had then reproduced themselves in the Black / White factionalism that led directly to his exile). The process continues with the episode of Pier delle Vigne (the emperor's unfortunate chancellor, as well as a poet of the Sicilian school), where Frederick appears as a capricious and violent ruler whose whims jeopardize the fortunes and the lives of his faithful councilors. Through a number of carefully structured parallels between Pier's circumstances and Dante's own, canto 13 clearly jeopardizes his convivial fantasy of the poet-philosopher's symbiotic relationship with an imperial master—along with any remaining hopes of implementing a rationally grounded political program in history. This palinodic structure is further articulated in a series of increasingly displaced allusions to Frederick via his family members, notably, Manfred, his son, in *Purgatorio* 3, and Constance, his mother, in *Paradiso* 3. In *Purgatorio* 24, as is well known, Dante establishes a fundamental rupture between his own *dolce stil nuovo* and the poetics of Il Notaio and the Sicilian lyricists.

While the *Commedia* apotropaically as well as palinodically invokes Frederick only to dismiss him, *Monarchia* is a very different story. As we have already seen, there no palinode is deployed—Frederick is simply excluded altogether. But why make so much of an absence, given the notorious difficulty of arguments, as it were, ex nihilo and in absentia? Because, as I have already said, so much of the material elaborated in *Monarchia* first appeared in *Convivio*, tightly linked to Frederick II. Because, as Dante says in *Convivio* (4.3.6), historically Frederick was the last occupant of the office he is discussing in *Monarchia* (or the next to last, depending on where the treatise is dated vis-à-vis Henry VII, who in any case is also excluded from the treatise) and this is a work whose specific goal is that of reinstating empire and emperor in the secular world. Because, finally, Frederick's open warfare with a series of popes is among the most pressing historical evidence, along with Boniface VIII's various escapades, of the need to find a solution to the problem of imperial vs. ecclesiastical claims to power.

This last item, of course, also tells us clearly *why* such an exclusion might be necessary: Frederick's historical existence, his empirical occupancy of the imperial throne, constitutes a virtual point-by-point refutation of Dante's logical arguments in *Monarchia*. Rather than bringing unity, Frederick created divisions; rather than reconciling reason with faith he is a reputed unbeliever and heretic; rather than submitting, with filial piety, to the spiritual authority of the church, he contested it fiercely; and so on and so forth. His name in itself would be a reminder of the disruptions in the imperial line that severed the institution not only from its Roman origins but even from the recent medieval past. The strain of recuperating the apparent violence and illegitimacy of the original Roman empire is, as I have argued elsewhere,[48] evident in the convoluted attempts of book 2 to show that Roman world domination is legal and even divinely sponsored. Frederick's presence in *Monarchia* would aggravate the problem: he is clearly too near in time, too obviously at odds with the rationalized fantasy of a rapport between church and state, in other words, too messily historical to be confronted within the boundaries of the treatise. And indeed, from the perspective of a rational human being scrutinizing the signs of recent history for expressive traces of the divine will, the twelfth and early thirteenth centuries offer very little support for the idea that God endorses the existence of a universal, Roman monarchy.

It was probably obvious from the outset why Frederick was excluded from *Monarchia* (and, for that matter, why Boniface VIII, as well as Clement V and Henry VII, if applicable, are not mentioned either). What I suspect was not obvious to start with, and what I hope is clearer now, is what the relevance of this exclusion is for our understanding of the palinode as a rhetorical-conceptual device for the textual inscription of history. Precisely because the telos of the treatise is the transformation of the historical scene, Dante is simultaneously asserting the priority of the secular world and suppressing significant features of it. A palinode would not work in this text because the prior contingent elements that would otherwise be offered only to be retracted cannot be allowed to appear for even the fleeting moment necessary to recant them, cannot (*pace* Dragonetti) be fully textualized. These elements cannot be subjected to palinodic reversal because they are, at base, neither an unmitigated fiction nor a pure concept of Dante's—instead they are *history*—or rather they are the historical significance of Frederick as it has pressed itself upon Dante and expressed itself in his writings.

Not, of course, that I would claim, simply inverting Dragonetti, that "history" in the person of Frederick II makes itself felt in an unmediated and / or irresistible way. No doubt that Dante could, like anyone else, ignore inconvenient historical facts, especially those a generation or two in the past, at his discretion. My case is based on two related points: (1) Dante's thought about language and politics in his postexilic experience was shaped in relation to the historical figure of Frederick in a way that points directly to *Monarchia* and makes his absence from it quite striking; and (2) Dante clearly prefers, as we see in the *Commedia* and elsewhere, to dominate and transform historical materials through the power of his representations, if this is possible at all. Frederick is missing, in other words, because he is too obviously at the origins of Dante's political discourse and yet cannot be recuperated and incorporated within that discourse, at least not in *Monarchia*.

What is it, then, that makes it possible for Dante to represent and reshape Frederick in the *Commedia* and not in *Monarchia?* And since he does do so there, why does that not imply a transcendence of the limited experience of *Monarchia* equivalent to what is achieved with respect to *Convivio* and *De vulgari eloquentia?* To sketch the relationship between the *Commedia* and *Monarchia*, let me now turn to the passage in the "poema sacro" with the most obvious and most obviously problematic connections to the political treatise. In *Purgatorio* 16, the "girone" of wrath, Marco Lombardo, responds to Dante's question concerning the origins, celestial or terrestrial, of the disappearance of virtue and order from the world by giving an account of the "anima semplicetta" whose innocent yet ignorant will requires law and guidance to teach it which pleasures to follow and which not:[49]

> Di picciol bene in pria sente sapore;
> quivi s'inganna, e dietro ad esso corre,
> se guida o fren non torce suo amore.
> Onde convenne legge per fren porre;
> convenne rege aver, che discernesse
> de la vera cittade almen la torre.
>
> (*Purg.* 16.91–96)

The guidance, which is now lacking from the world, should come from these same two sources:

> Soleva Roma, che 'l buon mondo feo,
> due soli aver, che l'una e l'altra strada
> facean vedere, e del mondo e di Deo.
> L'un l'altro ha spento; ed è giunta la spada

col pasturale, e l'un con l'altro insieme
per viva forza mal convien che vada;
    però che, giunti, l'un l'altro non teme. . . .

(*Purg.* 16.106–112)

As in *Monarchia*, here Dante derives the need for imperial, and papal, rule from the problem of regulating unstable human desire. And here too he divides that rule into a temporal and a spiritual domain and requires that there be a separation between them. Furthermore, as mentioned earlier, he here deploys, for his own, opposite purposes, an inverted version of the Decretalists' allegory of the "two lights" which he attacks in *Monarchia*. Unlike *Monarchia*, however, this passage, and the *Commedia* in general, stress the utter contemporary failure of these historical authorities. It is thus certainly no accident that Frederick is named for the last time in the poem immediately following the discourse on the "due soli," with specific reference to his troubles with the church which have now resulted in the banishment from Lombardy of the "valore" and "cortesia" that once dwelt there (16.115–120).

The reasons are not far to seek. In *Monarchia* Dante is reading the historical scene from the inside, as it were, from the perspective of human reason alone confronted with an array of dark and difficult signs to be interpreted [2.7.1, 4–9; 2.9.1]. To make his ideal project seem realizable he must, as he does with Frederick II, suppress as much as possible the overwhelming evidence that any attempt to reinstall universal monarchy is doomed to failure. In *Purgatorio*, by contrast, Dante represents himself surveying history not from the inside, and within the limited confines of reason, but from outside and above, where he has the benefit of an eschatological perspective beyond history, and thus direct knowledge of the divine will, as revealed to him by its many and various agents. From a secure position, above the fray, the violence and the failures of history can be contemplated with sorrow, yes, but also clarity and freedom.

In the *Commedia* Dante is also able to confront without obvious obfuscation or omission the paradox of his own "subject position" as theorist of the very earthly authorities to which he, along with any other "anima semplicetta," is technically bound in obedience. In *Monarchia* he confronts this paradox in two ways. On the one hand, he retreats into the impersonal and detached voice of reason which he has attempted to identify with the collective nature of humanity, avoiding the personal references which so consistently characterize his other works. On the other, he very indirectly confers on himself the status of a prophetic *nuntius* who declares God's will in certain matters independently of mediation by God's earthly vicars, pope or emperor as might be.[50] In the *Commedia*, however, he openly stages his own reacquisition of an autonomous authority over himself that would obviate any need for imperial and papal guidance, even if they were functioning properly. Since the need for guidance is tied to the conditions of fallen human existence, the problems of the tainted will and the darkened intellect in making proper choices for the individual, the recovery of a prelapsarian condition, with the attendant perfection of will and intellect, will liberate the individual soul from that need. And it is precisely the reacquisition of individual autonomy, not only from Virgil's guidance, but from that of the earthly "suns" as well, that is explicitly dramatized at the end of *Purgatorio* 27, when Dante passes out of Purgatory proper and back into the earthly Paradise, Eden itself:

> Tratto t'ho qui con ingegno e con arte;
> lo tuo piacere omai prendi per duce;
> fuor se de l'erte vie, fuor se' de l'arte.
>
> Vedi lo sol che 'n fronte ti riluce;
> vedi l'erbette, i fiori e li arbuscelli
> che qui la terra sol da sé produce.
>
> Mentre che vegnan lieti li occhi belli
> che, lagrimando, a te venir me fenno,
> seder ti puoi e puoi andar tra elli.
>
> Non aspettar mio dir più né mio cenno;
> libero, dritto e sano è tuo arbitrio,
> e fallo fora non fare a suo senno;
>
> per ch'io te sovra te corono e mitrio.
>
> (*Purg.* 27.130–140)

The passage seems specifically designed to refer back to canto 16— where Marco's assertion of free will is radically qualified precisely by the need for guidance. Where the "anima semplicetta" was only confused and corrupted when it followed its own "piacere," now Dante (not unlike the emperor of *Monarchia*) can make his desires his guide, because they are properly directed. The natural sun, figure of God, replaces the two temporal "suns." "Arbitrio" and "senno," will and intellect, are joined. And, last of all, Virgil symbolically confers on Dante the authority of monarch ("corono") and of pope ("mitrio") over himself.[51]

By thus removing himself from the taint of subjection to sinful desire and from legal servitude to the earthly authorities he both defines and criticizes, Dante in the *Commedia* is able to claim openly an authority, at once individual and transcendent, over the world of history, such as he could not in the *Monarchia*, where an earth-bound, exclusively rational perspective left him logically subordinate to both emperor and pope. At precisely this point in the *Commedia*, Dante is ready to receive a divine commission to report the allegorical vision of the intertwined histories of church and empire which unfolds in *Purgatorio* 32–33, as well as to deliver the prophecy of the DXV: "Però, in pro del mondo che mal vive, / al carro tieni or li occhi, e quel che vedi, / ritornato di là, fa che tu scrivi" (Therefore, for the profit of the world that lives ill, hold your eyes now on the chariot, and what you see, mind that you write it when you have returned yonder [32.103–105; cf. 33.52–54]), which can be seen as one of the poem's most elaborate and explicit accounts of its own genesis.

It could be argued further that the passage from *Purgatorio* 16 to *Purgatorio* 27 constitutes a palinodic narrative that doubles the possible relation of *Monarchia* to *Commedia*. The justification in canto 16 for the imposition of "two suns" is the need to guide the blinded human will and intellect in a postlapsarian world. It has not gone unnoticed, however, that in stressing the need for institutional guidance, Marco Lombardo all but suppresses the doctrine of the Fall and the consequent sinfulness of the human will.[52] In trying to hesitate between the two alternative explanations of the world's corruption, the "libero arbitrio" of men and the "necessità" of heavenly influence, he chooses a *via di mezzo* that defers the essential question. The stars cannot be blamed, since it would be unjust to punish men for faults not in their own control. And yet, the "anima semplicetta" cannot choose well on its own—not, it would appear, because of a faulty, fallen will, but rather because of simple ignorance. The sinfulness of the world, thus, is finally blamed neither on the heavens, nor on the individual, but rather on the failure of the institutional guides: "Ben puoi veder che la mala condotta / è la cagion che 'l mondo ha fatto reo / *e non natura che 'n voi sia corrotta*" (well can you see that ill-guidance is what has made the world wicked, and *not nature that is corrupt in you* [my emphasis]).

But how can one avoid blaming human nature for corruption, particularly, as Marco himself insists, in the context of individual sinners being subjected to purgation precisely for sinful acts of will? The reason is that the basic paradox of *Monarchia* is also operative, if far more effectively submerged, in the *Commedia*. Dante's political agenda requires that the temporal empire have a necessary and autonomous authority over the human will which, if properly exercised, would lead to the ideal condition of earthly peace and justice imagined in *Monarchia* book 1 and, fugitively and negatively, in *Purgatorio* 16 itself. The fallenness of the will, however, is the scandal, or stumbling block, that makes such a political utopia unrealizable, as Augustine had recognized long before in the *De civitate dei*. If it is the intractable sinful impulse of the will, rather than mere ignorance, that leads the "anima semplicetta" astray, no amount of guidance will ever succeed in completely domesticating human desire; and if that sinful impulse is universal, as universal as the empire itself, no human authority will ever escape from its shadow—no human emperor will ever be "free from desire" as Dante requires he must be in *Monarchia* (1.11.11–13; cf. *Convivio* 4.4.4).

But while a similar suppression of the intrinsically erroneous and insatiable character of human desire takes place in *Monarchia*, there Dante has no room for corrections, no perspective which can accommodate both the dream of empire and the vision of human history as the product of postlapsarian sinfulness. The *Commedia*, instead, makes use of a narrative dialectic, unfolding in time, palinodic in perspective, which allows him to offer an incomplete or even clearly false account at an early stage and supersede it at a later moment of greater vision. In the cantos which follow 16, the question of desire, and of "libero arbitrio" in particular, become ever more the center of attention. In particular, in canto 18, Dante returns to the "natural" desire of the soul for various objects and asks how it can be that the soul is rewarded or punished for its loves if it has no choice as to what it desires. Virgil's response is, in effect, a palinodic, now completely personal, revision of Marco Lombardo's institutional account, which itself refers us forward to a moment of even greater clarification when Beatrice will add revelation to Virgil's reason:[53]

innata v'è la virtù che consiglia
e de l'assenso de' tener la soglia.

Quest'è 'l principio là onde si piglia
ragion di meritare in voi, secondo
che buoni e rei amori accoglie e viglia.

Color che ragionando andaro al fondo,
s'accorser d'esta innata libertate;
però moralità lasciaro al mondo.

Onde, poniam che di necessitate
surga ogne amor che dentro a voi s'accende,
di ritenerlo è in voi la podestate.

La nobile virtù Beatrice intende
per lo libero arbitrio . . .

(Purg. 18.62–74)

From politics we move to ethics; from external powers which guide
and restrain, we are now told that the "podestate" to choose rightly
is in ourselves. But the corrective clarification is only partial. The
individual soul's freedom and responsibility are indeed made clear.
The politics that flowed from the earlier unclarity, however, remain
untouched, simply by omitting to point out the "contradizion che nol
consente" (to use Dante's own words against him [Inferno 27.120]).
The palinode, now intratextual rather than intertextual, has once
again worked its magic.

Why not then simply place Monarchia within the chronology of
palinodic transcendence as Nardi would have us do—after Convivio
but before the Commedia? The answer, at which I have already hinted,
is that we have no historical basis for doing so—poetic and rational
pretexts, yes, and the force of an overwhelming desire, ours and the
author's own, to confirm the ideal narrative order of Dante's thought
and his oeuvre, but no stable empirical evidence that supports us.
The fiction of the opere minori, subordinate to the master text, which
surveys and orders history but lies at its end in eschatological time-
lessness and transcendence, collapses under the pressure of chronology
and contingency.

Perhaps the simplest hypothesis, and one that allows us to set aside
the question of dating entirely, is that the differences between the
"voice of reason" as it manifests itself in Monarchia, and for that

matter *Convivio*, and the eschatological-prophetic perspective of the *Commedia* can best be accounted for "generically" and "rhetorically" by the different premises, purposes, and attendant argumentational and figurative strategies of the works, as easily as they can by a conjecture concerning intellectual or artistic development.[54] Nonetheless, it is important not to let such a hypothesis persuade us either that Dante was not conscious of the dangers of adopting contradictory perspectives or that palinodic inter- and intra-extuality is not a basic rhetorical fact of the *Commedia* and Dante's other works.

In fact, if we wished to insist on the "integral" character of the reference to *Paradiso* in *Monarchia*, we could even argue for a reverse palinode. We could argue, for example, that the literalist debunking of the Decretalists' allegory of the "two lights" is equally subversive of Dante's recourse to the metaphor of the "due soli" in *Purgatorio* 16. And we might claim that *Monarchia* recognizes, as the *Commedia* does not, that political history cannot finally be transcended or left behind, that once again the author of the *Commedia* (and the unfortunate Florentine prior of 1301) finds himself caught up in the historical fray. But even if we concede that the *Paradiso* reference was a later authorial interpolation, we still should treat it as a re-vision to be understood within the economy of Dante's complex revisionary practice. That is, even if the text that contains the retrospective reference to the *Commedia* belongs to a second or later draft, Dante clearly and deliberately invites the reader to understand *Monarchia* as postdating the *Commedia*, and thus himself opens the way to a reversal, or even a collapse, of the palinode.[55]

To conclude, *Monarchia* constitutes a scandal that disrupts the revisionary order, and the hierarchical system of textual value that sustains it, within the Dantean oeuvre. The undecidability of its chronological position in Dante's writerly itinerary, along with its urgent need both to engage and to suppress the political-historical order, reveal to us both the contingency and the rhetoricity of the palinode, its status as, among other things, a narrative trope. More than that, they confirm for us that Dante is, as Mazzotta has argued concerning the *Commedia* itself, always a poet of history and of exile, at once inside and outside of his troubled times—at once interpreting master and determinate consequence of the "secular world"—but in any case and in every way, a "historical subject."

NOTES

1. By "rhetorical reading" I refer to a practice of close textual analysis that stretches from New Criticism to Deconstruction. By "historical reading" I mean the broad spectrum of approaches commonly referred to as "New Historicism." As I hope will be clear, my relationship to both of these already very broad trends is eclectic and strategic, in the mode of bricolage.

2. On the resurgence of interest in the *opere minori* on the Anglo-American critical scene, see the review essay of Stephen Botterill, "Dante in North America: 1990–1991," *Lectura Dantis* 11 (1992): 3–25; as well as John Took, *Dante, Lyric Poet and Philosopher: An Introduction to the Minor Works* (Oxford: Clarendon Press, 1990). On the *rime petrose*, see Robert M. Durling and Ronald L. Martinez, *Time and the Crystal: Studies in Dante's "rime petrose"* (Berkeley and Los Angeles: University of California Press, 1990). On the *Vita nuova*, see Robert P. Harrison, *The Body of Beatrice* (Baltimore: Johns Hopkins University Press, 1988); and Thomas Clifford Stillinger, *The Song of Troilus: Lyric Authority in the Medieval Book* (Philadelphia: University of Pennsylvania Press, 1992). On *De vulgari eloquentia*, see Marianne Shapiro, *"De vulgari eloquentia": Dante's Book of Exile* (Lincoln, Neb., and London: University of Nebraska Press, 1990); Gary Cestaro. "'... Quanquam Sarnum biberimus ante dentes...': The Primal Scene of Suckling in Dante's *De vulgari eloquentia*," *Dante Studies* 109 (1991): 119–147; and Albert Russell Ascoli, "'Neminem ante nos': Historicity and Authority in the *De vulgari eloquentia*," *Annali d'Italianistica* 8 (1991): 186–231. On *Convivio*, Mario Trovato, "Dante's Stand against 'l'errore de l'umana bontade': *Bonum*, Nobility and the Rational Soul in the Fourth Treatise of the *Convivio*," *Dante Studies* 108 (1990): 79–96; and Albert Russell Ascoli, "The Vowels of Authority (Dante's *Convivio* IV.vi.3–4)," in *Discourses of Authority in Medieval and Renaissance Literature*, ed. Kevin Brownlee and Walter Stephens (Hanover, N.H.: University Press of New England, 1989), 23–46. See also, from the Italian side, the fundamental recent contributions of Maria Corti, *Dante a un nuovo crocevia* (Florence: Libreria Commissionaria Sansoni, 1981), and *La felicità mentale: Nuove prospettive per Cavalcanti e Dante* (Turin: Einaudi, 1983); and of Pier Vincenzo Mengaldo, *Linguistica e retorica di Dante* (Pisa: Nistri-Lischi, 1978).

3. For Gianfranco Contini, see the essays collected in *Un'idea di Dante* (Turin: Einaudi, 1970), particularly "Introduzione alle *Rime* di Dante," 3–20 (first published in 1938); "Dante come personaggio-poeta della *Commedia*," in *Un'idea di Dante*, 33–62 (first published 1958); "Un'interpretazione di Dante," 68–112, and "Filologia e esegesi dantesca," 113–142 (both from 1965). For Charles S. Singleton, see *An Essay on the "Vita Nuova"* (Cambridge, Mass.: Harvard University Press, 1949); *Dante Studies*, vol. 1: *Elements*

of Structure (Cambridge, Mass.: Harvard University Press, 1954); *Dante Studies*, vol. 2: *Journey to Beatrice* (Cambridge, Mass.: Harvard University Press, 1956).

4. The term was coined by Julia Kristeva, *Semeiotike: Recherches pour une sémanalyse* (Paris: Editions du Seuil, 1969). See the discussion by Cesare Segre, "Intertestualità e interdiscorsività nel romanzo e nella poesia," in *Romanzo e teatro: Due tipi di comunicazione letteraria* (Turin: Einaudi, 1984), 103–118 (first published in 1979). To this should be added much of the work of Roland Barthes. Operating with different terminology but related interests are Harold Bloom, *The Anxiety of Influence: A Theory of Poetry* (New York: Oxford University Press, 1973); Mikhail Bakhtin, *The Dialogic Imagination: Four Essays*, trans. Michael Holquist and Caryl Emerson (Austin, Tex.: University of Texas Press, 1981). An important alternative theorization / instantiation of intertextuality as a cultural-ideological phenomenon, with specific reference to Dante, is Corti, *La felicità mentale*, 38–71. Corti's emphasis, fostered by a confluence of philological method with formalist-structuralist theory, on the historical evolution of "culture" and "ideology" in language is a useful complement and corrective to the basically "psychological" and individual focus of intertextual, palinodic criticism of Dante on the North American scene.

5. Thomas M. Greene, *The Light in Troy: Imitation and Discovery in Renaissance Poetry* (New Haven: Yale University Press, 1982); David Quint, *Origin and Originality in Renaissance Literature: Versions of the Source* (New Haven: Yale University Press, 1983); Margaret Ferguson, *Trials of Desire: Renaissance Defenses of Poetry* (New Haven: Yale University Press, 1983); Leonard Barkan, *The Gods Made Flesh: Metamorphosis and the Pursuit of Paganism* (New Haven: Yale University Press, 1986). See also John Shearman, *Always Connect: Art and the Spectator in the Italian Renaissance* (Princeton: Princeton University Press, 1992), for a programmatic attempt to bring literary models of intertextual criticism to bear on Renaissance art.

6. For a recent interesting comparativist discussion of the palinode in the Renaissance, beginning with Petrarch and Boccaccio, see Patricia Phillippy, "Love's Remedies: Palinodic Discourse in Renaissance Literature" (dissertation, Yale University, 1990; abstract in DAI 51 [1990], 843A).

7. For example, the problem of the slippage from Beatrice 1 (the Beatrice of *Vita nuova*), to the "donna gentile" or Lady Philosophy of *Convivio*, to Beatrice 2 (the Beatrice of the *Commedia*) was the subject of an acrimonious debate between Luigi Pietrobono and Michele Barbi over most of the first half of this century. See, for example, Michele Barbi, "Razionalismo e misticismo in Dante," in *Problemi di critica dantesca*, 2d series (Florence: Sansoni, 1941), 3–86; and Luigi Pietrobono, "Filosofia e teologia nel *Convivio* e nella *Commedia*," *Giornale dantesco* 41 (1938): 13–71. See also Bruno Nardi, "Dalla

prima alla seconda *Vita nuova*," in *Nel mondo di Dante* (Rome: Edizioni di
Storia e Letteratura, 1944), 3–20 (first published in 1942 as "S'ha da credere
a Dante o ai suoi critici"); as well as *Dal "Convivio" alla "Commedia,"* fasc.
35–39 in the series Studi storici (Rome: Istituto Storico Italiano, 1960), 2–7,
127–131, and passim. More recently the question has been reviewed by Corti,
La felicità mentale, especially 146–155—and by Teodolinda Barolini, *Dante's
Poets: Textuality and Truth in the "Comedy"* (Princeton: Princeton University
Press, 1984), 15–23. It is now undergoing significant reconsideration by
Mario Trovato, in forthcoming work.

    8. The *Vita nuova* is broadly palinodic in at least three different ways:
(1) by recontextualizing separately written lyrics within the structure of
prose narrative and critical "divisions" it clearly assigns new meaning to
those poems individually; (2) by the episode of the "donna gentile" and
the vague promise of a future work to be dedicated to Beatrice, the book
anticipates its own later, palinodic supersession; (3) by ordering the poems
chronologically, it creates the impression that the modes of love represented
successively through the "libro della memoria" are constantly revising and
superseding earlier lyric experiences. To elaborate on the third of these: the
Vita nuova's individual lyrics and discreet episodes are organized, *Symposium*-
like, as upwardly hierarchical series (1) of objects and pseudo-objects of desire
(the "donna-schermo," the "donna gentile," and Beatrice herself) and (2) of
types of desire for Beatrice (love dependent on the "salute," love independent
of the "salute," love independent of a living object). The case of the *Vita
nuova* thus makes it clear that any distinction between "external" palinode
(recantation of an earlier work) and "internal" palinode (recantation of an
earlier part of the same work) in Dante's oeuvre is of heuristic value only—
a fact whose importance for reading the *Commedia* I return to at the end
of this essay. I am grateful to Thomas Stillinger for starting me on this
train of thought. Cf. Barolini, *Dante's Poets*, 15; Harrison, *Body of Beatrice*,
150. Martinez and Durling, *Time and the Crystal*, 164–167, see a similarly
revisionary pattern at work in what they take to be the clear sequence among
the four *rime petrose* composed after the *Vita nuova* but before Dante's exile.

    9. E.g., Bruno Nardi, *Saggi di filosofia dantesca*, 2d ed. (Florence: La Nuova
Italia, 1967; 1st ed., 1930), 297–310; as well as "Filosofia e teologia ai tempi
di Dante," in *Saggi e note di filosofia dantesca* (Milan and Naples: Ricciardi,
1966), 70–72. The need for these chronological gymnastics can be found in
Nardi's desire to ground his overall account of "dualistic" and "averroistic"
tendencies of the philosophical works (notably the *Monarchia's* reference
to the "possible intellect" [1.3.6–7; 1.4.1] and to the "two beatitudes" of
humanity [3.15.7] then overcome in the *Commedia* (*Dal "Convivio" alla
"Commedia,"* 83–120, and especially 309–313). The debate over which was
composed first, *De vulgari eloquentia* or *Convivio*, and even the controversy

over the authenticity of the so-called Epistle to Can Grande, depend heavily on speculative chronologies.

10. Luigi Pietrobono, "Il rifacimento della *Vita nuova* e le due fasi del pensiero dantesco," in *Saggi danteschi* (Turin: Nuova Biblioteca Italiana, 1954), 25–98 (first published in 1932). Cf. Corti, *La felicità mentale*, 146–155; Harrison, *Body of Beatrice*, 144–151. Pietrobono's conclusions are not now widely accepted.

11. Cf. Barolini, *Dante's Poets*, 29: "Dante's poetic career achieves such absolute retrospective coherence . . . that we are perhaps tempted to endow his earlier poetic shifts with too much teleological coherence."

12. The position is already sketched in Contini, "Introduzione," 4: "una costante della personalità dantesca [è] questo perpetuo sopraggiungere della riflessione tecnica accanto alla poesia, quest'associazione di concreto poetare e d'intelligenza stilistica." On the Dantean narrator-character, see "Dante come personaggio-poeta." The essays collected in *Un'idea di Dante* are, with the work of Auerbach (cf. notes 20–21, below), inspiring precedents for attempting a "historicist" reading of the Dantean oeuvre. As note 51, below, suggests, however, Contini's predominantly linguistic-stylistic focus creates certain problems of its own.

13. John Freccero, "Casella's Song (*Purg.* II.112)," in *Dante: The Poetics of Conversion* (Cambridge, Mass.: Harvard University Press, 1986), 186–194 (first published 1973). A related argument was made at the same time by Robert Hollander and recently reiterated by him: "*Purgatorio* II: Cato's Rebuke and Dante's 'Scoglio,'" in *Studies in Dante*, L'Interprete 16 (Ravenna: Longo, 1980), 91–105 (first published 1975); "*Purgatorio* II: The New Song and the Old," *Lectura Dantis* 6 (1990): 28–45. John Scott, "Dante and Philosophy," *Annali d'Italianistica* 8 (1990): 258–277, offers a specific critique of the palinodic hypothesis as applied to *Purgatorio* 2 by Hollander. His basic position is drawn from Kenelm Foster's insistence on the peaceable coexistence of two very different perspectives within the Dantean oeuvre ("The Two Dantes," in *The Two Dantes and Other Studies* [London: Darton, Longman, and Todd, 1977]). Scott denies the presence of the palinode even as rhetorical strategy, something he is able to do by sticking entirely to philosophical argumentation rather than attempting to account for the by now incontrovertible evidence that the *Commedia* systematically changes and contradicts passages from the *Convivio* and other texts. For a survey of some of the many revisions of the *Convivio* in the *Commedia*, see Nardi, "Filosofia e teologia," 75–79; and Ascoli, "Vowels of Authority," 42 and n. 47.

14. Freccero, "Casella's Song," especially 188–194.

15. Charles S. Singleton, "The Vistas in Retrospect," *Modern Language Notes* 81 (1966): 55–80. See also Amilcare Iannucci, "Autoesegesi dantesca: La tecnica dell' 'episodio parallelo' (*Inferno* XV–*Purgatorio* XI)," in *Forma*

ed evento nella "Divina Commedia" (Rome: Bulzoni, 1984), 83–114 (first published 1981); R. A. Shoaf's study of Narcissus in the thirtieth canto of each canticle, *Dante, Chaucer, and the Currency of the Word* (Norman, Okla.: Pilgrim Books, 1983), 21–100; and Franco Fido, "Writing Like God, or Better?—Symmetries in Dante's 26th and 27th Cantos," *Italica* 63 (1986): 250–264.

16. For the most comprehensive study of Dante's treatment of precursor poets, including himself, in the *Commedia*, see Barolini, *Dante's Poets.* For the near-contemporary vernacular poets, see Contini's seminal essays, "Dante come personaggio-poeta," and "Un'interpretazione di Dante." See also Patrick Boyde, *Dante's Style in His Lyric Poetry* (Cambridge: Cambridge University Press, 1971); Barolini, *Dante's Poets;* and Mazzotta, "Literary History," in *Dante, Poet of the Desert: History and Allegory in the "Divine Comedy"* (Princeton: Princeton University Press, 1979). On Arnaut Daniel, see, for example, Ronald L. Martinez, "Dante Embarks Arnaut," *NEMLA Italian Studies* 15 (1991): 15–28. For the classical poets generally see Barolini, *Dante's Poets;* and the overview of Kevin Brownlee, "Dante and the Classical Poets," in *The Cambridge Companion to Dante,* ed. Rachel Jacoff (Cambridge: Cambridge University Press, 1993), 100–119. For Ovid in particular, see, for example, Peter Hawkins, "Transfiguring the Text: Ovid, Scripture, and the Dynamics of Allusion," *Stanford Italian Review* 5 (1985): 115–140; Barkan, *Gods Made Flesh;* Brownlee, "Ovid's Semele and Dante's Metamorphosis: *Paradiso* XXI–XXIII," *Modern Language Notes* 101 (1986): 167–182; as well as two recent collections of essays—*Dante and Ovid: Essays in Intertextuality,* ed. Madison Sowell (Binghamton, N.Y.: Medieval and Renaissance Texts and Studies, 1991); and *The Poetics of Allusion: Virgil and Ovid in Dante's Commedia,"* ed. Rachel Jacoff and Jeffrey T. Schnapp (Stanford, Cal.: Stanford University Press, 1991). For Virgil, important examples are Robert Hollander, "Dante's Use of *Aeneid* I in *Inferno* I and II," *Comparative Literature* 20 (1968): 142–156, and *Il Virgilio dantesco: Tragedia nella "Commedia"* (Florence: Olschki, 1983), 117–154; Giuseppe Mazzotta, "Virgil and Augustine," in *Dante, Poet of the Desert;* Marguerite Mills Chiarenza, "Time and Eternity in Myths of *Paradiso* XVII," in *Dante, Petrarch, Boccaccio: Studies in the Italian Trecento in Honor of Charles S. Singleton,* ed. Aldo S. Bernardo and Anthony L. Pellegrini (Binghamton, N.Y.: Medieval and Renaissance Texts and Studies, 1983); Jeffrey T. Schnapp, *The Transfiguration of History at the Center of Dante's "Paradise"* (Princeton: Princeton University Press, 1986); and the essays collected in *Poetics of Allusion,* ed. Jacoff and Schnapp. For Statius, see Ronald L. Martinez, "Dante, Statius, and the Earthly City" (dissertation, University of California at Santa Cruz, 1977; abstract in DAI 38 [1978], 6707A); Winthrop Wetherbee, "Dante and the *Thebaid* of Statius," in *Lectura Dantis Newberryana,* vol. 1, ed. Paolo Cherchi and Antonio Mastrobuono

(Evanston, Ill.: Northwestern University Press, 1988), 71–92, and "'Per te poeta fui, per te cristiano': Dante, Statius, and the Narrator of Chaucer's *Troilus,*" in *Vernacular Poetics in the Middle Ages,* ed. Lois Ebin, Studies in Medieval Culture 16 (Kalamazoo, Mich.: Medieval Institute Publications, 1984), 153–176. For Cavalcanti, see Contini, "Cavalcanti in Dante," in *Un'idea di Dante;* Rachel Jacoff, "The Poetry of Guido Cavalcanti" (dissertation, Yale University, 1977; abstract in DAI 39 [1978], 1620A); Harrison, *Body of Beatrice,* especially 69–90; as well as Corti, *La felicità mentale,* 3–37.

17. Among many possible examples of critics who have explored the palinode in *Convivio,* in addition to Freccero and Hollander (see note 13, above), see Daniel J. Ransom, "'Panis angelorum': A Palinode in the *Paradiso,*" *Dante Studies* 95 (1977); Rachel Jacoff, "The Post-Palinodic Smile: *Paradiso* VIII and IX," *Dante Studies* 98 (1980): 111–122; and Barolini, *Dante's Poets,* 24–40, 57–84. On the palinode of the *rime petrose,* see Freccero, "Medusa: The Letter and the Spirit," *Poetics of Conversion,* 119–135 (first published 1972); and Sara Sturm-Maddox, "The *rime petrose* and the Purgatorial Palinode," *Studies in Philology* 84 (1987): 119–131. For *De vulgari eloquentia,* see Kevin Brownlee, "Why the Angels Speak Italian," *Poetics Today* 5 (1984): 597–610. See also Ascoli, "Vowels of Authority," 42–43 and note 47; and "'Neminem ante nos,'" 192–193 and note 12.

18. See Robert Hollander, *Allegory in Dante's "Commedia"* (Princeton: Princeton University Press); and Giuseppe Mazzotta, "Dante's Literary Typology," *Modern Language Notes* 87 (1972): 1–19, revised as ch. 4 of *Dante, Poet of the Desert.* On Dante's relation to the typological tradition more generally, see A. C. Charity, *Events and Their Afterlife: The Dialectics of Christian Typology in the Bible and in Dante* (Cambridge: Cambridge University Press, 1966).

19. Erich Auerbach, "Figura," in *Scenes from the Drama of European Literature: Six Essays* (New York: Meridian Books, 1959), 11–76 (first published 1944); *Mimesis; The Representation of Reality in Western Literature,* trans. W. R. Trask (Princeton: Princeton University Press, 1953 [first published in 1945]). See John Freccero's important critique of Auerbach in *Poetics of Conversion,* 103–104, 196–197; see also my "Boccaccio's Auerbach: Holding the Mirror up to *Mimesis,*" *Studi sul Boccaccio* 20 (1991–1992): 377–397.

20. This is to extend Auerbach's concept of the *Commedia's* figural relationship to history, as well as Freccero's more refined understanding of the narrative perspective of the *Commedia:* "The view from paradise is a spatial translation of what may be called a memory of universal history. The coherence of the whole poem may be grasped only with a view to its totality, a view from the ending, just as the coherence of the poet's life could be grasped only in retrospect, from the perspective of totality in death. Clearly the same may be said of universal history, whose coherence may be

perceived only from the perspective of eschatology . . ." ("Dante's Prologue Scene," *Poetics of Conversion*, 26, [first published 1966]). Cf. Mazzotta, *Dante, Poet of the Desert:* 17: "The palinode constitutes the temporal ground which sustains the possibility of dramatizing history's renewal."

21. Erich Auerbach, *Dante, Poet of the Secular World*, trans. R. Mannheim (Chicago: University of Chicago Press, 1961 [first published 1929]); see also "Figura," and *Mimesis*.

22. This is how Giuseppe Mazzotta summarizes the results of the earlier study in *Dante's Vision and the Circle of Knowledge* (Princeton: Princeton University Press, 1993), 3.

23. Other efforts, such as Antonio Mastrobuono, *Essays on Dante's Philosophy of History* (Florence: Olschki, 1979), and Schnapp, *Transfiguration of History*, enter more directly into the typical palinodic scheme: Dante's theological perspective, which places the world *sub specie aeternitatis*, allows him to dominate the realm of history from outside and from above.

24. Cf. Ascoli, " 'Neminem ante nos,' " 187–192. Contini certainly treats Dante in this way, at least as far as linguistic historicity is concerned. One interesting current version of this sort of approach is the criticism that has followed the work of A. J. Minnis on developing notions of the author (in *Medieval Theory of Authorship: Scholastic Literary Attitudes in the Later Middle Ages* [Philadelphia: University of Pennsylvania Press, 1984]); see also A. J. Minnis and A. B. Scott, *Medieval Literary Theory and Criticism, c. 1100– c. 1375: The Commentary Tradition* (Oxford: Clarendon Press, 1988). Another, related trend has focused attention on developments in medieval genre theory that subtend Dante's use of the terms "comedià" and "tragedia" in the *Comedy*, the *De vulgari eloquentia*, and, if it is indeed his, the Letter to Can Grande (see Lino Pertile, "*Canto-cantica-Comedìa* e l'Epistola a Cangrande," *Lectura Dantis* 9 [1991]: 105–123; and Zygmunt G. Barański, "*Comedìa*, Notes on Dante, the Epistle to Can Grande, and Medieval Comedy," *Lectura Dantis* 8 [1991]: 26–55, as well as " 'Prima tra cotanto senno': Dante and the Latin Comic Tradition," *Italian Studies* 26 [1991]: 1–36; see also the earlier essay of Amilcare Iannucci, "Dante's Theories of Genres and the *Divine Comedy*," *Dante Studies* 91 [1973]: 1–25). Mazzotta's placement of Dante in relation to the encyclopedic tradition (*Dante's Vision*, especially 15–33) at least implicitly constructs a generative intellectual, if not political and social, context for the *Commedia*, although the focus is on Dante's masterful synthesis and critique of the various texts and intellectual trends available to him. Also noteworthy is Corti, *La felicità mentale* and *Dante a un nuovo crocevia*; but also "Dante e la torre di Babele: una nuova *allegoria in factis*," in *Il viaggio testuale* (Turin: Einaudi, 1978), 243–256.

25. For the case of John Scott, "Dante and Philosophy," see note 13, above. Martinez and Durling, *Time and the Crystal* (especially 2–6), who

stress throughout the importance of the *rime petrose* in the development of the "microcosmic poetics" of the *Commedia*, make the important point that by reading the "minor works," in particular the *rime petrose*, exclusively through the filter of a presumed palinode in the *Commedia*, and not on "their own terms," significant interpretive opportunities are lost and a reductive image of Dante's development is reinforced.

26. In this sense at least I share with Teodolinda Barolini, *The Undivine Comedy: Detheologizing Dante* (Princeton: Princeton University Press, 1992), the project of reading Dante "rhetorically."

27. Cf. Harrison, *Body of Beatrice*. See also note 8, above.

28. See note 20, above.

29. On the question of "unfinishedness" see Albert Russell Ascoli, "The Unfinished Author: Dante's Rhetoric of Authority in *Convivio* and *De vulgari eloquentia*," in *Cambridge Companion*, ed. Jacoff, especially 49–50.

30. The *Monarchia* also plays an important role in Scott's critique of the theory of the palinode as applied to the *Convivio* in "Dante and Philosophy."

31. Cf. Mazzotta, *Dante, Poet of the Desert*, 9. See also Nardi, *Dal "Convivio" alla "Commedia,"* 186–207.

32. Nardi, "Filosofia e teologia," 71–109, especially 80–82; see also *Dante e la cultura medioevale* (Bari: Laterza, 1942), 133–138, and *Dal "Convivio" alla "Commedia,"* 116–131 and passim.

33. For Nardi, see note 9, above. For the other positions, see Pier Giorgio Ricci, "Introduzione," in Dante Alighieri, *Monarchia*, ed. P. G. Ricci, vol. 5 of *Le opere di Dante Alighieri*, Società dantesca italiana, Edizione nazionale (Verona: Mondadori, 1965); Prudence Shaw [James], "Sul testo della *Monarchia*," *Studi danteschi* 53 (1981): 181–217; Took, *Dante, Lyric Poet and Philosopher*, 147–151 and note 8; see Scott, "Dante and Philosophy," for a succinct and cogent review of the question (270–272 and notes).

34. Cf. Jeremy Tambling, *Dante and Difference: Writing in the "Commedia"* (Cambridge: Cambridge University Press, 1988), 7.

35. On scholastic practices from Abelard on for the resolution of logical conflicts between various texts and *auctores*, see Erwin Panofsky, *Gothic Architecture and Scholasticism* (Cleveland and New York: Meridian Books, 1957), especially 65–70 (I am indebted to Ronald L. Martinez for directing me to this work). On the so-called double truth espoused by the followers of Averroes, see Étienne Gilson, *Reason and Revelation in the Middle Ages* (New York: Scribner's, 1938), especially 54–63.

36. Nardi, "Filosofia e teologia," 56; Took, *Dante, Lyric Poet and Philosopher*, 150.

37. Ulrich Leo, "The Unfinished *Convivio* and Dante's Rereading of the *Aeneid*," *Medieval Studies* 13 (1951): 41–64. Cf. Nardi, "Filosofia e teologia," 51, 62–63; and *Dal "Convivio" alla "Commedia,"* 101–102 and passim; Hollander, "Dante's Use of *Aeneid* I."

38. Étienne Gilson, *Dante and Philosophy*, trans. D. Moore (New York: Harper and Row, 1949; reprint, 1963), 156.

39. Ascoli, "Vowels of Authority," 35–39 and notes; "Unfinished Author," 54–56.

40. See Mario Trovato, "Dante and the Tradition of the Two Beatitudes," in *Lectura Dantis Newberryana*, ed. Cherchi and Mastrobuono, 19–36; and "Dante's Poetics of Good: From Phenomenology to Integral Realism," *Annali d'Italianistica* 8 (1990): 231–256.

41. Cf. Ascoli, "Unfinished Author," 56; the relevant lines from the sonnet are cited in the notes of Cesare Vasoli to 4.3.6 in Dante Alighieri, *Convivio*, ed. Cesare Vasoli and Domenico De Robertis, vol. 1, part 2 of *Opere minori* (Milano and Napoli: Ricciardi, 1988), 544.

42. Citations are from *Monarchia*, ed. Pier Giorgio Ricci, vol. 5 of *Le opere di Dante Alighieri*, Società dantesca italiana, Edizione nazionale (Verona: Mondadori, 1965). Translations are my own.

43. This is Nardi's opinion, *Saggi di filosofia dantesca*, 299, reinforced by Allen Gilbert, "Had Dante Read the *Politics* of Aristotle?" *PMLA* 43 (1928): 606–613. See the entry under "Politica" in *Enciclopedia dantesca*, 5 vols. and appendix (Rome: Istituto dell'Enciclopedia italiana, 1970–1978), 4:585–586, for a convincing refutation. I have previously reviewed the question in Ascoli, "Vowels of Authority," 38 and note 39.

44. Cf. Ernst Kantorowicz, *The King's Two Bodies: A Study in Medieval Political Theology* (Princeton: Princeton University Press, 1957).

45. For historical background on Frederick, see Ernst Kantorowicz, *Frederick the Second, 1194–1250* (New York: Richard Smith, 1931); Thomas Curtis Van Cleve, *The Emperor Frederick II of Hohenstaufen: Immutator Mundi* (Oxford: Clarendon Press, 1972); David Abulafia, *Frederick II: A Medieval Emperor* (London and New York: Allen Lane, Penguin Press, 1988).

46. Roger Dragonetti, "Dante and Frederick II: The Poetry of History," *Exemplaria* 1 (1989): 1–15.

47. Citations are from *De vulgari eloquentia*, ed. P. V. Mengaldo, vol. 2 of *Opere minori* (Milano and Napoli: Ricciardi, 1979). Translations are my own.

48. Albert Russell Ascoli, "No Judgement among Equals: Authority and Division in Dante's *Monarchia*," paper delivered at the Northeast Modern Language Association annual meeting in Hartford, Conn., April 1991, to be published as part of a book on questions of authority and historicity in the postexilic prose of Dante.

49. All quotations and translations are taken from *The Divine Comedy*, 6 vols., trans. Charles S. Singleton (Princeton: Princeton University Press, 1970–1976).

50. Ascoli, "No Judgement among Equals."

51. Joan Ferrante, *The Political Vision of the "Divine Comedy"* (Princeton: Princeton University Press, 1984), 43. In an important "lectura" of this canto and this passage, Contini has argued that use of the *stilemi* "corono e mitrio" elsewhere in duecento verse suggests that the two actions do not correlate with pope and emperor—that, for example, both rulers might well possess both implements (Gianfranco Contini, "Alcuni appunti su *Purgatorio* XXVII," in *Un'idea di Dante*, 170–190 [first published 1959]). Contini's argument, however, makes external stylistic evidence take precedence over internal stylistic *and* "contentual" evidence that I find much more compelling. In addition to the clear textual echoes of *Purgatorio* 16 already mentioned, the canto itself virtually compels this type of reading, for example, by including the dream of Lia who contrasts her "active" life with that of the "contemplative" experience of her sister Rachel—a pairing that "mirrors" the emperor / pope pairing—as well as anticipating the Matelda / Beatrice dyad of the Earthly Paradise (to illustrate: Rachel sits at her "miraglio" [27.105]; Beatrice comes as an "ammiraglio" [30.58]). Contini's characteristic preference for historicizing "stylistically" rather than for exploring the relations between "style," or form more broadly understood, and signification defines, for me, the limits of his project historically and otherwise.

52. Charles S. Singleton, *Purgatorio*, vol. 2: *Commentary*, in Dante Alighieri, *The Divine Comedy*, 362 and 365.

53. See Mazzotta's recent synthetic review of this sequence of cantos in *Dante's Vision*, 116–134.

54. John Freccero, "Satan's Fall and the *Quaestio de aqua et terra*," *Italica* 38 (1961): 99–115, offers an example of this type of argument, alternative to the paliodic hypothesis, in his discussion of apparent contradictions between *Inferno* 34 and the *Quaestio de aqua et terra*.

55. Scott, "Dante and Philosophy," 272, makes this point, though he sees no contradiction whatsoever between the *Monarchia* and the *Commedia*, which I have suggested is not strictly speaking the case.

Part 3

Reception

R. A. Shoaf

"Noon Englissh Digne"

DANTE IN LATE MEDIEVAL ENGLAND

The title of my contribution to this collection is the fruit of twenty years' work. In those twenty years I have been studying the poets Dante and Chaucer and also the relationship between the two; I think now I can summarize the primary result of my work in the three words I have adapted from the *Man of Law's Tale*: "noon Englissh digne."[1] Because Chaucer, and the *Gawain* poet, too, in many circumstances, had "noon Englissh digne," they turned to other languages, other poetry, other cultures. Obviously, they turned to French and to Latin, but they also turned to Italian. Indeed, to C. S. Lewis's famous conundrum about Chaucer's *Troilus and Criseyde*, "What Chaucer Really Did to *Il Filostrato*," I would now reply, he "Dante-c/sized" it, all puns intended—in that single neologism expressing my sense of the extent, the size, of Chaucer's debt to Italy, as he translated and transformed one Italian poet, Boccaccio, by means of another, and greater, Italian poet, Dante.[2]

The three words, "noon Englissh digne," are found in a stanza that represents one of the more challenging of Chaucer's probable allusions or citations to Dante's *Commedia*, in this case, canto 33 of *Inferno*, the episode of Alberigo dei Manfredi. We will consider the episode and the allusion both at some length later. For now, first, I want to emphasize the extent to which this allusion to Dante approximates a direct citation by Chaucer. Even so rigorous a positivist as Howard Schless concedes that "Chaucer's lines [are] closely analogous to the passage from the *Inferno*."[3] I will argue that they are that and a good deal more.

I will argue a similar case for passages from the works of the *Gawain* poet.[4] Here, however, the issue is thornier. Although such sober empiricist scholars as P. M. Kean and Dorothy Everett have allowed as how the *Gawain* poet probably patterned the moral and geographical landscape of *Pearl* on that in the late cantos of *Purgatorio*—a male in a deep and complex erotic relationship with a female separated from him by a body of water—many scholars would consider the allusion at best questionable.[5] And these same scholars would perhaps cringe at the suggestion that a passage in *Cleanness* could have anything whatsoever to do with a passage from the end of *Paradiso*.

The sources of evidence I will be using, in short, by their juxtapositions, map the range of responses to the question of Dante in late medieval England, from no relationship to almost certain relationship. Other evidence could be adduced—for example, the Latin translation of the *Commedia* commissioned by two English prelates, Bubwich and Hallam, at the Council of Constance, and prepared for them by Giovanni Bertoldi (da Serravalle) in the breathtaking space of five months in 1416[6]—but these passages in their current order pose the question and define the controversy. If Dante is there, intertextually at play in the passages, then the poetry in each passage can be argued to assume both more point and more force than otherwise is possible. But what and where is the evidence that Dante is there?

The question so posed is the positivist's battle cry: Give me facts or give me nothing (some scholars, I have found, are fond of nothing). But it will be immediately evident that this is a caricature: no self-respecting historian is so positivistic as to think this way. Most historians of the past decade or so would readily see and urgently remark that the evidence is here in front of us, *in the literary texts we are reading*—after all, literature is also evidence.[7] And it is the evidence of the literature that I will investigate in this essay.

Let me begin, then, with admittedly the most difficult case, that of *Cleanness*:

> For when þat þe Helle herde þe houndez of heuen,
> He watz ferlyly fayn, vnfolded bylyue;

Þe grete barrez of þe abyme he barst vp at onez,
Þat alle þe regioun torof in riftes ful grete,
And clouen alle in lyttle cloutes þe clyffez aywhere,
As lauce leuez of þe boke þat lepes in twynne.
Þe brethe of þe brynston by þat hit blende were,
Al þo citees and her sydes sunkken to helle.
Rydelles wern þo grete rowtes of renkkes withinne,
When þay wern war of þe wrake þat no wyʒe achaped;
Such a ʒomerly ʒarm of ʒellyng þer rysed,
Þerof clatered þe cloudes, þat Kryst myʒt haf rawþe.
                    (Cleanness 961–972; 145 [emphasis added])

For when Hell himself heard the hounds of heaven,
He was gladdened to glean such a grisly event.
The abyss's great bars he broke, so that all
Of the region was wrecked; in a rift it was sunk!
The cliffs and the crags were cloven apart,
Like a book that is broken, whose binding explodes.
When the black smoke of brimstone had bled everywhere,
Those four cities had sunk; yes, they'd slipped into hell!
Their inhabitants, helpless, were harrowed with fear
When they saw no escape from destruction and death.
They clamored and called with such crying laments
That the clouds were cloven, and Christ would have wept!

As others before me have observed, the arresting point in the passage
I have cited is the line "þerof clatered þe cloudes, þat Kryst myʒt
haf rawþe": What can it mean that Christ is there having pity at
the destruction of Sodom? How can this possibly square with the
tone as well as the content of the rest of the poem?[8] There are
several approaches we might take to this question, but here I want to
propose that the poet remembers Paradiso and that Christ is present
at this moment, and feeling pity, as the Word (Logos)—the Word
that inscribes the book, the "un volume" of creation, that is springing
apart ("lepes in twynne") in this instant of divine retribution. In other
words, once we admit the corresponding image from Paradiso, we see
a structure of remarkable consistency:

Nel suo profondo vidi che s'interna,
legato con amore in un volume,

> ciò che per l'universo si squaderna:
> sustanze e accidenti e lor costume.[9]
>
> (Par. 33.91–92 [emphasis added])

> In its depth I saw ingathered, bound by love in one single volume, that which is dispersed in leaves throughout the universe: substances and accidents and their relations.

Moreover, the one volume that contains "ciò che per l'universo si squaderna" contains it in the form of a knot, "questo nodo,"

> La forma universal di questo nodo
> credo ch'i' vidi,
>
> (Par. 33.91–92 [emphasis added])

> The universal form of this knot I believe that I saw,

and I need hardly dwell on how important the figure of the knot is to the *Gawain* poet.[10] Christ the Word is the knot of the bound volume, "legato con amore," that infolds and unfolds the whole creation. At this moment of punishment, when the creation flies apart, "As lauce leuez of þe boke þat lepes in twynne," the author Christ takes pity on what should be "legato con amore" but is instead, in the poet's version of the biblical account, "in twynne," by "amor" perverted.[11] Dante's "si squaderna," the "unquiring" of creation, I suggest, is a source not only of the *Gawain* poet's image but also of his theology: he may have seen many a book "lepe in twynne" with his own eyes, but I think he saw a book's leaves "si squaderna," in the context of the Trinity's love, in Dante's *Paradiso*, and that love it is, as he recalls the image, that in the person of Christ, feels "rawþe" for the destruction of Sodom.[12]

Let me turn now to the second case, again drawn from the works of the *Gawain* poet, specifically the *Pearl*, which involves *Purgatorio* and St. Augustine's *Confessions*. Several years ago, I published an essay on *Pearl* and *Purgatorio* in which I set out many of the connections I am assuming,[13] some of which I will also discuss here, but in particular, I am adding to that earlier scholarship my subsequent study of a long and crucial passage from Augustine's *Confessions* (8.26–27):

Retinebant nugae nugarum et vanitates vanitantium, antiquae amicae meae, et succutiebant vestem meam carneam et submurmurabant, "Dimittisne nos?", et "a momento isto non erimus tecum ultra in aeternum", et "a momento isto non tibi licebit hoc et illud ultra in a eternum." et quae suggerebant in eo quod dixi, "hoc et illud," quae suggerebant, deus meus, avertat ab anima servi tui misericordia tua! quas sordes suggerebant, quae dedecora! et audiebam eas iam longe minus quam dimidius, non tamquam libere contradicentes eundo in obviam, sed velut a dorso mussitantes et discedentem quasi furtim vellicantes, ut respicerem. *tardabant tamen cunctantem me abripere atque excutere ab eis et transilire quo vocabar, cum diceret mihi consuetudo violenta*, "Putasne sine istis poteris?"

Sed iam tepidissime hoc dicebat. aperiebatur enim ab ea parte qua intenderam faciem et quo transire trepidabam *casta dignitas continentiae, serena et non dissolute hilaris, honeste blandiens, ut venirem neque dubitarem*, et extendens ad me suscipiendum et amplectendum pias manus plenas gregibus bonorum exemplorum. ibi tot pueri et puellae, ibi iuventus multa et omnis aetas, et grave viduae et virgines anus, et in omnibus ipsa continentia nequaquam sterilis, sed fecunda mater filiorum gaudiorum de marito te, domine. et inridebat me inrisione hortatoria, quasi diceret: "Tu non poteris quod isti, quod istae? an vero isti et istae in se ipsis possunt ac non in domino deo suo? dominus deus eorum me dedit eis. quid in te stas et non stas? *Proice te in eum! noli metuere.* non se subtrahet ut cadas: *proice te securus! excipiet et sanabit te.*"[14]

Vain trifles and the triviality of the empty-headed, my old loves, held me back. They tugged at the garment of my flesh and whispered: "Are you getting rid of us?" And "from this moment we shall never be with you again, not for ever and ever." And "from this moment this and that are forbidden to you for ever and ever." What they were suggesting in what I have called "this and that"—what they were suggesting, my God, may your mercy avert from the soul of your servant! What filth, what disgraceful things they were suggesting! I was listening to them with much less than half my attention. They were not frankly confronting me face to face on the road, but as it were whispering behind my back, as if they were furtively tugging at me as I was going away, trying to persuade me to look back. Nevertheless they held me back. I hesitated to detach myself, to be rid of them, to make the leap to where I was being called. Meanwhile the overwhelming force of habit was saying to me: "Do you think you can live without them"?

Nevertheless it was now putting the question very half-heartedly. For from that direction where I had set my face and towards which I was afraid to move, there appeared the dignified and chaste Lady Continence, serene and cheerful without coquetry, enticing me in an honorable manner to come and not to hesitate. To receive and embrace me she stretched out pious hands, filled with numerous good examples for me to follow. There were large numbers of boys and girls, a multitude of all ages, young adults and grave widows and elderly virgins. In every one of them was Continence herself, in no sense barren but "the fruitful mother of children" (Ps. 112:9), the joys born of you, Lord, her husband. And she smiled on me with a smile of encouragement as if to say: "Are you incapable of doing what these men and women have done? Do you think them capable of achieving this by their own resources and not by the Lord their God? Their Lord God gave me to them. Why are you relying on yourself, only to find yourself unreliable! Cast yourself upon him, do not be afraid. He will not withdraw himself so that you fall. Make the leap without anxiety; he will catch you and heal you."

Consider now the relevance of Augustine's tableau to both the episode of Dante and Matelda and that of the *Pearl* dreamer and the *Pearl* maiden. Augustine stands on one side of a divide and on the other side stands Continentia, figured as the mother of numerous chaste souls; she invites him to join them on the other side, but he still clings to his "nugas" and his "consuetudo" so that he hesitates to "transilire," to leap, to her on the other side. But it is only on the other side—and here is the crux of the matter for Dante and the *Gawain* poet alike—it is only on the other side that salvation and happiness are possible. Augustine by himself and of himself cannot get there: he must in fact first hear the child's voice in the garden shout "tolle, lege," so fierce is the grip upon him of his habits. But for Dante it is different, and for the *Pearl* dreamer even more different.

Dante stands on this side of a stream from Matelda. She is something more than the abstraction Continentia. To be sure, her name is a perfect anagram of "ad Letam," "toward Lethe," which is, of course, the first stream in which she immerses Dante, and she has about her numerous other hints of a literary device—she and the whole scene owe much to Cavalcanti's *pastorella*, "In una boschetta," for example.[15] But we feel that somehow Matelda exceeds these devices and emerges in Dante's fiction as an agent of a love more capacious than either

Augustine or Cavalcanti imagine (both of whom, we know, have a dark view of human sexuality).[16] If Matelda is John to Beatrice's Jesus, she is still a woman who inspires great desire. And the difference between Dante and Augustine is the value each places on woman and the desire of woman: Matelda carries Dante through and across the stream because Dante desires to be on the other side with her and with Beatrice—and this desire is good, very good.

Here then, too, is the similarity and the difference between Dante and the *Gawain* poet / *Pearl* dreamer. Like Dante, the dreamer desires to be on the other side with the maiden, but for him desire is not enough, and, perhaps, as with Augustine, too, desire is problematic, fraught with ambiguity. In 1990, I expressed it this way:

> Finally, it is the difference between two emphases in Christian theology: one, Dante's, an emphasis on form (and hence also on in-form-ation [Dante is the most informed of poets]), fundamentally optimistic of transcendence; and the other, the *Pearl*-poet's, a darker emphasis, on the recalcitrance of nature, uncertain of the reformability of the will. Or say, precisely, it is the difference between Beatrice and the *Pearl*-maiden, a grown woman and a child: Dante believes eros can encourage, enable, and sustain transcendence; the *Pearl*-poet is less secure about what nature can bear or perform.[17]

To this I would now add that the mediating influence of the passage from *Confessions* more sharply delineates the difference between Dante and the *Gawain* poet. Both of them desire the same fulfillment, transcendence through sensual, erotic union—perhaps the essential characteristic of Christian mysticism early and late[18]—but each has a very different assessment of this desire.

And yet that may be too simple a judgment, I fear. The *Gawain* poet was a far finer reader of Augustine and Dante than this judgment suggests. For if we look at the *Pearl* dreamer's self-condemnation in the penultimate stanza and compare it with Dante's closure of the *Purgatorio*, we see that the relationship between them is more complex yet.

> To þat Pryncez paye hade I ay *bente*,
> And ȝerned no more þen watz me *geuen*,
> And *halden* me þer in trwe entent,
> As þe perle me prayed þat watz so þryuen,

As *helde*, *drawen* to Goddez present,
To mo of His mysterys I hade ben *dryuen*.
Bot ay wolde man of happe more hente
Þen moȝte by ryȝt vpon hem clyuen.
Þerfore my ioye watz sone toriuen,
And I kaste of kythez þat lastez aye.
Lorde, mad hit arn þat agayn Þe stryuen,
Oþer proferen þe oȝt agayn Þy paye.
                    (*Pearl* 1189–1200; 100 [emphasis added])

Had I to please that Prince been bent,
Not craved more than was granted me,
But stood there, still, obedient
To my pure pearl's true decree,
I might have been to great God sent
And shown there still more mystery.
But mortals, madly, are intent
On making more than rightfully
Is theirs. Gone was my greatest glee.
I stood, exiled from ecstasies.
O Lord, he's lost who foolishly
Turns not to You Whom he should please!

    S'io avessi, lettor, *più lungo spazio*
da scrivere, i' pur cantere' in parte
lo dolce ber che mai non m'avria sazio;
    ma perché *piene son tutte le carte*
ordite a questa cantica seconda,
non mi lascia più ir lo fren de l'arte.
    Io ritornai da la santissima onda
rifatto sì come piante *novelle*
rinovellate di *novella* fronda,
    puro e disposto a salire a le stelle.
                    (*Purg.* 33.136–145 [emphasis added])

If, reader, I had greater space for writing, I would
yet partly sing the sweet draught, which never would
have sated me; but since all the pages ordained for
this second canticle are filled, the curb of art lets

> me go no further. I came forth from the most holy
> waves, renovated even as new trees renewed with new
> foliage, pure and ready to rise to the stars.

The restraint the *Pearl* dreamer laments he lacked is that very restraint
Dante submits to in "lo fren de l'arte": think then of *Pearl* as precisely
Purgatorio without the subsequent advent—the stream uncrossed—to
Paradiso. The *Gawain* poet, it seems to me, understands Dante well.

The final case I plan to consider, if it is in some ways the clearest,
in others is much less so; if it is difficult to dispute the allusion
to Dante in the passage from the *Man of Law's Tale*, the meaning
and the force of that allusion are open to debate. My own account
draws upon several papers I have published in the past decade on
Chaucer, portions of my book in progress, *"The Substaunce Is in Me":
An Essay on Error in the "Canterbury Tales,"* and it will be helpful
here to summarize the positions articulated and defended in them.[19]
Taking my cue from the description of the Man of Law in the *General
Prologue* to the *Canterbury Tales* that "he koude endite and make
a thyng, / Ther koude no wight pynche at his writyng" (he could
compose and write items such that no one could pinch at his writing
[*Canterbury Tales* 1.325–326 [my translation]]), I have argued that the
lawyer is obsessed with the perfect contract, written so flawlessly, so
error free, that no one can pinch at it, or find any fold in it that
would provide a purchase for altering or breaking it. This perspective,
applied to the tale the Man of Law tells, the tale of Constance,
yields an understanding of his obsessive concern with constancy: the
Man of Law desires the constant signifier, the trope that, wherever
it may go, remains always one and the same, unchanged, incorrupt,
in his own word "unwemmed" (the common Middle English word
for "immaculate").[20]

Within this perspective the Man of Law's condemnation of Donegild betrays his deepest anxieties. Recall at this point that Donegild,
mother of King Alla, who has wed Constance, forges letters to replace
those written to inform him of the birth of his son, her grandson,
by Constance; her forgeries misrepresent the child as a monster and
Constance as an "elf." Alla replies that he will accept the will of God,
but Donegild forges letters to replace these also, letters commanding
Constance and Mauricius to be exiled upon the sea. It is thus that
the Man of Law is moved to exclaim:

O Donegild, I ne have *noon Englissh digne*
Unto thy malice and thy tirannye!
And therfore to the feend I thee *resigne*;
Lat hym *enditen* of thy traitorie!
Fy, mannysh,—o nay, by God, I lye—
Fy, feendlych spirit, for I dar wel telle,
Thogh thou heere walke, thy spirit is in helle!
                        (*Canterbury Tales* 2.778–784 [emphasis added])

O Donegild, I have no English proper to express your malice and your tyranny. So I resign you to the fiend—let him make compositions about your treachery! Fie, you mannish creature—oh no, by God, I'm lying—fie you fiendly spirit; for I dare tell it, that though you walk up here on earth, your spirit is in hell!

It is precisely through the allusion to Dante's *Inferno* here that the Man of Law is exposed—and let us not forget that the entire episode hinges on *forged letters*, letters appalling to him at whose writing no one could pinch.

In the famous dialogue in canto 33 between Dante the pilgrim and Alberigo dei Manfredi (*Inf.* 33.109–150), Dante learns that a soul can be thrust into hell before its body dies, the body being assumed by a devil who manipulates it on earth for a certain space. In exchange for this and other information, Alberigo has asked Dante to clear the ice from his eyes so that he may weep a moment, and Dante has replied

Se vuo' ch'i' ti sovvegna,
dimmi chi se', e s'io non ti disbrigo,
al fondo de la ghiaccia ir mi *convegna*.
                        (*Inf.* 33.115–117 [emphasis added])

If you would have me help you, tell me who you are; if I do not relieve you, may I have to go to the bottom of the ice [but literally, let it be necessary or let it be agreed for me to go to the bottom of the ice].

Dante, in effect, makes a contract (*convegno*) with Alberigo.

To be sure, *convegna* here means primarily "be necessary," but this meaning does not mute or cancel the other meaning of contractuality or conventionality, a meaning important in many of the ten occurrences of the word in the final four cantos of *Inferno*.[21] And this is crucial since Dante *breaks the contract* with Alberigo:

> "Ma distendi oggimai in qua la mano;
> aprimi li occhi." E io non gliel' apersi;
> e cortesia fu lui esser villano.
>
> (*Inf.* 33.148–150)

> "But now reach out your hand; open my eyes." And
> yet I did not open them for him; and it was courtesy
> to show him rudeness.

But Dante does not break only the contract with Alberigo; he breaks another contract, too. Dante also breaks the contract or convention of language, according to which "cortesia" means "courtesy" and "villano" means "rude." Dante, in fact, commits an error—"cortesia" does not mean "villano" (though Dante writes "fu")—but this error is necessary to the truth: this flaw promotes the flow of truth. Here, in short, Dante insists that there is no a priori, immutable property of words: their property is a fiction agreed to ("convenire") by the community, and it is the poet who, on extraordinary occasion, must disturb the fiction, break the convention (contract), in order to establish anew what is proper to the word. It is the poet who must forge letters—if, finally, in a different sense from that of Donegild's forgeries.

Chaucer, then, has cited Dante at just that moment in the *Commedia* when Dante's poem exposes most clearly the Man of Law's anxiety. If we pursue the allusion, it leads us to the ground of that anxiety and the Man of Law's consequent narrative strategy; namely, there is no proper sense apart from human contract or convention: a signifier can be empty like the body of Branca, filled now with a demon—all signifiers are, ontologically, forgeries. And note how Chaucer reinforces this idea so alien to the Man of Law by means of the pun in "resigne": the Man of Law not only resigns, he also *re-signs* Donegild to the fiend; his words, even in his curse, are not completely in his control. We can pinch at them—he would say, forge them. And they exceed his control, we can pinch at them, precisely because there is no proper sense apart from convention.

But the Man of Law cannot abide this truth. He longs to write flawlessly. If he would write flawlessly, though, he must also write flowlessly: he must efface the contractuality or conventionality of his words, take them out of circulation (where the contract can always be renegotiated—as in the pun in "resigne") so as to insert them in a structure that ensures the return of the same, the unpinchable contract, where, no matter what the words say, they always refer to the predicted and prescribed meaning which he retains in his control, immune from forgery. Thus, for example, the Man of Law's words say that so many different catastrophes befell Constance, but everything they say, each catastrophe they narrate, refers always (for him) to the same end: Constance is constant, the unchanging because "unwemmed," signifier.

M. R. James, in his study at the beginning of this century of the catalogue of the fourteenth-century Augustinian library at York, sorrowed that

> The fact that an establishment so obscure as this of the Austin Friars at York should have owned a library of 646 volumes a century or more before its dissolution gives scope for serious and indeed depressing reflection. Depressing, because after a lengthy search among catalogues and libraries I cannot find that more than four of the whole number have survived.[22]

Less than 1 percent of a medieval English library survives (and if 100 volumes should turn up tomorrow, by wonderful surprise, still, even in that case, less than 20 percent would have survived). Who is to say there were no manuscripts of Dante in England in the fourteenth century? Not I. We need to honor the evidence of literature itself. Even as Dante, first in this as in so much else, understood that poetry without a theory of poetry is futile, the cacophony of voices dismembering Italy; let us also understand that interpreting texts without a theory of the evidentiality of texts is futile, too. Or worse, it forecloses our reading by denying a priori the data of texts themselves. It impoverishes us—"noon Englissh digne."

We are, needless to say, poor enough as it is, "noon Englissh digne." I have tried in this essay, as I have tried for the past twenty years, to overcome our poverty somewhat, to ensure that the logician's rule of parsimony does not turn, ogre-like, into the tyranny of miserliness, that Occam's razor not become a sword of Damocles. We have assembled this collection of essays to celebrate a poet-scholar who was also a consummate theoretician. I urge us, then, in conclusion to aspire to imitate his vision of our calling. As we continue to search the archive for contextual evidence of Middle English writers' awareness of Dante, we must also refine our concepts of evidence and the intelligibility of the literary text—as I have tried to do, by example, in this essay. A poem is a work of language in a mind ("in the act of finding what will suffice" [Wallace Stevens]), and no amount of contextualization will reduce a poem to complete determinacy (which is the anxiety of lawyers anyway—"And yet he semed bisier than he was" [*Canterbury Tales* 1.322]). To forget or, worse, ignore the polysemy of poetry is to dishonor a man—arrogant and abrasive as he may have been—who strove to enrich our lives with his art, who affords us means, and meaning, when we have "noon Englissh digne."[23]

NOTES

1. All citations of Chaucer's poetry in this essay are from *The Riverside Chaucer*, 3d ed., ed. Larry D. Benson (Cambridge: Houghton Mifflin, 1987) by fragment and line numbers; here *Canterbury Tales* 2.778.

2. C. S. Lewis, "What Chaucer Really Did to *Il Filostrato*," *Essays and Studies* 17 (1932): 56–75 especially 67–68.

3. Howard Schless, *Chaucer and Dante: A Revaluation* (Norman, Okla.: Pilgrim Books, 1984), 182.

4. All citations of the works of the *Gawain* poet are from the edition by Malcolm Andrew and Ronald Waldron, *The Poems of the Pearl Manuscript: Pearl, Cleanness, Patience, Sir Gawain and the Green Knight*, rev. ed. (Exeter: University of Exeter Press, 1987), as found in *The Complete Works of the Pearl Poet*, trans. Casey Finch (Berkeley: University of California Press, 1993), which is thus used for the convenience of both the edition and the translation in the same volume; I cite both line and page numbers.

5. P. M. Kean, *The "Pearl": An Interpretation* (London: Routledge and Kegan Paul, 1967), especially 120–132; Dorothy Everett, *Essays on Middle English Literature* (Oxford: Clarendon Press, 1955), 95.

6. See G. L. Hamilton, "Notes on the Latin Translation of, and Commentary on, the *Divina Commedia* by Giovanni da Serravalle," *Twentieth*

Annual Report of the Dante Society (1901) (Boston: Ginn, 1902), 17–37. See also G. Ferraù, "Bertoldi, Giovanni (Giovanni da Serravalle)," *Enciclopedia dantesca*, 5 vols. and appendix (Rome: Istituto della Enciclopedia italiana, 1970–1978), 1:608b–609a; and the biography by A. Vallone in the *Dizionario biografico degli italiani* (Rome: Istituto della Enciclopedia italiana, 1967), 9:574–576.

7. See H. Marshall Leicester, Jr., "Structure as Deconstruction: Chaucer and 'Estates Satire' in the *General Prologue*, or Reading Chaucer as a Prologue to the History of Disenchantment," *Exemplaria* 2 (1990): 241–261; see also his book, *The Disenchanted Self: Representing the Subject in the "Canterbury Tales"* (Berkeley: University of California Press, 1991), especially 16.

Heather Dubrow has announced (*MLA Newsletter* 25, no. 3 [1993]) a Special Topics Forum in a forthcoming *PMLA* on the status of literature as evidence.

8. I would like to recognize and thank Jim Rhodes of Southern Connecticut State University for our conversations together on this passage; we have quite distinct interpretations of it, but mine has certainly profited from being informed by his. He is currently finishing a book on Chaucer and the *Gawain* poet, *The Redemptive Design of Middle English Narrative*, centrally concerned with the poets' native English theological tradition.

9. The text and translation of Dante's *Comedy* cited in this essay is that prepared by Charles S. Singleton, *The Divine Comedy*, 6 vols., Bollingen Series, vol. 80 (Princeton: Princeton University Press, 1970–1975), here *Par.* 33.85–88 (emphasis added).

10. Of many recent studies, I would single out two, in particular: Geraldine Heng, "Feminine Knots and the Other *Sir Gawain and the Green Knight*," *PMLA* 106 (1991): 500–514; and Arthur Lindley, " 'Ther he watz dispoyled, with spechez of myerthe': Carnival and the Undoing of Sir Gawain," *Exemplaria* 6 (1994): 67–86. Both essays cite items from the extensive bibliography. I also offer comments in my own study, *The Poem as Green Girdle: "Commercium" in "Sir Gawain and the Green Knight"* (Gainesville, Fla.: University Press of Florida, 1984), especially 22, 66, 68, 74–75.

11. In attempting to understand the poet's theological position in his historical moment, I do not, implicitly or otherwise, forfeit my privilege to disagree with his theology or its consequences in my own life and time.

12. On images of the book in Dante's *Comedy*, see several essays by John Ahern: "Binding the Book: Hermeneutics and Manuscript Production in *Paradiso* 33," *PMLA* 97 (1982): 800–809; "Dante's Last Word: The *Comedy* as a *liber coelestis*," *Dante Studies* 102 (1984): 1–14; "Singing the Book: Orality in the Reception of Dante's *Comedy*," *Annals of Scholarship* 2 (1981): 17–40. I offer some comments of my own in "Dante, the Codex, and the Margin of Error," in *The Use of Manuscripts in Literary Studies: Essays in Memory of Judson Boyce Allen*, ed. Charlotte Cook Morse, Penelope B. R. Doob, and

Marjorie Curry Woods (Kalamazoo: Medieval Institute Publications, 1992), 1–17.

13. See R. A. Shoaf, "*Purgatorio* and *Pearl*: Transgression and Transcendence," *Texas Studies in Language and Literature* 32 (1990): 152–168, special issue of *Texas Studies: Beatrice dolce memoria: Essays on the "Vita Nuova" and the Beatrice-Dante Relationship*, ed. David Wallace.

14. The text of the *Confessions* I cite is that prepared by James J. O'Donnell, 3 vols. (Oxford: Clarendon Press, 1992), 1:99–100 (emphasis added); the translation is that of Henry Chadwick, *Saint Augustine, "Confessions"* (Oxford: Oxford University Press, 1991), 150–151.

15. See my essay "*Purgatorio* and *Pearl*," 153 and note 12; see also my study "'Lo gel che m'era intorno al cor' (*Purgatorio* 30.97) and 'Frigidus circum praecordia sanguis' (*Georgics* II. 484): Dante's Transcendence of Virgil," *Lectura Dantis* 5 (1989): 30–46, especially 44 and note 24.

16. See John M. Bowers, "Augustine as Addict: Sex and Texts in the *Confessions*," *Exemplaria* 2 (1990): 403–448; and Giuseppe Mazzotta, *Dante, Poet of the Desert* (Princeton: Princeton University Press, 1979), 215, 292.

17. Shoaf, "*Purgatorio* and *Pearl*," 161.

18. To my mind, expressed with special poignancy by Julian of Norwich: " . . . for I saw full sekirly that our substance is in God, and also I saw that in our sensualite God is; for the selfe poynte that our soule is mad sensual, in the selfe poynt is the cite of God, ordeynid to him from withouten begynnyng . . ." (*A Revelation of Love*, ed. Marion Glasscoe, Exeter Medieval English Texts [Exeter: University of Exeter Press, 1976], 66).

19. See R. A. Shoaf, "'Unwemmed Custance': Circulation, Incest, and Property in the *Man of Law's Tale*," *Exemplaria* 2 (1990): 287–302; and "Chaucer and Medusa: The *Franklin's Tale*," *Chaucer Review* 21 (1986): 74–90, scheduled for reprinting in Macmillan's New Casebook Series: *Chaucer, The "Canterbury Tales*," ed. Valerie Allen.

20. See Shoaf, "'Unwemmed Custance,'" 300, note 3, on the word "unwemmed."

21. See my study, "The Crisis of Convention in Cocytus," in *Allegoresis: The Craft and Meaning of Allegory*, ed. J. Stephen Russell (New York: Garland, 1988), 157–169.

22. M. R. James, "The Catalogue of the Library of the Augustinian Friars at York," in *Fasciculus Ioanni Willis Clark Dicatus* (Cambridge: Cambridge University Press, 1909), 2–96, at 16.

23. " . . . it should be understood that there is not just a single sense in this work [the *Comedy*]: it might rather be called *polysemous*, that is, having several senses" ("The Letter to Can Grande," in *Literary Criticism of Dante Alighieri*, trans. and ed. Robert S. Haller [Lincoln, Neb.: University of Nebraska Press, 1973], 99).

Literary Genealogy and the
Problem of the Father

CHRISTINE DE PIZAN AND DANTE

Christine de Pizan is the first literary figure in French whose identity as a women constituted not just a fundamental but also an explicit and elaborate part of her authorial persona.[1] At the heart of her preoccupation with self-definition in terms of gender is the sociohistorical fact that the dominant literary discourses of late fourteenth- and early fifteenth-century France excluded, by definition, a first person, female, speaking subject in the position of author/*auctor*. This is true, on the one hand, for courtly discourse—in which a desiring lyric subject marked as male addresses the female object of his desire (and his speech).[2] A similarly exclusionary gendering obtains for clerkly discourse—in which a learned male voice authorized by his control of a written corpus addresses (normally) a male audience, often on the topic of women. In order to succeed as a professional writer, Christine was thus—as it were—*obliged* to redefine courtly and clerkly discourse in terms of gender, so as to allow for a female author figure. At the same time, she had to link the issue of gender to that of authority, and to relate both to the question of her own gender in historically specific terms.

In this context, Christine utilized genealogy as a powerful figure in a variety of strategic ways, of which two are of particular interest for the present essay: "natural" genealogy—in particular, Christine's

relation to her father, Thomas de Pizan[3]—and literary genealogy, that
is, Christine's relationship to a privileged set of model authors, and in
particular, Dante. I will be concentrating on the first work in Christine's corpus where she systematically treats her relation both with
her father and with Dante: the *Livre du chemin de long estude* (1402–
1403). Indeed, in this pivotal work, I would like to suggest, these two
relationships are mimetically intertwined (and mutually illuminating);
that is, Christine's representation of Dante as a prestigious literary
father is linked to her deeply ambivalent representation of her own
father in specifically Dantean terms.[4] It is also important to note that
Christine's *Chemin de long estude* is the first serious reading—the first
rifacimento—of Dante's *Commedia* in French literature.[5]

Before turning to the text of the *Chemin*, a few preliminary remarks
are necessary in order to situate that work within Christine's larger
enterprise of self-representation and self-authorization in terms of
genealogy and literary models. Over the course of the first ten years
of Christine de Pizan's literary career (approximately 1395–1405; i.e.,
from her earliest lyric poems to *Lavision-Christine*), she elaborated an
empowering autobiographical narrative which served to authorize her
literary vocation, which enabled her to speak through, and by means
of, the dominant contemporary literary discourses—a highly selective
and stylized self-representation.

This fable of self-definition was elaborated in a series of different
works and involved a narrative core which provided Christine with
a gender-specific authority to utilize both courtly and clerkly discourse. To a large degree, this strategically significant autobiography
is founded on a radical opposition between Christine's present and
her past. This opposition is articulated in a series of overlapping and
interrelated contexts: national origin, family history, affective engagement, sociolegal status, political situation. Narratively speaking, what
we have is a gendered, personalized, secular retelling of the Fall. Let
me summarize the main points of this well-known story, from the
temporal perspective of 1402–1403, when she was writing—more or
less simultaneously—the *Chemin* (completed first, and "dated," in its
prologue, 5 October 1402 [vv. 185–188]), and the *Mutacion de fortune*
("dated" thirteen years afer her husband's death [i.e., 1403] in vv.
1395–1397).

Born in Italy, Christine moved to France as a child, because her
father, Thomas de Pizan, was appointed to the court of Charles V as

physician and astrologer.[6] She spent a happy childhood in Paris, where her learned father provided her with privileged access to the world of books, within the broader political context of the prosperous reign of his bibliophilic royal master. She was happily married at the age of fifteen and soon became the mother of three. This idyllic situation began to change with the death first of King Charles V (1380), then of her father (1387 / 1388).[7] The definitive rupture occurred in 1390 with the death of her husband, Étienne de Castel.[8] At the age of 25, Christine was left a widow, with three children to care for and serious financial problems which obliged her to earn a living. At the same time, there is a public parallel in the 1390s in terms of the somber events of the reign of Charles VI (whose first attack of madness dated from 1392), which contrasts strikingly with that of his father and predecessor. During the first decade of her widowhood, Christine progressively and with some difficulty established herself as a professional writer, an identity which is definitively set in place with the completion of a set of complementary works around the turn of the century: the predominantly courtly *Cent ballades* (1395–1400; in any case before 1402),[9] the *Epistre au dieu d'amours* (c. 1399), which combines courtly with clerkly discourse, and the clerkly *Epistre d'Othéa* (c. 1400).

The authorial persona which emerges from this autobiographical narrative is thus authorized in a variety of ways which simultaneously valorize her historically specific, gendered identity. First, she is a virtuous widow who had truly loved her late husband. She is thus able to speak at firsthand of the love experience, but from a position securely outside the economy of erotic desire. Second, she is the daughter of a professional scholar who passed on a portion of his learning to her. Genealogy thus provides Christine with an authoritative entrée into the exclusively male world of *clergie*. Yet this link—though undeniable—is also profoundly ambivalent for both parent and child in terms of gender.[10] By providing her with an intellectual education superior to that of a "normal" daughter, Thomas de Pizan enables Christine to assume a clerkly authorial identity as a kind of birthright. On the other hand, Thomas did not instruct Christine as he would have done with a son, and her education was thus "incomplete"—a lack for which she would have to compensate during her widowed adulthood as a professional writer.[11]

Christine's representation of her father as part of her literary autobiography is thus deeply ambivalent. In terms of clerkly learning, he both empowers and impedes her. A standard medieval topos which hierarchically genders language learning is also at issue here: Thomas provides his daughter with learning in the vernacular, i.e., the mother language,[12] while withholding a full clerkly formation in Latin, i.e., the father language.

Christine's representation of her relationship to model author figures over this same period is dominated by her spectacular polemic with the *Roman de la rose*, culminating in the famous dossier of the *Débat sur le "Roman de la rose"* (1402).[13] In Christine's reading of the *Rose*, what is at issue is a kind of negative genealogy in terms of gender: the *Rose*'s self-authorizing lineage of male lyric love poets—extending from Ovid to Guillaume de Lorris and Jean de Meun—excludes precisely the new kind of female authorial voice that Christine herself incarnates. Christine's confrontation with the single most influential and prestigious literary work in the French vernacular—the *Rose*—thus involves countering this overwhelming fact of literary genealogical *absence* (and exclusion) in terms of gender. First and foremost in her strategy of self-authorization is the equally overwhelming literary fact of her own *presence* as a female literary speaking subject—a female author figure in the process of writing, of producing new works. Various kinds of authorizing antecedents are implied by—*required* by—this present voice. Christine's ultimate treatment of this problem will take place in the *Livre de la cité des dames* (1405), where her project is to construct (to fully elaborate) a corrective female literary and cultural genealogy for herself (and, indeed, for women in general).[14] In this sense, the *Cité des dames* may be seen as Christine's ultimate *positive* response to the *Rose*—involving a master strategy of displacement and substitution (especially, from my present viewpoint, with regard to literary genealogy). In the *Débat* (completed two years before the *Cité*), a number of less definitive, less fully elaborated, more provisional solutions are utilized, in the context of Christine's ultimate *negative* response to the *Rose*, i.e., her most complete and explicit critique of the dominant text in the vernacular tradition in which she herself is writing.[15]

It is in the context of her polemical engagement with the *Rose* in the *Débat* that Christine explicitly refers to Dante for the first time in her oeuvre. Countering Pierre Col's valorization of Jean de Meun's treatment of Hell and Heaven, Christine cites Dante as an authoritative counterexample:

Mais se mieulx vuelz oïr descripre paradis et enfer, et par plus subtilz termes plus haultement parlé de theologie, plus prouffitablement, plus po-etiquement et de plus grant efficasse, lis le livre que on appelle le Dant, ou le te fais exposer pour ce que il est en langue florentine souverainnement dicté: la oyras autre propos mieux fondé plus subtilement, ne te desplaise, et ou tu pourras plus prouffiter que en ton *Romant de la Rose*,—et cent fois mieux composé; ne il n'y a comparison, ne t'en courouces ja. (*Débat*, ed. Hicks, 141–142)

But if you want to hear Heaven and Hell better described and theology discussed in more appropriate and subtle terms, more profitably, more poetically, and more effectively, then read the book of Dante—or have it translated for yourself since it is superbly composed in Italian: there you will find better arguments, more subtly presented (no offense), and from which you can derive more benefit than from your *Romance of the Rose*. It is also a hundred times better written; don't be upset, but there is simply no comparison.

As Jeffrey Richards has insightfully remarked, Christine's initial citation of Dante is thus part of her polemical response to the *Rose*, and, in Richards's words, other "explicit allusions to Dante seem to appear in Christine's work exclusively in this context."[16] For my present purposes, I would like to suggest that Christine counters the negative literary genealogy embodied for her by the *Rose* in the French vernacular with a positive literary genealogy embodied for her by the *Commedia* in the Italian vernacular. In this "provisional" solution, it is not gender but national origin that provides Christine with an alternative genealogical authorization in literary terms.

In the *Chemin de long estude*—to whose composition Christine explicitly turns at the end of the final letter in the *Débat sur le "Roman de la rose"*—a much more elaborate, and a clearly gendered, treatment of Dante is at issue. Christine uses Dante as a privileged model author in an elaborate strategy of regendering, in tandem with a complex play on identity and difference in terms of national origin. A drama of literary genealogy is thus, as it were, built into the very structure of Christine's poem. At the same time, the *Chemin* elaborately stages—in all its ambivalence—Christine's authorizing and limiting genealogical link with her father.

In order to explore the interrelations among these different aspects of the figure of genealogy and the problematic of authority, let us now turn to the text of the *Chemin de long estude* itself.[17]

The work is an allegorical dream vision, framed—and informed—by an autobiographical narrative. The poem opens with the solitary, widowed author in the present of 5 October 1402 (vv. 185–188), still lamenting her husband's death thirteen years earlier. This personal grief is doubled by a "public" grieving over the state of the world, which the first-person author perceives as engaged in perpetual and futile war. Immediately after she falls asleep (vv. 451–452), the grieving Christine has a dream-vision, which will last until virtually the very end of the poem. In this vision, the Cumean Sibyl comes to the sleeping Christine, whom the Sibyl claims as her intellectual daughter, and takes Christine on a long journey. This journey is divided into two qualitatively different but—I would argue—intricately interrelated parts. The first part (vv. 714–2554) involves a physical journey, as the Sibyl leads her charge first to Mt. Parnassus (vv. 714–1170), then on a tour of the earth (vv. 1171–1568), and finally on a celestial voyage (vv. 1569–2554) up to the Fifth Heaven (the "firmament"), then back down to the First Heaven (the "ciel d'aire," v. 2057), which provides the setting for the second part of the journey (vv. 2555–6270). A significant shift is involved in terms of mimesis, for this second part of Christine's vision does not involve spatial movement or physical representation. Rather, this will be a purely intellectual and discursive experience: an allegorical debate between Richece, Noblece, Chevalerie, and Sagece on how the self-destructive world can be set right. The debate occurs at the court of Raison, and centers on the choice of criteria to be used in determining who shall be the world-emperor, the political savior who can establish peace and prosperity on earth. During the debate sequence, the first-person protagonist virtually disappears from the story line, becoming no more than a "window" through which the reader experiences the long speeches of the various allegorical characters. The long discourse of Sagece (vv. 4080–6072) concludes and dominates the debate, with a dense sequence of learned citations of the Latin *auctores*.

The poem closes with the reintroduction of Christine as protagonist, as the Sibyl presents her to Raison as the messenger necessary to convey the substance of the debate to the court of France, where a final resolution can be effected. In the very last lines, the dream

frame is reevoked qua closing signal as Christine's descent from the
First Heaven back to earth is abruptly terminated by her awakening.

The first part of Christine's journey in the *Chemin* is explicitly and
programmatically modeled on Dante's *Commedia*. In the balance of
this essay, I will be focusing on the first two of the three key sections
in which this program functions most systematically and most visibly:
First, Christine's initial encounter with the Sibyl (vv. 451–712); second, their journey together to Mt. Parnassus (vv. 714–1170). I will
treat only cursorily the *Chemin*'s third Dantean episode, the celestial
voyage to the Fifth Heaven and back (vv. 1569–2044).[18] In all three
of these passages, the Dantean model functions through a process
of textual reminiscence and citation that involves simultaneously
authority and difference. That is, Christine programmatically evokes
Dante both to authorize her self-representation and to differentiate
herself from him.

This program begins with the initial encounter between Christine
and the authoritative female figure who comes to her in a moment of
despair (vv. 451–712). In terms of the genealogical construct that
concerns me in this essay, it is significant that her first word to
Christine is "fille" (v. 490). This genealogical trope is directly related
to Christine's identity as a learned woman, to what the Sibyl calls
"l'amour qu'as a science" (v. 492 [the love which you have for learn-
ing]). This love links Christine to the Sibyl, provides the narrative
motivation for the Sibyl's affection as well as her visit, and guarantees
Christine's future fame:

> Et ains que vie te decline,
> En ce t'iras tant deduisant
> Que ton nom sera reluisant
> Apres toy par longue memoire,
> Et pour le bien de ton memoire[19]
> Que voy abille a concevoir
> e t'aim et vueil faire a savoir
> De mes secres une partie,
> Ains que de toy soie partie.
>
> (*Chemin*, vv. 494–502)

And before your life is over, you will so rejoice in
(learning) that your name will be resplendent long

after your death; and because of the goodness of your memory, whose ability to conceptualize is powerful, I love you and want you to learn a part of my secret knowledge before I leave you.

The Sibyl then identifies herself in terms that emphasize her Virgilian origin and simultaneously recall the character Virgil's first words of self-identification to Dante-protagonist:

> . . . omo già fui
> e li parenti miei furon lombardi,
> mantovani per patrïa ambedui
> . . . poeta fui, e cantai di quel giusto
> figliuol d'Anchise che venne da Troia,
> poi che 'l superbo Ilïón fu combusto
>
> (*Inf.* 1.67–69; 73–75)

> . . . I was formerly a man, and my parents were Lombard, both born in Mantua. . . . I was a poet, and I sang of that just son of Anchises who came from Troy after the proud Ilium was burned.

Syntactic parallels with the introductory speech of the Dantean Virgil work to stress (and to remotivate) gender difference with regard to the authority of Christine's Sibyl as guide figure. At the same time, the status of writer (Virgil) is contrasted with that of actor (Sibyl) in such a way as to privilege Christine's guide from the point of view of chronology. Finally, Christine-protagonist is implicitly presented as a new *female* "Aenean" Dante figure, associated from the beginning with an "exile motif" that will be progressively redefined as the *Chemin's* plot line unfolds. In this context, of course, the initial evocation of Aeneas's meeting with Anchises in *Aeneid* 6 made by Christine's Sibyl serves (among other things) to set up—contrastively—the confrontation of Christine-protagonist with her father in the *Chemin:*

> Jadis fus femme moult senee,
> De la cité de Cumins nee. . . .
> Almethea fus appelee. . . .
> Celle suis, qui mena jadis
> Eneas l'exillié Troien;

Sanz autre conduit ne moien
Parmi enfer le convoiay. . . .
En enfer lui monstray son pere
Anchises et l'ame sa mere[20]
(*Chemin*, vv. 507–508; 511; 596–599; 613–614)

I was formerly a very wise woman, born in the city of
Cumae. . . . I was called Almethea. . . . I was she who
long ago led Aeneas, the exiled Trojan; with no other
guide or means I conducted him through Hell. . . . In
Hell I showed him his father Anchises and the soul
of his mother.

In the sequence that follows, the Sibyl sets forth a tripartite literary
genealogy which proceeds from herself through Virgil to Christine. It
is important to note that this involves a reversal of the *Aeneid* in
which Virgil as author spoke of the Sibyl as (authorizing) character.
In the *Chemin*, by contrast, Christine's character the Sibyl speaks of
Virgil as authorizing her "preexistent" truthful speech. Significantly,
Christine's Sibyl does this by referring directly to a Virgilian text that
is essential to the representation of the Dantean Virgilio: Eclogue
4.4–7.[21] This is, of course, the Virgilian textual locus that the *Commedia* presents as having saved Statius (*Purg.* 22.70–72). In Christine's
Chemin, the Sibyl explains that

Virgille, qui apres moy vint,
Long temps de mes vers lui souvint,
Car bien les avoit acointiez.
De moy parla en ses dictiez
Et dist: Or est venu le temps,
Ainsi com je voy et entens
Que Sebille Cumee ot dit:
Ainsi le recorde en son dit.

(*Chemin*, vv. 627–634)[22]

Virgil, who came after me, long remembered my
verses, for he knew them well. He spoke of me in
his poetry, saying: "Now has come (as I see and understand) the time that the Cumean Sibyl predicted."
Thus he wrote in his poem.

In the text of the *Chemin*, Virgil's authorization of the Sibyl's written prophecies is immediately followed by the Sibyl's appearance to Christine-protagonist:

> Or me suis je manifestee
> A toy que je voy apprestee
> A concevoir, s'en toy ne tient
> Ce que grant estude contient,
> Et pour ce me suis apparue
> Cy endroit. . . .

(Chemin, vv. 635–640)

> Then I revealed myself to you whom I see ready to understand what serious study leads to (even if you do not already possess it), and because of this I have appeared here.

The inscribed tripartite lineage Sibyl-Virgil-Christine sets in place the *Chemin*'s Dantean model, at the same time as it provisionally regenders this model.

What follows is the Sibyl's offer to take Christine-protagonist on an otherworldly journey in terms which recall and transform Virgilio's offer to Dante in *Inferno* 1.112–123. The initial response of Christine-protagonist conflates two key moments in what John Freccero has called the *Commedia*'s "prologue scene."[23] The first is Dante's response to the revelation of Virgilio's identity in *Inferno* 1.79–87, which combines *admiratio* and a plea for help, with the articulation of a direct link. In *Inferno* 1 this link involves reading; in *Chemin* 659–675, it involves a gendered love of wisdom. The second model Dantean locus is the extended moment of the protagonist's hesitation to undertake the otherworldly journey in *Inferno* 2.

Christine's first response to the Sibyl thus combines an admiring exclamation which emphasizes the latter's female identity, with an expression of Christine's own self-doubt and uncertainty with regard to her worthiness to be the object of the Sibyl's choice (vv. 666–675). The famous double negative comparison of *Inferno* 2.31–33 (in which Dante-protagonist contrasts himself with Aeneas and St. Paul) is here redone as Christine-protagonist makes a self-deprecatory comparison which is exclusively intellectual, at the same time as it invokes contrastively Aeneas's infernal journey (vv. 676–685). Christine-protagonist continues her reenactment in miniature (and in monologue) of *Inferno* 2's extended dialogic drama of hesitation and remotivation, as she affirms the authoritative rightness of the Sibyl's choice of her, at the same time stating her own willingness to undertake the journey (vv. 690–693). The scene concludes with Christine's self-presentation as a feminized pilgrim, ready to follow her female guide: "Si suis vostre humble chamberiere. / Alez devant! G'iray derriere" (vv. 697–698 [I am thus your humble handmaiden. Set out ahead! I will follow after]). As both Arturo Farinelli and Maria Merkel have noted,[24] this direct discourse recalls the final line of *Inferno* 1, a description (in the third person) of the initial beginning of the protagonist's journey with Virgilio as his guide: "Allor si mosse, e io li tenni dietro" (*Inf.* 1.136 [Then he set out, and I came on behind him]).[25]

The second section of the *Chemin* that is most systematically and visibly informed by the model of the *Commedia* is the first part of the voyage that Christine undertakes under the Sibyl's guidance, that is, their sojourn near Mount Parnassus (vv. 714–1170). The sequence opens as the two arrive at an elaborately described *locus amoenus*.[26] The Sibyl explains to Christine that the mountain which the latter sees to the right of the garden is Mount Parnassus or Mount Helicon (vv. 977–979), on whose slope is visible the "fontaine . . . de Sapience" (vv. 981–985 [Fountain of Wisdom]) where the "neuf muses . . . tiennent . . . l'escole sainte" (v. 992, 995 [nine muses hold their holy school]). Christine is here setting up a rewriting of Dante's Limbo, in terms of a use of classical mythology which stresses female authority at the level of textual mimesis: the *bella scola* of the classic epic poets in *Inferno* 4.94 is here re-presented as the *escole sainte* of the Muses.[27]

The detailed rewriting of Dante's Limbo which follows involves two key reversals of the model in *Inferno* 4. The first reversal involves mimesis. While Dante-protagonist is represented as actually having seen the souls of the great figures of pagan antiquity, Christine-protagonist is shown only the place which they used to frequent. Dante sees presence; Christine sees absence. In addition, Christine's *locus* is an emblematic mythographic fiction; while Dante's is presented as historical fact (based on *Aeneid* 6 conceived as *historia* rather than as *fabula*). Again, the contrast is between Dante's self-presentation as "actor" and Christine's, as reader: that is, Christine's journey is both a figure for, and a composite of, her reading of books. It does not claim either Dante's literal-historical or his figural truth.

The second reversal involves both sequential order and authorial self-presentation. In *Inferno* 4, Dante gives the poets pride of place—they come before the philosophers. In the *Chemin*, Christine reverses this order by presenting the philosophers first. The "philosophic" side of her conception of her own literary enterprise is thus emphasized, functioning as part of her programmatic self-authorization as a woman writer.[28] Christine's list of philosophers descends from Aristotle and follows closely (though with some modifications and omissions) the list in *Inferno* 4.130–144. The key change in Dante's basic *translatio studii* structure, however, is the striking addition of Christine's father as the final named philosopher:

> Ton pere meismes y savoit
> Bien la voie, si la devoit
> Savoir, car bien l'avoit hantee
> Dont grant science en ot portee.
>
> (*Chemin*, vv. 1045–1048)

> Your own father knew this place very well, and he certainly should have, because he often spent time there, and carried away great learning.

This personalization of the *translatio studii* involves, of course, a direct link to Christine. A corresponding link is, I think, suggested in Christine's list of poets, which clearly recalls the sequence in *Inferno* 4.88–90, where Virgilio explains to Dante: "Quelli è Omero poeta sovrano; / l'altro è Orazio satiro che vene; / Ovidio è 'l terzo, e l'ultimo Lucano" (That one is Homer the sovereign poet; the next who comes is Horace the satirist; Ovid is the third, and the last is Lucan). The *Chemin*'s enumeration of the poets who had frequented Parnassus starts with Virgil (vv. 1050–1053), thus emphasizing the fact that Christine's Sibyl has replaced Dante's Virgilio as the protagonist's guide. After Virgil, the *Chemin* enumerates "Omer, le poete souvrain" (v. 1061), "Ovide et Oraces satire, / Orpheus" (vv. 1065–1066).[29] The poet who links these classical models to Christine is implicitly presented as Dante himself.

In other words, in the *Chemin*'s version of the Dantean Limbo, genealogy functions to establish Christine's authority both in terms of philosophy and in terms of poetry. Two different kinds of genealogy are at issue, serving to link Christine to the authoritative canon of antiquity: her father, Thomas de Pizan, links her to the philosophers; her author, Dante, links her to the poets. In both these cases, Christine's national origin as Italian—significant, in a sense, only because she is writing in French for a French audience—doubles her biological, intellectual, and readerly genealogical links to her two father figures.

If, however, Thomas de Pizan and Dante thus function as mediators between Christine and the classical canon, her status vis-à-vis her prestigious philosophical and poetic predecessors is explicitly marked by a kind of radical difference: She will be like them, she will benefit from their learning, but she will not be identical to them, not one of their number,[30] as the Sibyl's words to her explicitly indicate: "s'estre de si haulte escole / Ne pues, tout au mains a seaux / Puiseras dedens les ruissiaux; " (vv. 1084–1085 [though you cannot be part of this noble school, at least you will dip your bucket into the fountain's water]).

It thus emerges that an important part of Christine's self-representation in the *Chemin* resides precisely in this difference, expressed as a kind of limitation vis-à-vis Dante. It is in this context that the Sibyl reveals to Christine the name of the path she is following on her journey: "ce chemin . . . a nom long estude" (vv. 1099; 1103 [the name of this road is long study]). Christine's *chemin*—as opposed to Dante's *cammino* (*Inf.* 1.1 ff.)—is a figure for her reading, her extensive and continuing study of authoritative books. Significantly, it is in connection with the Sibyl's revelation of the name of the path she is following (and, indeed, of the book she is writing), that Christine first explicitly invokes Dante as a model:

> . . . le nom du plaisant pourpris
> Oncques mais ne me fu apris,
> Fors en tant que bien me recorde
> Que Dant de Flourence el recorde
> En son livre qu'il composa
> Ou il moult biau stile posa
>
> (*Chemin*, vv. 1125–1129)

The name of this pleasant habitation was never taught to me, except in so far as I well remember that Dante

of Florence records it in in his book, which he wrote
in a very beautiful style.

This initial reference sets up Christine-protagonist as reader of Dante
in a way which retrospectively makes explicit Christine-author's use
of *Inferno* 4 as textual model for her Mount Parnassus sequence. At
the same time, a specific textual citation of the *Commedia* functions to
emphasize Christine's awareness of Dante's self-presentation as reader
of Virgil: The *biau stile* (v. 1129) with which Christine characterizes
the *Commedia* is a direct translation of the *bello stilo* (*Inf.* 1.87) that
Dante-protagonist claims to have learned from having read Virgil.[31]
    Christine then goes on to evoke in detail the narrative moment of
Dante's first meeting with Virgilio in the *Commedia*:

> Quant en la silve fu entrez
> Ou tout de paour yert oultrez,
> Lors que Virgille s'apparu
> A lui dont il fu secouru,
> Adont lui dist par grant estude
> Ce mot: Vaille moy long estude
> Qui m'a fait cerchier tes volumes
> Par qui ensemble acointance eusmes
>
> (*Chemin*, vv. 1131–1138)

> When Dante had entered the wild wood and was
> overcome by fear, at that moment when Virgil first
> appeared to help him, then Dante spoke with great
> learning the following words: "May the long study
> now avail me which has made me pour over your
> volumes, through which we first came to know
> each other."

Christine's recall of Dante's self-presentation as a careful and devoted
reader of Virgil simultaneously presents her as a similar kind of reader
of Dante. In addition to her use of the Italianism *silve* for Dante's
selva (*Inf.* 1.1 and 1.5), and of the French cognate *paour* for *paura*,
a key word in the *Commedia*'s opening canto where it appears no
less than five times (*Inf.* 1.6, 15, 19, 44, 53), Christine's narrative
summary involves (in vv. 1136–1137) a direct French translation of

Dante-protagonist's initial direct address to Virgilio for help: "vagliami 'l lungo studio e 'l grande amore / che m' ha fatto cercar lo tuo volume" (*Inf.* 1.83–84 [may the long study and the great love that have made me search your volume avail me!]).

When Christine-protagonist remembers this Dantean passage, she realizes that Dante's meeting with Virgil took place on the same "road"—the same *chemin*—as her present journey:

> Or congnois a celle parole
> Qui ne fu nice ne frivole
> Que le vaillant poete Dant
> Qui a long estude ot la dent,
> Estoit en ce chemin entrez,
> Quant Virgille y fu encontrez
> Qui le mena parmy enfer . . .
>
> (*Chemin*, vv. 1139–1146)

> Then I knew from this phrase, which was neither silly nor frivolous, that the valliant poet Dante, who was hungry for long study, had entered upon this very road when he met Virgil, who led him through Hell . . .

It is important to note that Christine's designation of "le vaillant poete Dant" is semantically overdetermined: First, the adjective "vaillant" has the same root (infinitive, *valoir*) as the imperative "vaille" (Italian, "vaglia"), which it also incorporates phonetically. A link is thus suggested between Christine's formulaic designation of her model author and the key citation which provides the name for her own book. Second, the prestigious title "poete" which Christine gives to Dante in this passage (but not to "Virgille," v. 1133) involves an important act of displacement vis-à-vis the Dantean model text. In the line immediately preceding the appeal to Virgilio for help which Christine translates, Dante had addressed his interlocutor as follows: "O de li altri poeti onore e lume" (*Inf.* 1.82 [O glory and light of other poets]). Christine strategically substitutes "Dant poete" for "Virgilio poeta"—that is, she presents her relationship to Dante as analogous to Dante's relationship to Virgil.[32]

At the same time, however, Christine re-emphasizes her *difference* from Dante. At the level of narrative event, Christine's *chemin* has already been explicitly presented as *not* leading to *enfer* (vv. 947–956). Thus, while Christine's journey in the *Chemin* is modeled on—and authorized by—Dante's journey in the *Commedia*, it is a qualitatively different kind of journey. In terms of mimesis, Dante distinguishes between his reading of Virgil's text and his encounter with Virgilio the character. Indeed, this distinction is absolutely fundamental to the theological poetics of the *Commedia*. Christine, on the other hand, does not make this kind of distinction. Her relationship with Dante is a purely literary, purely readerly one—it "takes place" in her library.

Thus, from the point of view of the *Commedia*, Dante's *lungo studio* of Virgil precedes the action depicted by the plot, in which Dante-protagonist, led by Virgilio the character, will follow a literal *cammino* on a literal journey. For Christine, her *long estude* of Dante (among others) not only precedes the journey recounted in the *Chemin*; it also constitutes that journey, which is an extended trope for Christine's reading of, and profound familiarity with, the *auctores*. This is, of course, directly related to the gendered problematic of Christine's authority as a clerkly writer, which is linked to her "autobiographical" mode. In the specific terms of Christine's use of paternal genealogy for self-authorization, two basic constructs are at issue with regard to gender.

First, with regard to the *Commedia* as the *Chemin*'s basic narrative model, a dramatic regendering has taken place. Christine maintains the Dantean first-person configuration, thus presenting herself as female protagonist. At the same time, she substitutes the Sibyl for Dante's Virgil as authoritative guide. On the one hand, this involves a "restoration" of Dante's own original Virgilian model: the Sibyl was, after all, Aeneas's guide on his (third-person) journey to the underworld in *Aeneid* 6. On the other hand, Christine's "restoration" of Aeneas's guide remotivates the Virgilian Sibyl in terms of gender. That is, in Christine's feminized narrative configuration, it is the Sibyl's identity as *female* authority figure that enables her to function as the mentor (the *magister*, the *maestro*) of Christine as first-person female protagonist. This use of the Sibyl confirms and valorizes Christine's literary vocation in terms that simultaneously recall and transform her Dantean model with regard to gender, at the same time performing a gendered rereading of Dante's transformation of Virgil.

In addition, Christine utilizes her Dantean model both to valorize and to undermine the intellectual status of her father, Thomas de

Pizan, whose ambivalent presence looms large in her empowering autobiographical narrative. In the transformed Dantean autobiographical journey undertaken in the *Chemin*, Christine-protagonist encounters her father in a rewritten version of Dante's Limbo—the First Circle of Hell where the souls of the virtuous pagan philosophers and poets reside. This is the single most ambivalent *locus* in the entire *Commedia*. From Dante's point of view, it is the "paradiso" of the pagan great—in which they achieve "immortality" on their own (limited) terms. It is the Elysian Fields from *Aeneid* 6 recontextualized in Dante's Christian universe, so that precisely by "winning" on their terms, the great pagan poets, heroes, and philosophers "lose" on God's terms. Highly significant from Christine's point of view is the fact that this is where the *Commedia* places Virgil, Dante's literary father. By assigning her natural father to her rewritten version of Limbo in the *Chemin*, Christine simultaneously represents both the positive and the negative side of her relationship with him in terms that recall and transform the figure of the Dantean Virgil. As she figures her father in literary autobiographical terms, he is at once the source of her learning, of her intellectual power, and the primary impediment to her full possession of *clergie*, i.e., *latinitas*. In both cases, gender is overdetermined as a feature in this father-daughter relationship.

It is in the context of the gender difference separating Christine from the natural and literary fathers to whom she is genealogically linked in the *Chemin* that the programmatic differences between her journey and Dante's must be read. For the purposes of the present essay, I would like to single out two of these.

First, there is Christine's use of the Dantean citation that constitutes her title as a "verbal golden bough" on her journey. This construct is set in motion immediately after the extended recall of Dante's first meeting with Virgil in *Inferno* 1, and involves the phrase "vaille moy long estude." Christine-protagonist declares:

> Si dis que je n'oublieroie
> Celle parole, ains la diroie
> En lieu d'ewangille ou de crois
> Au passer de divers destrois
> Ou puis en maint peril me vis;]
> Si me valu, ce me fu vis.

> (*Chemin*, vv. 1147–1152)

And I said that I would not forget these words, but
would use them rather than the gospel or the cross
when faced with the various difficulties and the many
dangers in which I later found myself; and this was
effective, in my opinion.

At a moment of danger in the course of her terrestrial journey with
the Sibyl, Christine-protagonist does in fact use this Dantean citation
as a verbal talisman. The episode takes place during the first stage of
an extended trajectory towards the East (*vers orient*, vv. 1355, 1408;
cf. v. 1512), while they are traversing the Great Kahn's territory.[33]
Here Christine encounters a multitude of threatening *bestes fieres* (v.
1383). This sequence recalls, I suggest, the famous scene in *Inferno*
1 where Dante-protagonist's initial attempt to climb the mountain
is impeded by the three beasts, and especially by the third, the *lupa*
(*Inf.* 1.49), called both *bestia* (*Inf.* 1.58, 88, 94) and *fiera* (*Inf.* 2.119).
As Dante is saved from the *bestia . . . fiera* by the arrival of his guide
Virgilio, so Christine is saved from the *bestes fieres* by the presence of
her guide, the Sibyl:

> Si m'eussent moult tost devouree,
> Se je fusse entre eulx demouree,
> Sanz le conduit qui me menoit;
> Mais tout ades me souvenoit
> Du bon mot qui vault en tel cas,
> Car quant j'estoie en un fort pas
> Ou a passer je fusse rude,
> Disant: Vaille moy long estude!
> Alors passoie seurement,
> Sanz avoir encombrement.
>
> (*Chemin*, vv. 1385–1394)

And they would have very quickly devoured me if I
had been there without the guide who was leading
me; but right away I remembered the good phrase
that is effective in such a case, for when I was in a
tight spot which was difficult to get out of, I escaped
safely and without hindrance by saying "May long
study avail me!"

This talismanic use of *Inferno* 1.83 ("Vagliami 'l lungo studio"/ "Vaille moy long estude") functions in several important ways in terms of the Dantean model text. First, it replicates the speech situation in *Inferno* 1, which is thus made to underwrite the scene in the *Chemin*. That is, Christine's cry for help in the face of her threatening beasts is a citation from Dante's cry for help in the face of his. This narrative and discursive overlap, this direct parallel, simultaneously functions, however, to bring to the foreground essential differences between Christine and Dante, in part in terms of literary genealogy. Dante-protagonist cries out to Virgil the character within the plot line of the *Commedia*. Christine-protagonist, by contrast, cries out, as it were, to Dante the author, outside the diegetic parameters of the *Chemin*.

Second, Christine's use of this construct also recalls another feature of the *Inferno*, i.e., Virgil's repeated use of a Christian verbal formula to overcome potential impediments to the Dantean journey, which he employs for the first time during his confrontation with Charon: "vuolsi così colà dove si puote / ciò che si vuole" (*Inf.* 3.95–96[34] [It is so willed where will and power are one]). This, as Robert Hollander (and others) have pointed out, represents Dante's Christian rewriting of the Virgilian golden bough in *Aeneid* 6.[35] The miraculous precious material which protects Aeneas is turned by Dante into an emblem of the protective power of the spirit: intertextually speaking, the point that is made is that the true gold is that of the Word. Christine takes this one step further, in a way which, once again, simultaneously takes Dante as model while marking her difference from him. Again, a literary genealogy is at issue: Christine rewrites Dante's rewriting of Virgil. And she substitutes for Dante's emblem of a transcendent poetics of divine election, a metonym for her own clerkly activity, for her authorially self-authorizing, studious reading of the *auctores*, epitomized by her knowledge of (and literary relationship to) Dante himself. Her key citation from the *Divine Comedy* is at once evidence of her clerkly credentials and a transformation of Dante's poetics for her own purposes—a transformation which is visible as such. The *Divine Comedy*'s "verbal golden bough" involved divine intervention in the life of Dante-protagonist at the literal-historical level (or, at least this is the claim Dante's poem makes). Christine's "verbal golden bough" is powerful precisely as evidence, as a sign of her *reading* of the *Divine Comedy*—and of her rewriting of it.

The second and final programmatic difference between Christine's journey in the *Chemin* and Dante's in the *Commedia* that I would like to consider in the context of the present essay involves the three explicit limitations which the Sibyl assigns to her charge's travels. The first of these limitations occurs at the outset of their voyage together, as the Sibyl clearly differentiates the path that they will be following from the one which leads through Hell (vv. 947–958). The second explicit limitation of Christine's journey vis-à-vis Dante's occurs at the end of the *Chemin*'s terrestrial peregrinations, as the Sibyl and her charge arrive at the place of the Earthly Paradise. The Sibyl explains that Christine cannot enter, but must take a different way (vv. 1546–1547; 1561–1567). Finally, at the end of Christine-protagonist's experience in the Fifth Heaven (the *firmament*), the Sibyl explicitly explains the limitation imposed on Christine's celestial voyage. She will not be allowed the direct experience of true Heaven—the highest sphere—because of her corporeality (vv. 2030–2044).

What Christine-protagonist will not be allowed to visit, in other words, is the Dantean spiritual heaven of the *Paradiso*, most specifically, the Empyrean, Dante's tenth and highest Heaven, which he visits in the culmination of the journey represented by the *Commedia* as a whole, that is, *Paradiso* 30–33.[36] This ultimate limit to Christine's voyage had already been anticipated by the Sibyl when she first differentiated—in the intellectual *locus amoenus* beside Mount Parnassus—the two *chemins* which lead to the Heavens. First there is the more narrow, the one Christine will not take:

> Le chemin que tu vois plus drois,
> Plus estroit et plus verdoiant,
> La face de Dieu est voiant
> Cil qui le suit jusqu'a la fin.
>
> (*Chemin*, vv. 902–905)

> The straighter, narrower, greener road that you see allows the one who follows it to the end to see the face of God.

Then there is the wider path, which leads only as high as the firmament (v. 910), and which is the one Christine will take:

Mais ceste voie est plus certaine,
Car par *science* est ordenee,
Mais celle autre est *ymaginee.*
Par celle nous fault toutevoie
Passer, car ceste estroite voie
Te seroit trop fort a suivir:
Si te convient l'autre ensuivir,
Qui est belle a qui bien emprise[37]
L'a, a ceulx qui n'ont ceste aprise.

(*Chemin*, vv. 914–922 [emphasis mine])

But this way is more certain, for it is ordered by
knowledge, while the other is *imagined*. By this one
we must go, for the narrow way would be too difficult
for you to follow: thus you must take this one which
is beautiful for those who have fittingly set out upon
it, for those who have not learned the other.

Here we have a proleptic epitome of Christine's representation of her
difference with Dante in terms of mimesis and poetic identity: *science*
vs. *ymagination*. But this differentiated identity is both articulated
and authorized in terms of the Dantean model from which Christine
explicitly deviates, even as she uses it to define her own vocation.
At the very end of the *Paradiso*, Dante-protagonist will see directly
the very "face de Dieu" that is denied Christine-protagonist from the
outset of her journey.[38] At the highpoint of her celestial voyage in
the *Chemin*, Christine dramatically confims this difference vis-à-vis
Dante in terms of narrative event, as she descends—in accord with
the Sibyl's prohibition—where Dante had ascended.[39]

The overall effect of these three limitations is quite striking in
terms of Christine's Dantean model. Unlike Dante in the *Inferno*,
she does not visit Hell. Unlike Dante at the end of the *Purgatorio*,
she does not visit the Earthly Paradise. Unlike Dante at the end
of the *Paradiso*, she does not visit the Empyrean. In a sense, all of
this represents the narrative elaboration of Christine's emblematic
initial self-representation on Mt. Parnassus/Limbo/Elysium as *not* a
full member of the *si haulte escole* (v. 1084), in contrast to Dante-
protagonist who, in *Inferno* 4, is explicitly received into the *bella scola*,

as the *auctores*—Virgil, Homer, Horace, Ovid, and Lucan—accept him
as one of their own:[40]

> e più d'onore ancora assai mi fenno,
> ch'e' sì mi fecer de la loro schiera,
> sì ch' io fui sesto tra cotanto senno
>
> (*Inf.* 4.100–102)

> and yet more honor did they show me, for they made
> me one of their group, so that I was sixth among so
> much wisdom

As Christine-protagonist is initially differentiated from Dante, the
act of reading whom has empowered her in her new, gendered version of *Inferno* 4, so the global narrative structure of the *Chemin*
differentiates her journey from that of her Dantean model in the
Commedia. She does *not* visit the farthest points, the "extremities"
reached by Dante-protagonist in each of the three *cantiche*. And this
is, I suggest, a fundamental part of Dante's function as model: to
represent Christine's differences, her "limits."

For "limitation"—ultimately presented in terms of gender—is an essential part of Christine's programmatic self-definition in the *Chemin*.
She uses both her father and Dante to dramatize this. But limitation
also means difference in a positive sense. Her use of Dante and of
Thomas de Pizan—precisely in the context of establishing limitation
and difference—proves her clerkliness, establishes her authority as
a woman writer. In this sense, absence becomes presence, negative
features become positive features in her progressive self-definition.
The genealogical connections with Thomas and Dante thus function
both as authorizing *links*, and as demarcating *lines*: an oxymoronic
lineage, then, connoting both these senses of the term.

By way of conclusion, I would like to suggest that Christine's
complex genealogical relationship to Dante in the *Chemin* must also
be read as part of her response to the *Romance of the Rose*. That
is, the negative genealogy that the *Rose* represented for Christine as
female author is in part made good in the *Chemin* by her privileged
relationship to Dante, in which literary genealogy is doubled by shared
Italian national origin.[41] In terms of gender, this construct is articulated through Christine-protagonist's relationship with the Sibyl at

the level of the plot. Not only does this regender the first-person configuration of the *Commedia* through a "restoration" of the original Virgilian guide, it also links the Sibyl and Christine as Italian women. Gender thus doubles "national origin" in this authorizing genealogy.

In terms of narrative event, all this becomes explicit near the end of the poem when the Sibyl proposes that Christine be the messenger who will transmit the debate at Raison's court in the First Heaven to the French royal court on earth. The final set of qualifications that the Sibyl adduces on behalf of her charge is as follows:

> Et si vient droitement a point,
> Car en France demeure celle
> Qui est de nostre escole ancelle,
> Et moult jeunete y fu menee,
> Combien que comme moy fust nee
> En Ytale . . .
>
> (*Chemin*, vv. 6286–6292)

> And this is just what we need, because she who is the handmaiden of our school lives in France, where she arrived at a very young age, although like me she was born in Italy . . .

In this context, Christine's biography is made to function as a kind of *translatio studii*, which extends and complements the various genealogical constructs used to define and authorize her writerly identity in the *Chemin*. First, this fact of Christine's biography links her to Italy as a *locus* of learning, in contradistinction to her French male opponents in the *Debate on the "Romance of the Rose."* At the same time, it authorizes her as a specifically French writer (in a kind of double-edged polemical use of national origin). Furthermore, this aspect of Christine's biography figures (and reinforces) her *reading* of Dante, which thus appears as (among other things) a literary (or writerly) version of her biographic *translatio*. This is even true at the literal level: Christine's *Chemin* is in part a "translation" of Dante's *Commedia* into French. In terms of the *Chemin*'s representation of French political history, both Christine's biographical *translatio* and her reading/translation of Dante into French double (and are authorized by) two key (and interrelated) political events: Charlemagne's transfer of *clergie* from Rome to Paris (vv. 5893–5906); and Charles V's *transla-cion* (v. 5016) of the Latin classics into French (vv. 5009–5030).

Finally, these various *translatio* constructs are of course directly related to Christine's father, who actually initiated the move from Italy to France.[42] Thus, in the poetic economy of the *Chemin de long estude*, Christine's biographic genealogy (in terms of Thomas de Pizan) doubles her literary genealogy (in terms of Dante). At the same time, Christine's gendered "problem of the father" is addressed through her use of the Sibyl figure. Here we have a gendered genealogy that fuses the female mythographic authority of the Sibyl with the historical specificity of Christine's individual life (as a writer), including the privileged issue of national origin with its insistence on the opposi-tion / *translatio* Italy / France.

In the closing lines of the *Chemin*, these various constructs of genealogy and *translatio*, gender and nationality are rearticulated in terms of a series of oppositions centering on that between the *Commedia* and the *Rose*, doubled by that between Christine's father and her mother. In the *Chemin*'s final scene, Christine-protagonist is making the descent back to earth after her sojourn in the First Heaven. She is in the process of effusively thanking the Sibyl for having taken her on the journey, when her dream is interrupted:

> Ja estoie bas desjuchee,
> Ce me sembloit, quant fus huchee
> De la mere qui me porta,
> Qu'a l'uis de ma chambre hurta,
> Qui de tant gesir s'esmerveille,
> Car tart estoit, et je m'esveille.
>
> (*Chemin*, vv. 6387–6392)

> It seemed that I had already descended quite a way when I was called by the mother who had carried me in her womb and who knocked on my bedroom door, astonished that I was still asleep, since it was late, and I awakened.

Christine effects closure by citing the celebrated final two lines of Jean de Meun's *Roman de la Rose*: "Ainsint oi la rose vermeille. / Atant fu jorz, et je m'esveille" (ed. Lecoy, vv. 21749–21750 [Thus I

obtained the vermillion rose; and then day broke, and I awakened]).
This witty citation *au second degré* (the citation of a closure to effect a
closure) functions to contrast, to distance Christine's dream from that
of the *Rose*.[43] At the same time, Christine has effected a dramatically
new kind of gendered authority and authorial self-definition, vis-à-
vis the stance she had adopted in the *Débat sur le "Roman de la
rose."* By the end of the *Chemin*, Christine's polemical response to
her dominant French predecessor-text has been significantly mediated
by her selective rewriting of the *Commedia*. It is thus significant—
in terms of literary genealogy—that in the *Chemin's* final lines, the
Rose is textually present, but informed (mediated) by the absent
Commedia, while—in terms of familial genealogy—Thomas de Pizan
is textually absent, the intellectual father having been displaced, at
least temporarily, by the corporeal mother.[44]

NOTES

1. An earlier and somewhat shorter version of this study appeared in the
Journal of Medieval and Renaissance Studies 23 (1993). All citations are from
the following editions: Dante Alighieri, *La commedia secondo l'antica vulgata*,
4 vols., ed. Giorgio Petrocchi, Società dantesca italiana, Edizione nazionale
(Milan: Mondadori, 1966–1968); Christine de Pisan, *Le livre du chemin de
long estude*, ed. Robert Püschel (Berlin, 1887); Christine de Pisan, *Le livre
de la mutacion de fortune*, ed. Suzanne Solente, SATF (Paris: Picard, 1959–
1966). Translations from Dante are based on Charles S. Singleton, *The Divine
Comedy of Dante Alighieri*, 6 vols. (Princeton: Princeton University Press,
1970–1975). Translations from French are mine.

2. The most important exception to this rule is the figure of Toute-Belle
in Guillaume de Machaut's *Voir-Dit*. See Jacqueline Cerquiglini, *"Un engin
si soutil": Guillaume de Machaut et l'écriture au XIVe siècle* (Paris: Champion,
1985), 91–103; and Kevin Brownlee, *Poetic Identity in Guillaume de Machaut*,
(Madison: University of Wisconsin Press, 1984), 94–156. Also relevant is the
figure of "La Guignarde" in the *Livre des cent ballades* of Jean le Sénéschal,
et al.

3. I will be dealing only tangentially here with Christine's representation
of her relation to her mother, which is of course linked in a variety of
important ways to her mimesis of her paternal genealogy in terms of gender
and authority. For Christine's ambivalent (and changing) representation of
her mother, see Renate Blumenfeld-Kosinski, "Christine de Pizan and the

Mysogynistic Tradition," *Romanic Review* 82 (1990): 279–292, and especially 285–289. See also Maureen Quilligan, "Allegory and the Textual Body: Female Authority in Christine de Pizan's *Livre de la cité des dames*," *Romanic Review* 79 (1988), 222–248; and *The Allegory of Female Authority: Christine de Pizan's "Livre de la cité des dames"* (Ithaca, N.Y.: Cornell University Press, 1991).

4. There is an important sense in which the *Chemin* can be seen as treating Christine's "problem of the father" implicitly while the *Mutacion* treats it explicitly.

5. The first known reference to Dante in French occurs in Philippe de Mézière's *Songe du viel pelerin* (1389), as discovered by Giuseppe di Stefano in his important article "Alain Chartier, ambassadeur à Venise," in *Culture et politique à l'époque de l'humanisme et de la renaissance*, ed. Franco Simone (Torino, 1974), 155–168. Cf. also Laurent de Premierfait's *Des cas des nobles hommes et femmes* 9.23 (1400); and Christine's letter to Pierre Col (dated 2 October 1402) which concluded the dossier of the *Débat sur le "Roman de la rose."* For the textual presence of Dante in the *Chemin de long estude*, see the two classic studies: Arturo Farinelli, "Dante nell'opere di Christine de Pisan," in *Aus romanischen Sprachen und Literaturen: Festschrift Heinrich Morf* (Halle: Niemeyer, 1905), 117–152; and Maria Merkel, "Le *Chemin de long estude*: Primo tentativo di imitazione dantesca in Francia," *Rassegna nazionale* 32 (1921): 189–211, 243–258.

6. For a good discussion of Christine's personal *translatio* from Italy to France, see Sandra Hindman, *Christine de Pizan's "Epistre Othéa": Painting and Politics at the Court of Charles VI* (Toronto: Pontifical Institute of Mediaeval Studies, 1986), 1–21.

7. Cf. Charity Canon Willard, *Christine de Pizan: Her Life and Works* (New York: Persea, 1984), 15–71; and Suzanne Solente, "Christine de Pizan," in *Histoire littéraire de la France*, vol. 40 (Paris: Imprimerie nationale, 1974), 335–422.

8. For Christine's representation of this event as part of her "autobiographic fable," cf. the *Cent ballades* (1, 5–20) and the *Débat sur le "Roman de la rose."*

9. See Charity Canon Willard, "Lovers' Dialogues in Christine de Pizan's *Cent ballades d'amant et de dame*: Criticism of Courtly Love," in *Court and Poet*, ed. Glyn S. Burgess (Liverpool: Cairns, 1981), 357–364.

10. See the prologue to the *Epistre Othéa*, especially p. 150, vv. 18–24, and p. 151, vv. 1–21 (ed. Loukpoulos); and the *Mutacion* 1.3–15; and especially 1.6, "Comment elle ne cueilli fors des racleures du riche tresor de son pere." It is important to note the double model in these two passages: Boethius's *Consolation* and Dante's *Convivio* (1.1). But cf. the "positive" portrait of her father in the *Cité des dames* 2.36. See also note 42, below.

11. See Christine's mimesis of her mother in this context in *Mutacion* 1.5 and 1.7; and in the *Cité des dames* 2.36 (where her mother is criticized in comparison to her father). See also Blumenfeld–Kosinski, "Christine de Pizan and the Misogynist Tradition."

12. Cf. the vast enterprise of translation / vernacularization at the court of Charles V. For the opposition between Latin as paternal language and the vernacular as maternal language in Dante, see Kevin Brownlee, "Why the Angels Speak Italian: Dante as Vernacular *Poeta* in *Paradiso* XXV," *Poetics Today* 5 (1984): 597–610.

13. Ovid as author figure is directly linked to this polemic; see Kevin Brownlee, "Ovide et le moi poétique à la fin du moyen âge: Jean Froissart et Christine de Pizan," in *Modernité au moyen âge: Le défi du passé*, ed. Brigitte Cazelles and Charles Méla (Genève: Droz, 1990), 153–173.

14. For the "female genealogy" established in the *Cité des dames*, see Kevin Brownlee, "Martyrdom and the Female Voice: Saint Christine in the *Cité des dames*," in *Images of Sainthood in Medieval Europe*, ed. Renate Blumenfeld-Kosinski and Timea Szell (Ithaca, N.Y.: Cornell University Press, 1991), 115–135.

15. See Kevin Brownlee, "Discourse of the Self: Christine de Pizan and the *Roman de la rose*," *Romanic Review* 79 (1988): 199–221.

16. See Jeffrey Richards, "Christine de Pizan and Dante: A Reexamination," *Archiv für Studium der neueren Sprachen und Literaturen* 137 (1985): 108.

17. I take as my global point of departure Howard Bloch's important insights concerning the centrality of genealogy as a construct in the discourses of medieval culture, especially the concluding section of *Etymologies and Genealogies: A Literary Anthropology of the French Middle Ages* (Chicago: University of Chicago Press, 1983), 198–227.

18. See Charity Canon Willard, "Christine de Pizan: The Astrologer's Daughter," in *Mélanges à la mémoire de Franco Simone: France et Italie dans la culture européenne*, vol. 1: *Moyen âge et renaissance* (Genève: Slatkine, 1980), 95–110. Cf. also Edgar Laird, "Astrology in the Court of Charles V of France as Reflected in Oxford, St. John's College, MS 164," *Manuscripta* 34 (1990): 167–176; and G. W. Coopland, *Nicole Oresme and the Astrologers* (Cambridge, Mass.: Harvard University Press, 1952).

19. Dante's "memory" (*mente*) evoked in *Inferno* 2 is a memory of events lived through; Christine's is a memory of books read. This will be one of the fundamental oppositions between Dante-protagonist in the *Commedia* and Christine-protagonist in the *Chemin*: Dante-actor vs. Christine-reader.

20. It is interesting to note that the figure of Aeneas's mother is here added by Christine.

21. See Ronald L. Martinez, "La *sacra fame dell'oro* (*Purgatorio* 22, 41) tra Virgilio e Stazio: Dal testo all'interpretazione," *Letture Classensi* 18 (1989): 177–193. See also, R. A. Shoaf, "'Auri sacra fames' and the Age of Gold (*Purg.* XXII, 40–41 ad 148–150)," *Dante Studies* 96 (1978): 195–199.

22. *Chemin* vv. 631–633 are a French translation of Eclogue 4.4 "Ultima Cumaei venit iam carminis aetas" (Now is come the last age of the song of Cumae). It is, I think, significant to Christine's rewriting of the *Commedia* that Dante's character Stazio (Statius) cites the next three verses of the Fourth Eclogue in an Italian translation as the text that converted him to Christianity: "Secol si rinova; / torna giustizia e primo tempo umano, / e progenïe scende da ciel nova" (*Purg.* 22.70–72 [The age turns new again; justice comes back and the primal years of men, and a new race descends from heaven]). Cf. Eclogue 4.5–7: "magnus ab integro saeclorum nascitur ordo. / iam redit et Virgo, redeunt Saturnia regna; / iam nova progenies caelo demittitur alto" (The great line of the centuries begins anew. Now the Virgin returns, the reign of Saturn returns; now a new generation descends from heaven on high).

23. See John Freccero, "The Prologue Scene," in *Dante: The Poetics of Conversion*, ed. Rachel Jacoff (Cambridge, Mass.: Harvard University Press, 1986), 1–28.

24. See Farinelli, "Dante nell'opere di Christine de Pisan," 127; and Merkel, "Primo tentativo di imitazione dantesca in Francia," 199.

25. Cf. also *Inferno* 2.136–142, and especially Dante's final words to Virgil and the re-beginning of the journey: "'Or va, ch'un sol volere è d'ambedue: / tu duca, tu segnore e tu maestro,' / Così li dissi; e poi che mosse fue, / intrai per lo cammino alto e silvestro" (139–142).

26. Within the poetic economy of the *Chemin*—i.e., within its functional network of literary models—this *plaisance* is a conflation of the Jardin de Deduit in the *Rose* and the Earthly Paradise in the *Purgatorio*. Cf. Farinelli, "Dante nell'opere di Christine di Pisan," 128.

27. Farinelli ("Dante nell'opere di Christine di Pisan," 129) and Merkel ("Primo tentativo di imitazione dantesca in Francia," 201–202) note the obvious reference to Dante's line.

28. At the same time, Christine suppresses the Dantean catalogue of virtuous active pagans (*Inf.* 4.121–129, thus depicting an exclusively intellectual Elysian Fields, which serves—appropriately—as her own (authorizing) point of departure. Interestingly, however, this also involves eliminating the only women in Dante's Limbo, for fully eight of the fourteen virtuous pagan "actives" listed in *Inferno* 4 are female.

29. Orpheus is taken from among the philosophers in *Inferno* 4 and placed among Christine's poets, where he substitutes for Dante's last-named "ultimo Lucano" (*Inf.* 4.90). Is Machaut at all at issue here, being implicitly evoked

as an "Orphic" poet? Cf. Machaut's *Prologue*, vv. 135–146; and Sylvia Huot's discussion of this aspect of Machaut's self-presentation in *The "Romance of the Rose" and Its Medieval Readers* (Cambridge: Cambridge University Press, 1993), 247, 270.

30. This involves a striking contrast to Dante's inclusion in the *bella scola* (*Inf.* 4.82–105).

31. All of this takes place before, it should be noted, his meeting with the character Virgilio in *Inferno* 1: "tu se' solo colui da cu' io tolsi / lo bello stilo che m'ha fatto onore" (*Inf.* 1.86–87).

32. For the literary importance of the prestigious term *poeta* and the "polemical" expansion of its semantic field by Dante to include vernacular writers, see Brownlee, "Why the Angels Speak Italian," especially 602–610; for the analogous phenomenon in French with the term *poète*, see Brownlee, *Poetic Identity in Guillaume de Machaut*, 3–23.

33. For Christine-protagonist's earthly journey in the *Chemin*, Mandeville's *Travels* also function as model. See Paget Toynbee, "Christine de Pisan and Sir John Maundeville," *Romania* 21 (1892): 228–239; and Richards "Christine de Pizan and Dante," 108–109.

34. Virgilio will use the same phrase again with Minos in *Inferno* 5.23–24. He uses a modified version with Plutus in *Inferno* 7.11 and with Malacoda (and the other devils) in the fifth Bolgia in *Inferno* 21.83–84.

35. See Robert Hollander, *Allegory in Dante's "Comedy"* (Princeton, N.J.: Princeton University Press, 1969), 3–56.

36. Also denied to Christine-protagonist is the Crystalline Sphere, or *primum mobile*, Dante's Ninth Heaven, where the nine orders of angels are presented in proper sequence. Cf. the *Chemin's* abbreviated angelology in vv. 2038–2040 and 2043–2044.

37. With regard to the term *emprise* (v. 921; in the rhyme position) referring to the setting out on Christine's path ("science") as opposed to Dante's ("ymaginee"), cf. the Dantean *impresa* used to refer both to the protagonist's journey (*Inf.* 2.41) and to the poet's literary project (*Inf.* 32.7).

38. The contrast between Christine and Boccaccio as readers of Dante in this regard is significant. Unlike Boccaccio, Christine does not deny Dante's transcendental poetics. Rather, she simply differentiates herself from this aspect of her Dantean model.

39. This limitation vis-à-vis her Dantean model is also inscribed into the opening scene of Christine's celestial journey, as the Sibyl prepares her to climb the ladder of Speculacion (v. 1643):

> Monter ou firmament te fault,
> Combien qu'autres montent plus hault,
> Mais tu n'as mie le corsage

> Abille a ce: toutefois say je
> Que de toy ne vient le deffault,
> Mais la force qui te deffault
> Est pour ce que tart a m'escole
> Es venue. . . .
>
> (*Chemin*, vv. 1673–1680)

It is important to note here the implicit link between Christine's limitation in terms of the Dantean journey and her limitation in terms of her "share" in her father's learning.

40. Cf. note 30, above. For the *bella scola* as a whole, see the important new collection of essays, *Dante et la "bella scola" della poesia: Autorità e sfida poetica*, ed. Amilcare Iannucci (Ravenna: Longo, 1993).

41. In this sense, the fact that Christine lives in France constitutes both a *translatio* and an exile.

42. In the works which precede the compositon of the *Chemin*, Christine's most graphic presentation of this aspect of her relation to her father occurs in the prologue to the *Epistre d'Othéa*. The dedicatee, Louis d'Orléans, is addressed in terms of genealogy and lineage, in part as a way of linking Christine to him (while simultaneously placing her in contrastive parallel with him), in terms of her own genealogy / translatio, which is tied to Charles V:

> D'umble vouloir, moy, povre creature,
> Femme ignorant, de petite estature,
> Fille jadis philosophe et docteur,
> Qui conseiller et humble serviteur
> Vostre pere fu, que Dieu face grace,
> Et jadis vint de Boulongne la Grace
> Dont il fu né, par le sien mandement,
> Maistre Thomas de Pizan, autrement
> De Boulongne fu dit et surnommé,
> Qui sollempnel clerc estoit renommé. . . .
>
> (*Epistre d'Othéa*, p. 150, v. 18–p. 151, v. 3)

Christine then presents her new work ("ceste oeuvre" [p. 151, v. 8]) itself in terms of a contrastive genealogical relationship with her father:

> Car moult en est la matiere nouvelle,
> Tout soit elle de rude entendement
> Pour pensee, car je n'ay sentement
> En sens fondé, n'en ce cas ne ressemble
> Mon bon pere, fors ainsi com l'en emble

Espis de ble en glenant en moissons,
Par mi ces champs et coste les buissons;
Ou mietes cheans de haulte table
Que l'en conqueult, quant li mes sont notable;
Autre chose n'en ay je recueilli
De son grant sens, dont il assez cueilli.

(Epistre d'Othéa, p. 151, vv. 11–21)

See *Mutacion* 1.6 ("Comment elle ne ceuilli fors des racleures du riche tresor de son pere") for an elaboration of this trope for Christine's gender-determined intellectual patrimony.

43. At the same time, Christine's rewriting suppresses the figure of the rose as object (of desire and action) which is epitomized in the poem's final two lines, thus effecting an emblematic erasure of the *Romance*'s poetic economy of erotic love, as well as of the gendered male subject/female object configuration of the *Rose* as a whole.

44. Cf. the combination of maternal genealogy and corporeal (female?) identity in the opening sequence of the *Cité des dames*, as Christine's mother calls her from her study to supper. See Blumenfeld-Kosinski ("Christine de Pizan and the Misogynist Tradition," 285–289) for the relation between these two sequences of maternal interruption—one at the end, the other at the beginning, of the *Chemin* and the *Cité*, respectively—in terms of Christine's ambivalent (even critical) representation of her mother.

Editing Dante's *Commedia*, 1472–1629

A customer intending to purchase an Italian printed edition of Dante's *Commedia* during the Renaissance could have been faced with a number of choices while browsing at a bookstall. He or she might have found copies differing considerably in size, heavy folios alongside tiny pocket-sized editions. Most of the larger editions would have offered one or even two commentaries on the text, with the commentaries themselves differing considerably according to their authors' approach to the poem. On the other hand, editions in octavo or smaller formats would have offered the bare text or only a minimum of annotation. At certain moments readers would have had a choice between different typefaces: gothic or roman in the 1470s, roman or italic in early and mid-sixteenth century, each of these typefaces possessing different cultural connotations. An edition might or might not have included a biography of Dante, or an index to help readers find their way around the poem, or illustrations or diagrams acting as a visual commentary. The text of the *Commedia* would almost certainly have differed from edition to edition. Looking more closely and perhaps reading between the lines, our potential purchaser could have detected rivalry, explicit or implicit, between one edition and another: rivalry between different Italian states, as might be expected, but also hostilities between scholars working within the same city.

Such diverse but complementary presentations of the *Commedia* were created, of course, in response to the perceived needs and tastes of the reading public, in all its variety. Printers and publishers naturally played an important part in the planning and execution of these presentations. If, however, there was to be any intellectual innovation in their edition of the *Commedia*, if it was intended to be more than just a straightforward copy of an earlier one, then they depended on the help of another figure: the editor.[1]

Who were the Renaissance editors of Dante? They are not always named, and this anonymity, presumably requested by them, reminds us that for some time many scholars preferred not to be publicly associated with the new-fangled process of producing books mechanically, with metal type rather than with the pen. It is particularly significant that Pietro Bembo, eldest son of one of the leading families of Venice, chose not to be named as editor in his Aldine Dante of 1502. Yet in many cases (as we can see from the list of editions provided in the table below) it is possible to name editors, from direct or indirect evidence. Many of them were Tuscans. Even among editors working in Venice we find the Franciscan friar and theologian Pietro of Figino or Figline near Florence; Alessandro Vellutello and Bernardino Daniello, both from Lucca; and Francesco Sansovino, born in Rome but brought up as the son of the Florentine sculptor and architect Iacopo Sansovino. This high proportion of Tuscans contrasts strongly with the publishing of Petrarch, whose lyric poetry had always been more widely read in courtly circles than in republican Tuscany and was consequently edited for the most part by non-Tuscans. On the other hand, in spite of the high number of editions of Dante printed in Venice, only two of his editors are known to have been from this city: Pietro Bembo and Lodovico Dolce, both of whom worked in the sixteenth century. In the fifteenth century, republican Venice, unlike Milan or Mantua or Naples, did not have its own native tradition of avant-garde, Tuscan-based, courtly vernacular literature, and so, before 1502, printers of Dante in Venice looked for help in at least two cases to immigrants: Cristoforo Berardi, from Pesaro in the Marche, and fra Pietro.

Most of these editors of the *Commedia* would only have worked for printers occasionally. In the 1470s and 1480s, they were predominantly humanists and teachers by profession. Some were well connected. Cristoforo Landino was one of the most highly reputed scholars of his time. Colombino of Verona and Martino Nidobeato were tutors to the families of marquises.[2] Francesco Del Tuppo, responsible for the Neapolitan edition of c. 1478, was the son of a notary in the service of the Aragonese court in Naples. From the 1490s, the social backgrounds of editors became more varied, ranging from the Franciscan convent of fra Pietro to the palazzo of Pietro Bembo. Vellutello and (probably) Bembo underwrote their own editions financially. But there was a different sort of financial involvement in the cases of Dolce and Sansovino, both of whom belonged to the new race of professional *poligrafi* who worked full-time in the Venetian printing industry from the 1530s onwards.

Having considered briefly who the editors of Dante were, we can now turn to consider their work. All editors had two principal functions. One was to provide a correct text; the other was to provide guidance and information for the reader. Since only the former function had to be undertaken by everybody, let us look first at how these editors fared as textual critics of Dante's poem.

It must be recognized that they were faced by an extremely difficult task. The number of manuscripts of the *Commedia* is very high (even today there are over 600), and the text became corrupt at a very early stage as scribes attempted to remedy real or apparent errors by borrowing from other manuscripts or by inventing their own corrections. It was hard for editors to know what manuscripts were available even locally and, if they had this information, it might be impossible to borrow the manuscripts unless they could pull the right strings. For example, when preparing the Florentine edition of 1595, members of the Accademia della Crusca had to wait for permission to consult books in the Biblioteca Laurenziana until the return to Florence of one of their members who happened to be related to the Grand Duke Ferdinando de' Medici.[3] Editors employed by printers had the additional problem of often having to work very rapidly. And once a text had been delivered to the printing house, whoever supplied it might have little control over the faithfulness with which it was reproduced. An example of the consequences of these conditions is provided by the *editio princeps* of the *Commedia*, the Foligno edition of 1472. A comparison of surviving copies has shown that after a certain number of the first ten sheets had been printed and the type distributed, the text was composed afresh, but that on this second occasion several new readings were introduced. The motive for these changes does not appear to have been correction either by an editor or by the printer. Although on certain pages one version is clearly superior to the other, on other pages each state of the text can contain different errors.[4] A better hypothesis is therefore that the resetting of the type took place for purely commercial reasons, because after a certain point it was decided to increase the print run, and that the press took insufficient care throughout the operation, failing to correct errors in the first printing and adding as well as correcting them during the second. In this period, then, the process of transfer from manuscript to print left a text very vulnerable to accidental change once it was in the hands of printers.

As well as facing these practical problems, editors had no scientific procedures to follow when preparing a text. Their method was simply to put two or more copies side by side and to select what seemed to make the best sense or to sound most beautiful. This had been essentially the method used by one of the very earliest editors of the *Commedia* in the manuscript age, a certain Forese. In 1330 (just nine years after Dante's death) he lamented the lack of skill of earlier vernacular scribes and said that he had written out a new text as soberly as he could by rejecting from various other copies what seemed to be false and by combining what seemed to be true or appropriate to the sense.[5] Similar comments were made time and time again by editors in the age of printing. Such a method was, of course, highly dangerous. It depended first of all on the editor's understanding of what Dante intended to say. Secondly, the editor had to be able to distinguish between what was stylistically appropriate for the trecento and what appealed to his own Renaissance taste. This was a distinction that the great majority of Renaissance editors did not think of making, or else did not want to make, because they were confident that their age could improve on the language of earlier times.

In spite of these difficulties, it must be said to the credit of Renaissance editors of the *Commedia* that many of them took the textual aspect of their work seriously. They were constantly in search of novelty. Some early editors, such as Berardi, Nidobeato, and Landino, appear to have given to the printer a manuscript rather than a corrected version of a printed text, even though those in the printing house would have found it easier to work from a printed source. But in most cases editorial enterprise consisted merely in "improving" a previous printing, sometimes but not always with the help of manuscripts or other printed editions. In at least one case an editor allowed his personal tastes to superimpose themselves on his sources. Lucius Laelius seems to have based his Venetian edition of 1478 on that of Colombino but, as the form of his name warns us, he was evidently persuaded that the vernacular would be ennobled by being brought closer to Latin. Lucius must also have felt that writing could legitimately be influenced by the speech of another region, even when the author was Tuscan. This combination of views was quite common in his period, but Lucius was unusual for his systematic attempt to convert Dante's early fourteenth-century Tuscan into something which could have been written in northern Italy in the mid-fifteenth century. For example, his version of the poem is full of northern-influenced single instead of double consonants, and Dante finds himself not in a "selva oscura" but in a Latinized "silva obscura." Lucius may also have had something to do with the decision, unique among editions of the *Commedia*, to print Dante's *terzine* without indentation, possibly so that the poem would look more like a Latin epic written in hexameters.

Lodovico Dolce's edition of 1555 seemed to offer a more authentic text. It announced to potential customers that the *Commedia*, or rather the *Divina commedia* as he now called it, had been "brought back to its true reading with the help of many very ancient exemplars," including a copy of a copy written in the hand of a son of Dante himself. This was a bluff typical of the mid-sixteenth century, as competition led editors and publishers to outbid each other with increasingly extravagant claim and counterclaim. All that Dolce did, in fact, was to follow the 1515 Aldine text for most of the time, occasionally preferring Vellutello's text of 1544. But one original device used by him was to give some variants in the margins. Dolce was thus the first editor to acknowledge explicitly that the text of the *Commedia* was far from fixed and to show some of the alternatives which he judged worthy of consideration.

Among the editors mentioned so far, even those who made use of manuscript sources could be accused of two failings: none had used any manuscripts of outstanding authority and none had made any attempt at a systematic survey of available manuscript evidence. There were, however, two editions of the cinquecento which respectively remedied these defects.

The first was the Aldine edition of 1502. In this, Pietro Bembo offered a revolutionary new reading of the *Commedia*. He did so thanks to a combination of his family connections and his remarkable dedication to an undertaking which, it seems, he had initiated himself. One of the treasures in the library of his father Bernardo was a manuscript of the *Commedia* dating from the mid-fourteenth century, probably the very copy sent by Boccaccio to Petrarch, now in the Biblioteca Apostolica Vaticana, MS Lat. 3199. By using this as his base text, Pietro Bembo was able to get closer to the source of the manuscript tradition of the poem, into waters which were not crystal clear but purer than those further downstream. To us, the authority of such a manuscript seems obvious. But that is a modern perception. Editors in the Renaissance did not necessarily seek out the oldest possible manuscripts and, when they had them, did not necessarily treat them with deference. Bembo's decision to use a fourteenth-century manuscript must have been influenced by the avant-garde of classical philology. In this respect too his father's library may have played an indirect but crucial role. It was here in 1491 that Pietro watched the greatest scholar of the time, Angelo Poliziano, collate a printed copy of Terence with Bernardo's fourth- or fifth-century manuscript of the Roman playwright. This memorable experience will have allowed Pietro to see at first hand the methodology of Poliziano, with its (for the time) quirky insistence on the respect to be shown to the oldest witnesses to a text.

However, as Bembo copied out his father's manuscript of Dante, he did not reproduce it letter for letter or even word for word. The first thing that we notice he changed was the very title of the work. Obviously uneasy with the term *commedia*, which as a humanist he would have associated with classical playwrights such as Terence, he replaced this with *Le terze rime di Dante*, thus opening the way for later Renaissance editors to experiment with other descriptions such as *La divina commedia* or *La visione*. As for the text, Bembo incorporated several readings from other sources, especially from one of the printed books owned by his father, a copy of the 1481 edition which had been sent as a gift by Landino himself. Bembo used conjecture very little and, as a rule, did not allow his personal views on Dante's language to intervene. As an example of his working method, we can compare (1) the text of his father's manuscript at *Paradiso* 30.22–33, with (2) that of Landino's edition, and finally with (3) that of the 1502 Aldine:

1. Bernardo Bembo's manuscript

Da questo passo uinto mi concedo   22
     piu ke giammai da punto di suo tema
     soprato fosse comico o tragedo
Che come sole in uiso in che piu trema   25
     cosi lorimembrar del dolce riso
     lamente mia da se medesma scema
Del primo giorno chiuidi ilsuuiso   28
     in questa uita insin a questa uista
     nol seguira ilmi cantar preciso
Ma or conuien kemio seguir desista   31
     piu dietra sua belleza poetando
     comalultimo suo ciascun artista

2. Florence, 1481 edition

Da questo passo uincto mi concedo   22
     piu che gia mai da puncto di suo thema
     soprato fussi o comedo o tragedo
Che come sole in uiso che piu trema   25
     chosi lo rimembrar del dolce riso
     la mente mia da me medesmo scema
dal primo giorno chio uidi elsuo uiso   28
     in questa uita infino a questa uista
     non e elsequire al mio cantar preciso
Ma hor conuien chel mio seguir desista   31
     piu drieto asua belleza poetando
     chomallultimo suo ciaschuno artista

3. Venice, 1502 edition

Da questo punto uinto mi concedo   22
     Piu; che giamai da punto di suo thema
     Soprato fosse comico, o tragedo.
Che come sole il uiso' che piu trema;   25
     Cosi lo rimembrar del dolce riso
     La mente mea da se medesma scema.
Dal primo giorno, ch'i uidi'l su uiso   28
     In questa uita, insin a questa uista:
     Non è'l seguire al mi cantar preciso:

> Ma hor conuien che'l mio seguir desista   31
> Piu dietr'a sua bellezza poetando;
> Com' a l'ultimo suo ciascun artista.

For most of the time, Bembo followed the manuscript, but in three places he preferred readings from the 1481 edition: "*dal* primo giorno" (28), "non è el sequire" (30, with the Latinizing *q* changed to *g*), and "che 'l mio" (31). He probably used at least one other source, from which he derived "punto" (22) and "il viso" (25), though these readings could of course be conjectures or errors. As he went through the text, Bembo also undertook two other major editorial operations. One was to revise the spelling, which is close to that of his sources but (as in the cases of "ke" (23, 31) and "sequire") not identical. The other operation was to add a great deal of punctuation and some accentuation. Punctuation had been all but absent in previous editions and in any case had not included the comma and semicolon, which were introduced for the first time by Bembo and Aldo Manuzio. Completely original too was their use of the apostrophe in order to divide words while signaling elision (as in line 33), and their use of the grave accent, mainly on the verb "è" (as in line 30). It would have been very easy for compositors to make errors with these unfamiliar signs, and a mistake was made in line 25 here when an apostrophe was inserted after "uiso" instead of a comma. A comparison between the complete absence of interpretive signs in the 1481 edition and their abundance in the Aldine provides a good illustration of one of the effects of printing described by Walter Ong in his stimulating book on *Orality and Literacy*. Ong suggests that, in manuscript culture and in some early printing, readers processed a text for meaning by concentrating on the sound of a word rather than on its appearance; but, as printing developed (and as one can see in the 1502 Dante), "sight-dominance" replaced "hearing-dominance" in the process of understanding a written text.[6]

Another prodigious feat of textual editing lay behind the Florentine *Commedia* of 1595. Since the middle of the century, Florentines had been trying to produce a text which would achieve what Girolamo Benivieni's edition of 1506 had failed to do, that is, to overthrow the preeminence of Bembo's Venetian version of the poem.[7] Then in 1572 appeared Vincenzo Buonanni's edition of the *Inferno*, intended as the first installment of a complete *Commedia*. This was full of eccentricities, including the editor's use of the spelling tz instead of z (as in his own first name "Vincentzio"), his suggestion that the title *Commedia* was intended to refer only to the first *cantica*, and the substance of the text itself. Buonanni did at least acknowledge explicitly that many of his emendations were either his own conjectures or found in perhaps only one manuscript. But his changes to the text were made on the shaky foundations of his own opinions about grammar, Florentine usage, or medieval history.[8] Buonanni's approach was all the more shocking, probably even embarrassing from a Florentine point of view, in that conjecture was a method of emendation used sparingly, if at all, by other Renaissance editors of Dante. Buonanni's *Purgatorio* and *Paradiso* never appeared. And so it was not until the last decade of the century that only the third complete Florentine *Commedia* was printed.

The impetus for it came in 1590 from the compilation of a dictionary by the newly established Accademia della Crusca. Florentines evidently favored a collegiate approach to the two literary texts which they esteemed most highly and regarded as most intrinsically Florentine, Boccaccio's *Decameron* and Dante's poem, and on this occasion the academicians resolved to collate about one hundred manuscripts, tackling this task by allotting one or more canti among over thirty of themselves. The results, however, were disappointing in relation to the effort involved. The academicians did not classify their manuscripts in any way. Their base text was that of Bembo and, somewhat overawed by its authority and perhaps also wanting to avoid the lure of conjecture for which Buonanni had fallen so spectacularly, they found it hard to bring themselves to change it. And the changes which they did make were based on subjective criteria. For instance, Dante uses the conjunction "tosto che" to describe the speed with which the damned souls react in horror to the words of Charon (*Inferno* 3.102); "tosto che" became "ratto che" in 1595, not because of the support which this second reading found in the manuscript tradition, but because "ratto" seemed to the editors to indicate greater rapidity. The Crusca edition did not, then, mark a significant advance in textual criticism of the *Commedia*, but credit must be given to the members of the Accademia for making the best attempt until the late eighteenth century to progress beyond the text of Bembo. Their efforts were all the more remarkable in that editors of the two other major poetic classics, Petrarch's *Canzoniere* and Ariosto's *Orlando furioso*, had ceased to give any serious attention to the texts of these works after the 1550s.

Among the variants in the margins of the Crusca edition were a very few explanatory annotations. In comparison with the first Florentine *Commedia* of 1481, however, the Florentine editions of the cinquecento did not go very far towards carrying out the second of the two editorial functions which I identified earlier: that of providing help for the reader. Looking at the evolving pattern of Dante editions in the Renaissance, one sees that this exegetic function was more of a Venetian speciality than a Florentine one. For a while it became even more important than the function of textual criticism. From 1477 to 1497 the *Commedia* was prefaced, surrounded, even submerged by additional material: biography, commentary, illustrations, indexes, and so on. Then in 1502 Bembo and Aldo went to the other extreme. They offered readers the naked text in a pocket-sized format which liberated the *Commedia* from its desk-bound existence. From that point on, printers, publishers, and editors had a choice between two basic ways of presenting the work: a traditional approach using a larger format, folio or quarto, with commentary, or the more modern approach in which the text was presented without commentary and in a smaller, more easily portable format, ranging from octavo to twenty-fours. This second option was slightly more popular once the second Aldine of 1515 had added its support to the first (see the figure below).

As editors prepared one or other of these two Dantes, what types of readership did they have in mind? The *Commedia* was one of the most widely known vernacular texts: "widely known" meaning both that it was widely read and, as far as Florence was concerned, that it was even, apparently, repeated orally among the less well educated, as two novelle of Sacchetti suggest.[9] Christian Bec's analysis of the books owned by Renaissance Florentines puts the *Commedia* as high as second place, behind the Gospels, until the mid-sixteenth century. Yet at the same time all the indications are that, in Italy as a whole, the *Commedia* was a work deeply appreciated by the most privileged and best educated members of society. Bec points out that the Florentine manuscript copies were often expensive, written on vellum and bound in leather, and that they were owned by the learned as well as by those of modest cultural interests.[10] The manuscripts of the *Commedia* from northern Italy show that there the poem was particularly appreciated among the aristocrats of Venice and members of the courts of princes.[11] In the words of Carlo Dionisotti, Dante was the poet of the powerful, "il poeta dei potenti," read by statesmen and senior members of the clergy.[12] That this perception held equally true in the age of printing is suggested by, among other things, the list of personages to whom our editors chose to dedicate their labors (see the table below). These included two popes, a cardinal, a grand duke, a duke, a marquis, the wife of a marquis, the Signoria of Florence, and various high-ranking functionaries and courtiers. Those to whom editions of Petrarch or Boccaccio were dedicated were not of such consistently elevated social rank. One must also remember that the *Commedia* was studied in the manner of an academic text, as is demonstrated by the long-established tradition of commentaries and public lectures devoted to it.[13]

It was this sophisticated audience which Renaissance editors of Dante predominantly chose to address. For many years they took an "all or nothing" approach to the exegesis of the *Commedia*. Their readers would include, on the one hand, men of letters with an academic background who would welcome rather than feel daunted by the sight of a tiny island of text surrounded by a dense black sea of commentary. On the other hand, many readers would be well enough educated to cope with the text and nothing but the text. In one sense, of course, the nakedness of the text tended to isolate the *Commedia* from contemporary actuality. But, quite apart from reawakening interest in the textual criticism of the poem, the publication of Dante according to the fashionable new octavo-and-italic formula ensured that he would be read by the influential courtiers and men of letters to whom such volumes were designed to appeal. For these users of the text, the empty margins were an open space which invited them to provide their own annotations. A copy of the Florentine edition of 1506 in Leeds University Library gives us an example of how such a reader might use this opportunity. The hand in which most of the text is copiously annotated is apparently that of a member of the Capilupi family, perhaps Lelio Capilupi, a courtier who served the Gonzaga of Mantua in the first half of the cinquecento and who was himself a poet.[14] The annotator went through this volume diligently jotting down in the margins any words, or grammatical forms, or points of metrical usage, which he considered noteworthy. Occasionally he added a further comment which shows he was well able to analyze Dante's language for himself. For example, on fol. G2r, at the end of *Inferno* 18, we see him writing correctly that "attinghe" is a subjunctive, that "unghia" is a plural, that "accosciarsi" means "to squat" ("seder su le coscie"), and so on. A survey of annotated early copies such as this one, similar to the census of early copies of Petrarch promoted by Giuseppe Frasso, could tell us a great deal about who read Dante in the Renaissance, and how.[15]

The approach taken by editors up to about 1550 to the question of whether and, if so, how to assist readers of the *Commedia* differed quite sharply from that found in editions of Petrarch's *Canzoniere*, Boccaccio's *Decameron*, and Ariosto's *Orlando furioso*. Bembo's influential *Prose della volgar lingua* of 1525 set the seal on the elevation of Petrarch and Boccaccio to the status of the best models of language and style. In the 1530s and 1540s Ariosto's verse also began to acquire classic status, as Daniel Javitch has shown.[16] As a result, editors of these three texts, especially those working in Venice, began to produce presentations which would help less well-prepared readers, including women and the young, to understand them and to use them as starting points for their own compositions. Although the *Commedia* was seen by some as a potential model early in the cinquecento, Dante's status as an author worthy of imitation was then irreparably damaged by his most influential cinquecento editor, Bembo. The Venetian would not have devoted so much time to the text of the *Commedia* if he had not recognized its stature and historic importance. But this did not prevent him from accusing Dante in the *Prose* of taking excessive liberties with language; he likened the *Commedia* to a field of fine grain overrun by weeds.[17] In the first half of the cinquecento there were therefore no editions of Dante with the glossaries or grammar notes which one could find in editions of the other three classic authors. Indeed, there were dips in the output of all editions of the *Commedia* in the years before and after the publication of the first two editions of the *Prose*, in 1525 and 1538 (see the table and figure below), while the same two years coincided with an upward surge in the publication of Petrarch's verse and Boccaccio's *Decameron*. Another probable reason for which the *Commedia* enjoyed less success was its philosophical and theological content, which would have made it particularly arduous for one important part of the new reading public which was deprived of education in such matters: the sector of women readers. It is significant that only one edition was dedicated to a woman, and that this woman was herself an unusually gifted poet, Vittoria Colonna.

However, if the quantity and editorial quality of editions of the *Commedia* dropped during the 1520s and 1530s, the period from the 1540s to the 1570s saw a rebirth of interest in the poem. What led to this mid-century revival? It must have been above all a response to a new intellectual and moral climate. The history of the reception of the *Commedia* up to modern times shows that there was particular interest in the poem at moments of religious and political crisis and renewal. Writing of the early quattrocento, Carlo Dionisotti noted how the message of Dante reacquired a prophetic value in the age of the Council of Constance, against a background of hopes for a reform of the church and of collaboration between church and empire, and in coincidence with the defeat of the French monarchy at Agincourt.[18] Dante's message had the same renewed power amid the religious and political turmoil of the cinquecento. In 1506 the *Commedia* was edited by Girolamo Benivieni, an ardent supporter of the reform movement led by Savonarola. The poem must have spoken even more directly to Italians in the mid-sixteenth century, after the emperor Charles V had driven the French from Italy, firmly establishing imperial power in the peninsula, and a council of the church had convened at Trent, inside imperial territory, with reform as well as doctrine on its agenda. The two popes to whom editions were dedicated were those who respectively opened the Council of Trent in 1545 and brought it to a conclusion in 1563. The edition of 1555 was dedicated to a figure who moved easily between the worlds of church and empire and the republic of letters: Coriolano Martirano, a humanist whose works include the Latin tragedy *Christus* and Latin translations of Greek tragedies and comedies, bishop and preacher at two sessions of the Council of Trent, secretary of the Emperor's Council in Naples and a member of "the moderate wing of the imperial group."[19] In general, the integration of the *Commedia*, on the part of editors, into contemporary religious concerns is reflected in the high proportion of the dedicatees chosen by them who belonged to the clergy: four out of nine in the cinquecento, four out of four in the crucial period from c. 1516 to 1564, against none at all in the preceding and the following centuries. As for the links between the *Commedia* and empire and church in the cinquecento, another small but interesting instance of how these could be indicated is found in a note written in 1556 by a certain Lodovico Nadalin in the British Library copy of the Venetian edition of 1478. Nadalin was in the service of Nicolò Madruzzo, colonel of the imperial army. He pointed out that Dante had lived under the empire of Lewis of Bavaria while he, Nadalin, was living under the reign of the emperor Charles V; he also noted loyally that his master's brother, Cardinal Cristoforo Madruzzo, had recently been sent to govern Milan on behalf of the emperor.[20]

As one would expect, fresh interest in the contents of the poem in the cinquecento led to new editorial initiatives in its exegesis. Benivieni's edition of 1506 contained a discussion on the layout of Hell illustrated with seven woodcuts. This idea was imitated by Bembo in new diagrams which appeared in the Aldine of 1515 and in the three Paganini editions. Its successful use by editors was made possible by another of the consequences of the invention of printing: the creation of "exactly repeatable visual statements," as Walter Ong has called them, or "uniform spatiotemporal images" in the phrase of Elizabeth Eisenstein.[21] Then, just before the Council of Trent, came the publication in 1544 of the first commentary on Dante since that of Landino. Its author, Alessandro Vellutello, tells us that, unlike his Florentine predecessor, he was interested only in the explanation of the text. He provided, too, new discussions and illustrations of the physical appearance of each realm of the afterlife.[22] Vellutello's method was popular enough to lead to further editions of the commentary either alone or yoked together with the extraordinarily long-lived commentary of Landino. It looks, though, as if Vellutello's first edition was not as successful as it might have been. In the rich John A. Zahm Dante collection at the University of Notre Dame is a reissue, unnoticed until recently, of the 1544 edition which was brought out in 1564 by the enterprising printer Francesco Rampazetto. Evidently several copies of the first edition had remained unsold, and Rampazetto decided to use the quite common trick of selling them as if they were new, in order, perhaps, to rival Sansovino's edition of the same year.[23]

Vellutello's commentary, relatively helpful though it was intended to be, would still for many readers have been too bulky and out of keeping with the new style of more sparingly annotated texts which were being produced by Gabriele Giolito and other leading Venetian printers. What was needed, given the revival of interest in the poem, was a Dante for a readership which had different tastes and which was probably rather wider than it had been earlier in the century. Many readers would now have appreciated a Dante manageable in size yet more "user-friendly" than the series of editions without commentary which began in 1502 but came to an end with the mid-century editions printed "al segno della Speranza." A first step in a new direction was taken in 1554 with the lightly-annotated *Commedia* printed by the obscure Giovanni Antonio Morando. This edition was only an imitation of the Lyon edition of 1551, one of two Dantes in sixteens recently produced in that city.[24] In the first decade of the sixteenth century, Lyon had plagiarized the Venetian innovations of Aldo Manuzio. From the 1540s onwards, the tide of influence in the printing of trecento verse tended to flow in the opposite direction, thanks largely to the initiatives taken in the French city by the merchant-bookseller Guillaume Rouillé, although it must be said that he owed a great debt to Italy, since he was a former apprentice of the Giolito family and he was assisted by a Florentine, Lucantonio Ridolfi.[25] Rouillé's Dante proved an eye-opener in the company where he had once worked. Giolito's principal editor, Lodovico Dolce, experienced though he was, evidently studied and learned from it before producing in 1555 his own cleverly designed *Commedia* which used techniques borrowed from contemporary editions of Boccaccio and Ariosto: a summary and an allegorical interpretation of each canto, brief marginal notes giving variants and some explanation of the text, and a list of difficult words with succinct explanations. This approach must have been encouraged by Dolce's opinion, expressed in the 1540s, that Dante was one of the vernacular authors who should be read by young women.[26]

But Dolce's role as editor went far beyond that of explaining Dante's language. His dedication shows that he believed the *Commedia* was to be appreciated not for its style but for its usefulness and its "dottrina," meaning learning but also doctrine. He used his "allegory" of each canto to present the lessons which he felt the poem had for his own troubled times. When Dante passes through the circle of the heretics in *Inferno* 9, 10, and 11, the pilgrim's attention is caught up above all in political and personal issues of the Florence of his youth. Yet Dolce draws our attention back after each canto to the danger of heresy. One must remember that 1555 was also the year in which one of the fiercest opponents of heretics, Gian Piero Carafa, became Pope Paul IV. So obsessed is Dolce with heresy that he completely distorts the sense of the first five lines of canto 11, interpreting the "alta ripa" which leads down to the seventh circle of Hell as a sign of the presumptuousness of heretics who wish to get too close to divine secrets, and then taking the stench which rises up from the lower part of Hell as a representation of the effects of heresy. In *Inferno* 28 Dolce draws attention to the fitting punishment of those like Mohammed who have introduced division and heresy into the faith. Later, in *Paradiso* (20 and 24), he talks of the need to accept the teachings of the pope and of the Holy Church. At various points in the last two *cantiche*, Dolce implicitly or explicitly urges obedience to Catholic teaching on contentious matters: free will (*Purgatorio* 16), grace (*Purgatorio* 17), the necessity of confessing one's sins (*Purgatorio* 31, *Paradiso* 24), the efficacy of praying for souls in Purgatory (*Purgatorio* 23), predestination (*Paradiso* 20), the efficacy of the intercession of the saints on our behalf (*Paradiso* 33). Dolce is also aware of the danger that the *Commedia* might be used to support the Protestant cause, and in his allegories and marginal notes on canti in which Dante rebukes popes for their conduct (*Inferno* 19, *Paradiso* 18 and 21) he reminds readers that the poet is referring only to *earlier* popes. Vellutello is rebuked for commenting on Forese Donati's attack on the shamelessness of Florentine women in *Purgatorio* 23 that anyone who tried nowadays to prevent women from wearing low-cut dresses would be laughed at even by husbands: to do so, Vellutello had said, would be as ridiculous as trying to convert the whole of Asia and Africa to Christianity. It is not clear whether Dolce disapproved of Vellutello's lack of faith in the authority of husbands or in the possibility of converting all heathens, or both. As for politics, Dolce uses his allegories to point out the importance of venerating the empire, whose rule, he says, has divine authority (*Purgatorio* 6, *Paradiso* 6).

As editor, then, Dolce had produced a Dante which, on the one hand, was more approachable than any before and, on the other hand, buttressed the positions of pope and emperor. Although Giolito did not print this edition again, it was copied at least twice in Venice by Domenico Farri and in 1629 (without the marginal notes) by Nicolò Misserini. More importantly, it was one of the three sources plundered by Francesco Sansovino for the volume which he edited in 1564. Sansovino's monumental edition was a summation of the exegesis of the past century. He surrounded the text of the *Commedia* with the commentaries of both Landino and Vellutello, including their introductory material, Vellutello's illustrations, and Dolce's summaries and allegories, only slightly revised. But Sansovino treated all this as a canvas to which he could add his own embellishments and highlights. This was not a new technique: in 1478 Nidobeato had inserted into Iacopo della Lana's commentary passages derived from his own classical learning and from his experience of contemporary politics.[27] The first message which Sansovino had to impart was patriotic. As well as making the style of Landino's defense of Florence more easily readable by contemporaries, and therefore potentially more influential, he updated Landino's list of famous Florentines with about one hundred new names of his own. Sansovino's second message was one of support for the papacy. His dedication praised Pius IV for having brought peace to the Christian world and for having healed souls with the medicine of the Council of Trent. Significantly, one of the modern Florentines to whom he gave prominence in his additions to Landino was Giacomo Nacchianti, bishop of Chioggia. Some of Nacchianti's contributions to the debates at Trent had smacked of heresy and had been investigated by the Roman Inquisition in 1548 and 1549.[28] Sansovino nevertheless described him as the chief defender of the church against heretics at the council, thus trying to smooth over the rift between the church and Nacchianti which was also a potential rift between the church and Florence. Sansovino, like Dolce before him, was using the *Commedia* in order to promote Catholic unity.

Another of the ways in which Sansovino built on the work of earlier editors was to take Dolce's list of difficult words in Dante but to make a few additions to it and above all to give more detailed explanations to readers. Here he made good use of his superior knowledge of early prose and of contemporary Tuscan in order to situate Dante's language more precisely in relation to past and present usage. For example, he pointed out that *ferute*, meaning "wounds," which Dolce had said was an archaic word, was still found in the living Tuscan language. Sansovino also added a few comparative references to the contemporary usage of northern Italy, where many of his readers would be found. Traces of the same approach are found in the commentary of Bernardino Daniello, published posthumously in 1568. These editors, then, linked Dante's language synchronically with other written evidence for medieval usage and diachronically with the spoken usage of Italy in the cinquecento.

This was just one of the ways in which, from the age of Nidobeato and Landino, through that of Bembo, to that of Dolce and Sansovino, editors sought to integrate the *Commedia* into the continuum of Italian thought and language. Responding to the needs of readers and to those of printers and publishers but also taking fresh initiatives of their own, they wrestled with the daunting task of improving the text and experimented with new methods of exegesis because, for them, Dante's poem remained a living text, from which one could learn much and with which one could still engage in dialogue, just as Machiavelli conversed with Dante within his *Discorso intorno alla nostra lingua.* In a recent series of lectures on "Bibliography and the Sociology of Texts," Donald McKenzie remarked that "History . . . confirms, as a bibliographical fact, that quite new versions of a work which is not altogether dead, *will* be created, whether they are generated by its author, by its successive editors, by generations of readers, or by new writers."[29] The new versions of the *Commedia* created by Renaissance editors, two or three centuries after the composition of the poem, certainly ran the risk of distorting its text and its meaning. Walter Ong has written of the associations between print and death and has warned that, if a work is to take on another life and thus pass to posterity, it must first, in a sense, "die."[30] On the whole, though, I think one should see these editors, not as assassins of the *Commedia*, but as midwives assisting its regeneration in ever new guises. The multiformity of the versions of the *Commedia* which they produced is among the best evidence we have that during this period the poem was very much alive.

ITALIAN EDITIONS OF DANTE'S COMMEDIA, 1472–1629

Date	Place	Printer(s)	Format	Editor(s)	Commentator(s)	Dedicatee(s)
1472	Foligno	Johann Neumeister and Evangelista Angelini	2°			
1472	Mantua	Georg and Paul Butzbach	2°	Colombino Veronese		Filippo Nuvoloni
1472	Venice	Federico de' Conti	2°			
1477	Naples	s.n.	2°			
1477	Venice	Windelin of Speyer	2°	Cristoforo Berardi	Iacopo della Lana	
1478?	Naples	Francesco del Tuppo	2°	Francesco del Tuppo		sei Eletti
1478	Milan	Ludovico and Alberto Pedemontani	2°	Martino Nidobeato with Guido Terzago	Iacoppo della Lana (revised)	Guglielmo marchese di Monferrato
1478	Venice	Filippo di Pietro	2°	C. Lucius Laelius		
1481	Florence	Nicolò della Magna	2°	Cristoforo Landino	Cristoforo Landino	i signori di Firenze
1484	Venice	Ottaviano Scoto	2°	(Cristoforo Landino)	Cristoforo Landino	
1487	Brescia	Bonino de' Bonini	2°	(Cristoforo Landino)	Cristoforo Landino	
1491/1492? (3 Mar.)	Venice	Bernardino Benali and Matteo di Codecà	2°	Pietro da Figino	Cristoforo Landino	
1491 (18 Nov.)	Venice	Pietro de Piasi	2°	Pietro da Figino	Cristoforo Landino	
1493	Venice	Matteo di Codecà	2°	(Pietro da Figino)	Cristoforo Landino	
1497	Venice	Pietro Quarengi	2°	(Pietro da Figino)	Cristoforo Landino	
1502	Venice	Aldo Manuzio	8°	Pietro Bembo		
1506	Florence	Filippo Giunta	8°	Girolamo Benivieni		
1507	Venice	Bartolomeo Zanni	2°	(Pietro da Figino)	Cristoforo Landino	
1512	Venice	Bernardino Stagnino	4°	(Pietro da Figino)	Cristoforo Landino	

Note: The table above and the figure which follows exclude the following Venetian editions which are listed by Mambelli or Parker (see note 1) but of which I have been unable to locate copies: Bernardino Stagnino, 1516; al Segno della Speranza, 1552; Francesco Marcolini, 1554; Domenico Farri, 1572; Domenico Farri, 1575. The *Inferno* printed in Florence in 1572 is counted as one-third of an edition.

Date	Place	Printer(s)	Format	Editor(s)	Commentator(s)	Dedicatee(s)
1515	Venice	house of Aldo Manuzio and Andrea Torresani	8°			Vittoria Colonna
1515?	(Venice)	(Gregori de' Gregori)	8°			
1516?	Venice	Alessandro Paganini	24°			Cardinal Giulio de' Medici
1518?	Venice	Alessandro Paganini	24°			Cardinal Giulio de' Medici
1520	Venice	Bernardino Stagnino	4°	(Pietro da Figino)	Cristoforo Landino	
1525?	Toscolano	Alessandro and Paganino Paganini	8°		Cristoforo Landino	
1529	Venice	Jacob da Borgofranco for Lucantonio Giunte	2°		Cristoforo Landino	
1536	Venice	Bernardino Stagnino for Giovanni Giolito	4°		Cristoforo Landino	
1544	Venice	Francesco Marcolini for Alessandro Vellutello	4°	Alessandro Vellutello	Alessandro Vellutello	Pope Paul III
1545	Venice	al Segno della Speranza	18°			
1550	Venice	al Segno della Speranza	16°			
1554	Venice	Giovanni Antonio Morando	8°			
1555	Venice	Gabriele Giolito	12°	Lodovico Dolce		Corliolano Martirano
1564	Venice	Domenico Nicolini for Giovanni Battista and Melchior Sessa and brothers	2°	Francesco Sansovino	Cristoforo Landino and Alessandro Vellutello	Pope Pius IV
1564	Venice	Francesco Rampazetto (reissue of 1544 Marcolini)	4°	(Alessandro Vellutello)	Alessandro Vellutello	
1568	Venice	for Pietro da Fino	4°	Bernardino Daniello	Bernardino Daniello	Giovanni da Fino
1569	Venice	Domenico Farri	12°	(Lodovico Dolce)		

Date	Place	Printer(s)	Format	Editor(s)	Commentator(s)	Dedicatee(s)
1572 (Inf. only)	Florence	Bartolomeo Sermartelli	4°	Vincenzo Buonanni	Vincenzo Buonanni	Francesco de' Medici
1578	Venice	heirs of Francesco Rampazetto for Giovanni Battista and Melchior Sessa and brothers	2°	(Francesco Sansovino)	Cristoforo Landino and Alessandro Vellutello	Guglielmo Gonzaga
1578	Venice	Domenico Farri	12°			
1595	Florence	Domenico Manzani	8°	members of Accademia della Crusca		Luca Torrigiani
1596	Venice	Domenico Nicolini for Giovanni Battista and Giovanni Bernardo Sessa	2°	(Francesco Sansovino)	Cristoforo Landino and Alessandro Vellutello	
1613	Venice	for Francesco Leni	16°			G. B. Minardi
1629	Padua	D. Pasquardi and partner	16°			Oddone Oddi
1629	Venice	Nicolò Misserini	24°			

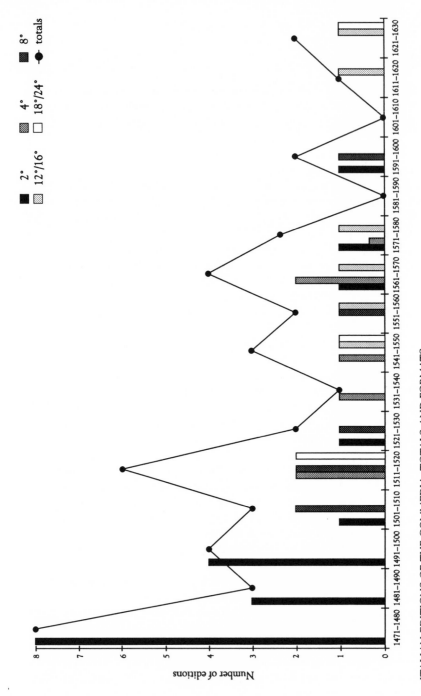

ITALIAN EDITIONS OF THE COMMEDIA: TOTALS AND FORMATS

NOTES

1. Two recent surveys of Italian Renaissance editing, in which more details will be found on many of the points discussed in this paper, are Paolo Trovato, *Con ogni diligenza corretto: La stampa e le revisioni editoriali dei testi letterari italiani (1470–1570)* (Bologna: il Mulino, 1991); and Brian Richardson, *Print Culture in Renaissance Italy: The Editor and the Vernacular Text, 1470–1600* (Cambridge: Cambridge University Press, 1994). Renaissance editions of the *Commedia* are discussed in Deborah Parker, *Commentary and Ideology: Dante in the Renaissance* (Durham, N.C.: Duke University Press, 1993), 124–158. The major bibliography is Giuliano Mambelli, *Gli annali delle edizioni dantesche* (Bologna: Zanichelli, 1931).

2. Colombino of Verona became tutor to the children of the marquis of Mantua in 1480: see A. Luzio and R. Renier, "I Filelfo e l'umanismo alla corte dei Gonzaga," *Giornale storico della letteratura italiana* 16 (1890): 119–217 (209–210); Nidobeato had been tutor to the marquis of Monferrato.

3. Severina Parodi, "Sugli autori della *Divina commedia* di Crusca del 1595," *Studi danteschi* 44 (1967): 211–222 (219).

4. On fol. 2r, for example, one state has "mi ritrovai" and "la nocte ch'io passai" (*Inferno* 1.2 and 21) against the other's mistaken "mi trovai" and "la nocte ch'io passi," and on fol. 9r (on the other side of the other half of the same sheet) the same state which was more correct for fol. 2r is also superior, with "disio" rather than "dissio," and "buia" rather than "buoia" (*Inferno* 3.126 and 130). On the other hand, one state of fol. 6v has the misprint "demendue" for "damendue" (*Inferno* 2.139), while the other has "succurse" (line 133) in rhyme with "-orse"; and, for the beginning of *Inferno* 6, one state of fol. 14v has the errors "ochi" (for "occhi") and "spirti" (for "spiriti"), but the other has the errors "cognate" (for "cognati"), "arta" (for "atra"), and "mestroce" (for "mostroce"). Forms possibly due to interference from the local Umbrian dialect, such as "quil" instead of "quel," remained unchanged. On this edition, see E. Casamassima, "L'edizione folignate della *Commedia* (1472)," *Bollettino della Deputazione di storia patria umbra* 62 (1965): 214–225, especially 218–225.

5. G. Vandelli, "Il più antico testo critico della *Divina Commedia*," *Studi danteschi* 5 (1922): 41–98 (53–54).

6. Walter J. Ong, *Orality and Literacy: The Technologizing of the Word* (London: Methuen, 1982), 119–122.

7. In the 1540s a group of Florentine scholars had made a careful collation of several early manuscripts of the Commedia, perhaps with a view to preparing a new edition (Richardson, *Print Culture*, 128). Here, too, vital inspiration must have come from the leading classical scholar of the day,

the Florentine Pietro Vettori, who had inherited Poliziano's respect for the oldest sources.

8. Examples of readings which Buonanni acknowledges to be conjectures are found in 4.1 ("roppemi," which he says is justified because the infinitive is "rompere" not "rumpere"); 9.109 ("come fui dentro" not "com'io fui dentro," justified because there would otherwise be two subject pronouns in three lines); 13.9 ("tra Cincelle" not "tra Cecina," because that is what these places are called); 13.149 ("Totila" not "Attila," for historical reasons); 14.79 ("brulicame," related to *brulicare*, not "Bulicame"). He says that he found his readings in 9.89 ("giunse alla porta") and 13.40 ("un titzon verde") in only one manuscript.

9. *Trecentonovelle*, nos. 114 and 115; see Gianfranco Folena, "La tradizione delle opere di Dante," in *Atti del Congresso internazionale di studi danteschi (20–27 aprile 1965)* (Florence: Sansoni, 1965), 1–76 (2–3).

10. Christian Bec, "I mercanti scrittori, lettori e giudici di Dante," *Letture classensi* 12 (1983): 99–111 (103–104); and *Les livres des Florentins (1413–1608)* (Florence: Olschki, 1984), 102–103.

11. Folena, "La tradizione," 2–3.

12. Carlo Dionisotti, "Dante nel quattrocento," in *Atti del Congresso*, 333–378 (334).

13. Dionisotti, "Dante nel quattrocento," 337–338.

14. The annotations are attributed to Lelio in a note probably written by a former owner, the bibliographer Antoine-Auguste Renouard. The hand seems identical to that which annotated an Aldine Petrarch of 1501, marked on fols. A1r and A7v as the property of "Camillo Cap.," i.e., Capilupi, and now located in the Biblioteca Nazionale Marciana, Venice (Aldine 498); see Paolo Trovato, "Per un censimento dei manoscritti di tipografia in volgare (1470–1600)," in *Il libro di poesia dal copista al tipografo*, ed. Marco Santagata and Amadeo Quondam (Modena: Panini, 1989), 43–81 (73, 75). On Lelio Capilupi, see the entry by C. Mutini in the *Dizionario biografico degli Italiani* (Rome: Istituto della Enciclopedia Italiana, 1975), 18:542–543. His *Rime* were published together with those of his brothers Ippolito and Camillo by Francesco Osanna in Mantua in 1585.

15. On annotated copies of Petrarch, see Giuseppe Frasso, "Per un censimento di incunaboli e cinquecentine postillate dei *Rerum vulgarium fragmenta* e dei *Triumphi*. I. London: British Library," *Aevum* 56 (1982): 253–262; later numbers of *Aevum* contain surveys of other libraries.

16. Daniel Javitch, *Proclaiming a Classic: The Canonization of "Orlando furioso"* (Princeton, N.J.: Princeton University Press, 1991).

17. See especially Pietro Bembo, *Prose della volgar lingua* 2.5, 2.20, 3.59.

18. Dionisotti, "Dante nel quattrocento," 335–337. For the eighteenth and nineteenth centuries, see especially Dionisotti's essay "Varia fortuna di

Dante," *Geografia e storia della letteratura italiana* (Turin: Einaudi, 1967), 205–242.

19. The description is from Hubert Jedin, *History of the Council of Trent*, trans. Ernest Graf, vols. 1–2 (London: Nelson, 1957–1961), 2:24, n. 1. On Martirano, see Giuseppe Alberigo, I *vescovi italiani al Concilio di Trento* (Florence: Sansoni, 1959), 208.

20. On Cristoforo Madruzzo, see Jedin, *History of the Council of Trent*, 1:566–574; Alberigo, I *vescovi*, 284–287; Massimo Firpo and Dario Marcatto, *Il processo inquisitoriale del cardinal Giovanni Morone*, 5 vols. (Rome: Istituto storico italiano per l'età moderna e contemporanea, 1981–1989), 1:341–342.

21. On Bembo's role, see Lino Pertile, "Le edizioni dantesche del Bembo e la data delle 'Annotazioni' di Trifone Gabriele," *Giornale storico della letteratura italiana* 160 (1983): 393–402. The relevance of illustrations to the development of modern science is discussed by Ong in *Orality and Literacy*, 126–128, and by Elizabeth Eisenstein in *The Printing Press as an Agent of Change*, 2 vols. (Cambridge: Cambridge University Press, 1979), 1:51–52.

22. See Ruth Mortimer, *Harvard College Library, Department of Printing and Graphic Arts: Catalogue of Books and Manuscripts*, part 2: *Italian 16th Century Books*, 2 vols. (Cambridge, Mass.: Belknap Press of Harvard University Press, 1974), 1:207–211.

23. This reissue was noted and described in the excellent exhibition "Renaissance Dante in Print (1472–1629)," prepared by Theodore J. Cachey, Jr., and Louis E. Jordan, III, with the assistance of Christian Y. Dupont, based on the John A. Zahm Dante Collection and held at the Hesburgh Library of the University of Notre Dame, Notre Dame, Ind., and the Newberry Library, Chicago, in 1993–1994.

24. The first was printed in 1547 by Jean de Tournes, with a dedication to Maurice Scève; *Inferno* and *Paradiso* had introductory canto summaries and explanatory notes in the margins. In the *Dante con nuove et utili ispositioni* published in 1551 by Guillaume Rouillé, each canto was followed by an "Annotatione" which summarized it and explained some terms and allusions; there were no marginal notes. Both volumes offered a life of the poet.

25. On Rouillé, see Henri and Julien Baudrier, *Bibliographie lyonnaise*, 12 vols. (new impression, Paris: Nobele, 1964), 9th série, 13–418; Natalie Zemon Davis, "Publisher Guillaume Rouillé: Businessman and Humanist," in *Editing Sixteenth Century Texts*, ed. R. J. Schoeck (Toronto: University of Toronto Press, 1966), 72–112, and "Le monde de l'imprimerie humaniste: Lyon," in *Histoire de l'édition française*, 4 vols., ed. Henri-Jean Martin, et al. (Paris: Promodis, 1982–1986), 1:255–277 (255–261). The Dante of 1551 is described in Baudrier, *Bibliographie*, 186–187; its preparation is mentioned in the Petrarch of 1550 (Baudrier, *Bibliographie*, 175–176), where it is stated that Ridolfi provided Rouillé with the text.

26. Lodovico Dolce, *Dialogo della institution delle donne* (Venice: Gabriele Giolito, 1547), book 1, fol. 19r. The first edition dates from 1545.

27. Dionisotti, "Dante nel quattrocento," 369–371; Gianvito Resta, "Martino Paolo Nibia," in *Enciclopedia dantesca*, 5 vols. and appendix (Rome: Istituto della Enciclopedia italiana, 1970–1976), 4:44.

28. Nacchianti's controversial views had been on the question of the relative authority of Scripture and Tradition. On him, see Luigi Carcereri, "Fra Giacomo Nacchianti vescovo di Chioggia e Fra Girolamo da Siena inquisiti per eresia (1548–1549), *Nuovo archivio veneto* 21 (1911): 468–489; Jedin, *History of the Council of Trent*, 2:64, n. 2; Firpo and Marcatto, *Il processo*, 1:269–271; William V. Hudon, *Marcello Cervini and Ecclesiastical Government in Tridentine Italy* (DeKalb: Northern Illinois University Press, 1992), 56, 122–123.

29. Donald McKenzie, *Bibliography and the Sociology of Texts* (London: British Museum, 1968), 29.

30. Walter J. Ong, "Maranatha: Death and Life in the Text of the Book," in *Interfaces of the Word: Studies in the Evolution of Consciousness and Culture* (Ithaca, N.Y.: Cornell University Press, 1977), 230–271 (232–240).

Dante in the Video Decade

> Man makes a picture,
> A moving picture.
> Through light projected
> He can see himself
> Up close.
> —U2, "Lemon"

When aired in Britain in July 1990, *A TV Dante* consisted of a sequence of eight video renderings, each approximately ten minutes in length, of the early cantos of Dante's *Inferno*.[1] Channel 4, London— an independent broadcaster with a history of blurring distinctions between high art (cinema or video) and low (television)—produced the series which was immediately dubbed one of its "most outlandish experiments": "Nothing quite like it," the *London Times* reported, "has been seen on television before."[2] Michael Kustow, commissioning editor in the 1980s for the channel's arts division, had both defined the nature of *A TV Dante* and selected collaborators Peter Greenaway and Tom Phillips for its initiating cantos.[3]

A controversial film- and videomaker with creative roots in painting, Greenaway is best known for such films as *The Draughtsman's Contract* (1982), *A Zed and Two Noughts* (1985), *The Belly of an*

263

Architect (1987), *Drowning by Numbers* (1988), and *The Cook, the Thief, His Wife and Her Lover* (1989). He is, however, arguably most innovative when he abandons "pure" film, which he refers to as a "dying" medium of expression,[4] to work in video or in video-film hybrids: examples from the period of *A TV Dante* include his Annales-inspired *Death in the Seine* (1989) and his Shakespeare-inspired *Prospero's Books* (1991).[5] In Greenaway, Kustow no doubt saw certain creative affinities with Dante—not only an intense investment in the visual but also a marked penchant for the encyclopedic, the catalogued, and the systematic: "I am a clerk," says Greenaway, "I like organizing material."[6] For example, *Drowning by Numbers* (completed in the same year as *A TV Dante*) centers on three "ladies" and opens with a child skipping rope who names and counts the stars until she reaches the number one hundred and stops. At that point, she explains, one must return to the beginning. Throughout the film, predictably sequential numbers appear in highly unpredictable places until the narrative itself culminates at one hundred.

Though recognized as a composer and critic, Tom Phillips is perhaps best known as an artist who works in "visual poetry," in the art of the page. His ongoing "treated" book *A Humument* is considered by some to be "the most important artist's book of the twentieth century";[7] indeed, he himself defines it as a meditation upon the technologies of cultural production, as "an anthology of the entire history of the book, from the medieval manuscript through the early printed book to the experimental and avant-garde book of recent vintage."[8] His 1983 translation and illustration of the *Inferno* prompted Kustow's interest in a Dante destined for broadcast. Phillips himself saw the video project as an extension of previous work, "as the equivalent of publishing a new edition of the book."[9]

Even before its 1990 broadcast *A TV Dante* provoked debate. Why, for example, was a series completed in 1988 shown to the Dutch, the Italians, and the West Germans well before the British? The press overtly wondered if even in the judgment of Channel 4 (now minus Kustow) the series was too "impenetrably obscure," too highbrow, for British television audiences.[10] Once aired, its relative unpopularity served to confirm such suspicions. And then, of course, there were the critics by profession. Consider, as but two examples, these diametrically opposed assessments. In the first, drawn from the final paragraph of *The Cambridge Companion to Dante* (1993), David

Wallace brings to his "reading" of A TV Dante the biases of the literary critic:

> Dante has now entered the television and video age, but not with any great conviction: the "TV Dante" of Peter Greenaway and Tom Phillips . . . has some nice touches (scholarly commentators at the margins of the screen), but seems likely to collapse of its own bombast and inertia. What gets lost, or diminished in this orgy of flashing images is the word— and it is through diligent attention to the word especially in many fine new translations of the Commedia, that most progress has been made in recent years. Tom Phillips has made a notable contribution to this effort."[11]

And in the second set of remarks, Robert Koehler brings to his "viewing" of the series the aesthetic investments of a video critic:

> It seems only natural that one of the highlights of the American Film Institute's National Video Festival—Peter Greenaway and Tom Phillips' TV Dante—has been described as "a thinking person's pop video." That's a glib label for a rich, unprecedented work, but it points to an overwhelming impression left by the festival. . . . TV Dante is a delirious celebration of video art and a genuinely post-modern examination of Dante's Inferno. . . . It's already a landmark in how video can interact with and enrich texts.[12]

Though wearing their professional allegiances on their sleeves in these conflicting assessments, Wallace and Koehler nonetheless share a common ground. Both feel compelled to place the video artifact in a relationship of relative value to the verbal artifact. For Wallace, A TV Dante "diminishes" the Commedia; for Koehler, it "enriches" it. I will argue that it does neither but, rather, asks of its audience a different order of question altogether. For the juxtaposition of these critical perspectives underlines in almost symptomatic ways the tension inherent in the transition we currently live—the transition from a culture of the dominance of the word to a culture of the dominance of the sound-word-image. This transition itself is, of course, located in an extended history of passages—from oral culture to the culture of the manuscript, to that of the printed book, to that of electronic reproduction. The challenge posed by A TV Dante is to articulate a dynamic relation between the technologies that have brought us the "Great Tradition" as we know it and those of contemporary media. To adopt Tracy Biga's terms, A TV Dante is most properly understood as a "translation" from the "language" of the book to the "language" of video. Following Walter Benjamin's "The Task of the Translator," Biga argues that "translations between media" mark the "continued lives" of texts by, in essence, lending them "new lives": *incipit vita nova.*[13]

Tom Phillips opens *A TV Dante* by speaking directly to his audience and boldly asserting that "A good old text always is a blank for new things." He provides further elaboration on the team's choice to explore the "vernacular" of contemporary media in his "Postscript" to the series' companion volume:[14]

> *A TV Dante* tries to answer the question, *Is there such a thing as television?* Is television a medium in its own right with an individual grammar that would make it an art form as independent of cinema as opera is of drama? . . . The test here was to bring the medium in its present potential to a great multi-layered text and see if it could stand the strain. Dante, in a letter to his patron says, "The work I have made is not simple; rather it is polysemous, by which I mean that it has many levels of meaning." The intention here was to try to match Dante's claim in visual terms, to have the richness of an illuminated manuscript combine with the directness and impact of a newspaper's front page.[15]

Here, the "good old text" or "blank" is understood to be the *Commedia*; and "the new thing," television. And the will to introduce the project by such a stark appropriation of the "old" by the "new" serves to locate self-consciously these eight video cantos upon a studied timeline within the history of artistic production. The series thus seeks, first and foremost, to define its own medium and to situate that medium in relation to the creative capabilities of earlier media. It is, for example, no accident that Greenaway's related "translation" of Shakespeare's *Tempest, Prospero's Books,* fixes obsessively upon books—upon how words become pages, and pages become pictures in the mind's eye. Since Prospero's volumes are magical, these pictures readily come to life—a spectacle we are permitted to behold through the intervention of video. "Prospero, sixteenth-century scholar and magus," says Greenaway, "would no doubt call upon the most contemporary state-of-the-art techniques that the legacy of the Gutenberg revolution could offer."[16] In Greenaway's opinion, the creative breakthrough afforded by postproduction video technology—the artist's vastly expanded ability to treat and to combine moving images—constitutes a "comparable revolution":[17]

I used to think that television had a much more reduced vocabulary than cinema—but I have come to realize that the language can be as rich. But it is a different language with different rules and characteristics. I think we should explore those characteristics to the utmost.[18]

What is striking in both this passage and in Tom Phillips's "Postscript" is the insistent use of a linguistic model to conceptualize television: it is a language; it has a grammar and a vocabulary. Indeed some critics, in contrast to Wallace, would consider A TV Dante too attentive to the word, too bound by its literateness to explore freely the full potential of sound and image. The series certainly resists any familiar notion of television as an ephemeral flow of programming; its dense intertextual field virtually demands a VCR. Greenaway even stipulates that "it is designed to be recorded on video and then watched by the audience at their own speed, stopping and starting at will like reading a book."[19] Thus both Greenaway and Phillips construct this Dante as "a new edition of the book," as a translation pressuring the limits of the grammar and vocabulary of video language.

In two groundbreaking articles Amilcare Iannucci has persuasively examined the affinity of this "new," rich language, as articulated by Greenaway and Phillips, with the "old," rich language articulated by Dante.[20] He argues for such a relationship by exploring in depth the notion of the Commedia's polysemy, its dense layerings of meaning that render it a "producerly" text—at once both "writerly" (dense, self-reflexive, multiple) and "readerly" (engaging, easily accessible). The Commedia, like television, addresses a wide variety of audiences. A TV Dante would clearly speak to multiple categories of potential spectators by deploying an encyclopedic range of images and sounds: it uses found footage and archival material (newsreels, weather reports, home movies, manuscript pages, books, films, etc.); it specially shoots footage of actors portraying Dante's characters; it employs computer-generated graphics. If these constitute its vocabulary, its grammar then becomes one of negotiating associations and juxtapositions. This is most often accomplished through postproduction techniques of layering image and sound, of creating a sort of video palimpsest. A dozen or more images may appear on the screen at once: they dissolve into or superimpose themselves upon one another; they are enclosed within one another by frames and boxes; they multiply in rapid succession. For example, when canto 4 enumerates its list of virtuous pagans, boxed commentators fill the screen to provide explanations. Their matter is that of the learned and literary traditions of the West; their manner is that of covering a sports event for broadcast television.[21] Here seemingly exclusive vocabularies collide; the "illuminated manuscript" meets the "newspaper's front page."

To examine how such category collisions generate meanings, I will focus the remainder of this essay on only one of A TV Dante's multiple registers of visual citations—on a "vocabulary" constituted by images drawn from, or inspired by, the photographic corpus of Eadweard Muybridge.[22] In the 1870s Muybridge began studies of animal and (later) human motion by sequentially triggering still cameras arranged in a row along a track. In the 1880s he toured Europe and America projecting his serial images by means of a rotating device, the Zoopraxiscope, which—in tandem with the innovations of Edison and Marey—constituted an essential link between stills and movies. Historian of photography Beaumont Newhall notes of Muybridge's animations that "motion pictures were born";[23] Tom Phillips alludes to Muybridge's pioneering of "a high-speed photographic procedure that prefigures the cinema."[24] In 1887 Muybridge published Animal Locomotion, an eleven-volume summary of his experiments accompanied by 781 photogravure plates which "made a major impact not only on photographers, but also on artists who had to revise the traditional conventions of representing animals in movement."[25] Characteristically, Muybridge's images are viewed in a series format which depicts the human or animal figure moving against the backdrop of a numbered grid. Shown individually, the frames stop motion; projected in sequence, they simulate it. "We regarded Muybridge's figures," writes Phillips, "as the timeless abstracts of being and moving."[26] In A TV Dante collaborators Greenaway and Phillips use Muybridge to articulate one of several visually insistent "refrains"; they either stage "Muybridge images" using naked actors and a gridlike set or they incorporate Muybridge's own photographs as "ready-made" footage.

Muybridge's images have, in and of themselves, produced a history of reception that belies their polysemy. His photographic series are equally at home in a medical library, an art history library, and a cinema-television library. They guide life drawing; they aid in the study of anatomy; they signify the "progress" of technology. It is also worth noting that both Peter Greenaway and Tom Phillips manifested a fascination with Muybridge well before A TV Dante.[27] Greenaway's obsession with systems and grids (not to mention bodies) marks him as a kindred spirit. Indeed, critic Michael Walsh goes so far as to define the Greenaway aesthetic as "a question of animation, a question of negotiating between two basics of the film image: the stillness it shares with painting and photography and the motion that decisively distinguishes it from the earlier visual arts."[28] To be even more specific, the 1985 A Zed and Two Noughts mounted its bizarre plot against the backdrop of a zoo (Muybridge had borrowed many of his subjects from the Philadelphia Zoo). The film's protagonists— the two noughts, Oswald and Oliver—work at producing a sequence of unmistakably Muybridge-staged photographic studies of animal decomposition. With the help of a proven apparatus—gridded platforms and cameras equipped with time-lapse triggering devices—they empirically examine bodies that have moved across the boundary between life and death.

Turning now to an example drawn from Tom Phillips, in his 1983 illustrated translation of the Inferno the first two frames of a Muybridge series of a bird in flight visually "translated" canto 5.82–84:

> Like doves with wings held high and motionless
> that drift on air supported by their will
> when drawn by longing for their pleasant nest.[29]
> (Inf. 5.82–84)

What Phillips here actualizes through studied borrowing is a visual remotivation of Dante's simile which, like a Muybridge photographic series, derives its power precisely from its tense balance between stillness and motion. This specific quotation of stills is in turn reanimated when it is quoted again in A TV Dante. By the time of broadcast, then, the "ideal" spectator "reads" Greenaway and Phillips citing Phillips citing Muybridge to "translate" Dante.

The opening credits to A TV Dante, the sequence that "figures" the series, proffers a twentieth-century emblem for dramas of descent and ascent across spatial levels; here the spectator views the interior of an elevator moving downward through the nine circles of Dante's Hell.[30] It is a boxlike construct containing twelve naked sinners staged against a grid of white on the familiar blue of a blank video screen, a blue also standardly used in blue-screen shots (a special effects process that literally permits the superimposition, or layering, of one cinematic or televisual image upon another).[31] "The gridded nature of the lift," writes Phillips, "is based on the grids in Muybridge's photographs."[32] In a gesture that evokes the scientific pretensions of an identifying series of mug shots, the criminals (or sinners) mechanically rotate for the camera: they are shot from the front, from the left, from the back, from the right, again from the front, and so on. The elevator reappears in canto 4 as unbaptized adults and children descend to Limbo and again as Adam, Eve, and the Patriarchs ascend when Christ harrows Hell: "This is the only *ascending* lift," notes Phillips "that will be seen in all the thirty-four Cantos."[33] When, in canto 6, Dante interrogates Ciacco to ascertain the whereabouts of distinguished Florentines, they too appear in the descending elevator.

The privileged motif of the elevator is but the first in a series of images staged to allude to the visual style of a Muybridge sequence. When in canto 2 boxed-in scholars describe and draw a diagram of the structure of Dante's Hell, the now familiar white-on-blue gridded lift figures as a backdrop that already connotes a spatial configuration of many levels. Here television's characteristic "talking head"—the stark close-up of, for example, the news anchor who speaks directly to the camera-spectator—becomes the Virgil of *Aeneid* 6. He even appears in his "book"; he is framed by a volume that is in turn superimposed on the surface of the grid. A set resembling the elevator is again used at the opening of canto 6 where, having descended to the next "floor," our quasi-scientific curiosity about animal (or, more accurately, monster) movement is satisfied by watching Cerberus consume mud cakes in an exaggerated and grotesque slow motion. What should seem clear from these examples is that the recurring suggestion of Muybridge's imagistic style works to construct a motif— a studied "visual theme whose reappearance will form connections."[34] These connections are, of course, all the more forcefully made when Muybridge's own photographs appear on the screen.

What is at issue here is not only the fact of incorporating "found" Muybridge "footage" but also the shaping of an aesthetics of its citation, not only the formulation of a vocabulary but also of a grammar. Given that the archival material in question consists of limited stills generally displayed in a series (typically ten to twelve photographs), they must first be projected in rapid sequence to create an illusion of motion and then repeated if the moving image is to be of any duration. The technique adopted to effect motion through repetition is called a "loop," meaning "a length of magnetic sound film or tape joined head to tail, that forms a circle, or loop, so that the recording is repeated again and again."[35] Just as figures of speech are differentially deployed to achieve desired effects, so visual "figures" may be artfully manipulated to varied ends. As but one of the many experiments constituting A *TV Dante*'s search for the "individual grammar" of television, Greenaway and Phillips fashion a "poetics" of video looping built upon the ground of Muybridge's stills. In this instance visual repetition (the very basis of looping) assumes two thematically driven and radically distinct modes: the first enacts a diabolical repetitiveness of sin; and the second, a divine repetitiveness of redemptive intervention.

A Muybridge series of a hound running is used to figure the she-wolf of canto 1;[36] as we have seen, one of his sequences of a bird in flight is doubled and superimposed upon itself to represent Paolo and Francesca in canto 5; his series of a man riding a white horse stands for Filippo Argenti in canto 8. In all three of these cases, Greenaway and Phillips both "box in" the looped figures (by situating them in frames, or in frames within frames—the television screen itself being yet another frame) and then manipulate the loop to create a repeated motion that goes nowhere. The figures move forward and fall back, move forward and fall back, in a seemingly endless gesture. Their motion is frantic but ultimately static; they make no progress; they are trapped within the futile pattern set by their eternal damnation.[37]

By contrast, in cantos 4 and 8 the same Muybridge sequence of a naked man in profile descending a staircase represents both Christ harrowing Hell and the Angel descending to rescue Dante and Virgil when their progress is blocked before the gates of Dis. Clearly the double use of this single Muybridge series connects the two moments of the poem; it invites the viewer to interpret the Angel's intervention in relation to that of Christ. It also separates these descents (by staircase) from the descents of the sinners (by elevator). More important, the figure of Muybridge's man is "treated" in such a way that he transcends the boxed-in status of the hound, the birds, and the rider; he enters the screen from the upper corner and moves diagonally across it to exit from the lower. As this flowing, unbounded movement is reversed and repeated the figure also moves closer to the viewer, ultimately seeming to pass out of the screen and into the viewing space. Working with what is in essence the same visual matter (stills of a figure in motion), looping here has been manipulated to an altogether different effect. The "videoed" Muybridge man (an image not only looped but also reversed, reverbed, and zoomed in the computerized editing process) appears to enter from and return to a world that transcends the infernal boundaries delimited by Greenaway and Phillips's television screen.

What is clearly accomplished through this looping of Muybridge citations is a video "translation" of thematic and structural principles at the center of the *Commedia*. At the literal level, each Muybridge image aptly represents a figure from Dante's text; in addition, symbolic separations between figures are marked by stylistic manipulation. But the polysemy of Muybridge quotation also moves the video in another direction: it helps constitute it as metavideo, as a meditation on the medium. Muybridge's sequenced stills signify a technological cusp; they stand for the critical passage from still to moving images. They are thus embedded in an early cinematic discourse of interest in relation to Dante—that of bringing the dead "back to life":[38] "So accurate are they," notes Phillips, "that when animated a hundred years later they come to life again."[39] Here, then, the technological passage from photography to cinema prefigures the passage from cinema to video;[40] a revolution of equal magnitude is postulated; Muybridge, like Dante, takes on "new life" through video "translation."

The title of *A TV Dante* was clearly studied to put in play the high cultural register now evoked by the name *Dante* and the low cultural register evoked by *TV*. What Channel 4 produced, however, was an imposing "breakthrough in fine art television" which, by Greenaway's own admission, remains "somewhat indigestible at times" and "needs repeated viewing."[41] For what is here sacrificed in experimenting with the medium are elements that would render the text more readily accessible to a broad audience: consider, for example, the disconnection created between Dante and Virgil when, as properly televisual "talking heads," they always speak directly to the camera-spectator and never to one another.[42] Such a strategy complicates any reading of the relationships between characters, obscures any ready comprehension of how such relationships motivate plot. Textual capacities for immediate and popular appeal risk being lost in translation.

In the months surrounding the British broadcast of *A TV Dante*, American comedian Eddie Murphy proposed an alternative "translation" of the *Inferno* for contemporary audiences. Interestingly his project was diametrically opposed to the stated goals of Greenaway and Phillips; he sought to create a version that would be "free of those pain-in-the-neck layers of meaning that English teachers are always hallucinating in the classics."[43] The as yet unrealized *Commedia* he projected would have reduced Dante's text to pure, albeit somewhat misconstrued, plot: guy dies, guy goes to Hell, guy tries to get out. The *TV Dante* that remains to be made is no doubt the text that, like Dante's, is at once high culture and low culture; that successfully articulates both impulses; that genuinely and radically undermines such distinctions.

NOTES

In the preparation of this article I have benefited greatly from the generosity of Tracy Biga and Amilcare Iannucci, both of whom shared with me not only their insights into, but also their as yet unpublished essays on, *A TV Dante*.

1. My "proof text" throughout this essay will be the eight cantos of *A TV Dante* (a KGP, Ltd.–Dante BV coproduction for Channel 4, London, 1988) as aired by Channel 4 in July 1990. I will allude neither to the text of the pilot of canto 5 nor to any subsequent cantos.

2. "Television Goes to Hell with Dante," *London Times*, 28 July 1990, 19d.

3. Michael Kustow, "How *A TV Dante* Came About," in *A TV Dante*, ed. Derek Jones (London: Channel 4 Television, 1990).

4. As quoted by Jonathan Hacker and David Price, in *Take Ten: Contemporary British Film Directors* (Oxford: Clarendon Press, 1991), 221.

5. Defining "the period" of *A TV Dante* requires some qualification: a pilot of canto 5 was completed by 1984; cantos 1–8 were completed for broadcast by 1988; they were broadcast in Britain in 1990. In 1991 *Prospero's Books* constituted a cutting-edge hybrid of cinema and video. Predominantly shot on film, it was transferred to video to enhance the creative possibilities of the editing process, then back to film for distribution in theaters, and then back to video for home distribution.

6. As quoted in Hacker and Price, *Take Ten*, 190.

7. Marvin A. Sackner, "Humumentism: The Works and Ideas of Tom Phillips," in *Human Documents: Tom Phillips's Art of the Page* (Philadelphia: Kamin Gallery, Van Pelt-Dietrich Library [University of Pennsylvania], 1993), 7. The book treated by Phillips is W. H. Mallock's, *A Human Document* (1892). Phillips's notion of the "treated" book involves using the actual pages of Mallock's volume as his ground; he layers images on the surface of

the nineteenth-century text, leaving some print still visible to articulate new meanings through the appropriation of old type.

8. Sackner, *"Humumentism,"* 14.

9. "Television Goes to Hell with Dante," 19d.

10. "Television Goes to Hell with Dante," 19d.

11. David Wallace, "Dante in English," in *The Cambridge Companion to Dante*, ed. Rachel Jacoff (Cambridge: Cambridge University Press, 1993), 255.

12. "Breakthrough TV: A Thinking Person's Festival," *Los Angeles Times*, 31 October 1990, F12.

13. Tracy Biga, "Cinema Bulimia: Peter Greenaway's Corpus of Excess" (dissertation, University of Southern California, 1994), 167–171. Amilcare Iannucci similarly uses the term "translation" to describe *A TV Dante* in "Dante Produces Television," *Lectura Dantis* 13 (Fall 1993): 40 and 44.

14. "Like Dante," writes Biga, Greenaway and Phillips "choose to create in the vernacular" ("Cinema Bulimia," 174).

15. *A TV Dante*, ed. Jones, 47.

16. Peter Greenaway, *Prospero's Books* (New York: Four Walls Eight Windows, 1991), 28.

17. Greenaway, *Prospero's Books*, 28.

18. As cited in Hacker and Price, *Take Ten*, 221.

19. Hacker and Price, *Take Ten*, 207.

20. Amilcare Iannucci, "Dante, Television, and Education," *Quaderni d'italianistica* 10, no. 1–2 (1989): 1–33; and "Dante Produces Television," 32–46.

21. See Biga, "Cinema Bulimia," 175.

22. Greenaway and Phillips explicitly identify Muybridge's images as one of the motifs in the eight-canto series (*A TV Dante*, ed. Jones, 14). In the closing credits to the video sequence they also include an acknowledgment to Muybridge. See also Biga, "Cinema Bulimia," 177.

23. Beaumont Newhall, *The History of Photography* (New York: Museum of Modern Art, 1982), 121. Though, as Noel Burch argues, Muybridge's status as an "inventor" of the motion picture may seem "somewhat ambiguous" today, it is nonetheless consistently at issue in the critical literature on early cinema (*Life to those Shadows*, trans. and ed. Ben Brewster [Berkeley and Los Angeles: University of California Press, 1990], 11). Brian Coe usefully qualifies: "Not only did [Muybridge] carry out the first successful analysis of motion by photography and not only did he project the first motion pictures based on such analysis but his work was the direct stimulus to others who carried on from the start he had made to create cinematography as it is known today" (*The History of Movie Photography* [New York: Eastview Editions, 1981], 47). Consider, as further examples of Muybridge's reputation as the "inventor," the following titles: Gordon Hendricks, *Eadweard Muybridge: The Father of*

the *Motion Picture* (New York: Grossman, 1975); and Kevin MacDonnell, *Eadweard Muybridge: The Man Who Invented the Moving Picture* (Boston and Toronto: Little, Brown, 1972). For an important recent analysis, see Linda Williams, *Hardcore: Power, Pleasure, and the "Frenzy of the Visible"* (Berkeley and Los Angeles: University of California Press, 1989), 34–57.

24. *A TV Dante*, ed. Jones, 14.

25. Coe, *History of Movie Photography*, 47.

26. *A TV Dante*, ed. Jones, 14.

27. On Greenaway and Phillips sharing Muybridge as a "hero," see John Dugdale, "Broadcast and Be Damned," the *Listener*, 26 July 1990, 26. See also Phillips in *A TV Dante*, ed. Jones, 14.

28. Michael Walsh, "Allegories of Thatcherism: The Films of Peter Greenaway," in *Fires Were Started: British Cinema and Thatcherism*, ed. Lester Friedman (Minneapolis: University of Minnesota Press, 1993), 258.

29. I cite here *Dante's Inferno*, trans. Tom Phillips (London: Thames and Hudson, 1985), 44.

30. The emblematic status of this image is demonstrated not only by its repeated use in opening credit sequences but also by its adoption for the cover of the companion volume to the series.

31. A blue-screen shot is defined as "a delicate and elaborate special effects process whereby the subject is filmed in front of a special, monochromatic blue background with normal film. Blue-sensitive mattes are made to replace the blue background with other footage. When combined the subject and background look as if they were shot simultaneously." "Chroma key" is a similar process used in television. See Ralph S. Singleton, *Filmmaker's Dictionary* (Beverly Hills: Lone Eagle Publishing, 1990), 20 and 31. This technology is deployed extensively in the visual layerings of *A TV Dante* (for example, the head shots of the footnote commentators in boxes) and is self-consciously staged in the moments described.

32. *A TV Dante*, ed. Jones, 14.

33. *A TV Dante*, ed. Jones, 29.

34. *A TV Dante*, ed. Jones, 14.

35. Singleton, *Filmmaker's Dictionary*, 98.

36. This image is also doubled and layered over itself as the she-wolf to represent the corrective "veltro." Since only half of the full body of the "veltro" is shown, this specific looped figure is not entirely "boxed in" by the television screen. As the backdrop to the simultaneous "footnote" in which Phillips explains the "veltro," Muybridge's sequenced stills of running hounds appear.

37. For a related discussion of "treating" stock footage to achieve signifying repetition in *A TV Dante's* canto 5, see Iannucci, "Dante Produces Television," 40–41.

38. The phrase is that of an associate of Marey, as cited by Burch, *Life to Those Shadows*, 26.

39. *A TV Dante*, ed. Jones, 14.

40. *A TV Dante* is not alone in making this connection. The mainstream music video (directed by Mark Neale) to U2's hit song "Lemon" is entirely based on staging the band members as pseudo-Muybridge figures. "Lemon," from the 1993 album *Zooropa*, is associated with the band's "Zoo TV Tour," a lengthy self-reflexive commentary on video stardom.

41. "Television Goes to Hell with Dante," 19d.

42. This phenomenon has long been at issue in relation to Greenaway's work. Peter Saintsbury, for example, states that as a condition of British Film Institute funding for *The Draughtsman's Contract* it was stipulated "that the characters spoke to each other instead of to the camera as before" (as cited by Hacker and Price, *Take Ten*, 198).

43. See the *Wall Street Journal*, 13 August 1990, A6.

Contributors

Albert Russell Ascoli is Associate Professor of Italian and Comparative Literature at Northwestern University.

Zygmunt G. Barański is Professor of Italian Studies at the University of Reading.

Kevin Brownlee is Professor of Romance Languages at the University of Pennsylvania.

Theodore J. Cachey, Jr., is Associate Professor of Romance Languages and Literatures at the University of Notre Dame.

Dino S. Cervigni is Professor of Italian at the University of North Carolina at Chapel Hill.

Christopher Kleinhenz is Professor of Italian at the University of Wisconsin, Madison.

Ronald L. Martinez is Associate Professor of Italian at the University of Minnesota, Minneapolis.

Giuseppe Mazzotta is Professor and Chair of Italian at Yale University.

Brian Richardson is Senior Lecturer in Italian at the University of Leeds.

R. A. Shoaf is Alumni Professor of English at the University of Florida.

Edward Vasta is Professor of English at the University of Notre Dame.

Nancy J. Vickers is Professor of French and Italian at the University of Southern California.

Index